Employment Relations in the 21st Century

Bulletin of Comparative Labour Relations

VOLUME 107

Founding Editor

The series started in 1970 under the dynamic editorship of Professor Roger Blanpain (Belgium), former President of the International Industrial Relations Association. Professor Blanpain, Professor Emeritus of Labour Law, Universities of Leuven and Tilburg, was also General Editor of the International Encyclopedia of Laws (with more than 1,600 collaborators worldwide) and President of the Association of Educative and Scientific Authors Authors. He passed away in October 2016.

General Editor

In 2015 Frank Hendrickx, Professor of labour law at the Faculty of Law of the University of Leuven (Belgium) joined as a co-Editor. Frank Hendrickx has published numerous articles and books and regularly advises governments, international institutions and private organisations in the area of labour law as well as in sports law. He is the Editor-in-Chief of the European Labour Law Journal and General Editor of the International Encyclopaedia of Laws.

Introduction

The Bulletins constitute a unique source of information and thought-provoking discussion, laying the groundwork for studies of employment relations in the 21st century, involving among much else the effects of globalization, new technologies, migration, and the greying of the population.

Contents/Subjects

Amongst other subjects the Bulletins frequently include the proceedings of international or regional conferences; reports from comparative projects devoted to salient issues in industrial relations, human resources management, and/or labour law; and specific issues underlying the multicultural aspects of our industrial societies.

Objective

The Bulletins offer a platform of expression and discussion on labour relations to scholars and practitioners worldwide, often featuring special guest editors.

The titles published in this series are listed at the end of this volume.

BULLETIN OF COMPARATIVE LABOUR RELATIONS – 107

Employment Relations in the 21st Century

Challenges for Theory and Research in a Changing World of Work

Edited by

Valeria Pulignano
Frank Hendrickx

Contributors

Antonio Aloisi
Wike Been
Andrea Bellini
Pete Burgess
Susan Corby
ACL Davies
Paul de Beer
Lisa Dorigatti
Roland Erne
Elena Gramano
Deborah Hann
Laurens Harteveld
Edmund Heery
Armin Höland
Richard Hyman
Arne L. Kalleberg
Panos Kapotas
Maarten Keune
Andreas Kornelakis
Marc Leemans
Evelyne Léonard
David Mangan
Cecilia Manzo
Hélène Michel
David Nash
Erik Pentenga
Silvia Rainone
Paul Soete
Adriana Topo
Marc van der Meer
Miet Vanhegen
Michail Veliziotis
Horen Voskeritsian
Manfred Weiss
Laurent Willemez
Paul Windey
Nuna Zekić

General Editor

Frank Hendrickx

Founding Editor

Roger Blanpain

Wolters Kluwer

Published by:
Kluwer Law International B.V.
PO Box 316
2400 AH Alphen aan den Rijn
The Netherlands
E-mail: international-sales@wolterskluwer.com
Website: lrus.wolterskluwer.com

Sold and distributed in North, Central and South America by:
Wolters Kluwer Legal & Regulatory U.S.
7201 McKinney Circle
Frederick, MD 21704
United States of America
Email: customer.service@wolterskluwer.com

Sold and distributed in all other countries by:
Air Business Subscriptions
Rockwood House
Haywards Heath
West Sussex
RH16 3DH
United Kingdom
Email: international-customerservice@wolterskluwer.com

Printed on acid-free paper.

ISBN 978-94-035-1764-3

e-Book: ISBN 978-94-035-1820-6
web-PDF: ISBN 978-94-035-1864-0

Printed in the United Kingdom.

Notes on Contributors

Antonio Aloisi Max Weber Postdoctoral Fellow, European University Institute, Florence (Italy).

Wike Been Researcher at AIAS-HSI, University of Amsterdam (The Netherlands).

Andrea Bellini Assistant Professor of Sociology at the Department of Political and Social Sciences (DSPS) of the University of Florence, Italy.

Pete Burgess Research Fellow at the University of Greenwich (UK).

Susan Corby Professor at the Department of Human Resources and Organisational Behaviour, Faculty of Business.

ACL Davies Professor of Law and Public Policy, Faculty of Law, University of Oxford (UK).

Paul de Beer Professor of Industrial Relations, AIAS-HSI, University of Amsterdam (The Netherlands).

Lisa Dorigatti Researcher at the University of Milan (Italy).

Roland Erne Professor of European Integration and Employment Relations at UCD School of Business and Geary Institute for Public Policy, University College Dublin (Ireland).

Elena Gramano Postdoctoral Research Fellow, Goethe University, Frankfurt (Germany).

Deborah Hann Lecturer in Human Resource Management at Cardiff Business School (UK).

Laurens Harteveld Senior policy advisor of the Dutch Employer's association AWVN (www.awvn.nl/).

Edmund Heery Professor of Employment Relations at Cardiff Business School (UK).

Frank Hendrickx Professor of Law and director of the Institute for Labour Law, Law Faculty, KULeuven (Belgium), Editor-in-chief of the European Labour Law Journal and General Editor of the International Encyclopaedia of Laws.

Armin Höland Professor at the Law Faculty of the Martin Luther University Halle-Wittenberg (Germany).

Richard Hyman Emeritus Professor of Industrial Relations at the London School of Economics (UK) and Founding Editor of the European Journal of Industrial Relations.

Arne L. Kalleberg Kenan Distinguished Professor of Sociology at the University of North Carolina at Chapel Hill (USA). His most recent book is *Precarious Lives: Job Insecurity and Well-Being in Rich Democracies* (Polity Press, 2018). He served as the President of the American Sociological Association in 2007-8 and is currently the editor of *Social Forces*, an International Journal of Social Research.

Panos Kapotas Senior Lecturer at the Law School of the University of Portsmouth (UK).

Maarten Keune Professor in Social Security and Labour Relations, AIAS-HSI, University of Amsterdam (The Netherlands).

Andreas Kornelakis Senior Lecturer in International Management at King's College London (UK).

Marc Leemans President of the Belgian Christian Trade Union, ACV/CSC.

Evelyne Léonard Professor at the School of Management, UCLouvain (Belgium).

David Mangan Lecturer at Maynooth University (Ireland) and Adjunct Professor at Osgoode Hall Law School (Canada).

Cecilia Manzo Assistant professor of Economic sociology, Catholic University of the Sacred Heart Milan (Italy).

Hélène Michel Professor of Political Science, University of Strasbourg (France).

David Nash Lecturer in Human Resource Management at Cardiff Business School (UK).

Erik Pentenga FNV Flex and principal negotiator of the Collective Labour Agreement for Temporary Agency Workers.

Valeria Pulignano Professor of industrial relations at the Faculty of Sociology, KU Leuven (Belgium).

Silvia Rainone PhD Researcher at the Law Faculty, Tilburg University (The Netherlands).

Paul Soete former CEO of Agoria (employers association of the technological industry), member of the European Economic and Social Committee, chairman of the Board of the Belgian Social Security Office.

Adriana Topo Professor of Labour and Employment Law at the University of Padova (Italy).

Marc van der Meer Professor of Education Labour Market Studies at Tilburg University (The Netherlands).

Michail Veliziotis Lecturer in Human Resource Management at the University of Southampton (UK).

Miet Vanhegen PhD researcher at the Institute for Labour Law, Law Faculty, KULeuven (Belgium).

Horen Voskeritsian Lecturer in Management, Birkbeck College, University of London (UK).

Manfred Weiss Professor emeritus of Goethe University, Frankfurt (Germany) and Former President of ILERA.

Laurent Willemez Professor of Sociology at the University of Versailles (France).

Paul Windey President of the National Labour Council (Belgium).

Nuna Zekić: Associate Professor in Labour Law, Tilburg University, Department of Labour Law and Social Policy (The Netherlands).

Summary of Contents

Table of Contents

Employment Relations in the 21st Century: Introduction and Overview

Valeria Pulignano & Frank Hendrickx

The multidisciplinary field of employment relations is confronted with many challenges nowadays, as the world of work is changing rapidly because of developments like globalisation, flexibilisation or digitalisation. These developments put traditional institutions and concepts in the field of employment (and industrial) relations and labour law (i.e., systems of collective bargaining and employee representation) under pressure. Therefore, scholars in the field of employment relations and labour law need to come together to reflect upon new approaches, theories and methods fitting the changing world of work. This may imply to focus on transnational regulatory structures and new forms of social protection and representation for different typologies and forms of work as a way to avoid increasing inequalities across (and within) countries. At the same time, and in order to respond to the aforementioned wide-reaching transformations, scholars need to study them from different disciplinary angles and at an international level in order to understand their broad effects and to come up with distinctive policy recommendations.

The three main aims of the book are to: (1) enhance current debates in the field of the current transformations affecting employment relations, (2) shape future research agendas in the light of the aforementioned transformations and (3) influence the policy agenda of national and international institutions.

To achieve these principal aims, we bring together contributions from different disciplines (such as employment (and industrial) relations, labour law, welfare state and social security, labour sociology, business and economics) to encourage a fruitful dialogue between them. As employment relations is per se an interdisciplinary field, the conference has provided a unique platform for dialogue and discussion among international experts, which we see as contributing to shape current and future research agendas on the changing world of work. In bringing this together, the book offers a more intensively in-depth understanding of the changing world of work, its main transformations and the challenges the latter poses to classical employment relations theories and methods as well as to labour law.

We especially focus on reflecting and discussing on why and how is work changing; how do collective actors deal with the changing world of work from both European and national perspectives; and look at the future of work. We do this in the light of contemporary challenges, cross-disciplinary theoretical and methodological innovation and renewed views on the changing world of work.

This publication is a follow-up from the IREC Conference held in Leuven from 10 to 12 September 2018. This interdisciplinary effort, jointly organised by KU Leuven's Centre for Sociological Research and the Institute of Labour Law and in conjunction with the European Sociological Association (ESA) RN17 Work, Employment and Industrial Relations and European Labour Law Network, brought together about 200 international scholars, all situated at the crossroads of the fields of employment (industrial) relations and labour law.

At the conference, we organised three main themes, which follow our parts in this book. For each theme we included two key-note addresses, to be found in each of the parts below, one from the field of social science and the other from the field of law. They are followed by various research contributions from these two disciplines.

In the first part of this book, we raise the question **why and how is work changing.** In his contribution, **Arne Kalleberg** gives a social science perspective and mentions the complex dynamics that play a role in the rise of precarious work. Experiences with precarious work are different in various countries. This may be due to differences in policies, which may lead to differences in the power relations of workers and in political dynamics. It is clear that labour market institutions affect the incidence of precarious work. Furthermore, the experience with labour market security or insecurity is closely connected with social welfare. The author brings up that the changing world requires a new social contract is that seeks to balance the needs for flexibility and security. **Anne Davies** makes her analysis from a legal perspective and asks how well labour law reponds to times of transition. New challenges are manifold, but she particularly indicates the rise of precarious work, workers' well-being, and effective dialogue between workers and management. Anne points out that the justifications for labour law are still relevant, which is to address inequalities of bargaining power, to protect workers' dignity, as well as to promote productivity. But she mentions that we need to think creatively about how to design the law in order to fit modern needs.

David Mangan uses a purposive approach and writes about the intersection between information technology and workplace regulation. He reveals that we must see the conflict between information technology and labour law. The facilitation of commerce may stand opposed to the protection of rights. David indicates that the dominance of economic liberalism has left many legal systems ill-equipped to address regulating the workplace and facilitating commerce. He expresses and connects many different interesting thoughts using the gig economy as an example. Striking is how he relates the legal discussion of distinguishing self-employed work from employment status in platform work with broader perspectives in our economies. Where the reality of the commercial relationship between the contracting parties in the gig economy may not be in conformity with the legal construction, or even undermine it, David nevertheless points out that Western economies believe in and rely upon small businesses. We wonder how this affects policy as well as legal practice in this field of employment relations and what this may mean for the future protection of those who are in work.

In their contribution, **Antonio Aloisi and Elena Gramano** present a succinct summary of the legal determinants of non-standard forms of employment (NSFE), which are on the rise in different sectors and various countries all over the world. Moreover, the chapter, which is largely exploratory, provides an analysis of existing legal frameworks regulating the organisation of non-standard forms of work and the negotiation of terms and conditions of work at the supranational level, with a particular focus on the implications related to competition law and its rigid limits in the European Union system. Technological and organisational change represents a major challenge for collective bargaining systems, given that they are often still predicated on the concept of a standard employment relationship. However, some innovative and spontaneous solutions are emerging. With this regards, the chapter sketches a mapping of nascent initiatives of workers' organisation, by distinguishing classic resources of unionisation from other tools (e.g., social media groups, strategic litigation, rating widgets) in a selection of European countries. The authors claim that in order for collective bargaining, unions, and business associations to continue to be impactful in the 'changing world of work', it may be necessary to adapt the way they currently operate. There may also be a need to adjust or update the relevant legal frameworks as well as to look into new ways to organise and build-up coalitions with other organisations and social movements.

The contribution of **Wike Been and Maarten Keune** presents a case of fragmented workplaces and illustrates their social implications. In particular, Wike Been and Maarten Keune look at work in the creative industry in the Netherlands where a paradox seems to exist as the industry combines (very) low levels of earnings with high levels of job satisfaction. Often this is attributed to creative workers 'just valuing other aspects of their work'. However, the authors illustrate that graphic designers and workers in the games industry do not generally perceive their income levels as low at an absolute level, but they do in relative terms. Also, they do point out specific groups as vulnerable with often very low earnings: starting entrepreneurs and freelance workers. These groups are central in the make-up of the sector as many start their own businesses at some point in their career. Workers indicate, however, that they are willing to forego earnings for the sake of working in the sector. This situation can best be understood as an interaction between personal preferences, labour market conditions and lack of interest in collective organisation. In addition, there seems to be a norm that 'true creative workers' should be willing to sacrifice earnings.

Nuna Zekić goes further into the issue of non-standard work, departing from the experience in the Netherlands. Although departing from her legal expertise, she uses insights from economic literature. This is applied to undertake a zoom in on the relation between non-standard work and economic inequality and to operate a discussion of the level of economic inequality in comparative perspective. Her conclusion is that the legislator has been very hesitant to interfere with the possibility of employers to conclude flexible employment contracts. Reforms have mainly focused on reducing employment insecurity. Their effectiveness can still be questioned and in her contribution, Nuna concludes that, overall, no real redistributive measures were introduced through recent labour law reforms in the Netherlands. That means, she argues, new labour laws are not likely to decrease income inequality in the near future and, thus, labour law should strengthen its redistributive commitment.

In the second part of this volume, the question is **how collective actors deal with the changing world of work? European and national perspectives**.

From his social science perspective, **Roland Erne** proses a new research agenda focusing on the EU, in particular with the aims to explore the challenges and possibilities that the EU's New Economic Governance (NEG) poses to labour politics. The question is how labour movements respond to it. Since the adoption of the 'Six-Pack' of EU law on economic governance in 2011, Roland sees the 'horizontal' integration be complemented by 'vertical' integration, through the direct surveillance of Member States' macroeconomic policies, including industrial relations and social policy. From this, he proposes a research design that is not based on national comparison, but which uses a design that compares the workings of NEG and labour movements in different areas of labour politics and in different economic sectors.

Although **Adriana Topo** writes basically from her legal expertise, her European, comparative and industrial relations know how comes to the fore in her analysis. She uses the concept of 'liquid unionism'. When there is 'liquid' representation of interests, labour interests are based on a direct method of expression of choices. That is facilitated by the digitalisation of communications. Adriana points out that 'in these situations, there is no a clearly defined agent, no traditional union, and only a volatile entity, which is almost impossible to identify and therefore bind under legal rules'. So it could indeed be questioned what this means for unionism, our the matter of representation itself, including not only the power relations but also its legal regulation.

This is also at the core of **Ed Heery**, **Deborah Hann and David Nash's** appealing contribution on 'The Involvement of Trade Unions in the Living Wage Campaign in the United Kingdom'. By using strong empirical evidence on the trade union response to the UK's Living Wage campaign, the author poses the interesting and challenging question whether trade unions coalitions with other types of progressive movement is to be considered the 'way' for union revitalisation. Have traditional methods of union representation become less effective over time, in the face of potent forces such as globalisation, neo-liberalism and austerity, and do unions have indeed lost the power effectively to represent their members? In the light of the findings, the author illustrates that although the adoption of radically new methods and the discovery of new power resources may be a valuable way for unions to act this is surely not the only and 'best' one.

Within a context characterised by increasing workplace fragmentation someone would expect the space for conflict being reduced. However, as the contribution of **Deborah Hann and David Nash** argue this may not be always the case. The authors analyse practices of workplace conflict management in Britain by drawing on a survey of private-sector employers. The focus is on the role that human resource professionals and trade unions play in regulating conflict at work. The impact of these two key actors in the employment relationship is assessed in three distinct ways: the experience of workplace conflict, its management and finally how organisations attempt to minimise it. First, the chapter outlines the nature and pattern of workplace conflict in Britain and evaluates how it is affected by the presence of HR specialists and trade unions. The second question it addresses is the extent to which trade unions and specialist HR professionals influence the management of workplace conflict. The analysis tests the various claims as to how employment relations actors shape the conflict management systems that firms adopt (Barret and O'Dowd 2005; Budd and Colvin 2005; Dobbin, 2011; Lewin, 2001). The final part of the chapter examines the ways in which firms seek to adopt pre-emptive practices designed to minimise workplace conflict. Roche and Teague (2012) claim that despite the interest in strategic HRM, little attention has been paid to how it relates to the area of conflict management. By analysing the prevalence of various progressive HR practices among employers the chapter determines the extent to which this conflict minimisation strategy is being adopted in Britain. It also assesses the relative priority that firms place on the minimisation versus management of workplace conflict and the extent to which this balance is shaped by the nature of the organisation's HR function and trade union relationship.

The theme of collective representation is further developed in an in-depth and complementary way by the **Andrea Bellini, Lisa Dorigatti and Cecilia Manzo**'s chapter where the authors pay particular attention to the role played by organisational choices in influencing the characteristics and the quality of creative work. By highlighting the centrality of professional and trade associations, the chapter illustrates how the arena of interest representation in the creative industry is considered as a space occupied by various actors, and where new actors can emerge in order to represent the voice of the creative workers by using both traditional and innovate organisational models and action strategies.

An interesting contribution, putting industrial relations and the legal world in perspective, is from **Pete Burgess, Susan Corby, Armin Höland, Hélène Michel and Laurent Willemez.** They look into three major systems (Germany, France and the UK) that use lay judges in labour courts. Lay judges in France and Germany, they conclude, are primarily industrial relations actors. They indicate that most lay judges spend more time on their industrial relations role than on their labour court role. Furthermore, these lay judges' origins and specific contribution are primarily derived from workplace knowledge. The UK's outlook is found to be different. This system, the authors show, has evolved away from this IR construction as state action has transformed the operation of labour courts and weakened the link to the industrial relations field.

In the third part of this volume, the contributions look into **the future of work**.

In this debate, some contributions reflect on key aspects of the future of work and how work in our societies will evolve. **Richard Hyman** reflects on the mechanisms ('sale and purchase') that govern labour power. He argues that there is no binary divide between voluntary and involuntary, or between free and unfree labour. It is for him a matter of degrees of freedom. In the broader global and political context, he points at the commodification of labour and the ways how policy makers, such as the European Union, once defenders of decommodification, have further liberalised economies and diminished protection on grounds of productivity and competitiveness. This has gone along with decreases in government spending and the rise of inequality. He wonders, somewhat rhetorically, if forced labour is the new normal.

Manfred Weiss draws our attention to the role of worker involvement in the European Union. EU policy has to deal with the variety and differences in industrial relations systems in the respective member countries. This is an important aspect, in fact a reality, behind the strategies in making legislation in the area of industrial relations and worker involvement. It has been a challenge to deal with these national differences, which are part of long standing traditions and the history of industrial relations. Manfred points out that it would be not only a mistake, but also impossible, to impose one national system to other countries. A way for this in a European context is to focus on proceduralisation in the legislative approaches. Beyond this, partly using the example of the European works councils, Manfred also points at new dynamics that have taken place in European industrial relations. Many European works council practices go beyond the strict confines of information and consultation and lead to the conclusion of European-wide agreements. This triggers the important issue that the legislative environment in this area may have allowed, or even created a stimulus for, the development of (European) industrial relations.

In their future-oriented contribution, **Horen Voskeritsian, Panos Kapotas, Andreas Kornelakis and Michail Veliziotis** focus on the issue of undeclared work. They focus on the interaction between institutional changes and their interplay with the informal sector of the labour market. In their chapter, they focus on the prevalence of undeclared work in the case of Greece during the economic recession. They conclude that while undeclared work is found in different sectors in the economy and existed also before the crisis, the fallback of the economy in Greece since 2010 due to the crisis has further advanced this phenomenon.

This part finalises with two rather legally oriented chapters. In her contribution, **Silvia Rainone** aims at unveiling the approach of the Court of Justice of the EU in the field of the law governing collective redundancies. This is done against the background of changing realities, but also an evolving (at least perceived) policy focus with emphasis on business freedoms in EU labour law and less than expected progress for workers' rights. Overall, Silvia concludes that, in the cases studied, the European Court shows rather a divergence in reasoning and does not adopt a uniform approach. She explains it as a systemic lack of coherence across the case law. It makes it also difficult to read the series of judgments of the Court as progress in terms of workers' negotiating powers.

Miet Vanhegen focuses on the law governing work incapacity and disability at the workplace, seen from an international legal point of view. The approach, both in policy and law, has been strongly influenced by the evolvement of anti-discrimination law but certainly by the adoption of the UN Convention on the Rights of Persons with Disabilities in 2006. This new and global UN strategy abandoned the mere medical understanding of disability and moved towards a focus on the social and environmental barriers that hinder full and effective participation in work and society. This leads to the so-called 'social model' of disability. Miet concludes that the European Court of Justice has taken significant steps in advancing a social model of disability, based on the strategy behind the UN Convention. However, there are still many legal questions and uncertainties. It is, for example, not very clear what the role is of environmental and socially constructed circumstances in creating a disability in terms of the law. The same matter plays in national case law. It does leave the question how far the social model has made its breakthrough, or whether the medical model is still not the prime zone of comfort for judicial application. It raises crucial questions for the future of work, putting the matter of workplace accommodation central for illness and disability, and thus basically asking whether we need to rethink the responsibilities between individual workers, employers and societies.

In the fourth and final part, we report about the debate that we organised on the current and future **challenges of industrial relations in the low countries: Belgium and the Netherlands**. We had the opportunity to bring together not only academics but also experienced industrial relations actors. This has allowed us to give insights in the current and future challenges of industrial relations, taking into account the action itself.

From an academic point of view, **Evelyne Léonard** gives a critical insight into the industrial relations system of Belgium. **Paul de Beer** and **Maarten Keune** do the same by looking into the system of the Netherlands. The insights are complemented by industrial relations actors of Belgium and the Netherlands. For Belgium, **Paul Windey, Paul Soete** and **Marc Leemans.** For the Netherlands: **Erik Pentenga** and **Laurens Harteveld.** In a broader overview, the outlook and challenges for the industrial relations systems in Belgium and the Netherlands are given by **Frank Hendrickx, Valeria Pulignano** and **Marc van der Meer**.

With this wide range of insights, analysis and reflection, we hope to deliver a unique volume and a fruitful contribution to the interdisciplinary study of industrial relations from both social sciences and the field of law.

This volume was finalised on 1 August 2019.

Part I Why and How Is Work Changing?

CHAPTER 1

Precarious Work, Precarious Lives: Changing Employment Relations in Rich Democracies*

Arne L. Kalleberg

§1.01 INTRODUCTION

The growth of precarious work since the 1970s has emerged as a serious challenge and major concern in the contemporary world. By 'precarious work' I mean work that is *uncertain, unstable* and *insecure* and in which *employees bear the risks* of work (as opposed to businesses or the government) and *receive limited social benefits and statutory entitlements* (Vosko 2010; Kalleberg 2011; Kalleberg and Hewison 2013). It has widespread consequences not only for the quantity and quality of jobs, but also for many non-work individual (e.g., mental stress, poor physical health, uncertainty about educational choices), family (e.g., delayed entry into marriage and having children) and broader social (e.g., community disintegration and disinvestment) outcomes. Moreover, precarious workers' insecurities and fears have spilled over to forms of protest that call for political responses to address these concerns.

While the growth of precarious work is common to countries, its incidence and consequences differ depending on the countries' social welfare protections and labour market institutions. I develop and demonstrate my arguments about the impacts of social welfare protections and labour market institutions on precarious work and its consequences by comparing six rich democracies that represent diverse models of capitalism: Social Democratic nations (Denmark); coordinated market economies (Germany, Japan); Southern Mediterranean economies (Spain) and liberal market

* This chapter is based on my keynote lecture at the 2018 IREC (Industrial Relations in Europe) Conference, Leuven, Belgium (10 September 2018), which summarized the main arguments of my book, *Precarious Lives: Job Insecurity and Well-Being in Rich Democracies* (2018, Polity Press).

economies (the United Kingdom and United States). These countries differ in their employment and social welfare regimes and exemplify the range of ways in which institutional, political, and cultural factors affect precarious work and its outcomes.

In this article, which is based on my 2018 IREC Lecture and recent book (Kalleberg 2018), I first discuss the rise of precarious work and then how differences among these six countries influence the incidence and consequences of precarious work. I next summarize some of the economic and non-economic consequences of precarious work, political reactions to precarious work and needed policies.

§1.02 COUNTRY DIFFERENCES

Different social, economic, and political structures typical of capitalist societies produce divergences among them in their employment systems and institutions. Two influential neo-institutional theories of diversity among capitalist countries identify the employment, labour market and social welfare protection systems that shape the nature and consequences of precarious work for individuals and their families: the 'Varieties of Capitalism' (VoC) or 'production regime' theory approach (Hall and Soskice 2001); and the Power Resources Theory (PRT) (e.g., Korpi 1985; Esping-Andersen 1990).

These theories help to explain differences among these countries in two key *social welfare protection policies*: (1) the generosity of *welfare spending*, or those monies (both public and required from private sources) that are designed to provide protection against illness, old age, disability, poverty and other kinds of difficulties faced by persons over the course of their lives; and (2) and the degree to which unemployed persons receive financial support (usually in the form of *unemployment insurance* payments). These financial supports provide a cushion or economic safety net to support people during times of unemployment.

In addition, there are country differences in several key *labour market institutions*: (1) the nature and extent of a country's *active labour market policies*, which are designed to help workers transition between jobs and from unemployment to paid work; and (2) the degree of *employment protections* for 'permanent, regular' workers and the rules governing the use of temporary and other nonstandard workers.

The generosity of public spending on welfare benefits and active labour market policies is relatively high in Denmark, Germany and Spain, and relatively low in Japan, the U.K. and U.S. Employment protections for regular workers are higher in Germany, Denmark and Spain compared to Japan, the U.K. and the U.S. (*see* Kalleberg 2018: Chapter 2).

[A] Varieties of Liberalization of Social Welfare Protection and Labour Market Systems

All of these countries have encountered pressures to liberalize their economies and labour markets and all have adopted some form of neoliberal policies, but they have done so in divergent ways, depending on the constellation and dynamics of political, economic and social forces that characterize the country (*see* Thelen 2014).

Embedded flexibilization (Denmark) involves the adoption of greater labour market and social welfare flexibility within an inclusive framework defined by a broad set of collective bargaining structures and strong union presence. Along with state policies to minimize wage inequalities, this has resulted in a relative collectivization of risks.

Dualization (Germany, Japan, Spain) entails the protection of 'core' workers from market risks at the expense of relatively unprotected 'peripheral' workers. A protected group of insiders or core workers enjoy long-term contractual relations and comparatively high levels of security while those in the periphery, or outsiders are generally employed in non-regular jobs with relatively few protections. Japan's economy has traditionally been dualistic, while dualism in Germany is more recent as it emerged within the past thirty years or so and was precipitated by de-industrialization and the failure of unions to organize workers in the private service sector. Spain has long been characterized by strong employment protections for regular workers and a strong insider-outsider divide.

Finally, *deregulatory liberalization* (in the U.K and the U.S.) involves the replacement of collective mechanisms of labour regulations by the imposition of market processes, shifting the risks of work to individuals.

§1.03 PRECARIOUS WORK

There are two main approaches to conceptualizing (and hence measuring) precarious work. One approach focuses on the form of the *employment relationship*, differentiating between the *standard employment relationship* and various forms of *nonstandard work arrangements*. Types of nonstandard work include: temporary work; contract work (comprising employees of contract companies as well as independent contractors and 'no account' self-employed persons who do not have any employees); irregular and casual employment; informal economy work; short-term work; and involuntary part-time work. In general, nonstandard forms of work are likely to be precarious because they are uncertain and insecure and, more importantly, lack social and statutory protections that have come to be associated with regular, standard employment relations in the early post-World War II period.

A second approach to precarious work emphasizes *job insecurity*. This is relatively low in Denmark, whether this is measured objectively by the risk and economic consequences of unemployment or perceived cognitive and affective job insecurity.

§1.04 WELL-BEING

I summarize the consequences for individuals resulting from precarious work in terms of three major aspects of well-being: economic insecurity; the transition to adulthood and family formation; and subjective well-being or happiness.

[A] Economic Well-Being

Economic insecurity denotes concerns about having sufficient economic resources to provide for oneself and one's family. Social welfare protection policies and institutions are important for shaping the consequences of precarious work for both objective and perceived economic insecurity. The data tell a consistent and coherent story: economic insecurity is lowest in Denmark and Germany; and highest in the liberal market economies of the U.K. and U.S. (Kalleberg 2018: Chapter 5).

[B] Transition to Adulthood and Family Formation

Precarious work has made it especially difficult in some countries for young people to make life course transitions such as gaining a firm foothold in the labour force, moving out of the home of one's origin, and marrying and having children. The inability to gain a solid foothold in the labour market is shown most dramatically in countries such as Spain and Japan, where young adults are taking longer to leave home due to not being able to find regular employment and young men (especially in Japan) are having difficulty finding suitable marriage partners because they have been unable to obtain a regular job that provides the promise of future advancement and economic security.

[C] Subjective Well-Being

Subjective well-being represents a person's overall affective evaluation of the quality of one's life. Labour market and social protection institutions affect subjective well-being directly by contributing to the overall social, economic and political contexts that shape external conditions (such as the extent of economic inequality and the degree and duration of unemployment) as well as by ameliorating or enhancing the impacts of these external conditions on subjective well-being.

§1.05 RESPONSES TO PRECARIOUS WORK AND LIVES

Precarious workers share experiences of anger (due to frustration over blocked aspirations), anomie (a passivity resulting from despair about not finding meaningful work), anxiety (due to chronic insecurity), and alienation (due to lack of purpose and social disapproval). These mutual understandings make the precariat a potentially dangerous class, capable of being mobilized by different groups for various ends, ranging from democratically based solutions – as in the New Deal in the United States in the 1930s – to authoritarian movements that blame immigrants and the poor for the precariat's insecurity (Standing 2011).

Workers have sought to counter this rise in precarious work and its consequences through both social movements and actions by organized unions and political parties. Moreover, political dynamics among the state, employers and workers have focused both on policies designed to help people adapt to precarious work through social insurance and skill acquisition, as well as emphasized ways of reducing precarious work by changes in labour and employment laws.

In order to address issues related to precarious work, policies in three general areas are necessary to produce a new social and political contract that is able to maintain flexibility for employers yet still provide individuals with ways to cope with the negative consequences produced by such flexibility. These include: (1) a safety net and various kinds of social protections to collectivize risk and help individuals cope with the uncertainty and insecurity associated with the growth of precarious work; (2) greater access to early childhood and formal education as well as lifelong education and retraining in order to prepare people for changes that will occur in jobs; and (3) changes in labour regulations and laws to protect those in both regular and non-regular employment.

§1.06 CONCLUSIONS

Why has there been a rise in precarious work in rich democracies, with their high standards of living and privileged positions in the world economy? And, how and why do people experience precarious work differently in countries with dissimilar institutions and cultures? The empirical evidence suggests the following five conclusions (*see* Kalleberg 2018).

First, the generosity of public spending on social welfare benefits and active labour market policies is relatively high in Denmark, Germany and Spain, and relatively low in Japan, the U.K. and U.S. Differences in these policies can be traced to differences in the power of workers and political dynamics in these countries.

Second, labour market institutions affect the incidence of precarious work. Temporary work is less common in the liberal market economies of the United Kingdom and United States and relatively high in Spain. These differences are associated with the low levels of employment protections in the U.K. and the U.S. and the high employment protections in Spain.

Third, generous social welfare benefits are linked to less economic insecurity, which is lowest in Denmark and Germany and highest in the liberal market economies of the U.K. and U.S. The latter countries differ, however, in their social wages due to the greater availability of economic and social supports in the U.K. that help people to mitigate various types of life course risks.

Fourth, young persons have difficulty gaining a solid foothold in the labour market especially in Spain, with its high levels of employment protection that relegates young workers to temporary jobs. Trouble establishing families is especially pronounced for young males in Japan, with its rigid markers of the transition to adulthood.

Fifth, the generosity of social welfare protections, along with high levels of active labour market policies, is associated with greater subjective well-being in a country.

The implementation of a new social contract – with its expanded and universal safety net, better managed labour market transitions, and appreciation for the needs of a diverse labour force – ultimately requires, of course, an associated political contract among the state, business and labour that seeks to balance employers' needs for flexibility and workers' needs for security. Achieving such a new social-political contract constitutes one of the great challenges of the first part of the 21st century.

REFERENCES

Esping-Andersen, Gøsta. 1990. *The Three Worlds of Welfare Capitalism*. Princeton, NJ: Princeton University Press.

Hall, Peter A. and David Soskice (editors). 2001. *Varieties of Capitalism: The Institutional Foundations of Comparative Advantage*. Oxford, UK: Oxford University Press.

Kalleberg, Arne L. 2011. *Good Jobs, Bad Jobs: The Rise of Polarized and Precarious Employment Systems in the United States, 1970s to 2000s*. New York, NY: Russell Sage Foundation.

Kalleberg, Arne L. 2018. *Precarious Lives: Job Insecurity and Well-Being in Rich Democracies*. Cambridge, UK: Polity Press.

Kalleberg, Arne L. and Kevin Hewison. 2013. 'Precarious Work and the Challenge for Asia.' *American Behavioral Scientist* 57: 271-288.

Korpi, Walter. 1985. 'Developments in the Theory of Power and Exchange.' *Sociological Theory* 3: 31-45.

Standing, Guy. 2011. *The Precariat: The New Dangerous Class*. New York, NY: Bloomsbury.

Thelen, Kathleen. 2014. *Varieties of Liberalization and the New Politics of Social Solidarity*. New York, NY: University Press.

Vosko, Leah F. 2010. *Managing the Margins: Gender, Citizenship, and the International Regulation of Precarious Employment*, Oxford, UK: Oxford University Press.

CHAPTER 2

Labour Law in Changing Times

ACL Davies[*]

It is clear that we are living in a time of significant transition in the labour market, brought about by technological change. This is not a new phenomenon – we can look back to the invention of the weaving loom, or the replacement of typewriters with word processors, among many other examples – but it does have a particular resonance in the modern age. The increasing sophistication of artificial intelligence means that a wide variety of jobs, at very different pay and skill levels, may be taken over by machines in the medium term. For example, driving jobs may be replaced by vehicles that are 'self-driving', and junior associates in law firms may be replaced by computers that can analyse large volumes of documents more rapidly. In other cases, jobs may change significantly because of technology. For example, medical professionals may have less of a role to play in diagnosing conditions as computers become more accurate than humans in performing this task. Although many commentators have speculated about the extent to which artificial intelligence will prove to be more significant than other rounds of technological development, only history will provide the answer to this question.

From a labour lawyer's perspective, the extent of change is, in any event, less important than the impact of that change on workers, who may face, at the very least, significant redefinitions of their roles and responsibilities, and in the worst cases, redundancy. In this short contribution, I ask how well-equipped labour law is for a time of transition, breaking that question down into two component parts. First, how suitable are current labour law norms for dealing with transitions themselves? In other words, how well does labour law respond to the needs of workers whose jobs are changing or disappearing? Second, I consider the broader question of how well-suited labour law is to a time of transition. Even if workers' jobs do not change or disappear,

* For reasons of space, this contribution focuses on EU and English law.

there are other consequences of rapidly changing workplaces that may need to be factored into the design of labour law regimes.

§2.01 THE LABOUR LAW OF TRANSITION

The traditional approach of labour law to transitions is to regulate the employer's decision to dismiss employees for economic reasons. In English law, this includes a requirement to follow a fair process when selecting employees for redundancy and to pay them compensation even in cases in which the dismissal of the employee on redundancy grounds is not unfair.[1] EU law contains a requirement to consult workers' representatives on ways of avoiding, reducing the number or mitigating the consequences of 'collective' redundancies, and to notify the responsible authorities.[2]

While these provisions are not problematic in themselves, they focus primarily on the job being lost, which is only a part of the transition process. The other part of that process is helping people to find another suitable job. Despite the Commission having adopted and pursued elaborate 'flexicurity' policies over a number of years, which have a particular emphasis on helping workers to move from job to job, this issue remains unresolved.[3] Of course, many of the possible solutions are matters of public policy rather than law. For example, generous social security benefits may help workers to move more easily from one job to another by reassuring them that they will be supported in any gaps between jobs.

However, there are various ways in which the law could be used to support more effective transitions. For example, it has long been argued that, while redundancy payments perform the important function of acknowledging that an employee is losing his or her job and is not to blame, they have no broader function in the labour market.[4] One option might be to link the payments to training in some way, for example, by requiring an enhanced payment where the employer has not provided the employee with training during the employment relationship, which can then be spent on training to help the employee find a new job.

§2.02 LABOUR LAW IN A TIME OF TRANSITION

It would be easy to assume that the law on redundancy should be our primary focus in changing times. However, I want to highlight three other issues that I think are important for workers who are living through upheaval in their workplaces, even if they are not facing redundancy themselves. These issues are the problem of precarious work, workers' wellbeing, and workers' voice.

1. Employment Rights Act 1996, ss 98 and 135.
2. Directive 98/59/EC, Arts 2 and 3.
3. Commission, *Towards Common Principles of Flexicurity: More and Better Jobs through Flexibility and Security* (COM(2007) 359 final).
4. For example Hugh Collins, *Justice in Dismissal* (OUP 1992), Chapter 5.

The problem of precarious work is already well-documented.[5] Casual working arrangements offer flexibility to employers, and it seems reasonable to assume that greater use will be made of these arrangements in times of uncertainty because they reduce the risk to employers of having to pay employees they do not need. Indeed, in some sectors, technology is already facilitating this by providing employers with ready access to a pool of casual workers via online platforms. The difficulty is that casual work transfers the risk of a drop in demand onto the workers themselves, leaving them with no guaranteed income and, in many cases, limited or no access to legal rights. Again, there has been a legal response: directives on agency and fixed-term working in EU law,[6] the development of 'worker' or other similar status to afford rights to individuals who are not employees,[7] and greater sensitivity on the part of courts to the possibilities of abuse.[8]

However, it may be questioned whether these developments have gone far enough. For example, it could be argued that the minimum wage is of such fundamental importance from a dignitarian perspective that it should be secured to all working people regardless of their employment status, by whoever is responsible for providing them with payment for work performed. Although this is a departure from the norms of labour law, it has the potential to reduce the impact of 'false' self-employment (though it is by no means a complete solution to this problem) and to provide a way of making certain types of platform responsible for monitoring the pay of workers who use their services to find work.

A second issue of importance in a time of transition is workers' well-being. The statistics suggest that there is a persistent and growing problem of mental ill-health at work. In the United Kingdom (UK), this is now one of the most common reasons for sickness absence from work.[9] While overall levels of sickness absence have declined in the past twenty years or so, absence on this ground has increased.[10] The relationship between work and a worker's mental health is a complex one. For an individual with an underlying mental health problem, being in work can have a positive effect, provided that the environment is supportive. However, issues at work can either trigger a worker's pre-existing condition or cause a mental health problem in an individual whose mental health was previously good.

The literature suggests that there are some common workplace phenomena that have a negative impact on workers' mental health.[11] These seem likely to be especially prevalent in times of transition. One is organizational change: knowing that there is a workplace reorganization in prospect, with the possibility of redundancies, is potentially problematic, particularly when management does not communicate effectively with the workforce about what is happening. Another is work intensification. In times

5. For example Mark Freedland and Nicola Kountouris, *The Legal Construction of Personal Work Relations* (OUP 2012).
6. Directive 2008/104/EC and Directive 1999/70/EC respectively.
7. For example National Minimum Wage Act 1998, s. 54.
8. *Autoclenz Ltd v. Belcher* [2011] UKSC 41, [2011] ICR 1157.
9. Paul Farmer and Dennis Stevenson, *Thriving at Work* (October 2017), 20.
10. *Ibid.*
11. Maria Hudson, *The Management of Mental Health at Work* (ACAS 2016), Chapter 2.

of uncertainty, workplaces may become more pressured environments, either because job cuts leave the remaining workers with more to do, or because the workers themselves feel the need to show their 'worth' in order to keep their jobs.

Again, there are legal measures in place to protect workers' mental health. Employers owe obligations under health and safety legislation to safeguard their workers' mental well-being, though critics argue that these obligations are less well-known and less clearly enforced than those relating to physical well-being.[12] In certain circumstances, a worker may be protected under the Equality Act 2010 when his or her mental health problem can be classified as a disability. However, there are significant difficulties both in determining when the Act applies and in elaborating the duties it places on employers.[13] More generally, it may be questioned whether these relatively specific legal regimes are likely to be effective in tackling broader problems such as work intensification.

This leads me neatly to a third significant issue in times of change: effective dialogue between workers and management. This is important both in ensuring that workers are informed about changes and that they have opportunities to defend their rights and interests.

The best way of representing workers is through strong, independent trade unions, but it is well-known that trade union membership is declining in many countries. In the UK, 23.2% of employees were trade union members in 2017, compared to 32.4% in 1995.[14] The causes of the decline in trade union voice are many and varied and, to some extent, specific to the UK, which has a particularly hostile legislative environment in respect of industrial action in particular.[15]

One way in which disgruntled workers may voice their concerns nowadays is through social media. While this is no substitute for effective trade union representation and collective bargaining, it does provide a potentially useful way for unions to identify workers who might be interested in joining and to target their organizing campaigns. However, employers are increasingly seeking to take disciplinary action against workers who are perceived to have damaged their reputation on social media.[16] As this area of law develops, it is particularly important that sufficient weight is given to workers' freedom of expression both as an end in itself and because of its implications for workers' ability to organize.

§2.03 CONCLUSION

In changing times, labour lawyers need to think carefully not just about legal protections for workers who might lose their jobs (the law of transition) but also about

12. Above n 9, Chapter 7.
13. Mark Bell, 'Mental Health at Work and the Duty to Make Reasonable Adjustments' (2015) 44 ILJ 194.
14. National Statistics, *Trade Union Statistics 2017* (May 2018).
15. For example Trade Union Act 2016.
16. Virginia Mantouvalou, 'I Lost my Job Over a Facebook Post: Was that Fair?' Discipline and Dismissal for Social Media Activity', (2019) International Journal of Comparative Labour Law and Industrial Relations (forthcoming).

other broader problems: the increasing use of precarious work, the negative impact of uncertainty on workers' mental health, and the need to ensure that workers have effective mechanisms to voice their concerns. It will by now be apparent that these broader problems are interlinked in various ways. Importantly, I do not intend to suggest that this creates a tangle of difficulties that is impossible to unravel. While we cannot hold back the tide of technological and economic change, we can use public policy to help and protect people who are adversely affected. The justifications for labour law are still relevant: to address inequalities of bargaining power, to protect workers' dignity, and to promote productivity. We just need to think creatively about how to design the law to fit modern needs.

CHAPTER 3

Ford, Taylor and the Gig: Workplaces in Transition

David Mangan[*]

§3.01 INTRODUCTION

Innovations in information technology mark the turn and ensuing years of the 21st century as a period of transition from an analogue to a predominantly digital means of interaction. Discussion of the impact of information technology in the workplace has been largely limited to 'gig' work or the platform economy. This chapter contends that current developments fit within a continuum.[1] The commercial focus in economic liberalism has been the ethos dating back to the early half of the 20th and continuing through the early 21st centuries. Models such as Fordism and Taylorism focused on maximizing the collective efforts of a labour force working as constituent elements of an enterprise. Production efficiencies were joined by cost reduction as similarly important aims. Models then started to deconstruct the (now) standard form of employment in order to effect these goals. Stimulation of the market economy soon became the dominant factor in employment regulation. The platform economy enters here.

The intersection between information technology and workplace regulation reveals a conflict in purposes[2]: information technology facilitates commercial access and has been imbued with a base of rights for consumers (such as data protection);

* My gratitude to Frank Hendrickx and Tonia Novitz for their comments on earlier drafts.

1. References to different jurisdictions have been made to illustrate the pervasive nature of the issues surrounding information technology and the workplace.
2. In labour law, the purposive approach has been employed by courts and in academic commentary. *See* for example, *Health Services and Support-Facilities Subsector Bargaining Assn. v. British Columbia*, 2007 SCC 27; *Autoclenz Ltd v. Belcher* 2011 UKSC 41. An academic contribution has been G. Davidov, *A Purposive Approach to Labour Law* (Oxford: OUP, 2016).

while labour law regulates its domain through reliance upon more rigid parameters (illustrated for example by the binary employment status distinction of employee or self-employed). Entrenchment of information technology within work and private life compounds the difference between facilitating commerce (where commercial law is a 'tool for its users')[3] and regulating the workplace. The consumer acts as a foil for the orthodox commercial approach, in which there is a presumption of relative equality among commercial parties. Regulations are organized around the concepts of those who are and are not commercial entities.[4] In contrast, the intersection of information technology and work reveals a significant tension (and the possibility of incompatibility) between the facilitation of commerce and the protection of rights. Consequently, difficult questions come to the forefront when assessing the regulation of employment as a tool for economic competitiveness. These queries centre around liberalism. On one side, the intensification of fragmentation in the labour market by commercial entities whose business models are premised on (often low-skilled) jobs being reduced to discrete tasks for fractional pay continue the path of economic liberalism. On the other, the permeability of liberal values (democratic freedoms), beyond economic liberalism, in the workplace is in question. Seemingly at the expense of the latter, the platform economy as well as regulation of information technology (such as the General Data Protection Regulation (GDPR)[5]) continue to primarily channel economic considerations through employment regulation.

§3.02 LIBERALISM AND THE WORKPLACE: FROM FORD & TAYLOR TO THE GIG

Liberalism underlies much of this discussion. A by-product of its changing history,[6] this contested word carries positive and negative connotations, depending upon the user and audience. In his 1997 article 'The rise of the illiberal democracy',[7] Fareed Zakaria identified decline in liberalism. His concern centred on freedoms (such as speech, assembly, religion, property) which he termed 'constitutional liberalism'. These 'natural (or "inalienable") rights' were to be respected by government. Illiberal democracies, he argued, casually ignored constitutional limitations, undercutting the aforementioned 'basic' rights. Zakaria's observation offers insight for contemporary events: 'Constitutional liberalism has led to democracy, but democracy does not seem

3. R. Goode, 'The Codification of Commercial Law' (1988) 14 Monash U. L. Rev. 135, 141. The drafter of the UK's original Sale of Goods Act 1893 (among other of his efforts to codify commercial law in the Victorian Era), Sir Mackenzie Chalmers' view of facilitation may have been particularly concerned with precluding litigation: M.D. Chalmers, 'Experiment in Codification' (1886) 2 L. Q. Rev. 125. McBride contends contract law in general 'facilitates the orderly workings of the marketplace': N. McBride, *Contract Law* (London: Bloomsbury, 2017).
4. In the UK, the Supply of Goods (Implied Terms) Act 1973 introduced the categories of consumer and non-consumer transactions.
5. Regulation (EU) 2016/679 of the European Parliament and of the Council of 27 April 2016 on the protection of natural persons with regard to the processing of personal data and on the free movement of such data and repealing Directive 95/46/EC [2016] OJ L 119/1.
6. H. Rosenblatt, *The Lost History of Liberalism* (New Jersey: Princeton, 2018).
7. F. Zakaria, 'The rise of the illiberal democracy' (1997) 76 Foreign Aff. 22.

to bring constitutional liberalism.' Recent publications on liberalism include those investigating its retreat[8] or even failure.[9] These studies and their recent proliferation speak to the on-going impact of The Great Recession.[10] The perception of outcomes linked to that period of time (correctly or otherwise) include: the increase in the wealth of the world's richest compared to the rising cost of living that wage increases do not match.[11] Liberalism has come under tremendous scrutiny in the early 21st century.

For labour law, liberalism offers two approaches which are best illustrated using the United Kingdom (UK) as an example jurisdiction. First, economic liberalism has been associated with the laissez-faire approach of allowing parties to arrange their affairs as they see fit and without government intervention. Otto Kahn-Freund characterized the UK as a locale for 'collective laissez-faire' labour relations.[12] While the (debated)[13] description no longer applied by the 1980s, labour law's role remained 'to regulate, to support and to restrain the power of management and the power of organised labour' and 'to redress any disequilibrium of power.'[14] Through the legislative interventions of the 1980s under Margaret Thatcher, labour market regulation was reconfigured as being 'in the interests of a free market economy'.[15] Since then, regulation in labour law has focused on enabling commerce by minimizing or removing restrictions on the competitiveness of businesses. Employment regulation has been drafted into a 'proactive role as an engine for trade'.[16] Second, liberalism also speaks to individual freedoms. The individual should not be unnecessarily encumbered. Here there is a role for the state to intervene so that there are equal opportunities.[17] The latter version of liberalism developed more recently. As these two visions of liberalism interact, criticism arises when freedoms are viewed as workplace protections that (arguably) attenuate commercial competitiveness. Consider the following rendition of the operation of the free market: 'In any free market system, a large proportion of wealth is concentrated in speculative interests held on share and futures exchanges. For this market to operate, it is essential that traders be kept to their

8. E. Luce, *The Retreat of Western Liberalism* (London: Abacus, 2017).
9. P.J. Deneen, *Why Liberalism Failed* (New Haven: Yale University Press, 2018).
10. For a detailed account of events surrounding the trigger for this financial crisis, *see* A.R. Sorkin, *Too Big to Fail* (New York: Viking Press, 2009).
11. *See* for example, J. Bersin, 'Why Aren't Wages Keeping Up? It's Not the Economy, It's Management' *Forbes* 31 October 2018 https://www.forbes.com/sites/joshbersin/2018/10/31/why-arent-wages-keeping-up-its-not-the-economy-its-management/#f75f5a5397ef.
12. O. Kahn-Freund, 'Labour Law' in M. Ginsberg ed, *Law and Opinion in England in the 20th Century* (London: Stevens, 1959), 224.
13. H.A. Clegg, 'Otto Kahn-Freund and British Industrial Relations' in K.W. Wedderburn, R. Lewis, J. Clark eds, *Labour Law and Industrial Relations: Building on Kahn-Freund* (Oxford: Clarendon Press, 1983), 14-28.
14. O. Kahn-Freund, *Labour and the Law* 3rd ed (London: Stevens, 1983), 15.
15. P. Davies & M. Freedland, *Towards a Flexible Labour Market* (Oxford: OUP 2007), 5.
16. Lord Irvine's comment on the nature of commercial law is not isolated to that discipline: 'the law ... assumed a proactive role as an engine for trade': 'The Law: An Engine for Trade' (2001) 64 Mod. L. Rev. 333.
17. This point was taken up in the UK through the Third Way and controversially Tony Blair's 'New' Labour. *See* for example, A. Giddens, *The Third Way and its Critics* (Cambridge: Polity Press, 2000), 86-89.

promises.'[18] The free market system requires as few encumbrances as possible. Commercial law aids in this effort by continuing the confidence first shown in the Victorian era to merchant law when it was codified into commercial legislation.[19]

For a large part of the 20th century, the development of industries garnered exclusive attention. Typified by adjectives such as Fordism and 'scientific management', the perceived synergy of interests between industrial growth and the well-being of citizens suggested that purposes aligned. This is not to undervalue the effect of trade unions or development of workplace rights which arose during this period. Rather, these protections came about within the existing collective framework. The perceived synergy has been subjected to increasing challenge. These criticisms have a long, continuing history[20] and are not elaborated upon here. The substance of these arguments for workplace protections has been premised upon classifications of worker cohorts, primarily employees (mostly union members) and self-employed individuals. This binary distinction has become an emblem of the current problems posed by the intersection of information technology and labour law.

The binary divide was evident in the earlier 20th century (largely American) influences on the organization of commercial activity. The Fordist model of employment has been the standard in the phrase non-standard employment. Referencing the factory assembly line of car manufacturer Henry Ford, this type of work would today perhaps seem ideal to those seeking the security of full-time, long-term employment. In the period after the Second World War, this bilateral agreement obligated employers to provide work and employees to perform it as instructed. Vertically structured, this classic format also entrenched the male breadwinner model.[21] Fordism sought the most efficient use of collective resources, leading to mass production of goods for mass consumption while also being profitable.

Another American industrialist sought to instil workplace production with scientific precision. Frederick Taylor devised 'scientific management'[22] which was itself a negative assessment of the industrial workforce; a cohort that he believed required an unusual amount of cajoling.[23] He believed there existed a formula for extracting the maximum worker output, resulting in the most efficient production. Taylor was less a scientist than the name of his model would suggest: 'Scientific

18. Irvine, n. 16, 337.
19. Two examples being the Bills of Exchange Act 1882 and the Sale of Goods Act 1893, both the products of Sir Mackenzie Chalmers. On the regard had for the 'mercantile' view at the time, *see* M.D. Chalmers, 'Codification of Mercantile Law' (1902) 2 Can. L. Rev. 146, 149: 'Our great mercantile judges have always kept the mercantile position in view.'
20. *See* for example, K.W. Wedderburn, *The Worker and the Law* (Harmondsworth: Penguin, 1965); P. Davies & M. Freedland, *Labour Legislation and Public Policy* (Oxford: OUP, 1993) as well as *Towards a Flexible Labour Market* (Oxford: OUP, 2007); T. Novitz, *International and European Protection of the Right to Strike* (Oxford: OUP, 2003), R. Dukes, *The Labour Constitution* (Oxford: OUP, 2014), J. Prassl, *The Concept of the Employer* (Oxford: OUP, 2016).
21. For critical commentary on this point *see* J. Conaghan, 'Women, Work, and Family: A British Revolution?' in J. Conaghan, R.M. Fischl, K. Klare eds, *Labour Law in an Era of Globalization* (Oxford: OUP, 2005), 53-73.
22. F.W. Taylor, *The Principles of Scientific Management* (New York: Harper Brothers, 1919).
23. Taylor called 'underworking' the 'greatest evil with which working-people in both America and England were afflicted': *Ibid* 13-14.

management was based upon the belief that all production knowledge could be described scientifically, reduced to written form, and transmitted as discrete instructions to each worker on a need-to-know basis.'[24]

The National Labor Relations Act 1935 (NLRA) (the long-standing United States (US) legislation also known as The Wagner Act) codified a collective view of work. It expressed several aims all premised on organized labour: to 'reduce industrial strife, restore mass purchasing power, promote a fairer distribution of economic resources, and further self-government by workers.'[25] It also established a dispute resolution mechanism coupled with a guaranteed period of industrial peace during the life of a collective agreement. Purposes aligned. Productive factories meant paid workers who raised their families with their earnings (though earnings barely met needs for many and the consequent gap was one of the lingering issues stoking subsequent industrial action). Organized labour was the engine set out by the NLRA.[26] By the 1970s, collective action had been usurped in focus by individual protections in the US[27] and other countries.

The UK legislative agenda from the 1980s illustrated not only a notable shift away from collective labour law, but also the embedding of employment regulation within macro-economic policies. Though appropriate to view them as anti-inflation strategies at that time,[28] 'the notion of a market economy as the ideal for industrial society'[29] pushed these changes to employment regulation beyond anti-inflation measures. It was a reconfiguration. The risks associated with employing individuals developed into perceived burdens of which companies had to divest themselves. Purposes diverged: a company could do well, but this would not necessarily confer commensurate benefits on workers. Control over the workforce for optimal efficiency eventually included control over labour costs. The latter grew over time in its importance.[30]

The use of information technology for labour purposes forms a thematic link between the approaches in the early 20th century with those employed in the early 21st century. Ostensibly, the tools provided by information technology (such as tracking

24. K.V.W.Stone, *From Widgets to Digits: Employment Regulation for the Changing Workplace* (Cambridge: Cambridge University Press), 35.
25. J.J. Brudney, 'Reflections on Group Action and the Law of the Workplace' (1996) 74 Texas L. Rev. 1563, 1564, 1565.
26. R. Blanpain, et al., *The Global Workplace: International and Comparative Employment Law: Cases and Materials* (Cambridge: CUP, 2007), 118.
27. Brudney, n. 27, 1564, 1571. In the US, discrimination and minimum standards legislation marked the movement away from the collective. Brudney posited: 'The inability of proponents to adapt the NLRA to changing circumstances and newly perceived problems raises doubts as to the extent of public interest in, or commitment to, the statute's basic approach.'
28. As described in H. Collins, 'The Productive Disintegration of Labour Law' (1997), 26 Indus. L. J. 295, 303.
29. P. Davies & M. Freedland, *Labour Legislation and Public Policy* (Oxford: OUP, 1993), 526.
30. Costs were an issue in the Ford and Taylor approaches. The focus over time had increasingly been upon continued searches for cost savings. The platform economy expresses those particular efforts.

software and algorithms)[31] afford the metrics to coax optimal effort in the Taylor spirit. It will be difficult to rebut this presumption without further understanding these technologies as well as additional data on their effectiveness. Still, a caveat remains: Taylor's was a belief not a science. These technologies, relying largely upon algorithms, are immune from neither critical analysis nor scrutiny.[32] Information technology does not necessarily offer an objective assessment of the workplace. In an interesting turn, commercial entities have increasingly relied upon consumer-driven metrics with thresholds set by employers. The platform economy does little to displace the observation that '[g]lobalization in its modern form is a process based less on the proliferation of computers than on the proliferation of proletariats.'[33]

Economic liberalism steered employment regulation in the direction of competitiveness, facilitating a change from a collective to individual focus. Labour law continues its discussion of collective examples including courts recognizing the right to collective bargaining[34] and the right to strike.[35] And yet, the widespread adoption of an individual focus at government and commercial levels has marginalized the collective structure of labour law.

§3.03 WORK AND THE PURPOSIVE APPROACH IN THE TWENTY-FIRST CENTURY

Much attention has been directed to platform work and how it parcels out the components of the employment contract for strategic business purposes. This effort falls short of originality; only the technology is novel. Under the Ford and Taylor approaches, employers effectively utilized the employment contract to establish employees' obligations and manage their efforts. With platform work, contract negates the costs associated with employment status. Although the employment contract connects them, the methods differ in their aims: the former seeks maximum efficiencies and adheres to a patriarchal system of management; the latter values minimizing costs while retaining a similar level of control. The flexibility of the contract is only outdone by the continued 'process of contractual formalization that is developing unimpeded'.[36]

31. A study of platform work in Germany outlines the monitoring mechanisms available with algorithms: M.Ivanova, et al., 'The App as a Boss? Control and Autonomy in Application-Based Management' Work in Progress interdisziplinärer Arbeitsforschung Nr. 2, Frankfurt (Oder): Viadrina, 2018.
32. For further discussion *see* D. Mangan, 'Labour Law: The Medium and the Message' and A. Seifert, 'Employee Data Protection in the Transnational Company' in F. Hendrickx and V. de Stefano eds, *Game Changers in Labour Law* (Deventer: Wolters Kluwer, 2018).
33. D. Coates, *Models of Capitalism* (Cambridge: Polity Press, 2000), 256.
34. *Health Services and Support – Facilities Subsector Bargaining Association v. British Columbia* 2007 SCC 27; *Demir and Baykara v. Turkey*, Application No. 34503/97, 12 November 2008.
35. *Saskatchewan Federation of Labour v. Saskatchewan* 2015 SCC 4.
36. A. Bogg & R. Dukes, 'The Contract of Employment and Collective Labour Law' in M. Freedland (ed) *The Contract of Employment* (Oxford: OUP, 2016), 99. Though these authors' comment relates to the profound effect of disintegrated forms of collective resistance in UK labour law, the topic of the present study fits within that overarching argument.

Collateral to the changes promulgated by information technology, other premises are being challenged such as the limitations of the largely binary approach to the workplace, workers or employers. The underdetermined area of self-employment has been a convenient tool utilized to facilitate commerce. Self-employment has also become an emblem of this transition period's effect on the labour market. The platform economy promises the individual the flexibilities and opportunities represented by economic liberalism. Conversely, these same platforms can also contribute to growing awareness of inequalities in the labour market.[37] This is the risk and reward for workers of the platform economy.

While 'gig economy' work has been found, so far, to be questionable on the analysis of mutual flexibility,[38] the argument persists that the 'gig worker' has more autonomy. Individuals participating in platform work acknowledge autonomy as a drawing factor; though evidence may be a matter of degree. In a German study of food delivery applications,[39] autonomy was construed as flexibility in timing, locations for carrying out work, and performance. These may not be orthodox elements of autonomy.[40] Nevertheless, riders found freedom in these aspects of their work. This form of autonomy and how it contrasts with an orthodox understanding can be disputed. Platform work appears to offer a restricted form of autonomy, where gig workers seek out their goals by making a more limited choice. The constrained choices in gig work offer sad commentary on the nature of jobs that the avoidance of human managers would constitute a key aspect of autonomy.[41] The disparity between what is perceived as autonomy as compared to a reality (here in a work relationship) raises an important question for further consideration: how is autonomy to be measured within a work scenario? Is autonomy a matter of degree,[42] thereby leading to a question of choices? To what extent may choices be curbed before autonomy has been lost? Overall, autonomy obtained in the 'gig economy' may come at a different cost: the fragmentation of work coupled with the commensurate fragmentation of remuneration. The larger picture is that 'gig' work contributes to the on-going decline of the standard employment relationship.

37. *See* for example, J.D. Ostry, P. Loungani, D. Furceri, 'Neoliberalism: Oversold?' (2016) 53 Fin. & Dev. 38.
38. For example, *Pimlico Plumbers v. Smith* [2018] UKSC 29 and *Uber v. Aslam* [2018] EWCA 2748 (leave to appeal to the UKSC has been granted).
39. Ivanova et al. n. 31, 11 ff.
40. Gardner wrote of an autonomous person being 'one who confronts a range of possible goals as objects of choice, and who sets some aside in order to pursue others': J. Gardner, *From Personal Life to Private Law* (Oxford: OUP, 2018), 223.
41. 'Perhaps the salience of this limited vision of freedom means that it is uniquely disempowering to have a fellow person order us about': D. Das Acevedo, 'Unbundling Freedom in the Sharing Economy' (2018) 91 South. Cal. L. Rev. 793, 812.
42. Writing about the imposition of risk, John Oberdienk commented – 'One nevertheless suffers the harm of having one's autonomy curtailed, for the risk imposition narrows one's safe option': J. Oberdienk, *Imposing Risk: A Normative Framework* (Oxford: OUP, 2017), 87.

[A] From Control to Fragmentation

The theme of control connects the different periods of work. The Ford and Taylor approaches relied upon detailed control over the workforce with the implicit threat of termination. The force of the potential for dismissal remains one of the most powerful tools for workplace discipline.[43] It is not, however, the only tool. The trend in 'gig' economy work has been fragmentation: parcelling out distinct tasks, each incurring remuneration, incentivizes workers to perform each task as instructed, thereby turning conformity to privately set standards of service into its own reward. The threat of termination has become the risk of not receiving another task. And yet, control has been retained.

The platform work business model depends upon the static nature of employment status: 'by characterizing the relationship as one of arms-length dealing with self-employed independent contractors, not employees.'[44] Labour law has, for some time, seen forms of work that diverge from the standard employment relationship. Moving away from this standard has been linked with cost savings for undertakings. And so, the 'gig' economy extends that commercial objective of profit.[45] Platform work is the first to premise its business model in such a wholesale manner on the malleability of employment status. By avoiding (or attempting to) the regulatory dimension of labour law entirely, these companies devised a means to limit labour costs and to implement a system designed to create efficiency; all while retaining the kind of control found in the Ford and Taylor models.

'Gig' work has also highlighted self-employment and revealed how profoundly influential the master-servant legacy has been. For much of the 20th century, the primary distinction of importance had been that between employers and employees. The hierarchy of the time had become plain and exclusive: while the primacy of employers' commercial judgment had been established, employees remained a recognized category[46] warranting attention. Those who fell outside of that binary classification were a sort of disregarded misfit. The 'gig' economy has pushed that misfit to the forefront of consideration. As 20th-century labour law transcribed the master-servant relationship into the employment contract, 'a set of hierarchical norms, about discipline and obedience and loyalty' had been included.[47] With the 'gig' economy, the observation may be expanded to add the limitation of the nomenclature; that is, not only was there a hierarchy which subordinated employees, but they were also viewed as (at least largely) incapable of moving up in this hierarchy. Platform work ostensibly conveys the (sometimes dubious) potential of being one's own employer.

43. *The Economist*, 'Too Many Chiefs' (26 June 2010), 72.
44. M.W. Finkin, *Beclouded Work, Beclouded Workers in Historical Perspective* (2016) 37 Comp. Lab. L. & Pol'y J. 603, 611.
45. House of Commons Work and Pensions Committee, *Self-employment and the gig economy* HC 847 (1 May 2017), para. 19.
46. Rights being granted to them to the exclusion of those the non-unionized worker: Bogg & Dukes, n. 38, 109.
47. M. Freedland, 'Otto Kahn-Freund, the Contract of Employment and the Autonomy of Labour Law' in A. Bogg, C.Costello, A.C.L. Davies, and J. Prassl eds, *The Autonomy of Labour Law* (Oxford: Hart, 2015), 29.

[B] The Shape of Liberalism

The purposes behind commercial law and employment regulation must also be situated within the larger context of liberalism. Disconnect has emerged between the two purposes leading to the subsuming of one area by the other. A narrative familiar in industrial relations, platform work extends the liberalization of workplace obligations and regulations in the name of economic competitiveness. It also asks how viable is the promise of the platform economy: are individuals actually their own bosses?

Information technology in the workplace reveals challenges to the purposive approach. First, the approach favours the consistent endorsement of a purpose. This becomes problematic when looking at settings where aims may conflict. Taking social media surveillance in the workplace as an example, conflict may be detected between an efficiency-focus of labour laws as adjunct to economic growth and the individual rights of privacy and speech accorded to workers through regulation and case law.[48] Although the GDPR attempts to balance commercial interests with individual rights, it is a confused guide when applied to the workplace. Moreover, it continues the emphasis on commercial concerns.

A few elements need to be unpacked. On a conceptual level, the platform economy approximates a red line for labour law – 'labour is not a commodity.'[49] Platform work overtly monetizes the provision of labour. The Philadelphia Declaration of 1944 has left the concept of self-employment without meaningful exploration in labour law. Instead, by default, it has fallen into commercial law.

Commercial law has also broadly operated as a binary classification system between consumers and commercial entities. The existence and importance[50] of small to medium-sized enterprise (SMEs)[51] question this simple division. Collective bargaining constituted a recognition of the imbalance of bargaining power between employees and employers. Consumers also fall under a similar circumstance. Bringing labour and commercial law together, do the self-employed (and those with few employees) fall into the SME category? Micro-employers constitute the smallest version in the range of SMEs. They have fewer than ten employees. Based on the absence of a minimum threshold, the self-employed (on their own or with a partner) would seem to be

48. For a comparative discussion of the topic *see*, D. Mangan, 'Online Speech and the Workplace: Public Right, Private Regulation' (2018) 39 Comp. Lab. L. & Pol'y J. 357.
49. International Labour Organization (ILO), Philadelphia Declaration 1944. Frank Hendrickx' challenge to this premise should be kept in mind: F. Hendrickx, 'Foundations and Functions of Contemporary Labour Law' (2013) 3 ELLJ 108.
50. SMEs account for two-thirds of employers in the EU and 99.3 % of private sector employers in the UK: respectively, European Commission, *Annual Report on European SMEs 2017-2018* (November 2018); Business, Energy and Industrial Strategy Committee, *Small Business and Productivity* HC 807 (5 December 2018).
51. SMEs are employing enterprises with between 1 and 249 workers. SMEs consist of three sub-groups: micros (1-9 employees); small (10-49 employees); and medium (50-249 employees). This is the breakdown used by the European Commission following EU recommendation 2003/361.

included.[52] This cohort must be seen as being in a vulnerable position compared to larger SMEs, let alone large companies. This complicates a universal approach to employment status whose 'goal is first and foremost to ensure protection to those who need it, rather than ensure determinacy'.[53] Such an approach relies upon the vulnerabilities characterizing employment relations. Vulnerability may be viewed as a by-product of the reification of contract and the façade of choice.[54]

The Ontario Court of Appeal decision in *Heller v. Uber Technologies Inc.*[55] illustrates a significant problem along these lines. The contract between Uber and Ontario-based drivers contained a dispute resolution/forum selection clause. It applied Dutch Law and required mediation and arbitration to be held in Amsterdam, under International Chamber of Commerce rules of mediation and arbitration.[56] *Heller* brought out an important question in the *Uber* litigation: if we accept Uber's argument that these drivers are their own commercial entities, is this case an instance of a larger entity taking advantage of a smaller and more vulnerable one? Additionally, if Uber drivers are self-employed, are there private law tools available which provide a means to contest a clause such as that found in *Heller*? The Court of Appeal ruled the provision was unconscionable. Treating all commercial entities as a homogenous group, then, can facilitate exploitation.

The gig economy implicitly criticizes the long-held understanding in labour law of the worker's subordination to the employer. The premise of platform-based companies has been that they contract with service providers independently; the relationship being that of two commercial parties. Taking the UK example, the Supreme Court has been consistent since its decision in *Autoclenz v. Belcher*[57] that it will not rely solely upon the written contract. It will also look at the 'the reality of the situation where written documentation may not reflect the reality of the relationship'.[58] The reality in each of *Uber*, *Pimlico Plumbers* and *Autoclenz* was not one of commercial parties forming a contract, but rather of workers and employers. Beyond the UK, on appeal from Spain, the Court of Justice of the European Union rejected Uber's self-identification as a technology company.[59] In 2019, the Paris Court of Appeal also found

52. European Commission, 'What is an SME?' https://ec.europa.eu/growth/smes/business-friendly-environment/sme-definition_en. The definitions are based upon EU Recommendation 2003/361.
53. G. Davidov, 'The Status of Uber Drivers: A Purposive Approach' (2017) 6 Spanish Lab. L. and Emp. Rel. J. 6, 9.
54. M. Albertson Fineman, 'The Vulnerable Subject: Anchoring Equality in the Human Condition' (2008) 20 Yale J of L. and Fem. 1, 2.
55. 2019 ONCA 1 (leave to appeal to the Supreme Court of Canada granted 23 May 2019).
56. The ICC's rules for mediation and arbitration, respectively: https://iccwbo.org/dispute-resolution-services/mediation/mediation-rules/; https://iccwbo.org/dispute-resolution-services/arbitration/rules-of-arbitration/.
57. [2011] UKSC 21. This decision built upon earlier case law such as *Snook v. London and West Riding Investments Ltd* [1967] 2 QB 786 and *Firthglow Ltd (trading as Protectacoat) v. Szilagyi* [2009] EWCA Civ 98.
58. *Ibid* [22].
59. C-434/15, *Associación Professional Elite Taxi v. Uber Systems Spain SL* (20 December 2017).

Uber drivers to be workers.[60] In each of these instances, a common point has been the tremendous amount of control exerted over the individuals who are alleged to be contracting as independent commercial entities. The protective aspect of labour law stands out here.[61] The construction of these impugned contracts emphasised the kind of control exerted by employers, not independent commercial entities. This implied paternalism has curbed meaningful discussion away from the less charted terrain between employee/worker and self-employed individual.

Although the reality of equal commercial parties contracting with each other was hollow in the Uber litigation, Western economies believe in and rely upon small businesses. Between 2000 and 2013, UK SMEs grew rapidly, increasing in number by about 41%.[62] While perhaps not necessarily grounded in empirical evidence, there is a rhetorical link between SMEs and the notion of innovation which keeps the theory of economic development moving. The potential must be there for an individual with her own car driving passengers to their destinations to subscribe to a modified form of autonomy at work in order for the platform economy to persist. The fact that so far courts have found the reality not to be one of commercial parties contracting measures how embedded within discourse the characteristic of subordination has been.[63] There is freedom to contract between commercial parties, but this freedom is antithetical to the subordination found in the employment scenario. The question here is how to separate the purpose of labour law (with regards to the vexed question of employment status) and a purpose of commercial law; facilitating entrepreneurial activity which requires the legal system to be 'flexible and responsive to rapid change.'[64]

[C] The GDPR and the Continuation of the Problem

The intersection between information technology regulation and the workplace has been a difficult terrain to map out given the many questions surrounding the GDPR.[65]

---

60. 'Le lien unissant un chauffeur et Uber reconnu "contrat de travail"' *Le monde* (11 January 2019). https://www.lemonde.fr/emploi/article/2019/01/11/le-lien-unissant-un-chauffeur-et-uber-reconnu-contrat-de-travail_5407507_1698637.html.
61. 'Labour law paternalism has taken on its mature form, seeing the market as an irreparably hostile environment for subordinate workers, so that the only way to serve their interests is to protect them from the market': R. Del Punta, 'Labour Law and the Capability Approach' (2016) 32 Int. J. Comp. Lab.Law and Ind. Rel. 32, 383, 398.
62. BIS, *Business Population Estimates for the UK and Regions 2013*, (2013) 5.
63. To illustrate: 'The employer-employee relationship is contractual, with particular rights and obligations on either side, and is characterised by legal subordination. It is governed by its own legal rules, which differ considerably from those generally applicable to relations between individuals': *Barbulescu* (Grand Chamber) [117] which is a translation of the Court of the Fifth Section's ruling in *Saumier v. France*, Application 74734/14, [60] (12 January 2017).
64. R. Goode, 'The Shaping of Commercial Law' in R. Goode, *Fundamental Concepts of Commercial Law: Fifty Years of Reflection* (Oxford: OUP, 2018), 169. Goode would seem to echo Chalmers' comment much earlier – '... the development of mercantile law ... ought to be a living and growing body of law ...': Chalmers, n. 19, 150.
65. For further discussion see D. Mangan, 'Beyond Procedural Protection: Information Technology, Privacy, and the Workplace' (2019) 44 Eur. L. Rev. 559. Many issues arise from the GDPR such as gender discrimination. On this point *see* further M. Kullmann, 'Platform Work, Algorithmic Decision-Making, and EU Gender Equality Law' (2018) 34 Int. J. Comp. Lab. L. Ind. Rel. 1.

The particular consideration here is the mixed purposes evident in the Regulation; protection for individualized rights as well as the facilitation of data flows for commercial aims. The GDPR furthers commercial purposes, while overlooking labour law aims.

The GDPR embodies the challenges of reconciling the purposes of labour and commercial law within one locale. It begins with the definitions in Article 4 of the GDPR. Employers may utilize the monitoring capabilities of information technology for the purpose of 'getting ahead' of any potential issues. They would then be gathering 'personal data' about their workers (data subjects) which is 'any information relating to an identified or identifiable natural person' and this data includes 'a name, an identification number, location data, an online identifier or to one or more factors specific to the physical, physiological, genetic, mental, economic, cultural or social identity of that natural person'. Collecting personal data could also be through automated means. The GDPR calls this 'profiling': the analysis of personal data including 'performance at work, economic situation, health, personal preferences, interests, reliability, behaviour, location or movements'. More broadly, this gathering process constitutes 'processing' which means 'any operation or set of operations which is performed on personal data or on sets of personal data, whether or not by automated means, such as collection, recording, organization, structuring, storage, adaptation or alteration, retrieval, consultation, use, disclosure by transmission, dissemination or otherwise making available, alignment or combination, restriction, erasure or destruction'. In either situation, employers are 'controllers' ('determines the purposes and means of the processing of personal data') and the entities which process this personal data are called 'processors' ('processes personal data on behalf of the controller'). The GDPR, then, seems to have been devised in a manner so as to capture a wide range of actions in which the data of data subjects may be processed or profiled.

This wide capture area expresses the importance placed by the European Union (EU) on protection of dignity of the individual. The aim has been highlighted in two articles of the *Charter of Fundamental Rights of the European Union.*[66] Article 1 states that human dignity 'is inviolable [and] ... must be respected and protected'. The connection to the workplace is identifiable in Article 31, which states: 'every worker has the right to working conditions which respect his or her health, safety and dignity'.[67] If a purpose of information technology regulation is protection of dignity (particularly given the importance of EU regulation in this area for non-EU countries), the question is whether this aim may be reconciled with the purposive approach to labour law in other jurisdictions.[68]

---

66. *Charter of Fundamental Rights of the European Union* [2012] OJ C 326/391.
67. This provision echoes the connection made by Hugo Sinzheimer: R. Dukes, 'Constitutionalizing Employment Relations: Sinzheimer, Kahn-Freund, and the Role of Labour Law' (2008) 35 J L Soc'y 341, 345.
68. This query may also be contemplated as one in which EU law views dignity as a fundamental right, though this status is not necessarily accorded to dignity in other jurisdictions. Still, here, the matter is not viewed as one of labour rights constituting fundamental rights. Rather, it is that there are certain rights (such as speech and privacy/dignity) that should permeate the artificial barriers of distinct regulatory settings.

Part of the difficulty in explicating the GDPR has been the evidence of differing purposes coming through in the final draft. The phrase 'is necessary for entering into, or performance of, a contract between the data subject and a data controller' illustrates the conflicting purposes embodied in the terms commercial and labour law. This wording arises in a few places within the GDPR, such as Article 7(4). Article 6(1)(b) expands upon the difficulty. It defines lawful data processing as including that 'necessary for the performance of a contract to which the data subject is part'. 'Profiling' algorithms for workplace outputs also pose similarly complicated questions.[69] Another example, Article 22 provides the data subject with a right to avoid a decision based solely on automated processing that carries a legal effect.[70] Putting aside the absence of clarity regarding the provision's application,[71] Article 22 does not apply when the decision arrived at by automated processing 'is necessary for entering into, or performance of, a contract between the data subject and a data controller'. The Article 29 Working Party in its *Opinion 2/2017 on data processing at work*[72] legitimated the phrase in writing 'performance of a contract and legitimate interests can sometimes be invoked, provided the processing is strictly necessary for a legitimate purpose and complies with the principles of proportionality and subsidiarity'. An employer may argue it must have the capacity to determine whether or not workers are adhering to contractual obligations. If (e.g.,) monitoring of employees (which would include gathering their personal data) is viewed as an aspect of the performance of the employment contract, the rights in the GDPR would seem to stop at the office door. The commercial purpose (facilitating trade) usurps the regulatory aim of labour law as governing the relations between workers and employers.

§3.04 CONCLUSION

From Ford and Taylor to the 'gig': this measures a period of transition in the workplace; 'a shift from vertically-integrated, nationally-based, standardized, Fordist production to increasingly transnational, post-fordist, "flexible" production'.[73] The intersection between information technology and the workplace poses questions regarding the purposive approach. The regulatory aim of labour law confronts the facilitative objective of a commercial approach, producing a purposive conflict. The dominance of economic liberalism has left many jurisdictions ill-equipped to address the disconnect of aims between regulating the workplace and facilitating commerce. Consequently, a preoccupation with commerce has created a situation in which GDPR protections arguably cease when a worker enters her workplace. There must be an on-going

69. Article 4(4) (profiling).
70. Article 21, the right to object, also raises difficult questions within a work context.
71. May a human manager simply rely upon the data produced by an automated source in making a decision? If so, the decision would seem to be largely arrived at through automated means with only a facsimile of human decision-making.
72. WP 249 (8 June 2017).
73. P. Ireland, 'From Amelioration to Transformation: Capitalism, the Market, and Corporate Reform' in J. Conaghan, R.M. Fischl, K. Klare eds, *Labour Law in an Era of Globalization* (Oxford: OUP, 2005), 197.

discussion regarding information technology and the workplace. Part of the discussion must include the distinctly individual but discrete conception of information technology rights as reconciled to the labour law framework.

CHAPTER 4

Workers Without Workplaces and Unions Without Unity: Non-standard Forms of Employment, Platform Work and Collective Bargaining

Antonio Aloisi & Elena Gramano

§4.01 INTRODUCTION, BACKGROUND AND RESEARCH QUESTIONS

In recent years, there has been a surge of interest in the impact of the organizational restructuring of firms and digital transformation of work, also in light of the advent of platform work. New working patterns in the gig-economy blatantly exclude workers (almost invariably categorized as independent contractors) from employment protections and social benefits traditionally afforded to employees. Concomitantly, technological change represents a major challenge for collective bargaining systems, given that they are often still predicated on the concept of a standard employment relationship (SER).

In spite of recent advances,[1] public debate on the changing world of work seems insufficiently focused on how technology is altering power relationships;[2] it also underestimates the role and implications of industrial relations patterns.[3] Accordingly,

1. H. Johnston, C. Land-Kazlauskas, *On Demand and Organized: Developing Collective Agency, Representation and Bargaining in the Gig Economy*, ILO Conditions of Work and Employment Series No. 94. 2018; K. Vandaele, *Will Trade Unions Survive in the Platform Economy? Emerging Patterns of Platform Workers' Collective Voice and Representation in Europe*, ETUI Research Paper. 2018.
2. B. Rogers, *People Analytics and Labor Standards*, Paper presented at the LLRN 3rd Conference, Labour Law Research Network, Toronto 25-27 June 2017.
3. A.C.L. Davies, *'Half a Person'. A Legal Perspective on Organizing and Representing 'NonStandard'* Workers, A. Bogg, T. Novitz (ed), *Voices at Work: Continuity and Change in the Common Law World*, (Oxford: OUP, 2014).

understanding the direction that work will take in the coming years must necessarily involve a greater emphasis on the collective dimension of non-standard arrangements, since the interrelation between innovation and jobs is mediated by how work is concretely organized and negotiated.[4]

Declining union power, falling union density, diminishing collective bargaining coverage, the shift toward individual decentralized bargaining, the individualization of the workforce, and the trend among firms to outsource core and non-core activities have molded a fragmented labor market by contributing to the spread of casual labor in developed and developing economies.[5] Non-standard forms of employment (NSFE) now makes up around one in three jobs in Organisation for Economic Co-operation and Development (OECD) countries.[6]

Against this backdrop, something unexpected is happening in sectors where working conditions are far from transparent, predictable, and sustainable.[7] Ways of generating social bonding at work and expressing collective action are taking on new forms.[8] In the "fissured workplace,"[9] workers find themselves confronted with the need to define or rebuild a specific identity in order to ensure recognition and overcome invisibility. The questions to be addressed are whether and to what extent non-standard workers can build impactful movements (or even unions) with a view of exercising the right to organize and bargain collectively. Moreover, how can traditional and institutional workers' organizations resist the trend toward precariousness and support actions aimed at bettering working conditions[10]?

After presenting the legal determinants of NSFE, this article investigates challenges to freedom of association and the effective recognition of the right to collective bargaining for non-standard workers, from a legal and practical perspective. In particular, the article examines the existing legal framework with a critical approach and stresses the relevance of legal hurdles that non-standard workers face, with a particular focus on the implications related to competition law and its rigid limits in the European Union (EU) system. Finally, the article sketches a mapping exercise of initiatives of workers' organization, by distinguishing classic resources of unionization from other tools (e.g., social media groups, strategic litigation, rating widgets) in a selection of European countries.

4. F. Hendrickx, *The Future of Collective Labour Law in Europe*, European Labour Law Journal, 1(1), 59-79, 2010.
5. International Labour Office, *Non-standard employment around the world: Understanding challenges, shaping prospects*. Geneva: ILO. 2016.
6. OECD, *In It Together: Why Less Inequality Benefits All*, Paris. 2015.
7. A. Broughton, et al., *Precarious Employment in Europe: Patterns, Trends and Policy Strategies* (Studies for the European Parliament's Committee on Employment and Social Affairs, 2016).
8. K. Vandaele, *Will Trade Unions Survive in the Platform Economy? Emerging Patterns of Platform Workers' Collective Voice and Representation in Europe*, ETUI Research Paper. 2018.
9. D. Weil, *The fissured workplace: Why work became so bad for so many and what can be done to improve it*, (Cambridge: HUP, 2014).
10. C. Garden, *Unions are wondering: Resist or assist?*, retrieved from https://goo.gl/cCm4dD. 2017, March 15.

§4.02 AN UPDATED NOMENCLATURE OF MISUSED DEFINITIONS

[A] Non-standard Forms of Employment

Non-standard forms of work can be investigated as a litmus test in order to get a better understanding of the state of the art of the "collective" dimension of digital transformation of work.

One of the key challenges to the research on this topic is the lack of a common definition and conceptualization.[11] This section will define the scope of a working definition of "non-standard," "atypical," "casual," "irregular," "alternative," "precarious," or even "contingent" forms of employment for theoretical purposes. It has to be acknowledged that the proposed labels cover various arrangements that might have widely different normative and social implications while sharing a significant number of features. Moreover, criteria for identifying what the legal system recognizes as an NSFE vary appreciably among local jurisdictions or may be influenced by the constantly evolving socioeconomic context.[12] For instance, at the European level, casual work can be distinguished from other NSFE, such as part-time, fixed-term or temporary agency work, which has already received growing political attention and consequent regulatory intervention.[13]

There is no universally accepted legal definition of non-standard employment other than "employment offering less security and fewer benefits than the standard employment relationship"[14] defined as a subordinate employment (full-time and of indefinite duration) that guarantees a stable income and secures pension payments and a wide range of benefits for the workers.[15] This generally acceptable characterization operates by contrast and encompasses a heterogeneous set of employment forms, mostly work that "deviates," along one or more axes, from the definition of SER which in turn is a rather strict classification, failing to take into account the "internal" diversity of this "prototype."[16]

11. A. Gillespie, et al., *Technology induced atypical work-forms. report for the office of technology assessment of the European Parliament* (Brussels: STOA, 1999).
12. A. Lo Faro, *Core and Contingent Work: A Theoretical* Framework, E. Ales, O. Deinert, J. Kenner (ed), *Core and Contingent Work in the European Union: A Comparative Analysis*, (Oxford: OUP, 2017): 7-23.
13. Council Directive 97/81/EC of 15 December 1997 concerning the Framework Agreement on Part-time work concluded by UNICE, CEEP and the ETUC, OJ [1999] L14/9; Council Directive 1999/70/EC of 28 June 1999 concerning the Framework Agreement on Fixed-term work concluded by ETUC, UNICE and CEEP, OJ [1999] L175/43; Directive 2008/14/EC of the European Parliament and the Council of 19 November 2008 on temporary agency work OJ [2008] L327/9.
14. M. Jeffery, *Not Really Going to Work? Of the Directive on Part-Time Work, 'Atypical Work' and Attempts to Regulate It*, Industrial Law Journal, 27(3), 193-213, 1998.
15. L. Delsen, *Atypical Employment Relations and Government Policy in Europe*, Labour, 5(3), 285-316, 1991.
16. I. Regalia (ed.), *Regulating new forms of employment: Local experiments and social innovation in Europe*, (London and New York: Taylor and Francis, 2006).

Although the contours continue to change, by using a broad and inclusive definition based on spatial, temporal and employment protection legislation divergences,[17] it could be said that NSFE include temporary employment, part-time work, temporary agency work, self-employment, dependent self-employment, disguised employment relationships, and other (new) forms of work such as platform-mediated arrangements. In this respect, Eurofound conducted a "mapping exercise" resulting in the identification of nine distinct forms of employment as new forms (or, better, ways) of work since 2000, namely employee sharing, job sharing, interim management, casual work, ICT-based work, voucher-based work, portfolio work, crowd and collaborative employment.[18]

It would be tedious and beyond the scope of this article to list and describe all forms in detail (for a preliminary attempt to identify sub-categories of NSFE according to four institutions, *see* Table 4.1). Needless to say, the incidence of these different types, and hence, the challenges posed for trade unions, vary considerably across countries.[19]

Table 4.1 Different Forms of Non-standard of Employment, According to Four Institutions[20]

	EU	*ILO*	*OECD*	*Eurofound*
Fixed-term or temporary contracts	✓	✓	✓	✓
Part-time work	✓	✓	✓	✓
Temporary agency work	✓	✓	✓	✓
Self-employment or independent contract work	✓	✓	✓	✓
Dependent self-employment		✓	✓	
Disguised employment relationship		✓		

17. A.C.L. Davies, *Regulating Atypical Work: Beyond Equality*, N. Countouris, M. Freedland (ed.), *Resocialising Europe in a Time of Crisis*, (Cambridge: CUP, 2013): 230-249.
18. Eurofound, *New forms of employment*, Luxembourg. 2015a.
19. R. Gumbrell-McCormick, *European Trade Unions and 'Atypical' Workers*, Industrial Relations Journal, 42(3), 293-310, 2011.
20. Authors' own elaboration. *See* European Commission, *Employment and Social Developments in Europe 2014*, Luxembourg, 2015; International Labour Office, *Non-standard employment around the world: Understanding challenges, shaping prospects*. Geneva: ILO. 2016); OECD, *New forms of work in the digital economy*, Digital Economy Papers No. 260. Paris. 2016, 17; Eurofound, *Exploring self-employment in the European Union*, Publications Office of the European Union, Luxembourg. 2017.

[B] Self-employment

Little attention has traditionally been paid to the situation of self-employment arrangements, which should be listed among the numerous non-standard forms of work.[21] A preliminary remark must be made about the distinction of two different forms that are often overlapping from a material point of view although they should be considered separately in strictly legal terms. The literature has commonly labeled these intermediate zones in the "grey area," identifying "work that lie[s] half-way between work under an employment contract and self-employment,"[22] as (i) "economically dependent work" and (ii) "bogus self-employment."

If the employee status is the "gateway" to full employment coverage, in several jurisdictions an intermediate category has been created to offer a "secondary entrance" to a limited set of social rights.[23] The acceptance, or tolerance, however called, of an intermediate category of "quasi-subordinate" workers is increasing. However, some authors have claimed that "[t]he description or definition of economically dependent workers starts from the premise that (1) such workers are not employees, and (2) economically dependent work must not be used to hide the true nature of the employment relationship."[24] Depending on the specific national rules, these workers are commonly outside the scope of labor law protection (e.g., the rules on dismissals) and collective bargaining coverage and are subject to "promotional" fiscal and tax regulations.

As noted in a previous article, such an intermediate category of worker is quite widespread.[25] Several legal systems have experimented with implementing a legal tool similar to an "in-between" category to cover economically dependent workers, but the level of protection afforded and even the definition of dependency vary among countries.[26] Among the countries identifying a third status, two main approaches exist: either the creation of a totally new hybrid worker status with specific rights or the recognition of a specific subcategory in the independent work domain.[27] Some jurisdictions have concentrated on a legal threshold of economic dependency (e.g.,

21. A. Burke (ed), *The handbook of research on freelancing and self-employment*, (Dublin: Senate Hall Academic Publishing, 2015).
22. A. Perulli, *Economically dependent/quasi-subordinate (parasubordinate) employment: Legal, social and economic aspects*, Study for the European Commission (Brussels, 2003).
23. Relevant examples can be found in Germany, *see* B. Waas, *What Role for Solopreneurs in the Labour Market?*, European Labour Law Journal, 8(2), 154-177, 2017; Italy, *see* M. Del Conte, E. Gramano, *Looking to the Other Side of the Bench: The New Legal Status of Independent Contractors under the Italian Legal System*, Comparative Labor Law & Policy Journal, 39(3), 579-605, 2018; Spain, F. Trillo Párraga, *Economía digitalizada y relaciones de trabajo*, Revista de Derecho Social, 76, 59-74, 2016.
24. F. Rosioru, *Legal Acknowledgement of the Category of Economically Dependent Workers*, European Labour Law Journal, 5(3-4), 279-305, 2014.
25. M.A. Cherry, A. Aloisi, *"Dependent Contractors" in the Gig Economy: A Comparative Approach*, American University Law Review, 66(3), 635-689, 2017.
26. M. Freedland, *Application of Labour and Employment Law Beyond the Contract of Employment*, International Labour Review, 146(1-2), 3-20, 2007.
27. M. Pallini, *Il lavoro economicamente dipendente*, (Padova: CEDAM, 2013).

Germany[28] and Spain[29]) while others have focused on the worker's strict coordination with the principal's business organization (e.g., Italy[30]).

In most cases, "economically dependent" and "bogus" or "false" self-employment share working conditions reflecting those of employees rather than of self-employed workers. But these commonalities aside, each expression emphasizes a different "prevailing feature." The first group represents a legal definition for an intermediate category (often singled out as a subset of self-employment), while the second formula relates to cases of evasion. When it comes to "false self-employment," the illicit and premeditated aim is to conceal an employment relationship and circumvent statutory or collectively agreed provisions, payroll taxes, and social security contributions.[31]

This fraudulent situation occurs when a company manipulates employment contracts in order to misrepresent the underlying reality, thus nullifying or attenuating legal responsibilities and protection afforded by the law.[32] For this reason, the most effective, yet unpredictable, way to contrast this condition is to challenge the formal

---

28. German law also recognizes a third category of employee-like person (*arbeitnehmeraehnliche Person*). An employee-like person must perform his or her duty to (1) the benefit of a client; (2) under service contract for a specific project; and (3) personally and largely without collaboration of subordinate employees. Importantly, the employee-like person works mainly for one client and relies on a single client for 50% of his or her income. These workers cannot claim unfair dismissal but do have access to labor courts, and conclude collective agreements with normative effect. Moreover, they are entitled to annual leave and protection against discrimination.
29. In Spain, a specific category for economically dependent autonomous workers has existed since 2007. The Spanish Statute for Self-Employed Workers crafted a third category of workers: *"Trabajador Autonomo Economicamente Dependiente"* (or TRADE). The TRADE workers were extended a fairly comprehensive package of benefits and protections that are almost as good as those given to employees. The crucial component is a dependence on the principal for at least 75 % of the worker's income.
30. In Italy, contracts of coordinated and continuous collaboration (*"contratti di collaborazione coordinata e continuativa"*) have existed since 1973 when Law 533 prescribed that the rules of procedure for labor litigation also applied to the "relationship of agency, of commercial representation and other relations of collaboration materializing in a continuous and coordinated provision, predominantly personal, even if not of subordinate character". The ultimate result is a return to the binary distinction of employee and self-employed workers, although the 2015 reform has extended employment protection to workers whose performance is organized by the client.
31. A. Thörnquist, *False Self-Employment and Other Precarious Forms of Employment in the 'Grey Area' of the Labour Market*, International Journal of Comparative Labour Law & Industrial Relations, 31(4), 411-429, 2015.
32. E. Ales, M. Faioli, *Self-employment and bogus self-employment in the European construction industry*, Expert Report, Self-employment and bogus self-employment in the construction industry in Italy. 2010, http://www.efbww.org/pdfs/Annex%2014%20-%20Final%20report%20italy.pdf. According to the Employment Relationship Recommendation, 2006 (No. 198), "disguised employment relationships" is the situation occurring "when an employer treats an individual as other than an employee in a manner that hides his or her true legal status as an employee". However, disguised employment relationships "may also involve masking the identity of the employer, when the person designated as an employer is an intermediary, with the intention of releasing the real employer from any involvement in the employment relationship and above all from any responsibility to the workers", International Labour Office, *The employment relationship*, International Labour Conference, 95th Session, 2006 Report V(1). 2006. *See also* J. Heyes, T. Hastings, *The practices of enforcement bodies in detecting and preventing bogus self-employment*, European Platform Undeclared Work, (European Commission, Brussels, 2017).

classification before a tribunal. The rise of NSFE and misclassification of employment relationships are strongly intertwined, not least because the emergence of the "hybrid" contractual templates could make the disguise of "bogus self-employment" even easier.

[C] Platform-Mediated Work

Coming now to platform-facilitated arrangements, the commonly used formulas are "sharing," "on-demand" or "gig" jobs. Despite that, very different models are lumped together under the umbrella definition of "platform-mediated work" in everyday parlance and this is not helpful. The literature seems to agree on a "*summa divisio*" between crowdsourcing and work on-demand through platform;[33] legal experts tend to "focus separately [...] on online and offline workers, because their places of work (remote versus face-to-face) and the relationship with clients (tele-mediated versus direct) create very different patterns of work, exposing workers to different risks."[34] A preliminary distinction between crowdsourcing and work on-demand can be drawn by taking into account the place of performance of work and the mechanisms through which work is requested or obtained. In the first model, the client and the service provider rarely (if ever) experience a face-to-face interaction, and services are electronically and globally transmittable, while the second form is often carried out in-person, locally, and with customer and worker in physical proximity.[35]

[D] Collective Rights, Focus on Collective Bargaining

From the worker's perspective, the organization of common interests along collective lines has traditionally proved to be the most effective way to achieve a countervailing power to the employer and re-establish a balance of forces in the employment relationship.[36] Hence, unionization is aimed at levelling the bargaining "playing field" between capital (or management) and labor. Because of the ever-present threat of a withdrawal of labor power, collective bargaining tends to be far more effective for workers than individualized bargaining.

33. V. De Stefano, *The Rise of the "Just-in-Time Workforce": On-Demand Work, Crowdwork, and Labor Protection in the "Gig Economy"*, Comparative Labor Law & Policy Journal, 37(3), 471-504, 2016, A. Aloisi, *Commoditized Workers. Case Study Research on Labor Law Issues Arising from a Set of 'On-Demand/Gig Economy' Platforms*, Comparative Labor Law & Policy Journal, 37(3), 653-690, 2016.
34. U. Huws, et al., *Work in the European gig economy. research results from the UK, Sweden, Germany, Austria, The Netherlands, Switzerland and Italy*, (Foundation for European Progressive Studies, 2017).
35. V. De Stefano, A. Aloisi, *European Legal framework for digital labour platforms*, (Luxembourg: Publications Office of the European Union, 2018).
36. S. Liebman, *Individuale e collettivo nel contratto di lavoro*, (Milano: Giuffré, 1993).

This section provides a definition for the "imprecise" notion of "collective bargaining"[37]—a process typically associated with workers in regular employment.[38] Collective bargaining is "a collective voice mechanism expressly based on a rationale which can be construed as "anti-competitive"—that labour is not a commodity and individual workers should not be required to compete over the terms and conditions on which they sell their labour."[39] Collective agreements and other expressions of collective voice and interests have been essential vehicles for securing decent working conditions for workers. Collective labor rights, together with corporate governance, active labor market policy, and work-life balance laws, may play a crucial role for mitigating dualism and rebalancing bargaining powers.[40] It has been demonstrated that, in those areas of the economy where collective agreements apply and work representatives are active, workers enjoy far better conditions and protection.[41] Indeed, collective agreements serve as important tools adjusting legal principles to specific economic situations of particular sectors.[42]

§4.03 THE CURRENT LEGAL FRAMEWORK, BETWEEN FUNDAMENTAL RIGHTS RECOGNITION AND ANTITRUST RESTRICTIONS[43]

This section explores the key legal issues pertaining to access to collective action and bargaining by providing a short summary of international legal standards.[44]

By operating as "enabling" or instrumental rights, freedom of association and the right to collective bargaining and collective action can make labor rights (more) effective for both employees and non-standard workers without the need to return to burdensome and intimidating individual protection and enforcement mechanisms, such as grievance procedures or individual lawsuits. Thanks to the "growing relevance

---

37. Understood as the legal tool (i) "determining working conditions"; (ii) "regulating relations between employer and workers"; and (iii) "regulating relations between employers' and workers' associations" (ILO Convention No. 154).
38. M. Rodriguez Piñero, B. Ferrer B., *International protection of collective bargaining, Labour law: Its role, trends and potential*, (Geneva: ILO, 2006).
39. P.A.J. Syrpis, S. McCrystal, *Competition Law and Worker Voice: Competition Law Impediments to Collective Bargaining in Australia and the European Union*, A. Bogg, T. Novitz (ed), *Voices at Work: Continuity and Change in the Common Law World*, (Oxford: OUP, 2014): 421-435.
40. C. Hobden, *Domestic workers organize—but can they bargain? Mapping collective bargaining and other forms of negotiation in the domestic work sector*, ILO's Work in Progress, retrieved from https://goo.gl/iqAeNW. 2015.
41. OECD, *New forms of work in the digital economy*, Digital Economy Papers No. 260. Paris. 2016, 17.
42. European Commission, *Green Paper, Modernising labour law to meet the challenges of the 21st century*, Luxembourg, 2006.
43. This section draws from V. De Stefano, A. Aloisi, *Fundamental Labour Rights,Platform Work and Protection of Non-standard* Workers, J.R. Bellace, B. ter Haar (ed), *Labour, Business and Human Rights Law*, (Cheltenham: Edward Elgar Publishing, 2019).
44. C. Rubiano, *Precarious Work and Access to Collective Bargaining: What Are the Legal Obstacles?*, International Journal of Labour Research, 5(1), 133-151, 2013; OECD, *Employment Outlook 2017*, Paris. 2017.

of legal intervention and action on a level above the state,"[45] freedom of association and the right to collective bargaining are guaranteed in numerous international treaties, incorporated into the universal catalog of human rights.

Within the Council of Europe legal order, the freedom of association and the right to collective bargaining were initially recognized by the Community Charter of the Fundamental Social Rights of Workers of 1989. Since the adoption of the Lisbon Treaty, the Community Charter has the same legal status as the European Treaties (Article 6 TEU). Moreover, the European Convention on Human Rights (ECHR) guarantees the freedom of association (Article 11). The European Court of Human Rights extended protection of freedom of association to self-employed persons[46] and the Grand Chamber held that the right to bargain collectively and to enter into collective agreements does constitute an essential element of Article 11.[47] Article 5 of the European Social Charter (Revised) (ESC) (adopted in 1996) sets out the right to form, join, and actively participate in associations designed to protect their members' professional interests. Article 6 of the ESC illustrates the content of the right "to bargain collectively" by listing the actions parties can undertake in order to ensure "its effective exercise," including active promotion. Article 28 of the Charter of the Fundamental Rights of the EU protects the right to collective bargaining, by specifically referring to "national laws and practices." The European Committee of Social Rights clarified that self-employed workers are protected under Article 6(2) of the ESC.[48]

The United Nations (UN) efforts for the protection of the right to association and collective bargaining include the Universal Declaration of Human Rights (UDHR) in 1948. Two of its provisions are of particular interest: Article 20(1) on the freedom of assembly and association and Article 23(4) on the right to form and join trade unions "for the protection of [one's own] interests." The International Labour Office (ILO) classifies four categories of Fundamental Principles and Rights at Work: freedom of association and the effective recognition of the right to bargaining collectively, elimination of all forms of forced or compulsory labor, effective abolition of child labor, and elimination of discrimination in respect of employment and occupation. These principles and rights are universal and, thus, apply to all workers.

In addition to this, according to ILO principles, the right to strike—an intrinsic corollary to the right to organize protected by Convention No. 87—is one of the essential means through which workers and their organizations may promote and defend their economic and social interests. It is not an absolute right; however, outside restricted situations (i.e., public servants, essential services and in case of acute national emergency), non-standard workers should be entitled to the right to strike, including the right to strike in solidarity. Article 2 of ILO Convention No. 87 provides that workers and employers, without distinction whatsoever, shall have the right to

45. F. Hendrickx, *The Future of Collective Labour Law in Europe*, European Labour Law Journal, 1(1), 59-79, 2010.
46. ECtHR, 17/07/2010, *Vörđur Ólafsson v. Iceland*, No. 20161/06.
47. ECtHR, 12/11/2008 (GC), *Demir a. Bayjara v. Turkey*, No. 34503/97, paragraph 153.
48. European Committee of Social Rights, *Irish Congress of Trade Unions* (ICTU) v. *Ireland*, Complaint No. 123/2016, 12 September 2018.

establish and, subject only to the rules of the organization concerned, to join organizations of their own choosing without prior authorization.[49] Article 4 of Convention No. 98 stipulates that measures appropriate to national conditions shall be taken, where necessary, to encourage and promote the full development and utilization of machinery for voluntary negotiation between employers or employers' organizations and workers' organizations, with a view to the regulation of terms and conditions of employment by means of collective agreements. According to Convention No. 98, governments have an obligation to promote collective bargaining for all workers and employers.

Despite that, a strict interpretation and enforcement of competition law effectively prevent self-employed and non-standard workers from bargaining collectively, on the grounds this could be considered illegal cartel action. In general, competition laws may operate as an impediment to the expression of collective voice by workers through collective bargaining. Where individual workers selling their labor are indeed classed as "undertakings," collective bargaining over pay by workers could constitute anti-competitive conduct. In most jurisdictions, this is avoided by providing that certain labor market transactions are exempted from antitrust prohibitions. Such exemptions may be expressly enacted or created through judicial interpretation. Indeed, "the rising prevalence of atypical forms of labour market engagement takes ever larger numbers of workers outside the scope of the competition law exemptions, in particular those workers engaged as 'independent contractors', and thereby risks limiting access to meaningful collective bargaining,"[50] unless workers are authorized or exempted to express their voices by courts or competition authorities.

In the EU's framework, despite the recognition of collective bargaining rights beyond a strict definition of "employee" (subordinate worker),[51] the Court's approach still falls short of a recognition of freedom of association and collective bargaining as universal labor rights, i.e., regardless of employment status. The Court of Justice of the European Union (CJEU) is still attached to its *Albany* decision,[52] the key case discussing the applicability of Article 101(1) TFEU to labor market collective agreements, decided by the European Court of Justice in 1999. In *Albany*, the question was whether a decision made by the organizations representing employers and workers in a given sector, in the context of a collective agreement, to set up a single pension fund responsible for managing a supplementary pension scheme, was contrary to what is

49. L. Fulton, *Trade unions protecting self-employed workers* (Brussels: ETUC, 2018); J. Hodges-Aeberhard, *The Right to Organise in Article 2 of Convention No. 87—What Is Meant by Workers Without Distinction Whatsoever*, International Labour Review, 128, 177-193, 1989.

50. P.A.J. Syrpis, S. McCrystal, *Competition Law and Worker Voice: Competition Law Impediments to Collective Bargaining in Australia and the European Union*, A. Bogg, T. Novitz (ed.), *Voices at Work: Continuity and Change in the Common Law World*, (Oxford: OUP, 2014): 421-435.

51. "The EU 'worker' concept is undoubtedly one that endorses a notion of subordination that includes 'control', but it also acknowledges more nuanced and loose concepts such as 'direction or supervision', that may include within its scope some domestic notions of quasi-subordinate work relations". N. Countouris, *The Concept of 'Worker' in European Labour Law: Fragmentation, Autonomy and Scope'*, Industrial Law Journal, 47(2), 192-225, 2017.

52. C-67/96 *Albany International BV v. Stichting Bedrijfspensioenfonds Textielindustrie* (1999) ECLI:EU:C:1999:430.

now Article 101(1) TFEU. After explaining the reasons why the agreement might be thought to be capable of infringing on what is now Article 101 TFEU, the Court stated that it was important to bear in mind that the Treaties contain not only goals of competitiveness but also social policy objectives. Thus, the Court concluded that:

> [i]t is beyond question that certain restrictions of competition are inherent in collective agreements between organisations representing employers and workers. However the social policy objectives pursued by such agreements would be seriously undermined if management and labour were subject to [Article 101 TFEU] when seeking jointly to adopt measures to improve conditions of work and employment.

First, when analyzing the nature of the agreement, the Court argued that the agreement "was concluded in the form of a collective agreement and is the outcome of collective negotiations between organizations representing employers and workers" (paragraph 62). Second, when it comes to defining its purposes, the Court stated that the scheme "seeks generally to guarantee a certain level of pension for all workers," thus "contribut[ing] directly to improving one of their working conditions, namely their remuneration" (paragraph 63). It is pivotal to underline that these features may well characterize an agreement potentially reached by non-standard workers' representatives.

Importantly, given the relevance that the Treaty of Lisbon also assigns to the ECHR, the *Albany* "exception-to-rule" approach does not seem consistent or even compatible with the jurisprudence of the Court of Strasbourg that considers the right to collective bargaining as an essential element of freedom of association under Article 11 of the ECHR and the importance assigned by this latter Court to the opinions of the ILO supervisory bodies when the Court determines the scope of the ECHR protection of collective rights. This is all the more relevant since the Court of Strasbourg also recognizes the freedom of association of the self-employed as protected under the Convention.[53]

Legal scholars cannot disregard these elements in treating future potential conflict between antitrust regulation and collective rights. Given the unequivocal recognition of these rights as fundamental and human rights—at least in European law and under ILO sources—these rights should be restricted only when they conflict with other human rights or, in ECHR terms, when a restriction is "necessary in a democratic society in the interests of national security or public safety, for the prevention of disorder or crime, for the protection of health or morals or for the protection of the rights and freedoms of others" (Article 11(2)).[54]

In addition, it is important that the existence of general exemptions for collective bargaining does not lead to complacency over the potential threat posed by competition law to worker voice expressed through collective bargaining. This is significant for

53. N. Countouris, *The Concept of "Worker" in European Labour Law: Fragmentation, Autonomy and Scope*, Industrial Law Journal, 47(2), 192-225, 2017.
54. V. De Stefano, A. Aloisi, *Fundamental Labour Rights, Platform Work and Protection of Non-standard Workers*, J.R. Bellace, B. ter Haar (ed.), *Labour, Business and Human Rights Law*, (Cheltenham: Edward Elgar Publishing, 2019).

two main reasons. On the one hand, workers continue to move toward more atypical forms of work, on the other, collective bargaining continues to fragment in many sectors of the economy. As a result, the protection afforded by the exemptions becomes ever narrower.

In 2014 the CJEU stated, in a judgment that has been harshly criticized,[55] that only "false self-employed" workers, disguised in order to avoid the application of some specific legislation (e.g., labor or fiscal regulations) which is considered unfavorable by the employer, have access to the right to collective bargaining.[56] The CJEU describes false self-employment as follows: "[o]n a proper construction of EU law, it is only when self-employed service providers who are members of one of the contracting employees' organizations and perform for an employer, under a works or service contract, the same activity as that employer's employed workers, [...] in other words, service providers *in a situation comparable to that of those workers*, that a provision of a collective labour agreement, which sets minimum fees for those self-employed service providers, does not fall within the scope of Article 101(1) TFEU" (paragraph 42, emphasis added). As a consequence, Article 101(1) TFEU does not apply "only when self-employed service providers who are members of one of the contracting employees' organizations and perform for an employer, under a work or service contract, the same activity as that employer's employed workers, are 'false self-employed'" (paragraph 42). To sum it up, only when the "condition" of self-employed workers is comparable to that of employees, collective bargaining agreements are exempted from EU legislation on cartels (price-fixing) and are thus legal.[57]

The EU exemption is a product of judicial interpretation. It is potentially more vulnerable, relying on a continuing shared judicial understanding of the nature of the relationship between competition law and labor law. The EU exemption is flexible and can much more easily grow so as to encompass more atypical forms of employment relationships.[58] Nevertheless, the tests used "may prove to be too strict for some quasi-dependent workers that are genuinely allowed a wide degree of autonomy in choosing the time, place and content of their work, and whose activities are mainly coordinated by the 'client/employer'."[59] As a consequence, "a number of workers that provide personal work or services with the support of some capital assets owned by

55. CJEU 4 December 2014, C-413/13 (FNV KIEM) ECLI:EU:C:2014:2411. The case was about a collective agreement setting a minimum salary for both employees and self-employed people (orchestra substitutes). The provision of a minimum pay, provided for by the collective agreement, can be applied to falsely self-employed workers, regardless of the national notion of worker and without prejudice to competition.
56. E. Grosheide, B. ter Haar, *Employee-Like Worker: Competitive Entrepreneur or Submissive Employee? Reflections on ECJ, C-413/13, FNV Kunsten Informatie*, S. Bellomo, N. Gundt, M. Łaga, M. Boto (ed.), *Labour Law and Social Rights in Europe: The Jurisprudence of International Courts. Selected Judgements* (Gdansk University Press, 2018): 21-39.
57. M. Freedland, N. Countouris, *Some Reflections on the 'Personal Scope' of Collective Labour Law*, Industrial Law Journal, 46(1), 52-71, 2017.
58. M.C. Lucey, *Should Professionals in Employment Constitute "Undertakings"? Identifying "False-Employed"*, Journal of European Competition Law & Practice, 6(10), 702-708, 2015.
59. N. Countouris, *The Concept of "Worker" in European Labour Law: Fragmentation, Autonomy and Scope*, Industrial Law Journal, 47(2), 192-225, 2017.

them, and thus be presumed to be a separate economic unit," will most certainly be exposed to the harsh realities of EU competition law.[60]

[A] Focus on Access to Collective Bargaining for a Subset of Non-standard Workers

As illustrated in Figure 4.1 below, while (traditional) atypical forms of employment (part-time, fixed-term, and temporary agency work), which are established under an employment relationship, currently face only practical difficulties in exercising their collective rights, two core issues arise when it comes to self-employed and platform-mediated workers. First, they are not entitled to collective bargaining unless they are falsely classified as self-employed. Second, they face inherent practical difficulties due to their temporal and spatial "non-standard" nature.

In many countries, legislatures and governments have been partly responsible for a relaxation of the rigid employee/self-employed "binary divide,"[61] and a floor of rights specifically has been "selectively extended" to a group of vulnerable workers.[62] Moreover, both in the common-law and civil law regimes, such sharp distinction relies on some assumptions that have been questioned only recently. First, the limitation of competition among employees finds justification under the monopsony of the labor market, where the labor supply structurally overcomes the demand, even on the most efficient markets. Second, the assumption that any form of coalition and collective bargaining process of independent contractors would hamper the functioning of the free market, leaving space for unlawful cartels,[63] seems exaggerated. The latter argument could not be justified under any substantial equity argument, given the fact that traditionally independent contractors are considered economic subjects capable of bargaining the conditions of their contract autonomously. Since many self-employed workers are in a very weak position in the market, it is debatable whether competition law is, in fact, the right frame of reference for them or whether different objects of legal protection come into play.

Where platform workers who work as self-employed contractors are able, within national legal systems, to engage in collective bargaining, they would have to demonstrate that they are in fact false self-employed (i.e., that they are in fact employees within the EU definition) in order to avoid the application of EU competition law to the substance of their agreements. Otherwise, genuine self-employed workers are prevented from joining force and negotiating over their terms and conditions of employment and work because such behavior among "undertakings" is considered "price fixing," to the detriment of final consumers.

---

60. *Ibid.*
61. M.A. Cherry, A. Aloisi, *"Dependent Contractors" in the Gig Economy: A Comparative Approach*, American University Law Review, 66(3), 635-689, 2017.
62. G. Davidov, M. Freedland, N. Kountouris, *The Subjects of Labor Law: "Employees" and Other Workers*, M.W. Finkin, G. Mundlak (ed.), *Comparative Labor Law. Research Handbooks in Comparative Law Series* (Cheltenham: Edward Elgar Publishing, 2015): 115-131.
63. C. Rubiano, *Precarious Work and Access to Collective Bargaining: What Are the Legal Obstacles?*, International Journal of Labour Research, 5(1), 133-151, 2013.

Figure 4.1 Right to Collective Bargaining According to Form of Employment in the EU[64]

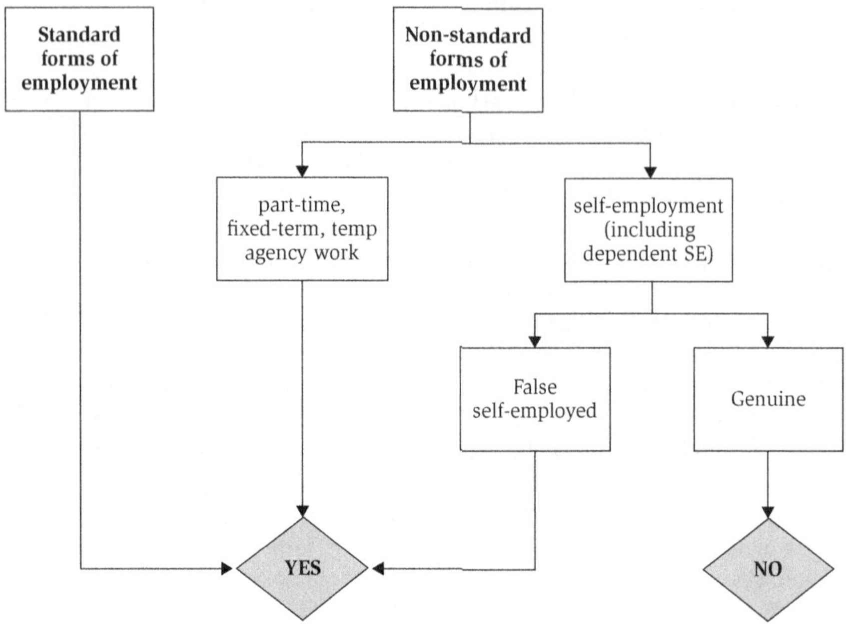

Concomitantly, a purposive interpretation of the CJEU's rulings may extend the scope of collective bargaining agreement by removing the exclusion of self-employed workers from the collective labor rights. The persistent (and ambiguous) overlap between independent contractors and ("micro" or "auto") undertakings must be challenged when taking into account the case of platform-coordinated workers whose autonomy is merely "nominal."[65] As a matter of fact, the overriding evidence confirms that transport services and delivery platforms exercise remarkable supervision, invasive direction, and far-reaching control over how the task is completed.[66] In light of what has been argued above, only self-employed individuals who do not provide "labor," but provide services by means of an independent business organization that they actually own and manage, and whose relevance in the provision of the service in terms of capital and work of other persons is considerably superior to the relevance of the individual's personal work, could be restricted in their right to bargain collectively.[67]

64. Authors' own elaboration.
65. W.S. Grimes, *The Sherman Act's Unintended Bias Against Lilliputians: Small Players' Collective Action as a Counter to Relational Market Power*, Antitrust Law Journal, 69, 195, 2001.
66. A. Aloisi, *"With Great Power Comes Virtual Freedom". A Review of the First Italian Case Holding That (Food-Delivery) Platform Workers Are Not Employees*, Comparative Labor Law & Policy Journal, Dispatch, 2018.
67. V. De Stefano, A. Aloisi, *Fundamental Labour Rights, Platform Work and Protection of Non-standard Workers*, J. R. Bellace, B. ter Haar (ed.), *Labour, Business and Human Rights Law*, (Cheltenham: Edward Elgar Publishing, 2019).

§4.04 PRACTICAL DIFFICULTIES AND SUCCESSFUL SOLUTIONS: INSTITUTIONAL AND GRASSROOTS INITIATIVES[68]

A historical perspective suggests that non-standard work is neither *atypical* nor new.[69] The history of unionism provides many examples of unions organizing in areas of casual or insecure employment,[70] more or less inclusive in defining their constituency and more or less restrictive in the issues they pursue. However, foundations, regulations, and processes concerning industrial relations are rooted in the pre-digital age and designed around a prototype of the "mass-collective worker."[71]

Understandably, the resurgence of highly standardized organizational modules encourages the mobilization of workers who had not previously been involved in political advocacy.[72] It has been claimed that, as labor markets have reacquired characteristics that were prevalent at the end of the 19th-century, the "labor movement" should engage to protect work and to give workers more of a say.[73] For this to happen, two pre-conditions need to be met: (i) structural conditions that make mobilization feasible (successful insurgency) and (ii) the existence of a subjective view among participants that collective action is likely to succeed (expectation to win).[74]

Having claimed that practical obstacles hinder or make less attractive the exercise of fundamental freedoms guaranteed by international conventions and national codes, this section lists a number of efforts to achieve effective representation and collective bargaining for non-standard workers carried out by both traditional and grassroots organizations.[75] In this respect, it is convenient to distinguish between classical resources of organization (e.g., representation, strikes, bargaining) and soft tools of organization (e.g., social media groups, manifestos, strategic litigation, rating widgets). Roughly speaking, the former initiatives are carried out by institutional unions, while the latter are implemented by informal and self-organized groups.

The share of non-standard workers can offer a new source of membership for traditional unions. Workers in entire sectors, from logistics to consulting, represent a

68. This section draws from A. Aloisi, *Negotiating the digital transformation of work: Non-standard workers' voice, collective rights and mobilisation practices in the platform economy*, EUI Working Paper MWP 2019/03. 2019, available at: http://hdl.handle.net/1814/63264.
69. S. Cobble, L.F. Vosko, *Historical Perspectives on Representing Nonstandard Workers*, F. Carre, M. Ferber, L. Golden, S. Herzenberg (ed.), *Nonstandard Work: The Nature and Challenges of Changing Employment Arrangements* (Ithaca: CUP, 2000): 291-312.
70. R. Saundry, M. Stuart, V. Antcliff, *It's More Than Who You Know—Networks and Trade Unions in the Audio-Visual Industries*, Human Resource Management Journal, 16(4), 376-392, 2006.
71. F. Murray, *The Decentralisation of Production—the Decline of the Mass-Collective Worker?*, Capital & Class, 7(1), 74-99, 1983.
72. J. Stanford, *The Resurgence of Gig Work: Historical and Theoretical Perspectives*, The Economic and Labour Relations Review, 28(3), 382-401, 2017.
73. E. Heery, B. Abbott, *Trade Unions and the Insecure Workforce*, E. Heery, J. Salmon (ed.), *The Insecure Workforce* (London and New York: Taylor and Francis, 2000): 155-180; K.V.W. Stone, *Unions in the precarious economy*, retrieved from http://prospect.org/article/unions-precarious-economy. February 21, 2017.
74. B.I. Sachs, *Law, Organizing, and Status Quo Vulnerability*, Texas Law Review, 96(2), 351-277, 2017.
75. M. Vicente, *Collective Relations in the Gig Economy*, E-Journal of International and Comparative Labour Studies, 8(1), 83-93, 2019.

new *constituency* for trade unions, but the central unions seem displaced, in the face of this change of paradigm, undecided whether to invest in the defense of traditional members or to lead a new generation of workers. In this respect, it must be acknowledged that the unions' approach toward NSFE has undergone substantial change: from the refusal to organize non-standard workers on the grounds that this would have legitimated these arrangements, to the settlement of specific "one-stop" trade-union offices in order to assist NSFE.[76]

In this respect, Pulignano et al. argue that the response of unions to atypical work arrangements has focused primarily on one of two strategies. The first has been to reject non-standard work arrangements, fighting instead for full-time, stable employment. The second has been to "adopt strategies aimed at improving working conditions, social rights and wages of such workers" (*ibid*). Therefore, unions responded to the needs of non-standard workers by creating specific representational opportunities in existing labor confederations for such workers.[77] While in the past unions used to found organizations specifically aimed at representing flexible workers, current strategies can be summarized as follows: (i) improve working conditions, (ii) promote litigations about misclassification of NSFE, (iii) influence the legislative process, (iv) mobilizing unorganized workers,[78] and (v) lobbying social actors such as insurance companies.[79]

Workers might prefer to organize around single issues, such as a hypothetical change to benefit provision that many employees a non-union setting feel was poorly handled by management or without adequate consultation.[80] Thus, in areas where hierarchical unions make little sense, networks (and social networks) may be a viable solution.[81] In this vein, network arrangements, internet platforms and the like may be favored by the more dispersed, occasional or individualistically-oriented workers. More importantly, another issue to be addressed is whether non-standard workers should be treated the same way as employees, treated differently within existing union structures or whether autonomous unions of atypical workers should be created.[82] By

76. R. Gumbrell-McCormick, *European Trade Unions and "Atypical" Workers*, Industrial Relations Journal, 42(3), 293-310, 2011.
77. V. Pulignano, L. Ortíz Gervasi, F. De Franceschi, *Union Responses to Precarious Workers: Italy and Spain Compared*, European Journal of Industrial Relations, 22(1), 39-55, 2016.
78. C. Benassi, L. Dorigatti, *Straight to the Core—Explaining Union Responses to the Casualization of Work: The IG Metall Campaign for Agency Workers*, British Journal of Industrial Relations, 53(3), 533-555, 2015 (Authors review the varied factors that encourage unions to engage with agency workers. They also state that high union density and strong collective agreements are two conditions that enable unions to bargain for greater protection for NSFE).
79. K. Boonstra, M. Keune, E. Verhulp, *Trade union responses to precarious employment in the Netherlands* (Amsterdam: Institute for Advanced Labour Studies, University of Amsterdam, 2012).
80. A. Bryson, et al., *The Twin Track Model of Employee Voice: An Anglo-American Perspective on Union Decline and the Rise of Alternative Forms of Voice*, IZA DP No. 11223. 2017.
81. B. Carneiro, *Trade Unions and Facebook: The Need to Improve Dialogue and Expand Networks*, ETUI Policy Brief, No. 5. 2018; A.J. Wood, *Networks of Injustice and Worker Mobilisation at Walmart*, Industrial Relations Journal, 46(4), 259-274, 2015.
82. M. Wynn, *Organising Freelancers: A Hard Case or a New Opportunity?*, A. Burke (ed.), *The Handbook of Research on Freelancing and Self-Employment* (Dublin: Senate Hall Academic Publishing, 2015): 93-103.

way of example, in Italy, the three unions have opened sections aimed at precarious and *freelance* workers (CGIL with *NiDIL*; CISL with *Alai* and, more recently, *vIVAce*; UIL with *CpO* and, more recently, *SindacatoNetworkers*).

To conclude, for collective bargaining and for unions and business and employers' organizations to continue to be relevant in the new world of work,[83] it may be urgent to adapt or reinvent the way they currently operate.[84] There may also be a need to adjust rules and practices. A main disadvantage is that a strategy of representation at the workplace level, based on the development of permanent workplace organization, is simply not plausible for many contingent workers who are not tied to a particular workplace or particular employer and who, in many cases, work at small work-sites in industries without an established union tradition.[85] Accordingly, the new organization of work must necessarily imply a shift in the locus of union representation beyond the traditional or physical workplace.[86]

[A] Focus on Platform-Organized Workers

This section presents an exemplary outline of union and non-union strategies to reinvigorate workers' contractual power and "from above and below" responses toward non-standard employment[87] by addressing practical obstacles such as geographical disaggregation, fear of retaliation, threat of dismissal/account deactivation, opportunistic relations and authentic reluctance, with a comparative approach.[88]

Challenges stemming from legal restrictions on platform-coordinated and other non-standard workers are compounded by the solitary structure of digital labor markets. Workers often operate independently, in isolation, over large geographical areas, and in direct competition with one another: dispersion of contracts over time and space inevitably leads to a fragmentation of bargaining, since they are not usually physically present at a single workplace or may not share a common "class consciousness." These practical difficulties are especially relevant for online workers. The short-term, task-based, and on-demand nature of platform work might place gig workers in direct competition with each other as online platforms seem designed to "foster a sense of competition rather than solidarity between workers."[89]

83. For a broader overview on non-standard forms of work and the collective, *see* V. Doellgast, N. Lillie, V. Pulignano (ed.), *Reconstructing Solidarity. Labour Unions, Precarious Work, and the Politics of Institutional Change in Europe*, (Oxford: OUP, 2018).
84. J. Wills, *Subcontracted Employment and Its Challenge to Labor*, Labor Studies Journal, 34(4), 441-460, 2009.
85. E. Heery, B. Abbott, *Trade Unions and the Insecure Workforce*, E. Heery, J. Salmon (ed.), *The Insecure Workforce* (London and New York: Taylor and Francis, 2000): 155-180.
86. E. Heery, et al., *Beyond the Enterprise: Trade Union Representation of Freelances in the* UK, Human Resource Management Journal, 14(2), 20-35, 2004.
87. R. Gumbrell-McCormick, *European Trade Unions and 'Atypical' Workers*, Industrial Relations Journal, 42(3), 293-310, 2011.
88. J. Berg, *Addressing the challenge of non-standard employment*, retrieved from https://goo.gl/ftt61i. April 1, 2017.
89. M. Graham, *Digital work marketplaces impose a new balance of power*, retrieved from https://newint.org/blog/2016/05/25/digital-work-marketplaces-impose-a-new-balance-of-power. May 25, 2016.

A firm's workforce may operate in multiple jurisdictions simultaneously (potentially on a global scale) thus inflating the workforce and creating conditions that encourage workers to undercut one another.[90] Furthermore, many platform companies have been unwilling to bargain with workers directly. In addition to this, technology may help employers to uncover and discourage emerging conflictual initiatives or may allow disconnection or exclusion for protest leaders and "troublemakers."[91] Many platform-organized workers, especially in the passenger transport and household services sectors, do not have the flexibility that real self-employment brings but are "subject to a subordinate labour relationship and should thus be entitled to a secure employment contract."[92] As a result, "these trends make it difficult to build collective voice; firms, however, are able to capitalize on the regulatory lacunae concerning worker agency and collective bargaining."[93]

Institutional and informal groups currently pursue a number of alternative strategies to help workers to organize and effectively express individual and collective grievances, involving the use of social media (e.g., commercial hashtag hijacking, according to the "name-and-shame" culture) and more traditional protest campaigns (e.g., mass disconnection from the staffing software during promotional initiatives and flyers inviting customers and restaurants to boycott unscrupulous or capricious clients). Several spontaneous initiatives have been developed with significant results at national level. In a few countries, examples of (traditional) industrial action have been identified, especially for time- and place-dependent on-demand work. The ease with which such workers can be replaced emphasizes insecurity, but close proximity makes organizing more feasible.[94] Moreover, public spaces help to foster social connections and promote collective engagement. As a result, couriers have triggered off a popularization of claims that until now had not been answered. They also built broader alliances of cooperation with civil society organizations (CSOs) and pressure groups in an attempt to avoid the isolation where platform workers are often confined, to represent mutual interests at the local level, to stimulate public opinion and to gain attention from institutions.[95] Taken together, these developments corroborate the idea that a strong awareness and resistance are emerging among workers.

90. V. De Stefano, *Non-standard Work and Limits on Freedom of Association: A Human Rights-Based Approach*, Industrial Law Journal, 46(2), 185-207, 2017.
91. K. Vandaele, *Will Trade Unions Survive in the Platform Economy? Emerging Patterns of Platform Workers' Collective Voice and Representation in Europe*, ETUI Research Paper. 2018.
92. T. Weber, *Time for a European dialogue on the platform economy*, retrieved from https://www.socialeurope.eu/time-european-dialogue-platform-economy. March 7, 2018.
93. H. Johnston, C. Land-Kazlauskas, *On Demand and Organized: Developing Collective Agency, Representation and Bargaining in the Gig Economy*, ILO Conditions of Work and Employment Series No. 94. 2018.
94. J. Woodcock, *#Slaveroo: Deliveroo drivers organising in the "gig economy"*, retrieved from http://novaramedia.com/2016/08/12/slaveroo-deliveroo-drivers-organising-in-the-gig-economy/ August 12, 2016.
95. M. Forlivesi, *Alla ricerca di tutele collettive per i lavoratori digitali: per i lavoratori digitali: organizzazione, rappresentanza,* contrattazione, Labour & Law Issues, 4(1), 36-58, 2018.

Moreover, independent unions are promoting a litigation strategy in many countries, with remarkable results (e.g., in the United Kingdom (UK) and the USA).[96] The international scholarly community is supporting the drafting of *Codes of Conduct* to be implemented by "fair" platforms.[97] International media outlets and militant researchers usually run extensive coverage of these activities sparking public outrage.[98] It is too early to point to concrete and systematic policy changes that resulted from these recent initiatives. However, unions, which have experienced difficulties trying to organize "new" workers, may benefit from this fresh wave of conflict. New networks can be "the launchpad for successful activism" for workplace conflict, membership renewal, and negotiation.[99]

In many industrialized and post-industrial countries, union engagement with non-standard workers has focused on applying existing collective bargaining frameworks to atypical workers. Many unions have sought to engage with non-standard and platform-based workers at times as part of a strategy to expand representation to incorporate non-standard workers more broadly.[100] In this vein, particular attention has to be devoted to initiatives of worker organization such as those carried out by traditional unions such as IG Metall,[101] NWW and Ver.Di in Germany as well as new union formations such as IWGB, a small base union,[102] and branches of the IWW across the UK.[103]

---

96. A. Aloisi, *"A worker is a worker is a worker". Collective bargaining and platform work, the case of Deliveroo riders in London*, International Labor Rights Case Law, 5(1), 36-40, 2019.
97. Austrian Chamber of Labour et al., *Frankfurt Paper on Platform Based Work*, Frankfurt. 2016.
98. C. Cant, *The wave of worker resistance in European food platforms 2016-17*, retrieved from https://goo.gl/vjDPUA. January 29, 2018, collecting data on informal strikes and protest tactics by "food platform workers" on a transnational scale; A. Tassinari, V. Maccarrone, *Striking the startups*, retrieved from https://www.jacobinmag.com/2017/01/foodora-strike-turin-gig-economy-startups-uber. January 23, 2017.
99. A.J. Wood, *Networks of Injustice and Worker Mobilisation at Walmart*, Industrial Relations Journal, 46(4), 259-274, 2015.
100. International Labour Office, *Non-standard employment around the world: Understanding challenges, shaping prospects*. Geneva: ILO. 2016.
101. In 2016, in Germany, IG Metall (*Industriegewerkschaft Metall*, Industrial Union of Metal Workers), the largest industrial trade union in Europe, changed its statute to allow the self-employed to become members. In 2016, IG Metall launched Fair Crowd Work, a type of watchdog organization run in collaboration with Austrian and Swedish trade unions. Fair Crowd Work collects information about crowd work platforms and produces a rating system based on the platforms' terms and conditions and worker reviews for online platforms. Additionally, it informs workers of their legal rights in an accessible language and lists trade unions they can join. *See* M.S. Silberman, L. Irani, *Operating an Employer Reputation System: Lessons from Turkopticon, 2008-2015*, Comparative Labor Law & Policy Journal, 37(3), 505-542, 2016.
102. The Independent Workers Union of Great Britain (IWGB) provides one of the best-known examples of new union formation for gig workers. The IWGB was formed explicitly to organize non-traditional, low wage and immigrant workers. The group opens membership to "all employees, workers and any other persons who accept the principles, objectives, and rules of the union" (Independent Workers' Union of Great Britain (IWGB), *"Constitution and Rulebook"*, retrieved from https://iwgbunion.files.wordpress.com/2017/12/policy-booklet-dec-2017.pdf. 2017).
103. A. Donini, et al., *Towards Collective Protections for Crowdworkers: Italy, Spain and France in the EU Context*, Transfer: European Review of Labour and Research, 23(2), 207-223, 2017.

On the one side, trade unions appear to support initiatives of platform workers rather than attempting to compete with their spontaneous actions. On the other, alternative movements are "better seen as complements rather than as substitutes to traditional labour unions" even because of their lack of ability to bargain collectively on behalf of their members.[104] As explained by Staunton,[105] informal, grassroots organizations can learn from more institutional unions about collective bargaining and social dialogue, while the latter can reproduce the mobilization capacity of the former. This interdependency is shaped by factors such as the dynamics and strategies of the clients, including platform internal design, country-specific labor market institutions and national regulatory frameworks governing the platforms, union cultures and identities.

As a consequence, it is crucial to "discard" the exclusionary distinction between employees and other categories of workers[106] and to develop new engagement and negotiation techniques. In this respect, successful collective bargaining is the best means to increase the attractiveness of collective autonomy in the digital era.[107] Notably, collective agreements can introduce measures to offset the imbalances that might result from the digital transformation of work in a way that is faster and more accurate than through legislative intervention.

§4.05 CLOSING REMARKS AND POLICY RECOMMENDATIONS

The future of organized labor depends on a more inclusive strategy that accommodates the interest of previously marginalized categories of workers.[108] Indeed, since collective action has been instrumental in achieving the existing labor regulations both at domestic and international level,[109] established social partners might play an active role in representing non-standard workers. While unions are usually perceived to be mainly concerned with securing wage rises, individual and collective grievance handling, a conspicuous aspect of their work will become increasingly important with intensified and technologically-driven managerial control, the growth of non-standard (and precarious) employment and the risk of technological displacement. "Negotiating the digital transformation of work" could become a crucial objective of social dialogue and action for employers' and workers' organization.[110]

---

104. OECD, *Issues Paper: Labour Relations in the Future World of Work,* Paris. 2018.
105. B. Staunton, *Grassroots action prominent in the platform economy,* retrieved from https://www.opendemocracy.net/en/can-europe-make-it/grassroots-action-prominent-in-platform-economy/. December 16, 2018.
106. C. Crouch, *Redefining Labour Relations and Capital in the Digital Age,* M. Neufeind, J. O'Reilly, F. Ranft (eds), *Work in the Digital Age Challenges of the Fourth Industrial Revolution,* (London and New York: Taylor and Francis, 2018): 187-197.
107. European Commission, *Employment and Social Developments in Europe Annual Review 2018,* Luxembourg, 2018.
108. Z. Jiang, M. Korczynski, *When the 'Unorganizable' Organize: The Collective Mobilization of Migrant Domestic Workers in London,* Human Relations, 69(3), 813-838, 2016.
109. K. Sisson, *Putting the record straight: Industrial relations and the employment relationship,* Warwick papers in industrial relations, No. 88, 2008.
110. V. De Stefano, *'Negotiating the algorithm': Automation, artificial intelligence and labour protection,* (Geneva: ILO, 2018).

Positive signs are indeed emerging all over Europe.[111] In May 2018, a territorial collective agreement was signed in Bologna by institutional trade unions, workers' autonomous collectives and the management of the company "Sgam-MyMenu." The "Charter" sets out a fixed hourly rate in line with the minimum wage in the respective industry, compensation for overtime, holidays, bad weather and bicycle maintenance, accident and sickness insurance. It also guarantees trade union rights.[112] In July 2018, a "historic collective agreement" was signed between the Danish trade union 3F and "Hilfr.dk," a platform providing cleaning services.[113] Thanks to the agreement, domestic cleaners, who were formerly invariably classified as self-employed, will be considered employees after completing 100 hours of work, unless they explicitly opt out of this status. The agreement sets a significant hourly minimum wage, protection in case of dismissal, data protection rights and a system regulating the cancellation of shifts. In February 2019, the British courier company "Hermes" negotiated an agreement with the GMB union,[114] offering drivers guaranteed minimum wages and holiday pay in a deal to provide trade union recognition.[115]

To counterbalance the challenges NSFE generate for the organization of workers, the recognition of shared problems, and the enforcement of collective interests, it is essential to identify ways to enable and strengthen collective action through trade unions and collective bargaining. Two layers of intervention are required. On the one hand, it is important to ensure that solo self-employed people have the fundamental right to negotiate collectively and that they are considered as individual workers rather than "undertakings," exempted from EU rules on anti-competitive practices if they act collectively. This can be done by updating the most obsolete regulations to accommodate new forms of work. On the other hand, it is vital to update unions' agendas in order to include NSFE in their constituency. To do so, collective agreements need to be enforced and modernized in order to extend existing protection standards to the digital economy workers. Interestingly though, collective autonomy and its mechanism may well represent a swift and flexible solution to ensure fair conditions for non-standard workers, while new legislation or legal claims might struggle to respond promptly and adequately to current challenges.[116]

111. A. Aloisi, *At the table, not on the menu: Non-standard workers and collective bargaining in the platform economy,* retrieved from https://euideas.eui.eu/2019/06/25/at-the-table-not-on-the-menu-non-standard-workers-and-collective-bargaining-in-the-platform-economy/. June 25, 2019.
112. V. De Stefano, A. Aloisi, *Employment and working conditions of selected types of platform work. National context analysis: Italy,* (Luxembourg: Publications Office of the European Union, 2018b).
113. J. Hale, *In Denmark, a historic collective agreement is turning the "bogus self-employed" into "workers with rights"*, retrieved from https://goo.gl/AjUbHH. July 4, 2018.
114. GMB, *GMB wins monumental victory in employment case against Uber,* retrieved from http://www.gmb.org.uk/newsroom/GMB-wins-uber-case. October 28, 2016.
115. S. Butler, *Hermes to offer gig economy drivers better rights under union deal,* retrieved from https://goo.gl/2SLzqB. February 4, 2019.
116. OECD, *Employment Outlook 2019,* Paris. 2019.

CHAPTER 5

That Is Just Part of Being Able to Do My Cool Job: Understanding Low Earnings but High Job Satisfaction in the Creative Industries in the Netherlands*

Wike Been & Maarten Keune

Work in the creative industries seems to be characterised by a paradox as it combines (very) low levels of earnings with high levels of job satisfaction. Often this is attributed to creative workers 'just valuing other aspects of their work'. There may be other explanations, however, such as labour market conditions and a lack of collective interest representation. In this study, we combine these explanations and aim to understand whether and why earnings in the creative industries are lower than might be expected for these workers. We focus on two sub-sectors of the creative industries: graphic design and the games industry. Semi-structured interviews were held with entrepreneurs, freelance workers and employees, as well as institutional-level actors. Results show that workers do not generally perceive their income levels as low at an absolute level, but they do in relative terms. Also, they do point out specific groups as vulnerable with often very low earnings: starting entrepreneurs and freelance workers. These groups are central in the make-up of the sector as many start their own businesses at some point in their career. Workers indicate, however, that they are willing to forego earnings for the sake of working in the sector. This situation can best be understood as an interaction between personal preferences, labour market conditions and lack of interest in collective organisation. In addition, there seems to be a norm that 'true creative workers' should be willing to sacrifice earnings.

* This chapter is based on the research project IR-CREA – Strategic but vulnerable. Industrial relations and creative workers, funded by the DG Employment, Social Affairs & Inclusion of the EC, agreement No. VP/2015/004/0121.

§5.01 INTRODUCTION

Inspired by Richards Florida's work on the creative class (2002), many governments in the developed world have established policies to support the creative industries with the expectation that it will contribute to economic growth and innovation in general, and more specifically to job creation (Chaston & Sadler-Smith, 2012). However, work in the creative industries presents us with an interesting paradox. On the one hand, many want to work in the creative industries, and those who do often state that they do so with pleasure and report high levels of job satisfaction; on the other hand, the creative industries are rife with low job quality, particularly in terms of low earnings and inadequate access to social security (e.g., De Peuter & Dyer-Whiteford, 2005; Eikhof & Warhurst, 2013; Menger, 2017; Neff, Wissinger & Zukin, 2005; Peticca-Harris, Weststar & McKenna, 2015; Thompson, Parker & Cox, 2016).

The literature offers three main arguments to explain this paradox (cf. Bellini, Burroni, Dorigatti, Gherardini & Manzo, 2018). The first concerns personal preferences and intrinsic motivation. Creative workers (including employees, interns, freelancers and business owners) are said to value other, non-monetary aspects of the work such as the possibility to express their creativity and doing what they love so much that they are willing to accept low earnings (Umney & Kretsos, 2015; Umney & la Palme, 2017). A second argument is that the nature of the creative labour market forces workers to accept low earnings. For example, the creative labour market is a portfolio labour market par excellence, which induces workers to accept low-paid jobs in order to increase the chances for getting more work in the future (Gill & Pratt, 2008; McRobbie, 2002; Peticca-Harris et al., 2015; Thompson et al., 2016). Third, the limited interest of creative workers in collective organisation is forwarded as an explanation, arguing that the resulting individual nature of employment relations puts workers in a disadvantaged bargaining position (McRobbie, 2009; Umney & La Palme, 2017; Umney & Kretsos, 2015).

In this study, we add to the literature by studying these various explanations together and in relation to each other. We discuss low earnings in the private, non-subsidised creative industries in the Netherlands and examine the validity of these three lines of argumentation. We ask three main questions: (1) to what extent do workers in the creative industries consider their earnings to be low? (2) to what extent are low earnings related to personal preferences, labour market characteristics and/or a lack of collective organisation? and (3) what are the reasons for large groups of creative workers not to organise collectively?

In the next section, we will review the literature concerning the three main arguments in more detail. Section §5.03 discusses the methodology and data. Section §5.04 presents the results of our research. Section §5.05 concludes.

§5.02 ANALYTICAL FRAMEWORK

[A] Workers' Preferences

The prevalence of low earnings among creative workers is often explained by these workers' preferences and intrinsic motivation, which downplay the importance of earnings as compared to other aspects of work (De Peuter, 2011; Dollinger, Burke & Gump, 2007). De Peuter (2011) distinguishes a number of worker prototypes and categorises creative workers as belonging to the group he names 'the precog', characterised by 'self-driven, passionate commitment to work; willingness to work for nothing; perpetual and personally financed reskilling; habituation to material insecurity; obsessive networking, bold enterprising behavior' (De Peuter 2011: 421). Also, creative workers often consider their work a hobby as much as work and are therefore highly intrinsically motivated (Arvidsson, Malossi & Naro, 2010; Siebert & Wilson, 2013; Wright, 2017). Passionate and highly intrinsically motivated, they are therefore willing to compromise on earnings just to have the opportunity to do the work they want to do, or so the argument goes (Wright, 2017).

Other authors have furthermore added that creative workers' prioritisation of aspects of work other than earnings may be grounded in their value orientations. Specifically, a desire to create reflects creativity as a core value, which is thus valued more than earnings (Dollinger et al., 2007). This value orientation is furthermore related to a strong desire to do 'their own unique thing', i.e., to be able to exercise autonomy over what they create, even if this means earning less (*ibid.*).

Finally, the importance attached to earnings may also vary with age. Young workers tend to have fewer responsibilities in terms of dependent partners, parents or children, and may not (yet) have a mortgage. Back-up options like temporarily living with one's parents or having a roommate to share costs make it easier to opt for less income for the sake of doing the work you love, as has been observed in the games industry (Bulut, 2015).

[B] Labour Market Characteristics

A second line of argument is that the specific labour market characteristics of the creative industries serve to reinforce the prioritisation of work over income. To begin with, creative work is often organised in specific projects with limited time durations, commonly referred to as project-based work. This is an argument for many contracting organisations to contract freelancers and/or temporary workers instead of permanent employees. The pressure to obtain work and sufficient earnings thus falls on the shoulders of the individual, who hops from project to project and is continuously engaged in securing new projects (McGuigan, 2010; Peticca-Harris et al., 2015). In the practice of the creative sector, this means that finding work, rather than finding well-paid work, is the main priority, although this is not to say that project-based work is necessarily poorly remunerated (Thompson et al., 2016).

In addition, the creative labour market is very much a portfolio labour market, in which building up a good portfolio – signalled by the inclusion of interesting and high-status projects and clients – is key for gaining status as a creative worker and increasing the chances for future work. Again, it is argued that this encourages creative workers to accept lower earnings just to secure work on a project that will look good in their portfolio. This is especially true under the conditions of an oversupply of labour characteristic of many creative industries (Bulut, 2015; Murdock, 2003; Peticca-Harris et al., 2015). Building up a portfolio is the most difficult for new entrants in the labour market, who, for lack of an established reputation and network, are even more pressed to accept very limited or no earnings to get their first jobs (e.g., Eikhof & Warhurst, 2013).

In these ways, the creative labour market pushes workers to become 'entrepreneurs of the self' (Foucault, 2010; *see also* Neff, 2012 specifically for the creative industries), constantly positioning themselves as miniature companies in a market competing with other such miniature companies. They continuously invest in their human capital by keeping their knowledge up to date, learning new skills and expanding their networks, and consider this to be their personal responsibility in order to remain marketable (Hennekam & Bennett, 2017; Eikhof & Warhurst, 2013). But where Foucault (2010) saw 'entrepreneurs of the self' competing for the maximisation of monetary rewards, creative workers are all too often competing to get jobs at all, preferably on the 'coolest' projects, disregarding to an important extent the aspect of earnings.

[C] Collective Organisation

Traditionally, an important mechanism for workers to improve their earnings is to organise collectively in trade unions or comparable organisations, which can then negotiate collective agreements or represent workers' interests in other ways. There is no inherent contradiction between creative work and trade unions, as demonstrated by, for example, the American Federation of Television and Radio Artists and the Screen Actors Guild, both set up in the 1930s and still existing today (jointly under the name SAG-AFTRA). Further examples exist of trade unions for orchestra musicians, architects, and others, as well as trade unions specifically targeting creative workers and organising them along lines of shared interests through measures of individual service provision. To a certain degree, they have also been found to be successful (Greer, Samaluk & Umney, 2018).

Despite these examples, however, creative workers are often described as being less likely to organise collectively (McRobbie, 2009; Umney & La Palme, 2017). A number of explanations prevail. First of all, workers who evaluate their work first of all in terms of creativity and autonomy may be less likely to join trade unions because these are associated with more 'traditional' aspects of job quality such as earnings. Also, workers in the creative industries tend to have fluid careers in terms of employment status, switching between employee, freelancer, and starting companies, often even combining different statuses at the same time (Hennekam & Bennett, 2017).

This may make it more difficult for them to identify with unions. Moreover, a labour market full of entrepreneurs of the self would seem to be thoroughly individualised, with little space for collective organisation based on solidarity, a core value for trade unions. It remains an empirical question however to what extent this is indeed the case, considering the above-mentioned examples of successful collective organisation in the creative industries.

§5.03 DATA AND METHODOLOGY

In an effort to answer the questions raised in the previous two sections, we exploratively studied the attitudes, preferences and practices concerning earnings in the creative industries in the Netherlands, a country where the weight of the creative industry is increasing rapidly and where the government is actively promoting its growth. Within the creative industries we limited ourselves to the private, non-subsidised segment, excluding the subsidised segment where we expect questions related to earnings to be affected by the role played by public money.

From the very diverse private, non-subsidised creative industries we chose two subsectors: the games industry and the graphic design industry. Trade unions are hardly present in these sectors and neither sector has a collective agreement, contrary to the Dutch economy in general in which some 80% of employees are covered by collective agreements (De Beer & Keune, 2017). The two sectors differ from each other, however, on several potentially important dimensions. To begin with the games industry, it is a young industry both in terms of its existence and in terms of the age of its workers. Also, most workers in the games industry are employees: about 5% are freelancers (Dutch Game Garden, 2018). The industry is characterised by an oversupply of labour, as the number of graduates from games-related educational programmes far exceeds the number of available positions (Koops, 2016). Finally, the games industry completely lacks any kind of collective setting of wages or reverence point for freelancer fees.

The graphic design industry is a much older industry with a more balanced age structure. It underwent radical changes as digital media replaced a major share of printed media in the last few decades, and the design work changed accordingly. This not only meant a change in the nature of the work but also in the place of work. Where workers generally used to be employed by large printing companies, nowadays 23% of the workers in the sector are freelancers, and most of the other workers work for independent design studios employing only nine people on average (BNO, 2017). In terms of collective interest representation this means that where workers were previously covered by the collective agreement of the printing companies, today they are not covered by any. Nevertheless, the organisation for professionals in the graphic design industry, the BNO, provides guidelines on working conditions including salary scales, which can be applied on a voluntary basis.

For this study, semi-structured interviews were held with employers, employees and freelance workers in the two sectors (Table 5.1). Interviewees were found through the internet, personal contacts and snowball sampling. In addition, semi-structured interviews were held with leading figures in national and local institutions representing or affecting these industries, i.e., professional organisations, trade unions, employers' organisations, the ministry of economic affairs, and municipalities. The interviews lasted between forty and ninety-five minutes, were recorded with consent and later transcribed ad verbum.

The interviews were analysed using MaxQDA. First, a broad coding structure was set up outlining the main categories of interest. Next, given the exploratory nature of the study, open coding was applied to allow topics to emerge from the data. After coding the first three interviews, the coding was discussed with the team of researchers and adjusted according to the issues emerging. Following this first round of coding, all codes were checked internally to ensure consistency. Then a phase of axial coding was entered, structuring and determining the codes given in the open coding phase and combining the codes into groups that each formed a different explanation for low(er) earnings (*see* appendix for a complete overview of categories, codes and sub-codes). We compared the graphic design industry and the games industry using the 'code frequencies' of the code tree for the two sectors, which allowed for the differences and similarities between the two sectors to show up clearly (Table 5.1).

Table 5.1 Number of Interviews

	Overall Creative Industries	*Graphic Design*	*Games*
National level	10	–	–
Local level	5	–	–
Workers' level:			
- Employers	–	*4*	*6*
- Freelance	–	*5*	*4*
- Employees	–	*3*	*3*

§5.04 RESULTS

[A] Earnings

The literature gives the impression that work in the creative industries provides very low earnings, with the exception of the lucky few. However, the experiences of the interviewees in the two subsectors actually showed much more variation with some having very low incomes but not all. Moreover, earnings are not generally experienced as very poor. The average hourly rates and yearly incomes published by BNO, the professional organisation in the graphic design industry, indeed exceed the modal income of the average person in the Netherlands (BNO, 2019).[1] Average incomes, however, do not say anything about the income distribution. Vulnerable groups can be extensive even if the average income level is above the national average. Although comparable figures are not available for the games industry, the levels of earnings described by our interviewees again show quite some variation, with some reporting very low levels but other reporting rather decent figures. Nevertheless, earnings do appear to be lower than what one would earn in a different (non-creative) industry doing the same kind of work: programmers in the games industry for example claim that they earn some 30% less than they would make in the Information Technology (IT) sector.

A few particularly vulnerable groups of workers can be found in both industries: beginning entrepreneurs partnering with others to form their own company, with or without employees (indie game developers frequently opt for this model in the games industry, but it is adopted by others in both industries as well), and freelance workers, particularly starting freelancers. In terms of numbers, these groups are quite central to the make-up of the industries, as many workers start a company at some point in their career, and freelance work is high and on the rise in graphic design (BNO, 2017).[2] The earnings of employees and more established entrepreneurs were described as better, although often still believed to be lower than what could be earned in comparable jobs outside the creative sector.

A direct consequence of low earnings for freelancers and entrepreneurs in both sectors is that most of them neither have an unemployment or disability insurance in place nor do they save up for retirement. Employees, on the other hand, are automatically covered by unemployment and disability insurance as regulated by law. Most freelancers, however, indicate that paying for private social security insurance is too expensive and that investing in their business takes priority. Nonetheless, they did not indicate to feel particularly vulnerable. They often relied on their social network, a partner or parents to fall back on, or regarded the basic level of social assistance in the Netherlands to be enough.

[B] Understanding Low(er) Earnings

Analysis of the interviews produced several explanations for the relatively low earnings in the sectors. In the table below the differences between the sectors are highlighted by indicating whether an explanation was found in both sectors or only one

1. The 2019 yearly report of BNO gives average hourly rates for 2017 of between € 75 and € 100 for different types of self-employed and of between € 85 and € 125 for persons working at design companies. At the same time, it shows that on average only 55% of the hours worked are indeed invoiced, pointing to substantial unpaid work in the sector.
2. The earnings level of interns is also notoriously low. This is also true however for interns in other sectors of the economy and not commonly problematised. It remains an open question whether internships in the creative industries extend beyond the education and training period, in other words, whether beginning workers aren't regularly employed as interns. Indications pointing in this direction were found in the interviews, as interviewees described how companies often make use of interns to keep the costs low and make ends meet. This would mean a third vulnerable group could be added. However, more research is needed to see whether this is the case.

of them (Table 5.2). We will now turn to discuss the explanations one by one. Differences found between the two sectors will be explored under the respective thematic headings.

Table 5.2 Understanding Lower Earnings in the Graphic Design and Games Industries

	Graphic Design	*Games*
Worker characteristics		
1. Valuing other work dimensions over earnings:		
a) Willingness to accept lower earnings for the sake of fun, creativity and doing what you love	X	X
b) Willingness to accept lower earnings to work on a cool project or at a certain company	X	X
c) Choice for a less profitable business model for the sake of autonomy and/or developing games that may become a success later ('hit')		X
2. Lacking true entrepreneurial spirit and skills	X	X
Labour market conditions		
3. Customer demands		
d) High pressure on costs resulting in low fees and a practice of free pitching	X	
e) Free apps		X
f) Insecurity about what will be a success		X
4. Oversupply of labour and portfolio labour market	X	X
Motivation to organise collectively		
5. Little interest in collective organisation	X	X
6. Culture of the 'true creative worker'	X	X

[1] Worker Characteristic: Placing Other Work Dimensions over Earnings

By far the majority of the interviewees indicated that they are willing to earn less than they could elsewhere just for the sake of working in the sector. They also stated that they attach more value to aspects of work other than earnings, such as fun, creativity and 'doing what you love' ('a' in Table 5.2). Many of the workers furthermore stated that they had high intrinsic motivation for doing their particular kind of work, emphasising how that they had aspired to do this work from a young age. They felt a sense of belonging to the sector and considered it an important part of their self-identity.

Employers in the sector also described how they do not attempt to attract workers by promising high earnings, but rather by offering them an attractive place to work in terms of atmosphere and content. According to the interviewed employers, this is what binds these employees to the organisation. As one graphic employee stated:

> *I would have liked to earn more, but I guess everyone would like to. No, for me it is more important that I like my job.*
>
> **Graphic 8, employee**

Not only did workers indicate a preparedness to earn less than in other sectors, but they also showed a willingness to forego immediate earnings for the sake of working on particularly 'cool projects' or at particular companies ('b' in Table 5.2). Employees not only described how they accepted lower salaries in order to get into A-rated companies, the ones with the large, cool, cutting-edge projects that look good in your portfolio but also into companies with socially relevant projects workers felt sympathy for. Similar mechanisms were at work for entrepreneurs and freelance workers. They strived to be part of the coolest projects, even to the detriment of earnings, and also regularly accepted jobs for reduced fees from companies with social goals in order to contribute to society, but also because they frequently offer creatively challenging jobs. As an employer in the graphic design industry mentioned:

> *We try to work according to the principle that we only accept clients that are willing to pay a certain budget or for clients that do not have much money but whom we believe to be a nice organisation or a nice project.*
>
> **Graphic 2, employer**

Particularly in the games industry, business owners and indie game developers deliberately opted for less profitable (in the short run) business models for the sake of more autonomy to develop their own projects without having to make concessions (*see* 'c' in Table 5.2). For example, indie game developers professed that the freedom to do 'their own thing' made up for poor earnings, sometimes even below the statutory minimum-wage level. A business owner of a larger company also favoured a business model that allowed them to maintain maximum autonomy in shaping both the direction of the company and the games they develop, rather than going for a larger earning potential. The desire for this kind of autonomy appears to be widespread among workers in the games industry, as it is common for employees and freelancers who work for hire to have their own 'indie' projects besides their jobs or assignments, dedicating one day a week or their weekends and evenings to it. At the same time, they all share the hope that, although they are aware that chances are slim, they will one day develop a very successful game, a 'hit', that will bring in loads of money. The dream to make a living off of your own project is illustrated by this quote from a freelance worker in the games industry:

> *I have the freedom to work on my own projects. That is very important. It is my goal. To be able to develop my own projects in the end and to make those generate money. To live from my own projects, to realize my dreams. That is very enjoyable.*
>
> **Games 5, freelance worker**

This desire for autonomy and the dreaming of a hit were less apparent in the graphic design industry where work on independent products is much less common.

[2] Worker Characteristics: Lacking True Entrepreneurial Spirit and Skills

The interviews showed that low financial returns are not only the result of worker preferences. Another important cause is a lack of business skills and entrepreneurial attitudes among freelance workers and entrepreneurs in the sector. Even if they are often motivated and very good at the creative work they do, they find it difficult to run their own business or to effectively sell their product. The interviewees stated that this is caused by a lack of interest in the business side of things and a lack of talent for sales, but is also the result of educational programmes not paying sufficient attention to business skills. A representative of the creative industries at the national level describes the situation as follows:

> *They are really, highly intrinsically motivated, so they can't think of anything else than making games. They love doing that, and in that journey where they want to build beautiful games, they really forget about business, and some of them even hate to do it.*
>
> **National 5**

[3] Labour Market Conditions: Customer Demands

In the graphic design industry, increasingly assertive client demands have made it increasingly difficult for workers to earn a decent income. The clients frequently put pressure on the price, which interviewees blame on a lack of awareness of the real added value of their work, especially since digital packages such as Photoshop give non-professionals the possibility to create their own designs. All too often designers give in to this pressure, both because they prefer working cheaply over not working at all and because of a lack of business skills. Another problematic practice described by interviewees is 'free pitching,' where clients invite several companies and/or freelance workers to 'pitch' for an assignment, but only pay the party who wins the assignment. This results in a lot of unpaid work for graphic designers preparing the pitches *see also* footnote 2). As a graphic design employer explained:

> *Our work is not always valued by the customer. This also has to do with the practices in our sector to agree to work for very low budgets or to participate in free pitching. [...] Customers often think 'we are a very cool company, so we can pay the creative less'. And often the creatives agree to this. I think this is a disadvantage of working in the sector, the free pitching etc. But we also let it happen to ourselves. Customers with a small budget nevertheless inviting six different companies to develop a proposal. I think this is ridiculous.*
>
> **Graphic 2, employer**

In the games industry, interviewees observed that customers do not expect and do not wish to pay for the games they play on their mobile devices, the fastest-growing section of the games industry, where mainly the indie companies are active. Ways to earn money through such games is either by offering paid add-ons or through advertisements. However, allowing advertisements in your game is often considered 'not done' among indie game developers, which leaves them fewer options to earn money, as described by one freelance worker:

> *For indie developers, it is a taboo. Advertisements? You wouldn't think about having advertisements in your game, surely? It is a moral issue. And having app purchases to increase the content of the game, it is like the devil for some. That makes it really hard.*
>
> **Games 5, freelance worker**

About the only other way of earning money as an indie game developer is to produce a game that becomes a huge success. This is an infrequent occurrence, however, meaning that many workers put in a lot of effort to produce games of which most will never yield much in terms of earnings.

[4] Labour Market Conditions: An Oversupply of Labour and Portfolio Labour Market

The interviewed workers indicate that structural characteristics of the labour markets in the games and graphic design industries also contribute to poorer earnings and working conditions. Both industries know an oversupply of labour in the Netherlands, albeit for different reasons: the graphic design industry has suffered a severe reduction of available jobs due to the economic crisis, whereas the games industry has an oversupply of graduates with games-related degrees. Under such conditions, starting your own company becomes a common way of entering the sector, either as a freelance worker (graphic design) or an indie game developer. Unsurprisingly in a context of many start-ups, the entrepreneurial risk associated with starting your own company contributes crucially to lower earnings. Even though the risk itself is not specific to the sector, the scale at which workers take this risk just to have a chance to work in the sector does seem to play a role.

The oversupply of labour in both sectors furthermore affects the bargaining position of those who have managed to find a position as an employee. After all, employers do not have to offer high salaries to attract good employees. The employees interviewed in the games industry, for example, indicate that they tend not to actively bargain about their salary with future employers but just accept their offer, the reasons being that money is not their prime motivation and that they feel lucky enough to have found a job in the industry in the first place. This is not equally true for all positions, however. According to the interviewees, programmers in the games industry generally have little difficulty in finding a position and have a good bargaining position because of the scarcity of their skills.

A labour market with an oversupply of labour makes it even more important for workers to distinguish themselves from competitors in order to secure positions and freelance jobs. In both industries the portfolio is an important means to this end. This is yet another reason why employees often do not bargain about their salary but just accept the offer: being able to add the work experience or the name of a certain company to their portfolio is valuable for their long-term career prospects, and more important to them than what they might earn in the short run.

[5] Motivation to Organise Collectively

Very few of the interviewees indicate any motivation for or interest in organising collectively. Many have never even considered it. To many workers, making their career a success has top priority. This is considered an individual responsibility, and workers perceive no benefit in collective organisation. However, they do consider the expansion of the respective sectors as a collective goal that will serve their individual needs. In this context they do see a role for the professional organisations which are active in the sub-sectors, as a graphic design employer states:

> *It would be good if they would do some missionary work. That they would show to business the strength of our sector and what we can contribute. Then maybe they get the idea to hire a local company.*
>
> **Graphic 2, employer**

Very few of the workers mention social security or a better bargaining position for wage or fee negotiations as interests potentially defended by collective organisations. The trade unions in the sector blame workers' lack of interest in these 'traditional' working conditions for their difficulties in organising the graphic design and games industries. According to them, individual creativity is prioritised by these workers, which is not conducive to great working conditions or realising a decent income, as voiced by a trade union representative:

> *It is more essential to produce work, to develop a game or to make animations, to draw, than to earn money. And that's the tricky part. It makes our position relatively weak because there tends to be low interest in organising, but also, well, people tend to take the job anyway.*
>
> **Representative of a trade union**

[6] Culture of the 'True Creative Worker'

During the interviews, it became clear that workers in the creative industry saw the willingness to earn less as a sign of being a 'true creative worker'. It was seen as an asset of those working in these industries. Employers made active use of this image of the true creative: it was mentioned by some of the employers as a strategy to select the sincerely intrinsically motivated people. On the contrary, wanting a higher salary signalled to these employers that the worker does not possess the qualities they desire in an employee: they perceived them as not sufficiently motivated and having a too relaxed attitude towards the work. As illustrated by this games employer:

> *I felt guilty at first that everyone had to take a step back, but at the same time it was convenient, because I want the intrinsically motivated people who really, really want to do something for our target groups. It became a kind of test or check to see whether someone is willing to give up earnings by choosing this job.*
>
> **Games 1, employer**

[7] Discussion and Conclusion

In this study, we set out to understand whether and why earnings in the creative industries are (relatively) low. First of all, we established that workers do not perceive the overall level of earnings in their sectors to be particularly low, and this is indeed often true in absolute terms. However, it is true in relative terms, as workers in comparable jobs in other sectors tend to earn more. Moreover, we identified several particularly vulnerable groups generally confronted with very low earnings that may be even below the level of the minimum wage: freelancers and beginning entrepreneurs (as mentioned, there are indications that interns are also particularly vulnerable, but more research is required on this group). These findings show, in line with Thompson et al. (2016), that the dominant view in the literature that earnings in the creative industries are uniformly low needs to be more nuanced, both distinguishing between relative and absolute levels of earnings, and between better and worse-off groups within the sector.

At the same time, we did find that it is common for workers in the sector to make compromises concerning their earnings, although some compromise more than others. We show that this can be understood as the result of a combination of three factors: personal preferences, labour market conditions, and a lack of collective organisation. We moreover found that these factors reinforce each other and therefore should not be considered in isolation. For example, considering together creative workers' great passion for their profession with the oversupply of labour in their specific labour market helps to understand why so many workers start their own business, even if they lack a specific desire to run a business as well as the skills to do so effectively, and are aware of the chances of low earnings. The centrality of entrepreneurship, in turn, reduces the likelihood that workers will organise collectively (cf. Neff, 2012), while the lack of collective organisation results in a weaker bargaining position for workers when negotiating about earnings.

This study furthermore unearthed a fourth explanation for lower earnings in the sector that had not been included in our original research design: a behavioural norm regarding the 'true creative worker'. We found in our interviews a notion of the 'true creative worker' as one willing to forego earnings for the pleasure of the work. This is illustrated for example by employers describing how they use the willingness to earn less as an indicator for the selection of good employees. More research is needed to better understand the extent to which such a norm exists and what it means for earnings, and possibly for entrepreneurial success.

There are many similarities between the graphic design industry and the games industry when it comes to understanding the prevalence of lower absolute and relative earnings. Nevertheless, there are some important differences. First, whereas customer demands make it difficult to earn money in both sectors, the nature of the problematic demands differ. Second, and most noticeably, we found a stronger desire in the games industry for autonomy and for being able 'to do your own thing'. Business owners in this industry consciously choose for less profitable business models because it provides greater autonomy and allows them to work on their own games. For the same reason employees often develop their own side-projects beside their jobs. An important driver behind these projects is the hope that their own game will become a 'hit', which in the meantime leads to the investment of great efforts for very insecure returns. We did not find this mechanism to play a role in the graphic design industry, possibly because of the different nature of the products: games are commercialised and may (or may not) generate profits, while graphic design products are mainly produced on demand for specific clients. The context of individual projects in the games industry puts additional emphasis on individual responsibility for success. This makes collective interest organisation even more unlikely, an additional explanation (besides the age of the sector and its employees) for the lack of any collective regulation of earnings, where the graphic design industry does have a voluntary guideline for the level of salaries.

REFERENCES

Arvidsson, A., Malossi, G., & Naro, S. (2010). Passionate work? Labour conditions in the Milan fashion industry. *Journal for Cultural Research, 14*(3), 295-309.

Bellini, A., et al. (2018) *Industrial relations and creative workers.* Overall report. IRCREA.

Beroepsorganisatie Nederlandse Ontwerpers (2017). *BNO branchemonitor 2017: De Nederlandse ontwerpsector in beeld en getal.* Amsterdam: BNO.

Beroepsorganisatie Nederlandse Ontwerpers (2019). *BNO branchemonitor 2019: De Nederlandse ontwerpsector in beeld en getal.* Amsterdam: BNO.

Bulut, E. (2015). Playboring in the tester pit: The convergence of precarity and the degradation of fun in video game testing. *Television & New Media, 16*(3), 240-258.

Chaston I., & Sadler-Smith E. (2012). Entrepreneurial cognition, cntrepreneurial orientation and firm capability in the creative industries, *British Journal of Management, 23*(3), 415-432.

De Beer P.T., & Keune M. (2017). Dutch unions in a time of crisis, in Lehndorff, S., Dribbusch H., & Schulten T. (eds) *Rough waters: European trade unions in a time of crisis, Brussels*, ETUI, 221-244.

De Peuter, G. (2011). Creative economy and labor precarity: A contested convergence. *Journal of Communication Inquiry, 35*(4), 417-425.

De Peuter, G., & Dyer-Witheford, N. (2005). A playful multitude? Mobilising and counter- mobilising immaterial game labour. *The Fibreculture Journal, 5*, 1-21.

Dollinger, S.J., Burke, P.A., & Gump, N.W. (2007). Creativity and values. *Creativity Research Journal, 19*(2-3), 91-103.

Dutch Game Garden (2018). *Games monitor: The Netherlands 2018.* Utrecht: Dutch Game Garden.

Eikhoff, D. & Warhurst, C. (2013). The promised land? Why social inequalities are systemic in the creative industries. *Employee Relations, 35*(5), 495-508.

Florida, R. (2002). *The rise of the creative class* (Vol. 9). New York: Basic Books.

Foucault, M. (2010). *The birth of biopolitics: Lectures at the College de France,* translated by Graham Burchill. Houndmills, Hampshire: Palgrave Macmillan.

Gill, R., & Pratt, A. (2008). In the social factory? Immaterial labour, precariousness and cultural work. *Theory, Culture & Society, 25*(7-8), 1-30.

Greer, I., Samaluk, B., & Umney, C. (2018) Better strategies for herding cats? Forms of solidarity among freelance musicians in London, Paris, and Ljubljana, in Doellgast, V., Lillie, N., & Pulignano, V. (eds) *Reconstructing solidarity: Labour unions, precarious work, and the politics of institutional change in Europe,* Oxford: Oxford University Press, 166-187.Hennekam, S., & Bennett, D. (2017). Creative industries work across multiple contexts: Common themes and challenges. *Personnel Review, 46*(1), 68-85.

Kenney M., & Zysman J. (2016). The Rise of the Platform Economy, *Issues in Science & Technology, 32*(3), 61-69.

Koops O. (2016). *Game monitor. The Netherlands 2005,* https://www.dutchgamegarden.nl/project/games-monitor/.

Mathieu C. (ed.) (2012). *Careers in creative industries,* Abingdon: Routledge.

McGuigan, J. (2010). Creative labour, cultural work and individualisation. *International Journal of Cultural Policy, 16*(3), 323-335.

McRobbie, A. (2002). Clubs to companies: Notes on the decline of political culture in speeded up creative worlds. *Cultural Studies, 16*(4), 516-531.

McRobbie, A. (2009). Reflections on precarious work in the cultural sector. *Governance der Kreativwirtschaft: Diagnosen und Handlungsoptionen. transcript-Verl., Bielefeld,* 123-138.

Menger, P.M. (2017). Contingent high-skilled work and flexible Labor Markets. Creative workers and independent contractors cycling between employment and unemployment. *Swiss Journal of Sociology, 43*(2), 253-284.

Morgan, G., Wood, J., & Nelligan, P. (2013). Beyond the vocational fragments: Creative work, precarious labour and the idea of 'flexploitation'. *The Economic and Labour Relations Review, 24*(3), 397-415.

Murdock, G. (2003). Back to work: Cultural labor in altered times. In *Cultural work* (pp. 27-48). Routledge.

Neff, G., Wissinger, E., & Zukin, S. (2005). Entrepreneurial labor among cultural producers: 'Cool' jobs in 'hot' industries. *Social Semiotics, 15*(3), 307-334.

Neff, G. (2012). *Venture labor: Work and the burden of risk in innovative industries.* MIT press.

Peticca-Harris, A., Weststar, J., & McKenna, S. (2015). The perils of project-based work: Attempting resistance to extreme work practices in video game development. *Organisation, 22*(4), 570-587.

Siebert, S., & Wilson, F. (2013). All work and no pay: Consequences of unpaid work in the creative industries. *Work, Employment and Society*, *27*(4), 711-721.

Thompson, P., Parker, R., & Cox, S. (2016). Interrogating creative theory and creative work: Inside the games studio. *Sociology*, *50*(2), 316-332.

Umney, C., & Kretsos, L. (2015). That's the experience' passion, work precarity, and life transitions among London Jazz Musicians. *Work and Occupations*, *42*(3), 313-334.

Umney, C., & Coderre-LaPalme. G. (2017). Blocked and new frontiers for trade unions: Contesting 'the meaning of work' in the creative and caring sectors. *British Journal of Industrial Relations*, *55*(4), 859-878.

Wright, A. (2017). 10 Understanding self-exploitation in the digital games sector. *The New Digital Workplace: How New Technologies Revolutionise Work*, 195.

APPENDIX

Worke characteristics

1. Valuing other work dimensions over earnings:

a) Willingness to accept lower earnings for the sake of fun, creativity and doing what you love
- Earning money less important
- Not much needed
- Creativity centered
- Intrinsic motivation
- Passion
- Informal and good atmosphere

b) Willingness to accept lower earnings to work on a cool project or at a certain company
- Strong pull factor/sexy
- Charity projects/societal relevance

c) Choice for a less prosperous business model for the sake of autonomy and/or developing games that may become a success later ('hit')
- Self-realization important
- Autonomy valued
- Provides freedom and flexibility

2. Lacking true entrepreneurial spirit and skills
- Lousy business models
- Not professional
- No mindset for earning money
- Difficult to sell/earn money/ lacking entrepreneurial skills
- Difficult outside representation

Labour market conditions

3. Customer demands

d) Low costs resulting in low fees and a practice of free pitching
- Difficult to ask high fees
- We agree to work for low tariffs easily
- Practice of free pitching

e) Free apps
- Indie culture

f) Insecure what will be a success
- Hit driven

4. Oversupply of labour and portfolio labour market
- Solo-self-employed not a free choice
- Good portfolio needed
- Competitive

Motivation to organise at a collective level
5. Little interest in collective organisation
- Do not want to be organised
- Never considered/thought about it
- (No) need for a C.A.
- Important to have a voice as a sector
6. Culture of the 'true creative worker'
- Selection of employees based on willingness to forego earnings

CHAPTER 6

Reforming Labour Laws in the Netherlands: An Assessment of the Redistributive Effects

Nuna Zekić

§6.01 INTRODUCTION

The rise of economic inequality is seen by many as one of the biggest current threats to our societies. Even organisations such as the Organisation for Economic Co-operation and Development (OECD) and International Monetary Fund (IMF) warn for unsustainable economic inequality in the future.[1] The debate on inequality is, however, often 'emotional and divisive'.[2] A widely proclaimed view is that only the tax (and social security) systems should concern themselves with distribution and redistribution of wealth.[3] The reason is that this kind of 'intervention' is considered to be most efficient because in this way the market is disturbed in the least possible way. Our tax and social security systems are indisputably important when we consider the legal systems in the light of economic inequality. However, when looking at the potential of legal frameworks to influence the level of economic inequality - and more specifically, income inequality - one cannot deny the role of labour law. Davidov, for examples, calls redistribution a 'major goal of labour law'.[4] The very fact that we have protective

1. OECD, *In it Together: Why Less Inequality Benefits All*, OECD Publishing, Paris 2015; OECD, *Divided We Stand: Why Inequality Keeps Rising*, OECD Publishing, Paris 2011; World Bank Group, *Poverty and Shared Prosperity 2016. Taking on Inequality*, Washington 2016; IMF, *World Economic Outlook*, April 2017.
2. S. Hsu, 'The rise and rise of the one percent: Considering legal causes of inequality', *Emory Law Journal Online* 2015 Vol. 64, p. 2045.
3. M. Dimick, 'Should the law do anything about economic inequality?', *Cornell Journal of Law and Public Policy* 2016 Vol. 26 No. 1, pp. 2-3.
4. G. Davidov, *A Purposive Approach to Labour Law*, Oxford: Oxford University Press 2016, p. 57.

labour laws assumes a certain intervention in the functioning of the (labour) market and a certain distributive effect.

It is important to scrutinise labour law's redistributive role, especially where it concerns the regulation of flexible work. The increase of non-standard employment has been indicated as one of the important contributors to rising inequality.[5] This contribution, therefore, examines recent labour law reforms in the Netherlands in terms of their distributive aims and effects. Are redistributive concerns part of the reform motives, and if so, what kind of redistribution do the legislators have in mind? Furthermore, what kind of legal mechanisms do they use to reach the redistributive goals and are these mechanisms likely to reach their goals considering what we know about economic inequality?

To answer these questions, first, non-standard work in the Netherlands is discussed, followed by a discussion of the level of economic inequality in a comparative perspective. The next step is to zoom in on the relation between non-standard work and economic inequality. For this end, this article mainly uses insights from economic literature. The main aim of this article is to examine – in section §6.03 – the recent legislative attempts in the Netherlands that deal with the growth of non-standard work and to consider them in the light of the rising economic inequality. Conclusions follow in section §6.04.

§6.02 NON-STANDARD WORK IN THE NETHERLANDS

[A] Non-standard Work in the Netherlands

The increase of the use of flexible types of employment contracts has been considerable in the Netherlands in the past decade.[6] Flexible employment as well as the number of independent contractors are rising. In 2015, 21% of the workers had a flexible contract, while in 2003, this was 13.6%.[7] It seems that especially the most flexible and unsecure types of employment contracts, such as zero-hours contracts, are on the rise.[8] Moreover, the transitions from flexible work to more permanent positions seem to be decreasing.[9] Some are speaking of a true segregation in the Dutch labour market: with a decreasing group of well-protected insiders enjoying permanent employment

5. For example OECD 2015, pp. 28-32.
6. L. Köster & W. Smits, 'Tijdelijk werk: Nederland in Europees perspectief', in: *Dynamiek op de Nederlandse Arbeidsmarkt*, CBS 2015, pp. 147-148; A. Heyma & S. van der Werff, 'De sociaaleconomische situatie van langdurig flexibele werknemers', Amsterdam: SEO 2013.
7. CPB, *De flexibele schil van de Nederlandse arbeidsmarkt*, CPB Achtergronddocument 17 November 2016. Other documents report an increase from 16% in 2003 to 27% in 2017, Statistics Netherlands (CBS), *Werkzame beroepsbevolking; positie in de werkkring*, https://opendata.cbs.nl/statline (website visited on 19 March 2018).
8. CPB 2016.
9. Köster & Smits 2015, pp. 147-148. Also *see* R. Dekker, 'Doorstroom van Flexwerkers', *ESB Arbeidsrecht* 2012 (4628), pp. 70-73.

contracts on the one side, and a growing group of employees on the other side working in flexible employment relations that offer little protection against the loss of the job.[10]

[B] The Extent of Economic Inequality in the Netherlands

The general perception is that the Netherlands is a fairly equal country. There is a developed welfare state that provides a good 'safety net' for those in need. There is a comprehensive system of progressive taxes and a social security system that can probably be placed among the best in the world.[11] But also in the Netherlands, economic inequality has been rising.[12] Particularly wealth inequality is relatively high in the Netherlands[13] and it has been rising in the recent years.[14] Income inequality is always much smaller than wealth inequality and it does not seem to be high in the Netherlands; it is average compared to other OECD-countries.[15] But the global trends in this context are visible here as well: since the end of the nineties, the gap between the highest and the lowest income groups has grown considerably.[16] The wages at the bottom are stagnating, while the wages at the top have grown substantially. Not only the top and the bottom have grown apart but also the disparity with the middle incomes has grown.[17] Furthermore, the labour income share – the part of national income allocated to wages – has been on the decline in the Netherlands,[18] just as it has been in the rest of the world.[19]

10. N. Gundt, 'Employment and security in the Netherlands', *European Labour Law Journal* 2015 Vol. 6 No. 4, p. 365.
11. *See* e.g., F. Pennings, *The International Encyclopaedia of Laws. The Netherlands*, Wolters Kluwer: Kluwer Law Online 2017.
12. Just like in general, there is discussion among economists in the Netherlands on how to measure economic inequality; there is no consensus on this matter yet. Furthermore, there is a lot of data missing, *see* e.g., G. Zucman, 'Wealth inequality', in *State of the Union. The Poverty and Inequality Report*, Stanford Center on Poverty and Inequality 2016, p. 43.
13. C. Balestra & R. Tonkin, 'Inequalities in household wealth across OECD countries: Evidence from the OECD Wealth Distribution Database', OECD Statistics and Data Directorate, Working Paper nr. 88, juni 2018, p. 8; B. van Bavel, 'Vermogensongelijkheid in Nederland: de vergeten dimensie', in M. Kremer, M. Bovens, E. Schrijvers & R. Went (eds.), *Hoe ongelijk is Nederland?*, WRR-verkenning 2014, p. 84.
14. R. Schulenberg, 'Toenemende vermogensongelijkheid in Nederland', *ESB* 2018, 4762 286.
15. M. Kremer, R. Went & M. Bovens, 'Economische ongelijkheid in Nederland', in M. Kremer, M. Bovens, E. Schrijvers & R. Went (ed.), *Hoe ongelijk is Nederland?*, WRR-verkenning 2014, p. 15.
16. *Ibid.*, p. 16.
17. CBS, 'Verschil in loon tussen top en gewone werknemer nam toe', mei 2018, https://www.cbs.nl/nl-nl/nieuws/2018/18/verschil-in-loon-tussen-top-en-gewone-werknemer-nam-toe (website visited on 3 July 2018).
18. DNBulletin: 'Flexibilisering arbeidsmarkt gaat gepaard met daling arbeidsinkomensquote', 1 February 2018, https://www.dnb.nl/nieuws/nieuwsoverzicht-en-archief/DNBulletin2018/dnb372062.jsp (website lastly visited on 11 June 2018).
19. European Commission, *Reflection Paper on Harnessing Globalisation*, 10 May 2017, COM(2017) 240, p. 9.

[C] Relationship Between Non-standard Work and Inequality

Globalisation and technological change are seen by most economists as the main drivers of inequality.[20] As a result of technological development, the demand for skilled labour increases which causes the wage gap between the low-educated and the high-educated workers to increase.[21] The decline in labour shares driven by technology and global integration has been particularly sharp for middle-skilled labour. The fact that routine-based technology has taken over many of the tasks performed by middle-skilled labour contributes to job polarisation towards high-skill and low-skill occupations.[22]

However, many believe that globalisation and technological change alone cannot explain the rise of economic inequality; they believe institutional changes have significantly contributed to the rise of inequality as well.[23] The declining strength of trade unions is one of the most important institutional changes in this regard, but the flexibilisation of the labour market seems to be important as well. The OECD observes that before the crisis, many OECD countries were facing a paradoxical situation: their employment rates were at record-high levels and yet income inequality was on the rise.[24] Arguably, this is due to the gradual decline of the 'traditional, permanent, nine-to-five job' in favour of non-standard work – typically part-time and temporary work and self-employment. The IMF, for example, explicitly urges the Dutch government to stop the further flexibilisation of the labour market in order to encourage wage growth.[25]

The Dutch researchers are, however, divided on the issue. On the one side, there is the view that the decline of the labour income share is indeed connected to the flexibilisation of the labour market.[26] Compared to 'standard workers', workers with flexible, non-standard contracts – such as temporary agency workers or workers with zero-hours contracts – have less job security and are hardly organised, all of which makes their negotiating position weak. At the same time, their presence on the labour market undermines the negotiating position of the 'standard' workers, because the two groups compete with each other. On the other side, however, there are the economists who say they cannot determine whether flexibilisation of the labour market really has this (negative) structural effect on wage growth.[27] They also see positive sides of a large number of people with flexible contracts: traditionally, unemployment has a (strong)

20. P. de Beer, 'Groeiende beloningsverschillen in Nederland', in Kremer et al., 2014, p. 63.
21. D.H. Autor, 'Skills, education, and the rise of earnings inequality among the 'other 99%', *Science* 2014 Vol. 344 No. 6186, pp. 843-851; A.B. Atkinson, *Inequality. What Can Be Done?*, Harvard University Press 2015; L. Tyson & M. Spence, 'Exploring the Effects of Technology on Income and Wealth Inequality', in H. Boushey, J.B. DeLong & M. Steinbaum, *After Piketty. The Agenda for Economics and Inequality*, Harvard University Press 2017, pp. 170-208.
22. IMF 2017, p. 125.
23. For example Atkinson 2015, pp. 82-83; De Beer 2014, p. 64.
24. OECD 2015, p. 28.
25. IMF Country Report No. 18/130, May 2018, p. 10.
26. DNBulletin: 'Flexibilisering arbeidsmarkt gaat gepaard met daling arbeidsinkomensquote', 1 February 2018, https://www.dnb.nl/nieuws/nieuwsoverzicht-en-archief/DNBulletin2018/dnb372062.jsp (website lastly visited on 11 June 2018).
27. CPB, *Vertraagde loonontwikkeling in Nederland ontrafeld*, CPB Policy Brief, 2018/12.

negative effect on wages, but a higher number of temporary workers reduces this negative effect of unemployment on real wages.[28] When unemployment is low, however, a high number of temporary workers can stagnate the wage growth. The researchers assume that in 'good times', temporary workers use their negotiating power to get a permanent job, instead of a higher wage. Therefore, they are not willing to accept a direct relationship between flexibilisation of the labour market and lower wage growth. Instead, they point to lower productivity growth as the main reason for stagnating wages. However, the same researchers cannot determine a link with globalisation, technological change, or shifting market power - even though there is a vast amount of literature that points in this direction –, because they have trouble 'operationalizing' these concepts.[29] This leaves us with disputable drives of inequality, but with a conclusion that the question of inequality cannot be approached with arithmetic means alone. There is a strong indication, however, that that the flexibilisation of the labour market and the increase of non-standard employment are among the drivers of economic inequality. It is, therefore, worth examining if and how the regulation of non-standard employment takes this into account.

§6.03 REGULATION OF FLEXIBLE EMPLOYMENT IN THE LIGHT OF ECONOMIC INEQUALITY

Most labour law systems in Europe have in common that they protect the employee as the weaker party. Some of these protective rules have clear redistributive effects, such as the rules on minimum wage and collective bargaining.[30] Collective agreements can be very effective redistributive mechanisms when they have a wide coverage. Many economists confirm the role of trade unions (and collective agreements) in lowering inequality and some of them urge the governments to strengthen that role.[31] However, there is an important restriction to (collective) labour law in this respect and that is the fact that most protective norms are in principle confined to employment relationships. That means that persons who do not perform labour under an employment contract, such as independent contractors, generally do not benefit from labour law protection or from redistributive measures through labour law. This is a long-acknowledged constraint of labour law.[32] The focus of this contribution is, however, on what is happening *within* the realm of employment: the rise of atypical or non-standard employment.[33]

The attempts on European Union (EU)-level to regulate atypical employment can be characterised as attempts with a double purpose. On the one hand, the aim has been

28. CPB, *Loongroei, een analyse op bedrijvendata*, CPB Achtergronddocument, 23 November 2018, p. 23.
29. *Ibid.*, p. 18.
30. Cf. Davidov 2016, 57.
31. Atkinson 2015, pp. 128-132.
32. For example G. Mundlak, 'The Third Function of Labour Law: Distributing Labour Market Opportunities among Workers', in G. Davidov & B. Langille (ed.), *The Idea of Labour Law*, Oxford: Oxford University Press 2011, pp. 315-328.
33. The terms atypical and non-standard are used interchangeably.

to improve the working conditions of atypical workers, while on the other hand, the aim has been to eliminate or scale down the existing barriers for flexible contracts. These goals are pursued simultaneously. This is also the case in the Netherlands. In 2015 major changes were introduced in Dutch labour law through the Act on Work and Security (*Wet Werk en Zekerheid*), which was based on a comprise between the social partners. The aim of the reform was to improve the position of employees with flexible contracts and at the same time to make dismissal of employees with permanent contracts less costly. In the end, the result of the changes should be that the flexible or temporary contracts have become less flexible and the open-ended contracts less permanent. Even though the reforms are quite recent, there are strong doubts about whether they have brought about the desired level of balance between the 'insiders' and the 'outsiders'. For example, dismissals might have become less costly, but it seems that the dismissal procedure was made more rigid with bigger risks for employers.[34]

In 2018, the new government proposed new changes with the Act on Labour Market in Balance (*Wet Arbeidsmarkt in Balans*). The main feature of this latest proposal for reform is the introduction of a so-called cumulating ground for dismissal in order to make it easier to dismiss employees. On many issues, the new reform is only a correction of the Act on Work and Security, which makes the Act on Work and Security still the most fundamental change of the Dutch labour law since the Second World War.[35] It is therefore interesting to see what changes were introduced in order to improve the position of flexible employees and to assess these changes in light of the discussion on economic inequality.

[A] Fostering Transitions into Open-Ended Contracts

One of the main goals of the Act on Work and Security was to prevent - what the legislator has called - ' the improper use' of flexible contracts.[36] This corresponds with the approach taken in the Pillar of Social Rights where the term 'abuse' of atypical contracts is used.[37] It is not clear when flexible contracts are used by employers in an improper way or when exactly we can say an employer is abusing flexible contracts. For the Act on Work and Security that is the case when workers are employed on flexible contracts on a long-term and involuntary basis, with little prospects of improving their position on the labour market.[38] In some aspects, this corresponds with the concept of precarious work. Indeed the ILO has stressed as well that nonstandard jobs are not necessarily precarious.[39] In other words, non-standard or flexible jobs are

34. A.R. Houweling, M.J.M.T. Keulaerds & P. Kruit, *VAAN-VvA Evaluatie-onderzoek Wwz 2016*, Den Haag, 2016, p. 12.
35. Gundt 2015, p. 364.
36. *Oneigenlijk gebruik*, *see* parliamentary documents No. 33 818/3 (*Kamerstukken II* 2013-2014, 33 818, nr. 3), p. 4.
37. Article 5 sub d of the European Pillar of Social Rights, p, 14.
38. *Kamerstukken II* 2013-2014, 33 818, nr. 3 (MvT), p. 10.
39. ILO, *Non-standard employment around the world: Understanding challenges, shaping prospects*, International Labour Office - Geneva: ILO 2016, p. 18.

not necessarily bad jobs. Therefore, even though the European and the Dutch legislator wish to tackle abuse of flexible employment, they both in the same (legislative) documents affirm the 'regular' use of flexible contracts and stress that they aim to ensure 'the necessary flexibility for employers, to adapt swiftly to changes in the economic context'.[40] Therefore, the range of flexible types contracts is not limited; the goal instead is to foster the transition towards open-ended forms of contracts. The Dutch government took a number of measures to achieve this goal. One of the main measures was limiting the use of *successive* fixed-term contracts from a maximum of three years to two years.[41] According to the government, the employer should be able to know after two years whether he has the possibility to hire that employee on a permanent basis.[42]

What non-standard work arrangements usually have in common besides in most cases *de facto* lower wages - which is obviously of great relevance to economic inequality and will be discussed below – is the fact that they give no or very little claim to job continuity in the future. The fixed-term contract is the best example of an atypical employment contract that gives no claim to job continuity after a fixed date or after a certain period of time.[43] Temporary agency work is another example of flexible employment that is legally designed in such way that it gives very little claim to job continuity (with the user undertaking). It is therefore not surprising that when seeking to improve the position of atypical workers, legislators have tried to advance their chances of obtaining an open-ended contract. The Fixed-term Directive for this purpose gives the Member States a choice in measures to limit the use of *successive* fixed-term contracts. A Member State may require objective reasons for justifying the renewal of such contracts, impose a maximum total duration of successive fixed-term contracts, or impose a maximum number of renewals of such contracts.[44] After the maximum duration or after the maximum number of fixed-term contracts, the employer can choose either to employ the worker in question on the basis of an open-ended contract or the employer can choose not to continue the employment relationship with the worker in question. When applying the Fixed-term Directive, the Court of Justice of the European Union (CJEU) has asserted that 'the benefit of stable employment (...) constitutes a major element in the protection of workers'.[45] This has been one of the central considerations in several CJEU rulings on flexible employment. The rulings of

40. Article 5 under b of the European Pillar of Social Rights.
41. Article 7:668a Civil Code.
42. *Kamerstukken II* 2013-2014, 33 818, nr. 3, pp. 15, 95. Furthermore, the interval between employment, after which a new 'chain' of employment contracts should start, has been prolonged from three to six months.
43. For example, after a certain project for which the worker was recruited has finished.
44. Article 5 of European Directive 1999/70/EC of 28 June 1999 concerning the framework agreement on fixed-term work concluded by ETUC, UNICE and CEEP.
45. CJEU 22 November 2005, C-144/04, *Mangold*, para. 64. The Court has later repeated such or similar considerations in several other rulings. For example CJEU 26 February 2015, C-238/14, *Commission v. Luxembourg*, para. 36, 50-51.

the CJEU have been interpreted as favouring permanent (i.e., open-ended) employment contracts as a rule over flexible ones.[46]

To sum up, one could say that the policy has been so far to allow for the use of flexible or non-standard work because flexible jobs do not have to be precarious or bad, but for workers, they should be stepping stones to more stable employment. Therefore, the policy is geared towards fostering transitions to open-ended employment namely by limiting the use of *successive* fixed-term contracts. As said, the Act on Work and Security reduced the use of successive fixed-term contracts in the Netherlands from a maximum of three years to two years.[47]

The law still does not require from the employer to show an objective reason to justify the recourse to fixed-term work. This approach of only limiting the use of successive fixed-term contracts may work in some sectors, but it has little effect in sectors where workers can easily be replaced by other workers and where the costs of recruiting and training new workers are low. This is often the case in the restaurant business, cleaning, supermarkets and other retail business, agriculture, delivering services, etc. In these sectors, the employer can employ a worker on a fixed-term contract for the maxim amount of time and then recruit and train a new worker to replace the old one. Especially when there are many job seekers, recruitment and training of new workers do not need to take longer than a few days. Only when the labour market is tight or the worker proofs to be exceptionally valuable, the employer will have an incentive to offer the worker a permanent position. Otherwise, the work is permanent, but the people have temporary positions.[48] Not coincidentally, these are the sectors that employ low-skilled workers, who already – as we have seen above – run the risk of receiving low pay. These are also types of work that large firms choose to outsource to other firms that are specialised in this type of work.

Many commentators have disapproved the reducing of the maximum number of successive fixed-term contracts to two years – instead of three years.[49] They have warned that this measure can have a counterproductive effect in the sense that it will change the position of the flexible workers for the worse: the employment contracts will last a shorter period leaving the worker without a job.[50] With the new measure, the worker has clarity about her prospects sooner in the process, but her prospects are not necessarily better. The new government has taken over this critique and in 2018, a proposal was introduced to extend the maximum use of successive fixed-term contracts to three years again.[51] However, there will still be no need to reduce flexible employment as such.

46. A.G. Veldman, 'The Coherency of European Social Policy: The ECJ Caught Between Flexible Employment Policies and Upholding European Employment Rights' in F.J.L. Pennings, Y. Konijn, & A.G. Veldman (eds) *Social Responsibility in Labour Relations: European and Comparative Perspectives,* Kluwer Law International 2008, p. 96.
47. Article 7:668a Civil Code.
48. For example Gundt 2015, p. 372.
49. *See* as one of the first commentators, F.B.J. Grapperhaus, 'De toren van Babel en het in het Wetsvoorstel Wet Werk en Zekerheid beoogde nieuwe ontslagstelsel', *TRA* 2014/22.
50. *Kamerstukken II* 2013-2014, 33 818, nr. 4, p. 2; A.R. Houweling, M.J.M.T., Keulaerds, and P. Kruit (eds.), *VAAN-VvA Evaluatieonderzoek WWZ 2016*, Den Haag: Boom juridisch 2016, p. 12.
51. *Kamerstukken I* 2018-2019, 35 074, nr. A, p. 4.

Even though there is plenty of criticism as to the effectiveness of the rules regarding the use of successive fixed-term contracts – especially regarding their ability to foster transition open-ended contracts – little attention is paid to the fact that the effectiveness is especially weak in the before mentioned low-wage sectors where workers are easily replaced. When proposing the Act on Work and Security, the Dutch government recognised that the probability that a temporary contract will be converted into an open-ended contract depends on the type of work and the type of employee who performs that work. The government acknowledges that high-skilled workers or workers in sectors where there is a great demand for labour (such as technology sectors) are likely more difficult to replace because they are scarce and they often perform work in which they build up specific knowledge. They have better prospects on the labour market in general and they have better prospects of obtaining open-ended contracts. However, the government simply remarks that this difference in labour market prospects between low-skilled and high-skilled workers is a long-standing fact and it is in the vision of the government not dependent to the maximum number of successive fixed-term contracts.[52] In other words, the government may wish to reduce the number temporary workers in the Netherlands, but it has no explicit desire to reduce the difference between the low-skilled and high-skilled workers with this measure. Consequently, it takes for granted that the measure will benefit high-skilled workers more than it will low-skilled workers.

[B] Equal Treatment of Atypical Workers

Besides treating flexible employment as stepping stones and fostering transitions into permanent contracts, prescribing equal treatment of workers with atypical contracts has been one of the main ways to improve the position of flexible workers and to prevent abuse of atypical contracts. The three main Directives on atypical work, Directive 97/81 regulating part-time work, Directive 99/70 on fixed-term work, and Directive 2008/104 on temporary agency work, all rely on equal treatment as a means to improve the quality of these forms of employment.[53] Any future attempts on EU-level for the improvement of working conditions of typical and atypical workers will presumably be guided by the new European Pillar of Social Rights.[54] The Pillar sets out a number of key principles and rights that are supposed to support 'fair and well-functioning labour markets and welfare systems'. In addition to emphasising the importance of the principles of equal opportunities and non-discrimination, the Pillar aims to extend the guarantee of equal treatment beyond the three forms of employment relationships (part-time, fixed-term, and agency work) currently covered by the Union

52. *Kamerstukken I* 2013-2014, 33 818, nr. C, p. 25.
53. M. Bell, 'Between flexicurity and fundamental social rights: The EU directives on atypical work', *European Law Review* 2012 Vol. 37 No. 1, p. 34.
54. European Commission, *Establishing a European Pillar of Social Rights*, Brussels 26 April 2017, COM(2017) 250 final. Also see the Commission Staff Working Document accompanying the Establishing a European Pillar of Social Rights, SWD(2017) 201 final.

acquis and to provide for equal treatment between workers irrespective of the type of employment relationship.[55]

The Dutch Act on Employment and Security did not include an explicit aim to foster equal treatment of atypical workers in general. However, equal treatment was part of the reform of dismissal law. Previously, employers in the Netherlands could choose out of two procedures when dismissing permanent workers: one procedure almost guaranteed a severance payment, while the other procedure did not. The employer was completely free in choosing the procedure, which led to arbitrary outcomes. The Act on Work and Security focused on *this* inequality of outcome of the termination process and introduced a right to a standardised severance payment for every employee who has a minimum of twenty-four months of seniority.[56] Important for our purpose is that the severance payment is due also in case the employer does not continue a (series of) fixed-term contract(s). In other words, a worker with a fixed-term contract will also receive a severance payment if her contract is not prolonged, providing that she worked for the same employer for a minimum of two years.[57] This is a step towards more equal treatment of atypical workers since before the reform, fixed-term employees were not entitled to any severance payment. In that respect, dismissal law has become more just for employees.[58] However, one of the main goals of the reform of dismissal law was to reduce the costs of employment termination in general.[59] Therefore, the amount of severance payments has been significantly lowered. The redistributive intent and effect of this particular reform are therefore very mixed.

The Dutch law did already provide for general rules on equal treatment of atypical workers. The Civil Code provides that employers may not discriminate between part-time and full-time employees when drafting employment contracts.[60] There should also be no discrimination between employees with fixed-term contracts and employees with open-ended contracts regarding the employment conditions.[61] In addition, the collective agreement applicable to temp agency workers now provides for same remuneration for temp agency workers as the workers directly employed by the user firm.[62] Arguably, the principle of equal treatment of atypical workers had already permeated Dutch labour law; there was no need to further develop this principle in the Act on Work and Security.

55. SWD(2017) 201 fin., p. 23.
56. Article 7:673 Civil Code. This severance payment is officially labelled 'transitory compensation' and should, according to the legislator, be used to ease the transition from one job to another.
57. The aforementioned new proposal for law reform – the Act on Labour Market in Balance – aims to introduce a right to severance payment for all employees regardless the length of their employment.
58. Gundt 2015, p. 370.
59. *Kamerstukken II* 33 818, nr. 3, p. 25.
60. Article 7:648 Civil Code.
61. Article 7:649 Civil Code. However, both provisions state that discrimination may be justified on objective grounds.
62. This collective agreement (*ABU-cao*) has been made generally binding for the whole temporary agency sector.

However, this argument fails to recognise the limitations of the (current) legal principle of non-discrimination. After analysing the three Directives on atypical work, Kountouris finds: 'While the "equal treatment" principle can - and ought to - play an essential role in the quest for an adequate level of protection of atypical workers, it cannot be seen as sufficient to achieve this end.'[63] Among other limitations and risks, he discusses the more 'technical' questions pertaining the identification of a 'suitable comparator' and the 'single source issue' and concludes that the idea of regulating for decent working conditions by reference to the equal treatment principle heavily relies on the assumption that the working conditions of comparable workers are indeed decent.[64]

Kountouris is right to question this assumption. The limitations of the reliance on the equal treatment principle become even more apparent when we consider its effectiveness in the light of economic inequality. When we concentrate on low-wage work, it is important to ask whom the atypical workers are compared to. Part-time workers and fixed-term workers are entitled to equal treatment with, respectively, full-time workers[65] and workers with open-ended contracts employed by the same employer. However, the wages of 'standard' workers have stagnated as well. Moreover, low-wage work tends to be outsourced to specialised companies. As a reaction to Piketty, David Weil specifically draws attention to the phenomenon of outsourcing.[66] He explains that 'instead of the old model of large corporations employing workers at all levels - skilled professionals, mid-level administrators, and manual workers, under a single roof as was the case in the past - increasingly jobs are outsourced by function, and workers who would once have been employees, and thus entitled to de jure and de facto privileges, are now forced to a race to the bottom'.[67] He dubbed this stratification of the labour market outside the walls of individual firms earlier as the 'fissured workplace'.[68] He argues that by shifting employment to smaller organisations operating in competitive markets, a large employer creates a mechanism to pay workers 'closer to the additional value they create', but avoids the problem of having workers with very different wages operating under one roof.[69]

For the principle of equal treatment, the fissured workplace means that atypical low-wage workers are compared to standard low-wage workers. For example, observing the rule that a worker employed by a cleaning company on the basis of a fixed-term contract or zero-hours contract needs to be paid the same wage as a 'comparable permanent worker' will probably not have large effects in the light of income

63. N. Kountouris, 'EU Law and the Regulation of "Atypical" Work', in A. Bogg, C. Costello, & A.C.L. Davies (eds), *Research Handbook on EU Labour Law*, Edward Elgar publishing 2016, p. 264.
64. *Ibid.*
65. Part-time workers should receive the same employment conditions as the full-time workers on a *pro-rata temporis* basis.
66. D. Weil, 'Income Inequality, Wage Determination and the Fissured Workplace', in H. Boushey, J.B. DeLong & M. Steinbaum, *After Piketty. The Agenda for Economics and Inequality*, Harvard University Press 2017, pp. 209-231.
67. *Ibid.*, p. 209.
68. D. Weil, *The Fissured Workplace: Why Work Became So Bad for So Many and What Can Be Done to Improve It*, Cambridge, MA: Harvard University Press 2014.
69. Weil 2017, p. 223.

inequality. The comparison concerns other workers employed by the cleaning company and not workers employed by the actual company or organisation where the worker is performing the work. This can be a hospital, a university, a big high-tech company, etc. However, because such big organisations have outsourced work like cleaning and catering, workers in these sectors become 'trapped' in low-wage work and have little chances for upward mobility.

This is related to the so-called single source issue. The economic literature on inequality has shown that different firms pay observationally equivalent workers different wages.[70] However, the legal approach is as follows: If there are differences in pay and other working conditions between workers who perform equal work or work of equal value, then these differences need to be attributed to the same source, otherwise the working conditions of the workers involved cannot be compared on the basis of EU equality law. The CJEU has reasoned that in that case there is nobody that is responsible for the inequality and that could restore equal treatment.[71] Due to the phenomenon such as fissured workplace, the requirement of non-discrimination can only marginally improve the position of the workers in the low wage-sectors in terms of wages.

§6.04 CONCLUSION

The Act on Work and Security was a comprehensive labour law reform. For the first time since the Second World War, considerable changes were introduced to the Dutch dismissal law. The discussion of the Act in this contribution did not touch upon all the matters involved in the reform. Instead, the goal was to review the Act in terms of its intended effects on economic inequality. After all, the economic literature suggests that the rise of atypical work is one of the important drivers of economic inequality today. The Netherlands has a large number of people employed in atypical contracts and with this Act, the government aimed to improve the position of flexible workers.

The conclusion must be that the legislator is still very hesitant to interfere with the possibility of employers to conclude flexible employment contracts. There is only the intent to tackle abuse of such atypical contracts. This is done by measures aimed at fostering transitions into open-ended contracts. Reforms are, therefore, mainly focused on reducing employment insecurity. The question is, however, whether such measures are effective enough. This is difficult to measure since many different factors can influence the behaviour of employers. It seems, however, that especially in low-wage sectors, there are little incentives to reduce flexible employment as such. That means that low-wage and low-skilled workers are less likely to benefit from these measures. The government explicitly acknowledges this probability but expresses no desire to reduce the difference between the low-skilled and high-skilled workers with this measure. The measure is not intended to be redistributive.

70. J. Lane, 'Inequality and the Labor Market: Employers', in B. Nolan, W. Salverda & T.M. Smeeding (eds), *The Oxford Handbook of Economic Inequality*, Oxford University Press 2011, pp. 204-205.
71. CJEU 17 September 2002, C-320/00, *Lawrence*; CJEU 13 January 2004, C-256/01, *Allonby*.

The Netherlands already had measures in place to realize equal treatment of atypical workers. One could assume that equal treatment is the most effective norm in terms of economic inequality: flexible workers may enjoy less employment security, but at least they receive equal pay compared to standard workers. As has been argued before, however, this argument fails to recognise the many limitations of the (current) legal principle of equal treatment. Especially with disintegrated ('fissured') workplaces, the requirement of non-discrimination can only marginally improve the position of the workers in the low wage-sectors in terms of their wages.

The Act on Work and Security did introduce a change to strengthen the equal treatment norm, in the sense that it introduced a right to a severance payment for fixed-term employees when their fixed-term contracts end, provided that they have worked for the same employer for at least two years. However, the amount of severance payments, in general, has been significantly lowered with the same reform. The redistributive effect of this particular reform is therefore very mixed.

It is interesting to note that in more or less the same time period that the Act on Work and Security was adopted, the Dutch government introduced caps on top incomes in the public and semi-public sectors and caps on bonuses in the banking sector. The government did not take specific action to improve the position of workers with low-incomes, but it did try to tackle the rise of top salaries. Even though these measures were not necessarily driven by redistributive motives - they were rather reactions to the financial crisis and the public outrage about top incomes - they would certainly fit in a list of redistributive measures. When included into consideration, they show that the Netherlands have seen very mixed reactions to the financial crisis and the growing economic inequality.

The overall conclusion is that no real redistributive measures were introduced through recent labour law reforms in the Netherlands. That means that new labour laws are not likely to decrease income inequality in the near future. However, the recent economic literature offers proof that in market economies, there is no natural force that will inevitably lead to a more equitable distribution of income and wealth. In that light, it can very well be argued that labour law should strengthen its redistributive commitment, rather than turning to a market-perfecting role.

Part II How Do Collective Actors Deal with the Changing World of Work? European and National Perspectives

CHAPTER 7

Labour Politics and the EU's New Economic Governance Regime: Methodological Challenges and Innovations of a New Research Agenda*

Roland Erne

Trade unions play a major role in democratic interest intermediation. This role is currently threatened by vertical interventions of political executives in the context of the European Union's (EU's) new economic governance (NEG) regime. We are therefore proposing a new research agenda that aims to explore the challenges and possibilities that the NEG poses to labour politics. Our agenda focuses on the way in which labour movements respond to the EU's NEG regime. Until recently, labour politics had been shaped mainly by 'horizontal' market integration through the free movement of goods, capital, services and people. Since the adoption of the 'Six-Pack' of EU law on economic governance in 2011, however, the latter has been complemented by 'vertical' integration affected through the direct surveillance of Member States' macroeconomic policies, including industrial relations and social policy (Erne, 2015). The resulting regime opens contradictory possibilities for labour movements.

On the one hand, the NEG's reliance on vertical surveillance makes decisions taken in its name more tangible, thereby offering concrete targets for contentious transnational collective action (Erne et al., 2015). On the other hand, the NEG mimics the governance structures of multinational corporations (Erne, 2015). By using performance indicators and coercive comparisons that put countries in competition with one

* This work was supported by the EU's Jean Monnet Chair programme [grant agreement 2016-2319] and the European Research Council grant 'Labour Politics and the EU's New Economic Governance Regime (European Unions)' [grant agreement 725240]. I would like to thank Andreas Bieler, Colin Crouch, Bianca Föhrer, Darragh Golden, Jamie Jordan, Imre Szabó, and Sabina Stan for their comments on earlier drafts. I have also used sections of my ERC project application (Erne, 2018).

another, it constitutes a deterrent to transnational collective action. NEG's interventionist strains and the country-specific focus of NEG interventions also increase the threat of nationalist counter-movements. This is undermining the structuring of the political space along transnational cleavages, including the class cleavage. The existence of transnational cleavages, however, is a necessary requirement for any multinational democracy. The central democratic functions, responsiveness and accountability 'are in fact diminished if voters are divided territorially along segmented electorates' (Caramani, 2015: 3).

§7.01 ANALYTICAL CHALLENGES

Labour mobilisations that followed the industrial revolution homogenised political behaviour within and across countries (Bartolini, 2000; Caramani, 2015). Neither democracy nor the mid-20th-century class compromise, on which national social systems were built, would be conceivable without the mobilisations of workers at workplaces and in national political arenas. A similar analogy can be made in an EU context (Erne, 2008). These democratic dimensions of labour politics are threatened by a 'silent revolution' (Barroso, cited in Erne, 2012).

Already before the shift to NEG in 2011, the formation of a supranational European centre was problematic, given the deficient parallel 'system building' in the area of transnational social integration and democratic participation (Bartolini, 2005). Yet, it is conceivable that transnational social integration will emerge after the creation of political authority at the EU level. Whether one is conceptualising the political in deliberative-democratic or in power-struggle-oriented terms, one should acknowledge that political authority over a population did not include democratic rights from the outset. The formation of political authority has usually been a product of 'coercion and capital' (Tilly, 2000). Citizenship rights followed afterwards, as a result of struggles by countervailing powers in response to social tensions created by the making of markets and political authorities. The formation of much more robust EU governance institutions can also be a precondition for the creation of a transnational democracy. As democracy is dependent on political authority to enforce the results of democratic consultations, there is a dialectical relationship between popular mobilisations and the creation of political authority.

Politicisation processes can be observed at three analytical levels, namely, at individual (micro), organisational (meso) and systemic (macro) level. Most studies in the field have favoured analyses located at either the micro or the macro level (Zürn, 2016). It is quite easy to analyse datasets about changing voter attitudes or to measure the salience of EU-related political issues in media debates. The growing socioeconomic inequalities have also been well documented. Yet, the emergence of new polarisations at a macro level and electoral divisions at micro level alone cannot explain the restructuring of the European political space. The formation of new social cleavages also depends on the emergence of corresponding 'organisational networks' (Bartolini, 2000: 26); hence, our focus on interest politics at the organisational (meso) level. Furthermore, a study of labour mobilisations regarding NEG makes sense methodologically only if European integration is considered as a process 'among distinct units indeed but, at the same time, units belonging to one single system' (Caramani, 2015: 283).

Whereas the questions about the politicisation of European integration are usually discussed by political scientists, questions about labour's capacity to enforce class compromises fall into the domain of industrial relations and social policy. For 'several decades now the study of labour issues has been a specialist field' (Crouch, 2015: 2). In the English-speaking world, this discipline used to be called industrial relations. In continental Europe, *la question sociale* was a domain of social policy. Now, NEG may be bringing industrial relations and social policy together once more. These disciplines not only offer complementary vantage points but are also directly affected by these changes in EU governance. The latter might bring the two disciplines back to the big questions about capitalism and democracy that led to the creation of the social sciences in the first place. Paradoxically, the closer alignment to management enabled industrial relations scholars to capture the governance by 'coercive comparisons' (Marginson and Sisson, 2004: 11) long before other scholars theorised 'governance by numbers' (Supiot, 2015). 'The increasing attention paid to "governance" may appear as reinventing the wheel. Industrial relations have always been characterised by interactions between public and private actors' (Leonard et al., 2007: 6). Industrial relations also suggest that NEG's governance by numbers will not lead to an end of social contestation. Multinational firms try to benefit from international competition by subjecting unions from different sites in whipsawing games. And yet, 'competition can frustrate cooperation, but it also motivates it' (Anner et al., 2006: 24).

In addition, the re-framing of socioeconomic conflicts in nationalistic terms by political and socioeconomic elites has been an important feature of labour politics since its inception. Labour parties and unions are facing an increasingly Eurosceptic working class. But an analysis of the restructuring of the European political space cannot only rely on quantitative data on voter attitudes or the salience of EU politics in national media (Béthoux et al., 2018). Equally important are organisational mobilisations and the political structures of opportunities in which they are taking place. These processes are *social* processes. Individual attitudes become a social force only if they are mobilised. Mobilisations depend on organisational networks located in the forecourt of party politics. This explains our interest in unions, as they play a key role in the 'organisational dimension' of cleavage structuring (Bartolini, 2000). Our new research agenda, therefore, aims to (1) understand the interrelation between vertical (political) and horizontal (market) integration processes (2) open up new analytical approaches that are able to capture both national *and* transnational social processes; and (3) analyse the responses of labour movements in different areas of labour politics, and their feedback effects on NEG.

§7.02 METHODOLOGICAL INNOVATIONS

The more labour movements (old and new) politicise NEG in a transnational context, the more this will lead to restructuring the European political space along transnational class lines. In contrast, the more they politicise NEG in nationalist counter-mobilisations, the more this will lead to a fracturing of the European political space along national lines. Given the strong bias of NEG's 'corporate governance type' structure in favour of intra-European competition, labour can also contribute to the fragmentation of the EU along national lines through competitive adjustments. Table 7.1 outlines the corresponding actor strategies and indicates observable activities, which allow their operationalisation in empirical research.

Table 7.1 Actor Strategies Leading to Different Structures of the European Political Space

Action Framework	*Observable Actor Activities*	*Leading to a Restructuring of the Political Space:*	
		Along Transnational Lines	*Along National Lines*
Politicising NEG (EU level)	EU-level contentious action Euro-strikes and demonstrations, ECI	**Yes**	**No**
Depoliticising NEG (EU and/or national level)	No contentious action Support for NEG and competitive adjustments of labour policies	**No**	**Yes**
Politicising NEG (national level)	National contentious action Nationalist counter-mobilisations	**No**	**Yes**

Source: Adapted from Erne (2015: 305 and 2008: 25).

So far, most studies on the popular responses to the Euro crisis and the new EU's economic governance regime have relied on comparisons of different national cases (Stan et al., 2015). This is not surprising, given the dominance of methodological nationalism in the field, which mirrors approaches in terms of varieties of capitalism, unionism or welfare regimes. However, designs that are exclusively based on national variables are unable to capture the restructuring of economy and society along transnational supply and value chains in the sphere of production as well as transnational care chains in the sphere of reproduction. Accordingly, the workings of NEG cannot be adequately captured by national datasets either. Social mobilisations that politicise NEG must be studied (a) at the meso level of interest politics and (b) within *and* across national boundaries. Hence, I am making the case for the disaggregation of the units under study. This contextualised approach to the study of labour politics will enable us to capture and compare social dynamics that often fall under the radar of macro level comparisons.

We are proposing a research design that is no longer based on the comparison of national units. Instead, we are proposing an alternative design that compares the workings of NEG and labour movements in different areas of labour politics and in different economic sectors. This includes investigations at EU level, but also enquiries in selected countries as well as parallel case studies. In contrast to the approaches in terms of varieties of capitalism, unionism and welfare states however, the selection of locations for empirical analysis will not be informed by different 'types' of national regimes. Instead, territorial locations will be selected in order to capture both central and peripheral locations in the integrated but also uneven European political and socioeconomic space.

Concretely, we will examine the workings of NEG in two areas of labour politics (wage policy and the provision of public services) and in three sectors (public healthcare, urban transport, and water services). These areas and sectors are all directly affected by NEG, albeit in different ways. Wage policy is affected by interventions targeting wage bargaining and labour law. The provision of public services is directly affected by NEG's interventions in national budgets and social services. This selection enables us to capture not only vocal reactions, e.g., contentious action, but also cooperation with NEG, e.g., union cooperation in the implementation of requested competitive wage adjustments. Our selection of areas and sectors allows us to observe actor activities in relation to both politicisation *and* depoliticisation (*see* Table 7.1). Wage policy and the provision of public services also differ in relation to the social actors involved. Whereas unions tend to prioritise wages, social movements are more concerned about citizens' access to public services. At times, these two concerns converge as in the case of the '*right2water*' European Citizens' Initiative (ECI) of European Federation of Public Sector Unions (EPSU). At times, they do so to a lesser extent, as in the case of the 'fair transport' ECI of the ETF (European Transport Workers Federation) (Erne and Blaser, 2018). Our research design allows comparisons across areas of labour politics that are usually studied by distinct disciplines. Moreover, the healthcare, transport and water services sectors are not only relevant because they are all directly affected by NEG interventions. They are also affected by horizontal federalising dynamics, caused for example by the free movement of workers, services, and patients. Therefore, our research design allows us to compare NEG also with horizontal EU integration processes.

Finally, the big questions addressed in our ERC project are relevant not only for the future of democracy and social justice but also for the predominately institutionalist approaches in comparative industrial relations, labour law and social policy. I, therefore, believe that the growing horizontal and vertical integration of Europe, and the counter-movements that these processes are triggering, are obliging us to pursue new methodological paths that go beyond the methodological nationalism in our fields.

REFERENCES

Anner M, Greer I, Hauptmeier M, Lillie, N and Winchester, N (2006) The industrial determinants of transnational solidarity. *European Journal of Industrial Relations* 12(1): 7-27.

Bartolini S (2000) *The Political Mobilization of The European Left, 1860-1980.* Cambridge: Cambridge University Press.

Bartolini S (2005) *Restructuring Europe: Centre Formation, System Building and Political Structuring Between the Nation-State and the European Union.* Oxford: Oxford University Press.

Béthoux, E, Erne, R, and Golden, D (2018) 'A primordial attachment to the nation? French and Irish workers and trade unions in past EU referendum debates' *British Journal of Industrial Relations*, 56 (3): 656-678.

Caramani D (2015) *The Europeanization of Politics: The Formation of a European Electorate System in Historical Perspective.* Cambridge: Cambridge University Press.

Crouch C (2015) *Governing Social Risks in Post-Crisis Europe.* Cheltenham: Edward Elgar.

Erne R (2008) *European Unions: Labor's Quest for a Transnational Democracy.* Ithaca, NY: Cornell University Press.

Erne R (2012) 'European industrial relations after the crisis. A postscript' In: Smismans, S. (ed.) *The European Union and Industrial Relations.* Manchester: Manchester University Press, 225-235.

Erne R (2015) Politicizing the New European Economic Governance Regime? Explaining Transnational Trade Union Action in Times of Crisis. *Labor History* 56(3): 345368.

Erne R (2018) Labour politics and the EU's new economic governance regime (European Unions): A new European Research Council Project. *Transfer,* 24(2), 237-247.

Erne R and Blaser M (2018) 'Direct Democracy and Trade Union Action', *Transfer* 24(2): 217-232.

Erne R, Bieler A, Golden D, Helle I, Kjeldstadli K, Matos T and Stan S (2015) Introduction. Politicizing the Transnational. *Labor History* 56(3): 237-245.

Leonard E, Erne R, Smismans S and Marginson P (2007) *New Structures, Forms and Processes of Governance in European Industrial Relations.* Luxembourg: Office for the Official Publications of the European Communities.

Marginson P and Sisson K (2004) *European Integration and Industrial Relations: Multi-Level Governance in the Making.* Basingstoke: Palgrave Macmillan.

Stan S, Helle I and Erne R (2015) European collective action in times of crisis. *Transfer* 21(2): 131-139.

Supiot A (2015) *La Gouvernance par les Nombres.* Paris: Fayard.

Tilly C (2000) *Coercion, Capital, and European States, AD 900–1990.* Malden: Blackwell.

Zürn M (2016) Opening up Europe: Next steps in politicisation research. *West European Politics* 39(1): 164-182.

CHAPTER 8

'Liquid' Unionism and the Future of Industrial Relations

Adriana Topo

'What is the future of labour law[1] is THE question academics face when focusing on the many changes occurring in technology, communication and expression of political e professional interests and therefore in the labour arena. The emerging of new parties[2] and opinion movements[3] spreading beside traditional agents, the development of direct democracy supported by the digitalization of communication means, the digitalization of work and of working places[4], the potential breaking of traditional boundaries between work time and lifetime, are facts that none would deny. All these situations affect labour and therefore its regulation so that the issue formulated at the beginning of these comments should be translated into the question: Is the current labour regulation adequate in respect to the satisfaction of workers' interests in the new social and technological context? Answering on the future of labour law is a too ambitious task because the future is always and for everybody unpredictable. What it is possible is the analyses of the changes affecting work and society and the discussion on the pros and cons of different legal approaches to work and industrial relations. This presentation is therefore focused on the impact of the abovementioned changes on the shapes of industrial relations regulations and practices.

---

1. 'The Future of Labour Law' is the title of a book dedicated to Sir Bob Hepple QC, edited by C. Barnard, S. Deakin, G. Morris, in 2004; earlier A. Supiot, Beyond Employment: Change in Work and the Future of Labour Law in Europe, 2001.
2. Already: S. Hug, Altering Party Systems: Strategic Behavior and the Emergence of New Political Parties in Western Democracies, 2001; T.N. Clark, V. Hoffmann - Martinot, The New Political Culture, 2018; D.A. Snow, S.A. Soule, H.J. McCammon, H. Kriesi, Social Movements, 2nd edition, 2019; G. Passarelli, D. Tuorto, The Five Stars Movement: Purely a Matter of Protest? The Rise of a New Party Between Political Discontent and Reasoned Voting, Party Politics 2016.
3. T.N. Clark, P.H. Merkl, When Parties Fail: Emerging Alterative Organization, 1998.
4. M. Cherry, Beyond Missclassification: The Digital Transformation of Work, 37 Comp. Lab. L. & Pol'y J., 2016.

The intellectual task is realizing the friction point between consolidated industrial regulations and practices, and the impact of the mentioned changes in the world of work.

A possible criterion for describing how these changes affect the world of work comes from distinguishing between endogenous changes and exogenous changes. The latter in not a necessary distinction and is instead just a possible one, for the purpose of indicating that some events are external to work and to work relations and nevertheless impact on work regulation. The fact of being qualified as exogenous means that regulators cannot avoid these events.

One among the exogenous changes is the fragmentation of the work place: 'fissured workplace[5] is not simply another term for subcontracting, outsourcing, or offshoring. Nor does it solely arise from lead companies seeking to avoid payment of private or socially required benefits. Rather, the fissured workplace reflects the fundamental restructuring of business organizations.

The fragmentation of the work place is so relevant that also platforms such as Amazon Turk could be interpreted as a sort of extreme management through the fragmentation of the business.

The fragmentation is then supported and boosted by the digitalization of communications and the digitalization of work. Digitalization is nevertheless a process exogenous in respect of industrial relations. None of us can prevent the progressive application of digitalization to many if not all spheres of human life. At the moment nevertheless, not all the work force operate in the digital market. In conclusion digitalization of work does not totally affect the labour regulation. In the manufacturing and in the services sectors there is still the traditional method of work where digitalization is not that important, may be differently important. One nevertheless could comment that labour law is inspired by models of production and businesses models impact on the efficiency of industrial relation in the sector.The coherent conclusion of the latter comment is that unions have to face the technological evolution and act in a manner that are adequate to the specific work context.

A third exogenous event is the globalization of the market. The globalization of the market has been supported by the introduction of containers in the transport service (in the future, 3D printing will enhance in a similar way globalization) and as well by the doubling of the world work force since the nineties of the last century, when China entered the capitalistic society and skilled workers from India started to compete in the services sector[6].

It is possible nevertheless to figure out also a different sort of changes in the world of work, changes endogenous to the dynamic of social collective relations.

Among these changes, there is the loosening of the links between unions and political parties[7] especially where (Italy, France, some central Europe countries) new

5. D. Weil, The Fissured Workplace, 2014.
6. R.B. Freeman, America Works: Thoughts on an Exceptional U.S. Labor Market, 2008.
7. K. Hamann, Union Revitalization Through Political Action? Evidence from Five Countries, lerachapters.org, 2018; R. Hyman, Trade Unions, Politics and Parties: Is a New Configuration Possible?, Etui, 2010.

nationalist parties and popular movements have overcome the traditional consolidated political parties, whose action since a long time has been intertwined with trade unions' action. The consequence has been the discontinuance of the social dialogue that was the basis for work regulation.

One might define as exogenous another circumstance such as the 'liquid' representation of interests, which is the manifestation of labour interests on the basis of a direct method of expression of choices. This method is only facilitated by the digitalization of communications, but the facility means a lot. In these situations there is no a clearly defined agent, no traditional union, and only a volatile entity, which is almost impossible to identify and therefore bind under legal rules. The direct manifestation of choices by individual produces in fact the vanishing of the representation itself. The latter situation is evident in the case of strike promoted or organized by liquid entities on electronic chats: in the circumstance it is difficult to encapsulate the action in a traditional legal frame, because opinions expressed and action promoted by volatile groups not necessarily are coherent with principles that relate to the definition of the common interest inside a specific group. Dubious is also if the result of consultations or ballots, between members of indefinite groups, reflect an interest which one would define as 'collective' on the basis of the traditional labour law vocabulary.

The former and latter endogenous and exogenous factors may be subject to a critical exam that would be excessive for the purpose of this discourse. In order to get to a conclusion, which is also a hypothesis about the future of labour law. As such it is necessary to accept them as effectual qualifications and to continue the drawing of a divide between highly (United States and United Kingdom) versus lowly (Italy) structured legal schemes on industrial relations. In order to explain the difference, is important to make clear that the latter means that the regulation of industrial relations by statute is minimal and the freedom of association is widely interpreted so that the principle of pluralism of representation of workers' interest applies under few limits.

The above-described changes in work organization and in the labour market affects in different manner the two frameworks.

The increased pool of available workers, which is one of the reasons for the weakening of unions' efficacy of action, is an exogenous cause of change of the world of work. The issue should be approached through a legislative support to unions, which should be effective on transnational level. The same solution seems necessary for the purpose of tackling the impact on workers of the fragmentation of the undertaking. In this case, widening the accountability of the various employers in the chain is fundamental. It is extremely problematic if not impossible, for unions and for workers on their own, to tackle these epochal changes, without the support by an upper authority.

In respect to the digitalization it is clear that the unions' challenge is adapting traditional methods of recruiting and affiliation to the virtual working place and to the new means of communication. The concurrence of regulation by statute and the adaptation of unions to the changing of working models is fundamental as pointed out before.

Besides, it may be interesting to distinguish the impact of the endogenous changes in the highly regulated systems, and, on the contrary, in the lowly regulated systems.

Reasoning on the basis of the former distinction, the highly regulated industrial systems seem less adequate in respect to the phenomenon of liquid representation of interests. Where the process of collective bargaining is highly defined by statute and is also demanding, the process may not mirror the increased and increasing fluidity of workers' opinions. The complicate and length process of representation seems not coherent with the fluidity of interests, so that representative agents are not capable of reacting on time to workers' opinion. As well, the strict regulation of strike may detach people from traditional unionism. If direct democracy, facilitated by digitalization of communication, seems to respond rapidly and widely to the workers' needs of expression, demanding systems of representation discourage workers from trusting the efficacy of traditional unionism and push workers to adhere to informal organizations that operate outside the formalized frame. The highly regulated systems, therefore, have to be adapted not only to the features of the virtual work place. The main issue is facilitating a timely reaction by unions and its capacity to capture the fluidity of workers' opinions and needs.

Also the lowly regulated systems suffer the impact of liquid representation. Groups competing against unions relent or disrupt the process of collective bargaining. The circumstance is evident in case of strike in the essential services[8]. The overleaping of workers' representative is a problem because the employer does not know with whom to negotiate and the authority does not have an interlocutor, and cannot mediate between workers and employers.

In both cases, the pacification of the dispute is lengthy and complicate and the damage is great for everybody who is interested in the termination of the conflict or is victim of the conflicts, as users of essential services.

The weakening of the links between political parties and unions in the lowly regulated systems has also a relevant impact on industrial relations. Political parties in low regulated systems play an important role within the social dialogue process while operating side by side with unions. The rupture of links between political parties and unions seems therefore relenting if not blocking the dialogue, which has a substantial role in the composition of industrial conflicts where the law does not interfere with the dynamics of industrial relation.

Eventually, the liquid representation of workers' interests by not structured entities is problematic under another perspective. The liquid unregulated representation does not guarantee a democratic process of definition of the collective interest. In industrial relations, the definition of the collective interest is of pivotal importance. How an informal, unstructured, volatile entity would transparently represent interests that should result from a transparent and democratic process?

Notwithstanding the application of a schematic approach to the evolution of industrial relations, the prediction on how the future of labour law will evolve is

8. A. Topo, in M. Mironi, M. Schlachter (Eds.), Regulating Strikes in Essential Services: A Comparative 'Law in Action' Perspective, 2018.

complicated as well of the prediction of which model will be more adequate for the interpretation and the regulation of workers' collective interests. What appears difficult to understand is how the political and social dynamics, that are at the core of the phenomenon of unionism, will develop in reaction to problems that are less related to technology and new models of work and instead are to be linked to the foundations of unionism, to the idea of democracy and to the limits of the freedom of thought.

The endogenous changes in industrial relations represent in fact and probably the evolution of something more important than labour law, or industrial relations. It would be misleading to believe that only labour law is affected by the definition of what is democratic and what is not.

The transformation of industrial relations is a profile of a more general issue concerning the idea of democracy and the individuation of its limits for who believes that outside the democratic principle there is no justice.

CHAPTER 9

Going It Alone? The Involvement of Trade Unions in the Living Wage Campaign in the United Kingdom

Edmund Heery, Deborah Hann & David Nash

§9.01 INTRODUCTION

A prominent theme in recent writing on trade unions has addressed the union relationship with new institutions of worker representation. Unions, it has been widely suggested, should work collaboratively with other civil society institutions that engage with the world of work, forming alliances and coalitions to advance the interests of working people (Doellgast et al. 2018; Tattersall 2010). Moreover, it has been further argued that unions can learn from institutions of this type, adopting the methods of community organizations and campaigning social movements to generate a fresh capacity to mobilize their members (Tapia 2013). For proponents of social movement or community unionism these two responses to new employment actors, coalition and organizational learning, can lie at the heart of union revitalization, recreating unions themselves as social movements (Holgate 2015; Luce 2014).

In this article we use empirical research on the trade union response to the United Kingdom's (UK's) Living Wage campaign as a means of evaluating this argument. In the UK, the Living Wage is a voluntary employment standard that has been promoted for nearly twenty years by Citizens UK, the British arm of the international community organizing movement. The standard itself comprises an hourly rate of pay, calculated annually on the basis of independent research commissioned from the Resolution Foundation into the expenditure needs of low-wage workers. Separate rates are calculated for London and the rest of the UK, both of which are substantially higher than the confusingly titled National Living Wage, the UK's statutory minimum rate of pay for workers aged 25 and over. The standard requires that the Living Wage be paid to all employees of 18 years and over who work for at least two hours a day and who have at least eight weeks' experience and applies both to direct employees and to the employees of contractors permanently located on the employer's premises, such as cleaners, catering staff and security guards. Since 2011, a system of accreditation has operated, whereby organizations can be designated Living Wage Employers if they sign up to the standard. This system of accreditation is operated by the Living Wage Foundation, an offshoot of Citizens UK, though with this work subcontracted to partner organizations, the Poverty Alliance and Cynnal Cymru, in Scotland and in Wales respectively.

The UK's Living Wage campaign presents a striking example of a civil society-led initiative to shape the operation of the labour market and combat the pressing problem of in-work poverty. At its heart lies Citizens UK and its sister organizations, an emblematic 'new employment actor' that aspires to speak on behalf of and address the interests of working people. In what follows, we use original research to describe the extent and manner of union involvement in the Living Wage campaign, seeking to establish whether it has been characterized by coalition and joint-working in the manner suggested in the social movement unionism literature. We also seek to establish whether unions have adopted the methods of Citizens UK and the Living Wage Foundation, applying the techniques of civil society to their own attempts to tackle the UK's problem of low pay.

The research that we use to explore these two avenues of enquiry has made use of multiple methods. The primary method upon which we draw in this article is a programme of semi-structured interviews with trade union officers, officers of employers' organizations, managers in accredited Living Wage Employers, and Living Wage campaigners. A total of fifty-five interviews of this kind were conducted between July 2015 and March 2019. This programme of interviews has been supplemented by the collection of archive material and by extensive observation of Living Wage campaign events in London and in Wales. We have attended planning meetings for the campaign, policy workshops, public assemblies to promote the Living Wage, demonstrations, and launch events in Living Wage Week, held each November when the new annual rates for the Living Wage are publicly announced. Third, we draw upon a survey of accredited Living Wage Employers carried out in late 2016, which was completed by the Living Wage Foundation's primary contact in each accredited organization and which included questions on the extent of trade union involvement in the decision to introduce the Living Wage.[1] Finally, we report evidence from a dataset of all Living Wage Employers that have been accredited since 2011. This dataset contains information on nearly 6,000 accredited organizations, including their characteristics and the impact of the Living Wage measured by the number of workers covered and the number and types of worker that have received pay awards as a result of accreditation. In March 2019 approximately 1.8 million workers were directly employed by Living

1. The survey was administered to a total of 2,851 accredited organizations, 845 of which (29.6%) responded. Responses were broadly representative of the survey population in terms of size, sector and geographical location and the data provide a reliable foundation on which to generalize about the employer experience of the Living Wage campaign.

Wage Employers and nearly 175,000 employees had received a pay increase since accreditation began, 52% of whom worked part-time and 33% of whom were indirect workers employed by contractors.

§9.02 UNION INVOLVEMENT IN THE LIVING WAGE CAMPAIGN

In the literature on union revitalization it is frequently suggested that unions should forge coalitions with civil society organizations. It is through formal alliance-building, it is argued, that unions can best develop a cooperative relationship with non-labour organizations that can supplement their internal resources and enable them to pursue goals that would otherwise lie beyond their reach. The institutional form that is often recommended for a coalition of this type is an umbrella-body, a meta-organization to which unions and civil society organizations can affiliate, which is jointly governed by both parties and which can direct and coordinate their campaign activity on a particular issue (Turner 2006).

It is further suggested that for such coalitions to be successful they should pursue the distinct but complementary interests of both parties. Examples of separate but complementary interests identified by researchers, include the interest of public sector unions in maintaining levels of employment and the interest of service-user organizations in maintaining levels of service and the interest of manufacturing unions in reducing worker exposure to toxic substances and the interest of sustainability organizations in reducing harmful emissions into the natural environment (Mayer 2009; Tattersall 2009). Successful coalitions may also make use of complementary methods, with civil society organizations and trade unions mobilizing different types of resource to exert pressure on employers or governments. The mobilization of consumer pressure by campaigners for global labour standards alongside the mobilization of workers by unions for improvements in pay and conditions is an example of complementarity of this kind (Donaghey et al. 2014; *see also* Preminger 2019). A final thing to note about the research literature on union-community coalitions is that it reports extensive joint activity, involving the leaders and activists of both types of organization. Accounts of campaigning activity describe joint participation in demonstrations, street theatre, petitioning and lobbying of public authorities and commissioning of research and legal advice (Tapia 2014; Tattersall 2010). The coalition, in these accounts, serves to channel the activism of both unions and civil society organizations towards a set of complementary goals.

The initial objective of our research was to establish if the Living Wage campaign was characterized by this coalitional pattern of interaction between trade unions and civil society organizations. As a first step, we concentrated on the formal institutions with primary responsibility for the campaign, Citizens UK and the Living Wage Foundation and sought to ascertain whether they displayed three characteristics. First, can these bodies accurately be described as umbrella organizations that have been jointly created by unions and civil society, such that they embody a labour-community coalition? Second, are they meta-organizations that include trade unions as a core group within their membership? Third, do unions participate centrally in the governance and formal decision-making of these organizations, such as to exert substantial influence over their policy and operations?

With regard to the first condition, the research established that trade unions did not play any role in the creation either of Citizens UK or of the Living Wage Foundation and in this sense neither should be regarded as the embodiment of a union-community alliance. Citizens UK is the British arm of the international community organizing movement and was established initially as the Citizens Organizing Foundation in the mid-1990s by activists seeking to transpose American community organizing techniques to the UK (Jamoul and Wills 2008). Its roots lie in community activism rather than the labour movement and from the outset, it has been a strongly faith-based organization. The Living Wage Foundation is a rather different entity, essentially an operational offshoot of Citizens UK, established in 2011 because it was felt that a dedicated organization was necessary to run the Living Wage campaign and accredit employers. In its absence, it was believed that the success of the Living Wage campaign would swamp Citizens UK's other activities and distract from its broader community organizing mission. The motivation for creating the organization, therefore, had a strong efficiency component and emerged from within the citizenship movement rather than from a relationship with external forces.

While Citizens UK may not be the product of a union-community coalition, it is certainly a meta-organization and operates through a network of local chapters that draw membership organizations into their campaigning activity. There are currently fifteen chapters, six of which include local union branches among their membership or report that trade union representatives form part of their leadership group. In at least two of these chapters, Greater Manchester and Birmingham, unions were founding members. Trade unions form part of the Citizens UK network, therefore, though they constitute only a small proportion of total membership, which is comprised primarily of faith organizations, community organizations and educational institutions, such as schools, colleges and universities. Moreover, affiliation to Citizens UK is confined to a small group of unions (Unite, UNISON, the University and College Union (UCU) and the Royal College of Nursing (RCN)) and among these only UNISON and RCN have a presence in more than one chapter.

The Living Wage Foundation is not a meta-organization and while it has formal arrangements for consulting with stakeholders it is not a membership body as such. It does accredit other organizations, however, which contract with the Foundation to pay the Living Wage and which are then licensed to describe themselves as Living Wage Employers. One of the notable features of this system of accreditation is that trade unions have participated as employing organizations. Both the Trades Union Congress (TUC) and Scottish Trades Union Congress (STUC) are accredited Living Wage Employers as are thirty-one individual trade unions and trade union branches. Through accreditation, trade unions have demonstrated their support for the Living Wage in a tangible way in a manner that is similar to the common union practice of affiliation to charities, campaigns and other good causes (Heery 2009). It is notable though that this relatively weak form of participation – seeking accreditation to signal backing for the Living Wage – is more widespread than is membership of local

Chapters of Citizens UK, with its associated commitment to engage in campaigning activity.

Evidence for the third condition of the coalitional pattern, trade union involvement in the formal governance and decision-making, is also rather limited. There is no union representation on the main Board of Trustees of Citizens UK though unions do play a part in the governance arrangements of the Living Wage Foundation. The TUC is represented alongside employers, civil society organizations and independent experts on the Living Wage Advisory Council, established to provide a sounding board for the Foundation, and is also represented on the Living Wage Commission, the body that oversees the setting of the Living Wage on an annual basis and which has broad oversight of the campaign (Sellers 2017). Below the level of formal governance, trade union inclusion in decision-making within Citizens UK and the Foundation is uneven. Unions have been consulted over key policies, such as a change in the method of calculating the Living Wage, have participated in groups to promote the Living Wage in particular regions or industries and have taken part in 'accountability assemblies', public meetings at which Citizens UK sets out its programme and seeks to win support from political leaders seeking election. Trade unions are not always involved in forums or events of these kinds, however, and they are notably absent from the Living Wage Foundation's list of Principal Partners, which consists of large employers and social justice organizations that campaign to promote the Living Wage. Moreover, when participation does occur it is often ad hoc, dependent on the commitment of individual trade unionists rather than formal institutional ties. Unions participate in the activities of Citizens UK and the Living Wage Foundation therefore but the degree of participation is limited and arguably falls well short of coalition. Other external partners, particularly major employers and other civil society organizations that campaign alongside Citizens UK, occupy a more central position in the Living Wage network than do trade unions and seemingly exert greater influence over policy.[2]

§9.03 UNION INVOLVEMENT IN LIVING WAGE ACCREDITATION

Another way of testing for the coalitional pattern is to gauge the extent to which unions are involved in joint campaigning with Citizens UK and the Living Wage Foundation to spread the Living Wage and persuade individual employers to become accredited. Our interview and observation work yielded several examples where unions had campaigned jointly with local Chapters of Citizens UK to secure the Living Wage at individual employers. These examples came from central government, local government and universities and involved union activists from FDA, UCU and UNISON (*see also* Holgate and Wills 2007; Lopes and Hall 2015). In several cases, it was notable that union activists were campaigning for the Living Wage to be paid, not to their own members but to outsourced staff providing cleaning and other ancillary services who

2. Scotland is a possible exception to this judgment as the Scottish TUC is a prominent member of the Poverty Alliance, the organization that promotes the Living Wage in Scotland, and UNISON in particular, has been an active participant in the group that exercises oversight of the Scottish campaign.

typically were not union members. Their relationship to the workers targeted in the campaign, that is, was identical to that of external activists from faith and other organizations, articulating a social justice rather than a representational case for action on low pay.

Additional information on union involvement in accreditation campaigns came from the survey of Living Wage Employers. This indicated, firstly, that most accredited employers are not unionized: only 18% reported that they deal with trade union representatives on a regular basis. This impression of the Living Wage flourishing in the UK's extensive non-union economy was reinforced by the dataset of accredited employers: 26% of accredited employers are concentrated in industries such as hospitality, professional services and finance where union density falls below 10%, while only 5% are found in the heavily unionized public sector. A second key finding from the survey was that even in organizations where unions were recognized, employers reported that they had only limited influence over the accreditation decision. Among the minority of employers dealing with unions, it was reported that unions had campaigned for the Living Wage to be adopted in only 19% of cases, in only 13% was the Living Wage subject to collective bargaining, and in fewer than 10% of cases had unions attempted to shape the application of the standard post-implementation.

This pattern of relatively limited union influence over the employer decision to become accredited, moreover, contrasted with that of relatively greater influence exerted by Citizens UK and the Living Wage Foundation. Across the entire population of respondents to the survey (unionized and non-unionized), just under 20% reported that union representatives had exercised at least some influence over the decision to become accredited, while 70% reported that Living Wage campaigners had exerted influence. These estimates are positively correlated, indicating that where unions have influence so do Living Wage campaigners: a finding that suggests the two groups have sometimes worked jointly, cooperating to encourage employers to sign up to the Living Wage. In most cases, however, Citizens UK and the Living Wage Foundation have worked independently of unions and have succeeded in persuading employers to become accredited where unions are absent. There is evidence from the survey of the kind of joint activity between trade union and civil society activists identified in the coalitional model, therefore, but this is confined to a minority segment of the Living Wage campaign and has not been a defining characteristic of the latter.

§9.04 CONFLICT BETWEEN LIVING WAGE CAMPAIGNERS AND TRADE UNIONISTS

While the research identified cases of unions becoming involved in the Living Wage campaign it also uncovered examples of the reverse situation, of tension and conflict between Living Wage campaigners and trade unionists. Representatives of both sides attested to the fact that their relationship was sometimes difficult. Such tension could take the form of mutual recrimination. Some trade unionists complained that when they had worked closely with Citizens UK, the latter tended to claim sole responsibility for campaign success, while others reported that attempts to obtain advice or support from the Living Wage Foundation when trying to secure the Living Wage for union members met with minimal response. One London-based union representative stated bluntly that Citizens UK was, 'Not always a great partner' (*see also* Sellers 2017). Living Wage campaigners for their part expressed disappointment that unions had offered only modest support to the campaign and complained that they had been rebuffed when seeking to forge closer links.

On occasion, these tensions have led to withdrawal from joint cooperation. At least one regional TUC has declined an invitation to join a multi-stakeholder 'leadership group', established to promote the Living Wage in its area on the grounds that Living Wage campaigners have appealed directly to unionized employers to adopt the Living Wage without involving trade union representatives. We were also informed that in another part of the country an attempt by the regional TUC to develop a joint programme with Citizens UK in the early phase of the campaign had been rejected by the latter, a response that was attributed to a wish by Citizens UK to retain full control of the campaign. More recently, new initiatives launched by the Living Wage Foundation have often proceeded with minimal, if any trade union involvement. Attempts to encourage the funders of charitable activity to promote the Living Wage or to develop Living Wage towns and cities through a Living Wage Places programme, have largely been implemented without union participation.

There is also evidence of both sides developing, or considering alternatives to cooperation. The left-led Bakers' Union has developed a campaign for an alternative living wage standard, set at £10.00 an hour, which has attracted support from other unions, including the GMB and Unite. This initiative has been inspired by the American Fight for Fifteen movement and the £10.00 target has featured in union campaigns to organize fast-food workers.[3] How impactful this alternative standard has been it is difficult to say though it has registered a striking success in being adopted by the Labour Party, which has pledged to implement a statutory minimum of £10.00 an hour in 2020 for all workers aged 16 and over if it is elected to power.[4] The alternative that has been considered by campaigners has been the development of a dedicated membership organization for low-wage workers that can build on the success of Living Wage campaigns and extend them to encompass other workplace issues. We were asked by one campaigner whether there was any UK equivalent to American worker centres that might serve this purpose. Consideration of this alternative has been born of frustration with the trade union movement and what is seen as its failure to cooperate fully with the campaign but has not resulted in any concrete action to date.

3. We are grateful to Katy Huxley and Helen Blakely of the Welsh Institute of Social and Economic Research, Data and Methods at Cardiff University for sharing with us their unpublished data on the fast-food campaign.
4. Unlike the Living Wage, the alternative £10.00 standard is not based on research into the expenditure requirements of low-wage employees and is not uprated on an annual basis. It is substantially higher than the UK-wide Living Wage promoted by the Living Wage Foundation of £9.00 an hour but is below the London Living Wage of £10.55 (2018-2019 rates). Some employers have adopted the £10.00 standard – it is the bottom rate of pay for employees of the Labour Party – but the direct impact of the campaign on wage rates to date is probably limited.

Why have tensions of this kind arisen when both types of organization seemingly want the same thing, to raise the pay of low-wage workers as a means of addressing in-work poverty? In the research literature on union-community coalitions, tension has often been explained in terms of the cultural differences between the two types of organization; that they possess differing values, assumptions, personnel and modes of behaviour (Fine 2007; Holgate 2009, 2015; Tapia 2013). Researchers supportive of coalitions have also complained that trade unions can be conservative institutions, resistant to experimenting with new methods (Holgate 2015). Explanations of this kind are valid. For example, a notable feature of Citizens UK is that it is a largely faith-based coalition and this characteristic can be off-putting to secular trade unionists, committed to a liberal position on questions of sexuality and reproduction. In addition though, our research identified two further, structural reasons for tension in the relationship between trade unions and the Living Wage campaign, both of which contradicted the argument about complementarity outlined above. On the one hand, campaigners and trade unionists were pursuing competing and not complementary objectives, while on the other the methods they used to promote the Living Wage followed competing, not reinforcing logics.

A notable feature of the Living Wage campaign is that it involves a direct attempt by civil society organizations to determine the pay of employees, long the central activity of trade unions. Moreover, this attempt intrudes on the same 'regulatory space' (MacKenzie and Martinéz Lucio 2019) occupied by unions to the extent that Citizens UK and its allies are trying to shape the behaviour of individual employers, a proportion of which already have recognition agreements and collective bargaining arrangements with trade unions. Both the substantive issue at the heart of the campaign and the locus of campaigning activity, therefore, are shared with trade unions. While this sharing of territory can lead to mutual reinforcement through the involvement of unions in Living Wage accreditation campaigns in the manner described above, it can also, perhaps inevitably, lead to rivalry. The breakdown of relations between campaigners and the regional TUC body, referred to previously, arose from rivalry of this kind. The local chapter of Citizens UK launched a campaign to secure the immediate payment of the Living Wage to employees at the regional airport when recognized unions were involved in pay bargaining for the same group of workers and had negotiated an agreement that the Living Wage would be paid in the future once the business returned to profitability. There was direct rivalry between the two types of organization therefore over which would determine the pay of a group of workers and which would shape the policy of a single employer. Other cases of conflict between Citizens UK and trade unions we believe have arisen for similar reasons (*see* Holgate 2009; Wills et al. 2009). As one of our union interviewees expressed it, 'If you've got an independent organization setting your wage rate, what's the point of joining a trade union?'

While unions and Living Wage campaigners have shared the objective of seeking to raise the pay of low-wage workers, they have often used rather different methods in attempting to do so. For unions, joint regulation through collective bargaining remains a primary method and progress in addressing low pay has often been secured through single or multi-employer collective agreements. For Citizens UK and the Living Wage Foundation, in contrast, the primary method is that of unilateral regulation, in which employers are pressured or persuaded to adopt a predetermined labour standard, formulated within civil society, and are accredited if they agree to do so. The application of these different methods to promote the Living Wage has been another source of conflict between unions and campaigners. Thus, unions were critical of the accreditation process used by the campaign because it focused solely on the Living Wage and largely ignored other aspects of the employment relationship. Union representatives explained that short or unpredictable working hours were a more significant problem for many low-wage workers and objected that accreditation could amount to the endorsement of otherwise bad employers.[5]

For their part, campaigners criticized union negotiators for collective agreements that set rates below the Living Wage, arguing that this was a failure of union representation and that basic standards such as the Living Wage should not be negotiable. In response to criticism of this kind, unions replied that they had to represent their members as best they could and that while pay rates may be low it was often possible to secure compensating improvements in other employment terms, such as fringe benefits, flexible working or training provision. Underlying disputes of this kind are the competing logics of the two modes of regulation being used. Joint regulation implies mutual concessions between employer and union, often encompassing trade-offs across multiple issues, within the context of a long-term bargaining relationship. Unilateral regulation by civil society organizations, in contrast, leaves no space for concessions, is confined to a discrete standard or set of standards and relies upon a limited, transactional relationship with employers, in which compliance with the standard is exchanged for accreditation. When this method of unilateral regulation has been imported into a unionized context characterized by collective bargaining, its separate, competing logic has often been the source of conflict.

§9.05 TRADE UNION APPROPRIATION OF THE LIVING WAGE

Our interview and documentary research revealed the existence of a substantial 'shadow' Living Wage, where employers paid the Living Wage to at least a portion of their employees but refrained from accreditation. The evidence also indicated that in many cases trade unions had played an important part in spreading the Living Wage standard in this way, negotiating with employers or exerting campaigning pressure to persuade businesses to adopt the Living Wage, quite independently of the 'formal' Living Wage campaign (*see also* Johnson 2017; Moore et al. 2018; Prowse and Fells 2016). In this section we examine union activity of this kind, looking in turn at Living Wage disputes, collective bargaining to secure the Living Wage at industry and enterprise levels and separate union campaigns for the Living Wage. In each of these areas, there has been an effective union appropriation of the Living Wage, in which the standard has been detached from the Citizens UK-led campaign and incorporated within the ongoing, representative activity of trade unions. In other words, unions

5. It should be noted that partly in response to criticism of this kind, the Living Wage Foundation is launching a new Living Hours standard in 2019, which will seek to address the problem of short and unpredictable hours for many low-paid workers.

have relied upon their existing repertoire to promote the Living Wage. It may nevertheless be the case, however, that unions have learnt from the Living Wage campaign and incorporated some of the methods of community organizing into their own, separate activity. In examining Living Wage disputes, bargaining and union campaigns therefore, we also consider whether there is convergence with the methods used by Citizens UK and its sister organizations.

Strikes and other forms of collective conflict are at a historical low-point in Britain but against this background of labour quiescence, there has been the spread of, often small scale, disputes involving low-wage workers over the past five years. A distinctive feature of these disputes is that a demand to be paid the Living Wage or the London Living Wage has been a focal point. Perhaps the most noteworthy disputes of this kind have been initiated by small, so-called indy unions, such as the Independent Workers' Union of Great Britain (IWGB), Industrial Workers of the World (IWW), United Voices of the World (UVW) and the Cleaners and Allied Independent Workers' Union (CAIW), which have been most active in London (Alberti and Peró 2018; Peró 2014). These unions, most of which are newly formed, have led militant campaigns to secure the London Living Wage for delivery workers in the gig economy and for outsourced cleaners in universities, museums, newspapers, retail and luxury services, many of whom are recent migrants to the UK. Other, more established unions have also initiated disputes of this kind, partly as a result of the competitive pressure exerted by indy unions. Recent strikes which have included the Living Wage as a core demand include: a Public and Commercial Services Union (PCS) strike of outsourced cleaners in Whitehall in May 2019; Unite-led strikes of cleaners at Luton Airport in December 2018; a UNISON organized strike ballot at the University of Bath in 2018 which secured the reintroduction of the Living Wage for cleaners after it had been withdrawn; a strike of outsourced cleaners at retailer, Top Shop organized by the GMB in 2017; and the long-running dispute of members of the cinema, television and theatre technicians' union at the Ritzy cinema in London. Another, related development has been the 'fast-food' strikes in MacDonald's and other food and drink chains in 2018, though in this case, the demand for a living wage references the alternative £10.00 an hour standard favoured by the Bakers' Union and its allies. A final way in which the Living Wage has impinged on dispute activity is as part of the resolution of strikes initially called over other issues. The acceptance by the National Gallery that it would ensure its contractors paid the Living Wage brought to an end a long dispute with PCS over the outsourcing of gallery attendants in 2015, while a threatened strike in NHS Wales over the non-implementation of Pay Review Body recommendations was averted in the same year by the introduction of the Living Wage for all directly employed staff, benefiting about 4,000 employees.

It is important to note that in these disputes, neither Citizens UK nor the Living Wage Foundation was involved as participants. The standard formulated by the Living Wage campaign was often a core demand but those who were interviewed averred that there was virtually no contact with Living Wage campaigners. The disputes also differed from the 'official' Living Wage campaign in certain important respects. First, they were typically strongly adversarial in their relationship to employer and often made use of militant tactics, including picketing, flash-mobs, and temporary occupations. The Living Wage campaign, in contrast, is strongly pro-employer in its orientation, seeking to elicit responsible behaviour from businesses persuaded that there is a business case for the Living Wage. Moreover, even when Citizens UK has used pressure tactics to target resistant employers these have tended to assume a moderate, 'responsible' form that exposes poor behaviour to the public gaze but without a strongly adversarial rhetoric. As Bunyan (2016) has noted, the campaign has tempered the use of 'agitational' with 'conciliatory' methods and reliance on the latter has become more accentuated over time. Second, the demand for the Living Wage has sometimes been linked to other objectives that contradict the policy of the Living Wage campaign. The key issue here is a demand in disputes led by several of the indy unions and by PCS and UNISON that outsourced work should be brought back in-house. In contrast, the Living Wage campaign has sought to encourage 'responsible' outsourcing and it is for this reason that indirect employees working on the primary employer's premises are included in the standard. The Living Wage Foundation has also introduced a supplementary Service Providers standard, which can be awarded to contractors that undertake to include a Living Wage option whenever they tender for work. Some of the UK's primary outsourcing companies, such as ISS and Sodexo have been accredited under this scheme.

Another way in which the Living Wage has been appropriated by unions is through its inclusion in collective bargaining. In recent years the Living Wage has been adopted as the base, entry-rate in several industry-level agreements. The Living Wage settlement in NHS Wales has already been mentioned and there are now equivalent agreements in NHS England and NHS Scotland. Other branches of public service with Living Wage agreements include further education in Scotland and Wales, Scottish cooperative housing and Scottish local government. In 2019 a new pay spine was implemented for English and Welsh local government that sets the bottom rate at £9.00 an hour, equal to the Living Wage, though without referencing the standard as such. There have also been some, more novel multi-employer arrangements. Unison has negotiated framework agreements for the adoption of the Living Wage by faith schools and cooperative schools, while the construction union (now part of Unite) has secured tacit agreements with a number of property companies to ensure the Living Wage is paid by contractors on major construction sites in London. These developments at industry level have been echoed within enterprise-level agreements. A substantial number of local authorities in the UK have negotiated Living Wage agreements with the GMB and UNISON (Johnson 2017; Prowse and Fells 2016) and we have collected examples from a range of other industries, including manufacturing, entertainment, universities and cultural institutions, including theatres, galleries and museums.

In some cases, these agreements have led directly to the accreditation of employers by the Living Wage Foundation. A number of union representatives expressed the view that this was desirable because it underscored the employer's commitment to the Living Wage and made it difficult to withdraw at a future date. In many other cases, however, negotiation has not led on to accreditation, resulting in the phenomenon of the shadow Living Wage described above. One reason for this failure is the opposition of union representatives, concerned both that accreditation involved sharing the credit for improvements in wages with an 'outside' organization and that the standard might impose a ceiling, blocking further increases in rates of pay. Another reason is that union negotiation of the Living Wage, particularly within multi-employer contexts, has often been confined to directly employed workers and has not been extended to employees of contractors. In this regard, union agreements can fall short of the Living Wage standard.

Another feature of union bargaining for the Living Wage, which also distinguished it from the Living Wage campaign, is that it has often included concessions, such as the introduction of flexible working practices or the reduction of overtime and other premium payments in order to fund the higher base rate. Trade-offs of this kind were particularly a feature of enterprise-level agreements. In contrast, our survey of Living Wage Employers found little evidence of clawback of this kind within the campaign directed by the Living Wage Foundation, with only very small percentages of employers reporting that they had reduced hours or cut benefits or premium payments to fund the Living Wage. What this suggests is that when the method of joint regulation has been used employers have responded rather differently, seeking to elicit reciprocal concessions in the time-honoured manner of collective bargaining.

A final point to note about union bargaining for the Living Wage is that we encountered very few reports of successful negotiation in industries dominated by low pay, such as retail, social care and hospitality. In this regard, joint regulation echoed the experience of the wider Living Wage campaign. While the latter has recruited some employers in low-wage industries, the population of accredited organizations is skewed towards high paying sectors, such as energy, information and communication technology, construction, professional services and financial services. Accreditation has often benefited low-wage workers in high-wage industries and to a degree union bargaining has reproduced this pattern, with the bargaining power of well-organized groups in health, education, public administration and the arts being used to lift the pay of the less-well organized. Joint regulation through collective bargaining and unilateral regulation through accreditation have displayed a similar, constrained property: their reach into the lower levels of the labour market has been limited.

The third main way in which unions have appropriated the Living Wage standard is by including it in their own, separate campaigning activity. In some cases, unions have launched dedicated campaigns to secure the Living Wage in particular industries or businesses. In others, the standard has been included within a broader campaign, intended to secure a more general improvement in working conditions. An example of the former is the campaign launched by PCS in 2011, to secure the Living Wage for its membership in national museums and galleries, the main area of low-wage employment within the civil service. This campaign was described to us as embodying the characteristic of PCS as a 'campaigning union' and was targeted at a number of different cultural organizations, including the Liverpool Museums and Galleries, the Tate Galleries, the National Gallery, the Wallace Collection, and the Victoria and Albert Museum. It was developed and implemented without any involvement of Citizens UK or the Living Wage Foundation. Two more recent Living Wage campaigns of this type have been directed at Heathrow Airport and at social enterprise, Greenwich Leisure Limited (GLL), by the GMB and Unite respectively. The GMB campaign is intended to secure coverage by the London Living Wage for all contractors operating on the

Heathrow site, while the Unite campaign is seeking to have the standard adopted at leisure centres across London and has targeted Labour-controlled local authorities which contract with GLL for the provision of leisure services. In both of these campaigns, the union is effectively seeking to build on commitments already secured by the Living Wage Foundation. Heathrow Airport is an accredited Living Wage Employer and its accreditation has already led to increases in pay for several thousand, mainly contracted workers. The London boroughs targeted by Unite, such as Waltham Forest and Tower Hamlets, are also accredited Living Wage Employers. Despite this link, the campaign materials of the two unions have little to say about the Living Wage campaign and both initiatives are presented as discrete and solely union-authored.

An example of a broader union campaign that incorporates the Living Wage is UNISON's campaign for the Ethical Care Charter. The latter comprises a set of employment and care standards for the provision of social care by local authorities, including provision through outsourced services. The standards include payment of the Living Wage, alongside occupational sick pay, restrictions on the use of zero-hours contracts, opportunities for care staff to meet and discuss service issues and the allocation of sufficient time for home visits to ensure a high-quality service. Notable features of the campaign include linking improvements in employment conditions to improvements in service quality and the use of an explicitly moral, social justice language to frame the campaign. To date, more than forty local authorities have committed to implementing the Charter within their care services.

It is in their campaigning for the Living Wage that the activity of trade unions most closely resembles that of the Living Wage campaign itself. Several of the methods employed in the latter can be seen in the campaigns described above. Thus, PCS organized protests at opening events at museums attended by celebrities and other public figures, threatening the reputation of cultural institutions as a form of leverage, in precisely the manner that Citizens UK has done. The Unite and UNISON campaigns are focused on public authorities and include lobbying councillors to try and persuade them to use procurement as a way of promoting the Living Wage, again in exactly the same way that the Living Wage Foundation has acted. The GMB's targeting of Heathrow Airport also echoes the campaigning activity of the Foundation, both in its focus on an 'anchor institution' with an extended supply chain that can shape employment practice in a particular region and in its use of street theatre to highlight the problem of low pay. Again, both elements feature in the Living Wage campaign, with the targeting of anchor institutions such as transport hubs forming an important part of the Living Wage Places initiative launched by the Foundation in 2019.

The parallels are particularly marked in the case of the Ethical Care Charter. In certain respects, this represents a union venture into unilateral regulation through the attempt to persuade local authorities to sign up to an ethical standard; albeit with the proviso that the implementation of the Charter commitment should be undertaken jointly by councils and local UNISON branches. The Charter campaign has also made use of worker testimony, in which care workers on low-pay and zero-hours contracts have directly addressed councillors to report on the difficulties of their situation and the failings of care services. Delivering testimony of this kind is a pronounced feature both of the Living Wage campaign and of the wider community organizing movement

(Walls 2015). UNISON reported to us that they were not aware of this but the adoption by unions of this kind of direct, morally loaded speech by ordinary workers to those in power is perhaps the clearest example of unions learning from community organizing.[6] The use of other techniques found within the Living Wage campaign is probably best viewed as representing convergence rather than direct learning. In developing Living Wage campaigns, unions have drawn upon a broad campaigning repertoire that originates in numerous sources and which is available to a wide range of campaigning organizations, including both unions themselves and the civil society organizations behind the Living Wage.

§9.06 CONCLUSION

The purpose of this article has been to use the case of the Living Wage campaign to test the claim within the literature on union revitalization that unions can and should develop coalitions with other types of progressive movement to advance the interests of their members. Writers who make this argument have often also claimed that traditional methods of union representation have become less effective over time and that, in the face of potent forces such as globalization, neo-liberalism and austerity, unions have lost the power effectively to represent their members. Revitalizing unions it therefore follows, requires the adoption of radically new methods and the discovery of new power resources. Developing coalitions with other, often more potent social movements and adopting their seemingly more effective methods have been presented as ways in which this revitalization can be achieved (Turner 2006).

The evidence we have gathered from the Living Wage campaign is most striking for the fact that it does not conform closely to this account. With regard to coalition the research has identified four key findings as follows: (1) The Living Wage campaign is not a formally constituted coalition between unions and civil society organizations but rather has originated in the transfer of American community organizing institutions and methods to the UK. (2) Unions form part of the network of organizations that have become involved in the Living Wage campaign but in many regards their involvement is marginal and less significant than that of other campaign 'partners'; for many unions involvement has taken the form of supportive affiliation rather than active participation. (3) Central to the campaign has been the accreditation of Living Wage Employers who give a formal, contractual agreement to conform to the Living Wage standard. Unions have been involved in this accreditation activity, encouraging or pressurising employers to adopt the Living Wage alongside community campaigners but this involvement is confined to only a minority of employers and appears often to assume

6. Union use of worker testimony is not restricted to the Living Wage campaign and may be spreading to other campaigns. In May 2019 a worker from one of Amazon's UK warehouses provided testimony about poor working conditions to the company's major investors at an event organized by Trade Union Share Owners. The use of worker testimony to investors is also a feature of the Living Wage campaign. It has often been arranged by Share Action, an organization that campaigns on ethical investment, and which has worked jointly with the Living Wage Foundation to promote the Living Wage to large, publicly invested companies. In this case, worker testimony has typically been given at annual shareholder meetings.

a minimal form even in organizations where unions have formal recognition. (4) While there has been involvement of unions in the Living Wage campaign there has also been tension, leading in some cases to a breakdown in the relationship between trade unions and Living Wage campaigners. In many parts of the UK contact between the two groups of campaigners is limited and relations are frosty. These difficult relations have arisen, we believe, because neither the goals nor the methods of unions and Living Wage campaigners are complementary in the manner suggested by theorists of coalition. On the contrary, the research identified competing objectives and competing logics in the methods used by the two sides.

With regard to the transfer of campaigning methods from community organizing to the trade union movement, the research again provided little supporting evidence. Unions have begun to use worker testimony before powerholders in the manner of Living Wage campaigners and their own campaigning activity to promote the Living Wage often resembles that of Citizens UK and the Living Wage Foundation. This resemblance, however, is probably best interpreted as convergence rather than imitation, arising from both types of organization drawing from a common pool of campaigning techniques. The main finding of the research with regard to union methods is that unions have appropriated the Living Wage standard and have sought to promote it through their established means of representation. Thus, there has been a recent growth of Living Wage disputes, the standard has been absorbed within collective bargaining at both industry and enterprise levels and unions have launched their own distinct Living Wage campaigns, completely separate from the activity of Citizens UK and the Living Wage Foundation. There has been innovation with regard to substance – union appropriation of the Living Wage standard – but continuity with regard to method – primary reliance on collective bargaining. This arrangement is precisely the reverse of that suggested in the theory of union revitalization.

A final conclusion is that the case suggests that the extensive literature on union revitalization possibly exaggerates both the extent of change within trade unions and the pressures upon them to engage in radical innovation. An alternative concept to revitalization has recently been advanced by Moore et al. (2018). Writing about collective bargaining in the UK, they identify what they term 'resilience'. Such resilience has two aspects, first a continuing capacity for collective bargaining to secure material gains for workers in terms of improved wages and better employment conditions and, second, a substantive flexibility, such that new issues have been imported into collective bargaining as the challenges unions face have changed. This notion of resilience, we believe, captures the union response to the Living Wage. In many respects, unions have kept their distance from the Living Wage campaign but they have seized upon the standard and the opportunity it presents to make progress in representing the interests of low-wage workers. They have done so by entering into disputes with employers, through collective bargaining and by campaigning to pressure employers and public authorities to adopt the Living Wage. In doing so they have materially improved the condition of many in low-paid employment, even in a context of austerity. The case attests to the stubborn resilience of British trade unions but not to their revitalization.

REFERENCES

Alberti, G. and Peró, D. (2018). 'Migrating industrial relations: migrant workers' initiatives within and outside trade unions', *British Journal of Industrial Relations*, 56 (4), 693-715.

Bunyan, P. (2016). 'The role of civil society organizations in reducing poverty and inequality: a case study of the living wage campaign in the UK', *Local Economy*, 31 (4), 489-501.

Doellgast, V., Lillie, N., and Pulignano, V. (2018). 'From dualization to solidarity: halting the cycle of precarity', in V. Doellgast, N. Lillie, and V. Pulignano (eds), *Reconstructing Solidarity: Labour Unions, Precarious Work, and the Politics of Institutional Change in Europe*. Oxford: Oxford University Press, 1-41.

Donaghey, J., et al. (2014). 'From employment relations to consumption relations: balancing labor governance in global supply chains', *Human Resource Management*, 53 (2), 229-252.

Fine, J. (2007). 'A marriage made in heaven? Mismatches and misunderstandings between worker centres and unions', *British Journal of Industrial Relations*, 45 (2), 335-360.

Heery, E. (2009). *Amnesty International and Trade Unions in Britain: Thirty Years of Solidarity for Human Rights*, London: Amnesty International UK.

Holgate, J. (2009). 'Contested terrain: London's living wage campaign and the tension between community and union organising', in J. McBride and I. Greenwood (eds), *The Complexity of Community Unionism: A Comparative Analysis of Concepts and Contexts*. Basingstoke: Palgrave, 49-74.

Holgate, J. (2015). 'An international study of trade union involvement in community organizing: same model, different outcomes', *British Journal of Industrial Relations*, 53 (3), 460-483.

Holgate, J. and Wills, J. (2007). 'Organizing labor in London: lessons from the campaign for a living wage', in L. Turner and D.B. Cornfield (eds), *Labor in the New Urban Battlegrounds: Local Solidarity in a Global Economy*. Ithaca NY and London: ILR Press, 211-223.

Jamoul, L. and Wills, J. (2008). 'Faith in politics', *Urban Studies*, 45 (10), 2035-2056.

Johnson, M. (2017). 'Implementing the living wage in local government', *Employee Relations*, 39 (6), 840-849.

Lopes, A. and Hall, T. (2015) 'Organising migrant workers: the living wage campaign at the University of East London', *Industrial Relations Journal*, 46 (3), 208-221.

MacKenzie, R., and Martinéz Lucio, M. (2019). 'Regulation, migration and the implications for industrial relations', *The Journal of Industrial Relations*, 61 (2), 176-197.

Mayer, B. (2009). *Blue-Green Coalitions: Fighting for Safe Workplaces and Healthy Communities*, Ithaca NY and London: ILR Press.

Moore, S., et al. (2018). 'The resilience of collective bargaining: a renewed logic for joint regulation?', *Employee Relations*, 41 (2), 279-295.

Luce, S. (2014). *Labor Movements: Global Perspectives*, Cambridge: Polity Press.

Però, D. (2014). 'Class politics and migrants: collective action amongst new migrant workers in Britain', *Sociology*, 48 (6), 1156-1172.

Preminger, J. (2019). 'Creating a multi-layered representational "package" for subcontracted workers: the case of cleaners at Ben-Gurion University', *Industrial Relations Journal*, 49 (1), 34-49.

Prowse, P. and Fells, R. (2016). 'The living wage in the UK – an analysis of the GMB campaign in local government', *Industry and Labour*, 26 (1), 58-73.

Sellers, P. (2017). 'The UK living wage: a trade union perspective', *Employee Relations*, 39 (6), 790-799.

Tapia, M. (2013). 'Marching to different tunes: commitment and culture as mobilising mechanisms of trade unions and community organizations', *British Journal of Industrial Relations*, 51 (4), 666-668.

Tapia, M. (2014). 'The United Kingdom: dialectic approaches to organizing immigrant workers, postwar to 2012', in L.H. Adler, M. Tapia and L. Turner (eds), *Mobilizing Against Inequality: Unions, Immigrant Workers and the Crisis of Capitalism*. Ithaca NY and London, ILR Press, 52-68.

Tattersall, A. (2009). 'Using their sword of justice: the NSW Teachers' Federation and its campaign for public education between 2001 and 2004', in J. McBride and I. Greenwood (eds), *Community Unionism: a Comparative analysis of Concepts and Contexts*. Basingstoke: Palgrave MacMillan, 161-186.

Tattersall, A. (2010). *Power in Coalition: Strategies for Strong Unions and Social Change*, Ithaca, NY and London: ILR Press.

Turner, L. (2006). 'Globalization and the logic of participation: unions and the politics of coalition building', *The Journal of Industrial Relations*, 48 (1), 83-97.

Walls, D. (2015). *Community Organizing*, Cambridge: Polity Press.

Wills, J., et al. (2009). 'Religion at work: the role of faith-based organizations in the London living wage campaign', *Cambridge Journal of Regions, Economy and Society*, 2 (3), 443-461.

CHAPTER 10

The Role of HRM and Trade Unions in the Resolution of Workplace Conflict in Britain

Deborah Hann & David Nash

§10.01 INTRODUCTION

Conflict in the workplace is pervasive with estimates by the United Kingdom's (UK's) Confederation of British Industry estimating that it costs the UK economy £33 billion per year (Everett 2017). The nature of such conflict can take a wide variety of forms and how such conflict manifests changing over time, but what is clear is that the management of conflict is now a core part of the management of the employment relationship (Saundry and Dix 2014; Teague, Roche and Hann 2012). While the ubiquitous nature of conflict is well documented, the management of such conflict at the workplace level is still not clearly understood (Dix 2012). This gap in understanding of how conflict is addressed at an organisational level has led to an increased interest in conflict resolution both as a focus of academic research (Lipsky et al., 2012; Roche, Teague, and Colvin 2014), but also in policy development (Department for Business, Innovation and Skills 2011).

While employment relations, in general, has often been the focus of strategic decision making within organisations (Kochan, McKersie and Cappelli 1984), decision making with regard to the approach taken to conflict management is less understood. The research that does exist concerning the relationship between strategy and conflict management focuses on how policies can be designed to improve organisational efficiency (Lipsky, Avgar, and Lamare 2017). While the aims of organisations in designing an approach to conflict management are beginning to be understood, the role played by key actors in making these decisions is under-explored. This paper considers what impact the presence of key employment relations actors can have on the nature and implementation of conflict management strategies at a workplace level.

This paper draws on data from a large-scale survey of firms located in Great Britain. The survey asked questions on organisations' experience and management of conflict, as well as the presence and role of various key employment actors. The article draws on these data to argue that the presence of key actors, in this case, Human Resource (HR) specialists and trade unions, can significantly impact on the approach taken and that different actors have different approaches that they seek to develop. The article finds that HR specialists actively look to develop innovative approaches to conflict resolution, and more specifically approaches that keep the conflict within the organisation, while in contrast, trade unions also encourage the development of more innovative approaches, but they focus on approaches that include very specific actors.

§10.02 LITERATURE REVIEW

A key focus of recent developments in research and policy development relating to the management of conflict in the workplace has been the role and development of Alternative Dispute Resolution (ADR), with workplaces increasingly looking at wide options to resolve conflict (Bendersky 2006; Lipsky, Seeber and Fincher 2003). ADR is the focus of much current interest as its interest-based approach often results in more effective outcomes, offering flexible and innovative solutions that aim to resolve issues as close to the source as possible (Ury, Brett and Goldberg 1993). The traditional route to the resolution of conflict in the workplace has been through organisational grievance and disciplinary procedures, usually involving successively higher levels of management and offering opportunity for appealing such decisions. In contrast, ADR focuses on opportunities to generate trust and create settlement with the intention that outcomes are less traumatic to the parties involved and less public (Davis 2002). These flexible approaches are increasingly popular, however the majority of the empirical studies are focused on the United States (US) (*see*, for example, Bendersky 2006; Lipsky et al., 2003). Research outside the US is limited but suggests that the growth of ADR is perhaps less prevalent (Hann, Nash and Heery 2019; Teague, Roche and Hann 2012). This paper will first investigate the extent to which ADR is present within organisations within Great Britain.

While existing research, even beyond the US, suggests that the use of ADR is growing within organisations, how decisions are made in relation to strategic choices around conflict management approaches is less understood (Nash and Hann 2019). In particular, there is a lack of understanding concerning the relationship between employment relations actors and the strategies that organisations use to manage conflict at a workplace level. This paper will consider the role of two key actors, HR specialists and trade unions, in determining the approaches an organisation takes. In short, the article is interested in whether different actors lead to different approaches to policy and practice.

Although the impact on conflict management is underexplored, research evidence suggests that HR professionals have the ability to impact policy and practice developments more generally within organisations (Dobbin 2011; Ulrich 1998). Lewin (2001) argues that HR specialists focus on internal mechanisms driven by trained managers as opposed to reliance on processes involving external actors to resolve adversarial conflict. This approach tries to keep conflict 'in-house' and in the control of HR rather than allowing the conflict to enter the public sphere. In contrast, however, Hann, Nash and Heery (2019) found that where HR is present there is an increased use of external processes in addressing conflict, suggesting that HR may be willing to experiment beyond the borders of their organisation where this is seen as appropriate.

The impact of union presence on conflict management is equally unclear in existing research. Initially, ADR was associated with non-union firms as a way to 'fill the gap'. While grievance procedures and processes are long-established within unionised sectors, non-unionised sectors have often lacked adequate or established mechanisms to address conflict (Budd and Colvin 2005; Lipsky et al., 2003). In these cases, ADR has been used as a union substitution strategy rather than being embraced by unions and thus it would be assumed that where a union is present we might see less occurrence of ADR practices (Barrett and O'Dowd 2005). More recent research suggests, however, that dispute resolution techniques are now present in both unionised and non-unionised organisations (Lipsky, Avgar, Lamare et al., 2012; Lipsky and Seeber 2000; Roche and Teague 2012). Unions may seek to actively use ADR especially when it comes to collective disputes and often with a focus on approaches that keep the conflict internal (Hann et al., 2019; Heery and Nash 2011). In short, while it is clear that key employment relations actors have an impact on the approach taken to conflict management in the workplace, the direction of such impact is not always obvious. The intention of this paper is to begin to address this gap in understanding.

§10.03 METHODS

The work presented below is based on evidence collected using the survey method. The survey, undertaken in 2018, is an extension of previous work undertaken in the Republic of Ireland in 2009 (Teague et al., 2012) and Wales in 2015 (Hann et al., 2019). The research instrument was developed in conjunction with Advisory Conciliation and Arbitration Service (Acas), Britain's public body responsible for workplace dispute resolution, and was further defined and adapted through cognitive testing with a range of HR professionals.

The sample frame was derived using data from Companies House (the source of official data on the characteristics of UK employing organisations) to identify those organisations whose head office is located in Great Britain. A sample frame was derived to include all organisations with 20 or more employees and covered all industries in the private sector (excluding agriculture, in common with other organisational based surveys). A sample frame of over 99,600 was identified and from this, a sample of 4,833 surveys, representative of both size and sector, were sent out.

The questionnaire was addressed to the senior executive in the company who it was assumed would have responsibility for dealing with workplace conflict, where possible this executive was the HR Specialist. In the event of it not being possible to identify an HR specialist, the questionnaire was sent to the company secretary or to a general management contact with a specific request in the covering letter that it be passed on to the most appropriate person. The questionnaire was distributed by post, with an option for electronic completion. Two postal reminders were issued and organisations also received a telephone call encouraging them to complete the survey. The number of valid responses received was 402.

Within the survey, three forms of conflict were considered: conflict that occurs between individual employees and their employers, defined as individual disputes; conflict that occurs between colleagues but doesn't directly involve the employer (e.g., bullying and harassment), defined as inter-employee disputes; and conflict between groups of employees and their employer, defined as group disputes. Although data have been collected on all three of these forms of conflict, this paper will only consider that relating to individual conflict. The reason for this specific focus is that this is the most common form of conflict within organisations.

This paper will use this data to answer two key research questions:

(1) How do employers manage workplace conflict in the UK?
(2) How is their approach mediated by the presence of specialist HR and trade unions?

§10.04 RESULTS

What is clear from the survey results is that conflict is ubiquitous in British organisations. Almost all firms reported that they had experienced some form of conflict. Table 10.1 shows that a range of employee-initiated conflicts from the most informal disagreements to the most serious manifesting in employment tribunal cases is evident throughout all parts of the UK economy, but the table also indicates that the most common form of conflict is employer-initiated, namely disciplinary cases.

Organisations were asked to rank the extent to which various forms of conflict occurred within their organisation on a scale from 1 to 4 (1 = Never; 4 = Often). All organisations, regardless of size, sector, union presence, or type of HR function report experiencing all but the most serious forms of conflict at least once. Only in the case of employment tribunals and conflict that requires the involvement of external experts do organisations report that the frequency is, on average, less than once in the previous two years.

Further analysis of the data suggests that organisations with an HR specialist are more likely to experience all forms of conflict. With the exception of the use of external experts other than Acas (where there is no statistically significant difference), the presence of an in-house HR function was associated with a higher frequency of reported disputes (often or occasionally). In contrast, where in-house generalist managers were responsible for dealing with HR issues, then reporting of the presence of disputes within an organisation was seen as lower. Trade union presence has the same impact on the level of disputes as the presence of an HR Specialist, although in the case of unions the impact is slightly less pronounced.

Table 10.1 Presence of Conflict with UK Organisations

	All Firms	*Specialist HR*	*Generalist HR*	*Unionised Firms*	*Small Firms*	*Medium Firms*	*Large Firms*	*Manf. Firms*	*Service Firms*
Informal disagreements	2.64	2.78	2.18	2.69	2.18	2.72	3	2.52	2.67
Grievances brought by employees	2.21	2.37	1.68	2.21	1.7	1.97	2.8	2.13	2.18
Disciplinary initiated by the organisation	2.72	2.93	2.07	2.75	2.17	2.75	3.24	2.73	2.69
Bullying or Harassment cases	1.69	1.83	1.24	1.7	1.3	1.58	2.1	1.64	1.67
Disputes referred to Acas	1.55	1.63	1.29	1.53	1.27	1.45	1.91	1.43	1.59
External experts involved in resolving disputes	1.49	1.54	1.34	1.51	1.35	1.55	1.56	1.43	1.5
Disputes resulting in an Employment Tribunal claim	1.39	1.47	1.16	1.38	1.1	1.32	1.72	1.4	1.36

One final point of note is that respondents in British organisations take an overwhelmingly unitarist orientation in their attitude toward conflict, i.e., that conflict primarily arises as a result of 'misbehaviour, poor performance or misunderstanding'. Seventy-eight per cent of organisations adopt this unitarist stance, while only 10% view conflict as inevitable and unwelcome and a further 12% view conflict as potentially constructive. It should be noted however that the position adopted is not significantly influenced by the presence of an HR specialist of a trade union.

§10.05 IMPACT OF KEY ACTORS ON DIMENSIONS OF CONFLICT MANAGEMENT

The overall impact of the key industrial relations actors on the management of conflict will be explained using four dimensions reflecting the breadth of activities involved in resolving workplace disputes. First, the paper examines the formality of the approach taken, comparing dispute resolution policy with practice. Examining this potential disparity is important as the reality of what happens in the workplace may not match management's rhetoric (Argyris 1990; Legge 1994). Second, the paper considers the implementation of more innovative approaches to dispute resolution, here interpreted as the adoption of ADR, as there is evidence that particular types of organisation are more likely to establish non-traditional approaches to dispute resolution than others (Lipsky and Seeber 2000; Lipsky et al., 2012; Roche and Teague 2012; Hann et al., 2019). Third, the extent of training for the key actors in dispute resolution will be examined in line with previous studies, which have highlighted its importance in effective conflict management strategies (Conbere 2001; Keep 2014). Finally, the paper will look for evidence of firms adopting more general HR practices that may constitute a pre-emptive approach to minimising or eliminating conflict prior to its occurrence. This will allow for an investigation of the extent to which conflict management is part of a broader HR approach (Lepak and Snell 1999). The following sections will consider each of these dimensions briefly.

[A] The Formality of the Approach Taken

When considering the formality of the approach taken, this analysis focuses on the extent to which different dispute resolution mechanisms are included in the formal written policy. The mere existence of a formal policy, in and of itself, is a signifier that a firm likely takes a more formalised approach. The vast majority (87.9%) of organisations have established a formal policy to handle disputes in the workplace to address individual conflict. In addition, in the case of individual conflict the vast majority of organisations tend to employ their policy in a flexible manner, using their discretion to reflect the circumstances at hand. The results in Table 10.2 suggest that the presence of in-house HR function is influential in how an organisation might respond to conflict. Where an HR specialist is the first point of contact, then a greater number of organisations will have a policy, which is either rigidly or flexibly applied.

Interestingly, trade union presence has no significant impact on the existence of a policy

Table 10.2 Formal Conflict Management Policy by HR Presence

	Firms with Formal Policy		*Firms With No Formal Policy*	
	No.	*%*	*No.*	*%*
In-house HR specialist	244	91.0	24	9.0
In-house general manager	69	78.4	19	21.6
Contracted out HR function	24	85.7	4	14.3
Total	*337*	*87.8*	*47*	*12.2*

The survey considered the presence of fifteen practices which organisations may adopt to deal with conflict in the workplace; two traditional approaches and thirteen more innovative approaches. The fifteen practices are outlined in Table 10.3. The ADR approaches can be further divided down into those which aim to keep the dispute internal to the organisation (use of organisation's own internal mediation service through to use of personal development/improvement plans) and those which utilise external actors. This taxonomy was utilised by Hann, Nash and Heery (2019).

The majority of organisations utilise the two approaches that would be considered as traditional when it comes to individual conflict (54.2 % state that a process involving progressively higher levels of management is contained within their policy, whilst 57.7% offer a right to appeal decisions within their policy). The presence of an HR specialist or a trade union has no significant impact on the presence of traditional approaches in their formal policy.

Table 10.3 Conflict Management Practices

Category	*Practices*
Traditional approaches	• Progressively higher levels of management resolving disputes • A right to appeal decisions made by management
ADR Practices with a focus on internal resolution	• Use of organisation's own internal mediation service • Use of review panels comprised of managers or peers • Use of formalised open-door approach • Discussions facilitated by HR • Intensive communication regarding change with a view to avoiding disharmony • Use of conflict coaching • Informal conversations with line-manager(s) • Use of personal development/improvement plan

Category	*Practices*
ADR Practices utilising external actors	• Use of Acas conciliation, to help prevent an Employment Tribunal claim • Use of Acas mediation • Use of professional mediation by a third-party provider (excluding Acas) • Use of lawyers • Use of an external HR expert

Employment relations actors have a limited impact on the content of conflict management policies. The impact of specialist HR on the inclusion of more innovative approaches in formal policy is also limited. Bivariate analysis indicates that only in the case of discussions facilitated by HR, informal conversations with line managers, use of personal development plans and the use of lawyers is there a significant relationship. The presence of HR specialists appears unrelated to the inclusion of the other nine practices. In contrast, the presence of a trade union within an organisation has no significant influence on the content of conflict management policies where they exist. Of the thirteen more progressive approaches to deal with conflict in the workplace, only the use of review panels comprised of managers or peers is more commonly found in company policies where a trade union is present within an organisation compared to where a trade union is not present.

Whilst the presence of HR specialists and/or trade unions within an organisation is only weakly associated with the presence of various approaches within organisational policy, there is a much stronger relationship in terms of the usage of such approaches. It is worth noting that more traditional approaches to conflict management (the use of a process involving progressively higher levels of management and the right to appeal decisions made by management) are more common in organisations with a either a HR Specialist or a trade union present. The pattern of use of both traditional and innovative conflict management practices is associated with the presence of specialist HR and or trade unions.

[B] Adoption of ADR Practices

The presence of an HR specialist within an organisation means that ten of the thirteen innovative approaches to dispute resolution are more frequently used to resolve conflict. This is illustrated in Table 10.4, which compares the average use of ADR practices by firms with and without a specialist HR function. This increase in usage is particularly noticeable when considering practices that aim to keep matters 'in-house'. All but the 'use of review panels comprised of managers or peers' are significantly more frequently used in organisations with HR specialists. It is also notable that the presence of HR specialists is associated with a strong preference to try to keep conflict 'in-house' with the use of external actors only being marginally more prevalent (albeit statistically significant). In the case of approaches using external actors, while the differences in three out of five practices are statistically significant, they are of a smaller magnitude.

Table 10.4 Use of ADR Practices by Type of HR Function

	HR Specialist	*General Manager*
Internal approaches		
Use of organisation's own internal mediation service	1.73**	1.47**
Use of review panels comprised of managers or peers	1.27	1.28
Use of formalised open-door approach	2.46***	1.94***
Discussions facilitated by HR	3.05***	1.52***
Intensive communication regarding change with a view to avoiding disharmony	2.50***	1.90***
Use of conflict coaching	1.58***	1.24***
Informal conversations with line-manager(s)	3.43***	2.75***
Use of personal development/improvement plan	3.15***	2.37***
External approaches		
Use of Acas conciliation, to help prevent an Employment Tribunal claim	1.54***	1.25***
Use of Acas mediation	1.22	1.20
Use of professional mediation by a third-party provider (excluding Acas)	1.30**	1.15**
Use of lawyers	2.19**	1.56**
Use of an external HR expert	1.85*	1.61*

* significant at .1, ** significant at .05, *** significant at .001

As with the presence of HR, the presence of a trade union within an organisation means the usage of ADR practices is more common than in non-union organisations. The results in Table 10.5 show that nine of the thirteen ADR approaches are more frequently used in organisations with trade unions than those without. The differences in the use of internal approaches, while still statistically significant are less marked than when considering the presence of an HR specialist. What is notable when considering the impact of a trade union is the differences evident when looking at which external actors are involved. Where a trade union is present within an organisation, Acas or lawyers are more commonly involved than external HR specialists or non-Acas professional mediators. This difference suggests that more emphasis is placed on external actors who are perceived as genuinely neutral over those that may have an affiliation with the 'purchaser' or the employer.

Table 10.5 Use of ADR Practices by Presence of Trade Union

	Union Present	*Non union*
Internal approaches		
Use of organisation's own internal mediation service	1.78	1.64
Use of review panels comprised of managers or peers	1.45**	1.23**
Use of formalised open-door approach	2.67**	2.26**
Discussions facilitated by HR	3.22***	2.59***
Intensive communication regarding change with a view to avoiding disharmony	2.84***	2.24***
Use of conflict coaching	1.60	1.48
Informal conversations with line-manager(s)	3.56***	3.20***
Use of personal development/improvement plan	3.22***	2.90***
External approaches		
Use of Acas conciliation, to help prevent an Employment Tribunal claim	1.70**	1.42**
Use of Acas mediation	1.33*	1.18*
Use of professional mediation by a third-party provider (excluding Acas)	1.26	1.25
Use of lawyers	2.39***	1.97***
Use of an external HR expert	1.70	1.81

* significant at .1, ** significant at .05, *** significant at .001

[C] Training for Actors

The third dimension where the presence of particular employment relations actors is linked with the management of conflict is the degree to which said actors have been trained to deal with its occurrence. The presence of HR specialists is associated with higher levels of formal training for a range of actors who may be expected to offer advice or guidance on workplace conflict. This includes line managers, trade union representative, non-union representatives, senior managers, HR professionals themselves, occupational health workers and diversity/equal opportunities officers.

The presence of a trade union within an organisation also has an impact on the degree to which actors are trained to manage conflict, although a more limited one. Here the focus of training is narrower with higher numbers of representatives, both union and non-union, receiving training in organisations where there is a trade union present than where there is not. HR Professionals are also more likely to be trained to deal with conflict where a trade union is present. In short, employment relations actors are associated with the provision of training that is designed to ensure that conflict is effectively handled, but this effect varies depending on the nature of the actor considered.

[1] Pre-emptive HR Practices

The final dimension considered in the survey was the presence of more general HR practices which could serve to address or reduce conflict prior to its occurrence. Respondents were asked to identify which, if any, more general HR practices they used with the aim of reducing or avoiding conflict, and the results are shown in Table 10.6. The focus of this practice was primarily around voice mechanisms, both where they actively seek the views of employees, but equally where management unilaterally communicates information. Respondents were also asked whether external consultants were asked to review and advise the organisation on its dispute resolution policies in an attempt to pre-empt conflict. In other words, the organisation didn't just have these particular practices, but that one intention of having them was addressing conflict before it started. The analysis found that there is a significant difference in the use of these pre-emptive HR practices according to the presence of a trade union or an HR specialist. Unionised organisations were found on average to adopt 5.5 such policies, compared to 4.2 for non-unionised firms. Organisations with HR specialists adopted an average of 4.7 practices, whereas those firms without a specialist HR function only adopted three practices.

Table 10.6 Use of Pre-emptive HR Practices to Reduce/Avoid Workplace Disputes by HR and Union Presence (% of Firms Adopting Practice)

	HR Specialist	*General Manager*	*Union Present*	*Non Union*
Notice boards	71.5	62.9	80.0*	69.4*
Suggestion schemes	48.3	39.3	42.9	47.9
Regular use of newsletters/email	67.9***	49.4***	82.9***	61.2***
Information posted on company intranet	51.7***	25.8***	61.4**	43.2**
Regular coffee sessions, lunches etc. to identify areas of concern	27.5	20.2	28.6	25.6
Regular meetings with employee representative bodies	42.7***	18.0***	62.9***	32.2***
Use of focus groups	24.8**	10.1**	31.4**	19.9**
Periodic surveys of employee satisfaction	52.6***	23.6***	60.0**	43.8**
Use of external consultants to review dispute resolution practices	5.6	4.5	2.9	6.0

	HR Specialist	*General Manager*	*Union Present*	*Non Union*
Employees have training in coaching techniques	25.8**	12.4**	27.1	22.1
Employees have training in handling difficult conversations	38.4**	24.7**	50.0**	32.2**
Employees have training in other dispute resolution techniques	15.6	9.0	20.0	12.9

* significant at .1, ** significant at .05, *** significant at .001.

Of the twelve pre-emptive approaches used to reduce or avoid conflict, the presence of an HR specialist or trade union appears is associated with greater use of consultative voice mechanisms such as the use of regular meetings with employee representative bodies to identify growing areas of concern, the use of focus groups and periodic surveys of employee satisfaction. The use of more one-sided approaches to employee voice (Management communications on notice boards and suggestion schemes) do not appear to vary significantly dependent on the presence of an HR specialist or a trade union within the company, although the use of a company intranet and emails does appear to be greater. The presence of an HR specialist or a trade union is not associated with the use of external consultants to review company practice.

§10.06 CONCLUSIONS

The findings of this research indicate that the ubiquity of conflict in the workplace is clearly evident, although this conflict is often expressed as low-level disagreements rather than more serious manifestations, such the occurrence of tribunal cases. While conflict is pervasive, the survey data show that there is a clear impact of employment relations actors. The higher levels of disputes occurring where an HR specialist is present could reflect the nature of the type of organisation, i.e., organisations with specialist HR tend to be large firms, who, as established above, have higher levels of conflict. Alternatively, where HR professionals are in place, they may have established policies and practices that allow for the expression of views and opinions more easily. These voice mechanisms might, in turn, 'incentivise' people to speak out or disagree with established policies and practices. Identical trends are also noted for the presence of a trade union as to the presence of an in-house HR function. Similar explanations may apply here, in that larger organisations are more likely to be unionised and these unions may support employees in voicing disagreements where they occur. That is not to say that these employment relations actors cause more conflict, but this may simply be a function of creating more pathways for the expression of said conflict or even a better understanding of the presence of conflict within an organisation (Hirschmann 1970).

In answer to the first research question, organisations in Great Britain employ a wide range of approaches in addressing conflict. The presence of innovative approaches builds on the US literature and begins to demonstrate that contrary to earlier research, ADR is perhaps not just a US phenomenon (Teague et al., 2012). The difference between the study in Ireland and the data found in this paper is the focus on policy over practice. The evidence suggests that the inclusion within policy is limited, as per the Irish research but that the use of ADR practices is fairly widespread.

It is evident from the findings above is that both HR specialists and trade unions are clearly associated with the usage of conflict management policies within organisations, but this relationship varies depending on the actor and the dimension considered. In both cases, these employment relations actors appear to drive the inclusion of the ADR approaches within the practice of their respective organisation. In particular, the findings refute the earlier research (Barrett and O'Dowd 2005; Budd and Colvin 2005) that where a union is present ADR is less likely to be located. Unions in Great Britain appear to be consistent with the use of ADR, especially where those practices link to their own objectives.

The increased level of training evident where an HR Specialist is present is reflective of a desire to formalise and provide robust support for handling conflict in the workplace, which would be consistent with the professionalised nature of the HR function (Legge 2004). These differences could simply be a reflection of the nature of the organisations responding, i.e., an organisation with a trade union present is, by definition, more likely to train union representatives. An organisation with a union (probably a large organisation) is also more likely to have HR professionals in place and thus be more likely to train said HR professionals. Alternatively, the increased evidence of training of representatives in organisations with a trade union could equally be a reflection of the aims and goals pursued by trade unions, i.e., to ensure those representing the employees are able to undertake the tasks required of them.

In short, the findings in this paper suggest that employment relations actors influence the manner with which conflict handled within an organisation. The evidence suggests that HR specialists are associated with a more formalised approach to conflict approach, but one, as suggested by Lewin (Lewin 2001), that looks to keep conflict internal within organisations. While they do not reject the help of external actors in addressing conflict, the analysis suggests a clear preference for practices that occur without outside help. Unions, in contrast, also have a clear and significant impact, but a narrower focus in how they look to drive conflict management. They concentrate on particular external experts in supporting conflict management and they appear to encourage training of selected actors when it comes to handling disputes in the workplace

REFERENCES

Argyris, C. 1990. *Overcoming Organizational Defences: Facilitating Organizational Learning*. Needham Heights: Allyn and Bacon.

Barrett, J. and J. O'Dowd. 2005. *Interest-Based Bargaining: A User's Guide*. Oxford: Trafford Publishing.

Bendersky, C. 2006. 'Complementarities in Organizational Dispute Resolutions Systems: How System Characteristics Affect Individuals Conflict Experiences.' *Industrial and Labor Relations Review* 60(2): 204-222.

Budd, J. and A. Colvin. 2005. 'Balancing Efficiency Equity and Voice in Workplace Dispute Resolution Procedures.' *Human Resources Research Institute Working Paper*. Available at: Legacy-Irc.Csom.Umn.Edu.

Conbere, J. 2001. 'Theory Building for Conflict Management System Design'. *Conflict Resolution Quarterly* 19(2): 215-236.

Davis, S. 2002. 'ADR: What Is It and What Are the Pros and Cons.' Pp. 1–11 in *ADR and Commercial Disputes*, edited by R. Caller. London: Sweet & Maxwell.

Department for Business, Innovation and Skills. 2011. *Resolving Workplace Disputes: A Consultation*. Available at: https://assets.publishing.service.gov.uk/government/uploads/system/uploads/attachment_data/file/31435/11-511-resolving-workplace-disputes-consultation.pdf.

Dix, G. 2012. 'Dispute Resolution and Policy: Past, Present and Future.' *ESRC Seminar Series – October 2012*.

Dobbin, F. 2011. *Inventing Equal Opportunity*. Princeton: Princeton University Press.

Everett, C. 2017. 'Could Technology Help to Reduce Conflict at Work?' *Personnel Today* https://www.personneltoday.com/hr/technology-help-.

Hann, D., D. Nash, and E. Heery. 2019. 'Workplace Conflict Resolution in Wales: The Unexpected Prevalence of Alternative Dispute Resolution.' *Economic and Industrial Democracy* 40(3): 776-802.

Heery, E. and D. Nash. 2011. *Trade Union Officers and Collective Conciliation: A Secondary Analysis*.

Hirschmann, A. 1970. *Exit, Voice, and Loyalty – Responses to Decline in Firms, Organizations, and States*. Cambridge, MA: Harvard University Press.

Keep, E. 2014. Corporate Training Strategies: The Vital Component? In Storey, J. 'New Perspectives on Human Resource Management (Routledge Revivals)' Routledge: London 109-125.

Kochan, T.A., R.B. McKersie, and P. Cappelli. 1984. 'Strategic Choice and Industrial Relations Theory.' *Industrial Relations* 23(1): 16-39.

Legge, K. 2004. *Human Resource Management: Rhetorics and Realities*. Chippenham: MacMillan.

Lepak, D. and Snell, S. 1999. 'The Strategic Management of Human Capital: Determinants and Implications of Different Relationships'. *Academy of Management Review* 24: 1-18.

Lewin, D. 2001. 'IR and HR Perspectives on Workplace Conflict – What Can Each Learn from the Other?' *Human Resource Management Review* 11: 453-485.

Lipsky, D., A. Avgar, and J.R. Lamare. 2017. 'Organizational Conflict Resolution and Strategic Choice: Evidence from a Survey of Fortune 1000 Companies.' P. Retrieved [18/1/18], from Cornell University, ILR in *Paper Presented at Conflict and Its Resolution in the Changing World of Work: A Conference and Special Issue Honoring David B. Lipsky, Ithaca, NY*.

Lipsky, D., A. Avgar, J.R. Lamare, and A. Gupta. 2012. *The Antecedents of Workplace Conflict Management Systems in U.S. Corporations: Evidence from a New Survey of Fortune 1000 Companies. Presented to International Labour and Employment Relations Association.* Ithaca: ILR School, Cornell (draft paper).

Lipsky, D. and R. Seeber. 2000. 'Resolving Workplace Disputes in the United States: The Growth of Alternative Dispute Resolution in Employment Relations.' *Alternative Dispute Resolution in Employment* 2: 37-49.

Lipsky, D., R. Seeber, and R. Fincher. 2003. *Emerging Systems for Managing Workplace Conflict.* San Francisco: Jossey-Bass.

Nash, D. and D. Hann. 2019 'Strategic Conflict Management? A Study of Workplace Dispute Resolution in Wales.' *Industrial & Labor Relations Review.* Online First: https://doi.org/10.1177/0019793919874031.

Roche, W. and P. Teague. 2012. 'Human Resource Management and ADR Practices in Ireland.' *The International Journal of Human Resource Management* 23(3):528-549.

Roche, W., P. Teague, and A. Colvin. 2014. *The Oxford Handbook of Conflict Management in Organizations.* Oxford: Oxford University Press.

Saundry, R. and G. Dix. 2014. 'Conflict Resolution in the United Kingdom.' Pp. 475–93 in *The Oxford Handbook of Conflict Management in Organisations*, edited by W.K. Roche, P. Teague, and A. Colvin. Oxford, UK: Oxford University Press.

Teague, P., W. Roche, and D. Hann. 2012. 'The Diffusion of Alternative Dispute Resolution Practices in Ireland.' *Economic and Industrial Democracy* 33(4): 581-604.

Ulrich, D. 1998. 'A New Mandate for Human Resources.' *Harvard Business Review* 76: 124-135.

Ury, W.L., J.M. Brett, and S.B. Goldberg. 1993. *Getting Disputes Resolved: Designing Systems to Cut the Costs of Conflict.* Cambridge, MA: The Harvard Law School.

CHAPTER 11

Interest Representation in Graphic Design and Video Game Development in Italy: Demand, Supply and Influence on Working Conditions*

Lisa Dorigatti, Andrea Bellini & Cecilia Manzo

This paper explores the supply and demand side of interest representation in two creative industries in Italy and how they influence working conditions. Relying on semi-structured interviews with key informants in graphic design and video game development, we will show that the arena of interest representation is dominated by non-traditional actors - such as trade and professional associations, and informal communities - which, differently from traditional ones, do not focus on market regulation, but rather on the promotion of workers' individual capacity to stay on the market. We argue that this is connected with the peculiar way in which workers define their demands which are characterised by a strong individual orientation. As a consequence, the influence of interest representation actors on working conditions in the two sectors is rather limited.

* This paper has benefited from over two years of intense work within the working group of the IR-CREA Project (*Strategic but Vulnerable. Industrial Relations and Creative Workers*), funded by the European Commission, DG Employment, Social Affairs and Inclusion (Agreement No. VP/2015/004/0121), and carried out by research teams at the Universities of Florence, Amsterdam and Copenhagen. We are particularly grateful to the coordinator of the project, Luigi Burroni, and the other members of the group - Wike Been, Alberto Gherardini, Maarten Keune, Trine P. Larsen and Mikkel Mailand - for the many fruitful discussions. We also thank Valeria Pulignano for giving us precious feedback on a previous version of the paper.

§11.01 INTRODUCTION

The creative industries have not been a strong focus of enquiry in industrial relations research. The specialist literature has scarcely investigated the relationship between interest representation and working conditions in these sectors. What we know about work in these industries comes from media and communications scholars who, since the pioneering studies of Ursell (2000), McRobbie (2002) and Ross (2003), have analysed the characteristics of creative labour in different economic sectors. In particular, the literature highlights the existence of a tension between relatively poor working conditions and a high emotional attachment to work (Hesmondhalgh and Baker 2011). The 'passion' for work and the aspiration to work in glam sectors characterised by a crowded and competitive labour market often work like a trap, which masks and feeds a tendency towards 'self-exploitation' (Ross 2003).

The discussion of creative labour has, instead, ignored the issue of interest representation, assuming the absence of trade unions and workers' indifference to collective action as a given. This paper aims to contribute to this literature by exploring workers' demands, interest representation and working conditions in two creative industries, graphic design and video game development, in Italy. The research questions are the following. How do workers articulate their interests? What are the characteristics of interest representation? Which is the impact of interest representation on working conditions?

The empirical findings show that the actors of industrial relations do not play a significant role, while professional and trade associations and informal communities are relevant actors. The stronger role played by these actors can be explained by the fact that they seem better able to respond to the way workers articulate their interests. These, in fact, have a marked individual orientation and mostly demand support for their capacity to stay in the market (rather than regulating it, as trade unions typically do). We also show that, because of their specific characteristics, these organisations have limited impact on working conditions, the latter being influenced by other factors.

This paper provides a threefold contribution to the literature on creative labour and industrial relations in creative industries. First, by adopting a broad approach to interest representation, we highlight the existence of different types of organisations, mostly neglected by the (still limited) literature on interest representation in the creative industries, which focuses on labour (i.e., trade unions and new forms of representation), stressing the minimal relevance of collective actors. On the contrary, we show that these latter are indeed present in these sectors, but they are of a different nature (mostly trade and professional associations). Second, and relatedly, we show that the limited impact of collective organisations on working conditions is not because the former are inexistent, but because they deal with other issues, not including labour regulation. Finally, our situated comparison of two creative industries confirms the importance of recent calls to provide a more nuanced representation of creative workers. In this sense, the focus shifts from individual motivations to organisational differences and the position occupied in the labour market. This leads to questioning – at least partially – the exceptionalism of the creative industries.

This contribution unfolds as follows. The next section reviews the available literature on interest representation in the creative industries. Section §11.03 introduces the research design and the methods used and draws a picture of the contexts of the sectoral studies. Section §11.04 examines how workers articulate their interests and demands. Section §11.05 focuses on the actors of interest representation and explores their strategies, while section §11.06 focuses on their impact on working conditions. The last section discusses the research results and draws some conclusions.

§11.02 INTEREST REPRESENTATION IN THE CREATIVE INDUSTRIES: THE STATE OF THE ART

As anticipated, the literature on creative labour mostly dealt with working conditions, leaving aside issues concerning labour regulation and interest representation. The few contributions dealing with those issues can be clustered into two main streams.

The first of these looks at the attitudes of creative workers towards collective action, hence focusing on the *demand* for representation. Here, scholars converge on the idea that creatives are little inclined to collective action, for three distinct reasons. First, the constraints posed by a competitive labour market, whose functioning is based on personal reputation (Antcliff et al., 2007; Gandini 2016), reduce willingness to express grievances and join collective organisations, due to the risks of being labelled as 'troublemakers' (Hesmondhalgh and Baker 2011). Second, the individual motivation to do a job that guarantees creative autonomy and self-fulfilment often induces a certain 'fatalism' regarding the conditions in which this work is carried out, even if unfavourable (Greer et al., 2018). Several authors highlighted how the logic of union action 'discourages' unpaid or poorly paid work, which workers, instead, perceive as necessary for career development (Saundry et al., 2007; Umney and Coderre-Lapalme 2017). Third, the presence of a robust entrepreneurial mentality among creative workers, which sees good working conditions as praise for individual success and considers bad ones a sign of failure, reinforces an 'entrepreneurial self' (Dardot and Laval 2009), hardly attuned to collective action.

The second stream – not always dealing with creative labour per se, but often using the creative industries as an empirical locus of research – deals with the *supply* of representation and, particularly, with the strategies implemented by trade unions and other collective actors to organise creative workers. This literature most strongly highlighted that, to represent these workers, both traditional unions and new organisations – also referred to as 'quasi-unions' (Heckscher and Carré 2006) or 'proto-unions' (Sullivan 2010) – developed strategies focused more on the provision of services than on market regulation (Heery and Adler 2004; Saundry et al., 2007).

This contribution aims to combine the insights provided by these two literature strands to analyse the relationship between the way workers articulate their interests, the configuration of interest representation, and working conditions. The comparison between two sectors enables us to contextualise these dynamics.

§11.03 THE RESEARCH

[A] Scope, Design and Methods

This contribution is based on the results of a broader research project (for further details, *see* Bellini et al., 2018a, 2018b), which examined interest representation in two creative industries: graphic design and video game development. The choice of sectors aimed to explore the heterogeneity of creative industries. Indeed, they represent radically different cases, with graphic design originating partly in traditional and strongly unionised industries, such as publishing and printing, and video game development being a new sector with no traditions in industrial relations.

The research design was based on a multilevel analytical approach. First, we mapped interest representation at the national level, through interviews with key informants (i.e., union and employers' representatives, policymakers, experts). Then, we focused on company cases and individuals (employers, employees, freelancers), investigating their needs and demands, as well as the strategies pursued to advance them.

A total of forty-five semi-structured interviews were carried out: fifteen at the national level, nine in graphic design and twenty-one in video game development (*see* Table 1, Annex). At the company level, specifically, we selected at least three company cases per sector to guarantee a variety of business models, occupational positions and membership statuses. Different sources were used to identify the interviewees: preliminary explorations with the associations and professional social networks (e.g., LinkedIn) gave rise to the first contacts; then, word of mouth, following a 'snowball' procedure, allowed for a larger sample.

[B] The Contexts of the Sectoral Studies

Graphic design and video game development differ significantly in their essential features, which makes the comparison between them meaningful. Graphic design is a typical business service sector and is highly segmented, based on the field of activity and the type and size of clients. Video game development is part of the video game industry and contributes to the production of different products: personal computer C and console games, mobile games, and applied games.

Both sectors are relatively small in size and fragmented. Small firms are prevalent, and freelance work is common, although this is far more pronounced in graphic design. More than 80% of about 13,000 companies in the graphic design industry are individual firms or self-employed workers (Istat, based on the *Statistical Register of Active Enterprises*, 2015), compared to 40% of only 120 companies in video game development (AESVI, *Third Census of Italian Game Developers*, 2016).

Freelancers represent the dominant employment model, especially in graphic design, where they practise either alone (in individual studios, co-working spaces or at home) or in informal partnerships. In video game development, they also are a significant number, although they mostly work 'for hire' in other companies and are integrated into the production process on a project basis.

A first model of business organisation is that of *small teams*. They are based on informal coalitions of freelancers, either stable (i.e., aimed at sharing fixed costs or collaborating under a common brand) or not (i.e., built around a specific project and terminating with that). In video game development, these organisations are concentrated in the segments of mobile and applied games, since they do not have the financial or human resources to develop complex games. A second model is constituted by *small firms*, which are often the 'juridification' of a (previously informal) small team. Usually, they are built around a core of salaried workers and a variable geometry of freelancers, hired as needed to carry out specific activities. Lastly, we find *larger companies*, which typically rely on more stable forms of employment. Still, job mobility is reported to be high, and workers frequently move after completing a project.

The rise and persistence of these models have been significantly influenced by technological innovations. In video game development, for example, the diffusion of mobile devices has reduced development costs, 'democratising' access to the market and making it possible for small teams and firms to enter the business (Parker et al., 2014). In graphic design, the emergence of the disruptive phenomenon of online work platforms opened up the market of 'online freelancing'. However, the dominant trigger of freelancing was the transformation of the way graphic designers' usual employers, like publishing and printing companies, organise their production process. Indeed, over the last twenty years, these companies have outsourced more and more functions, facilitating the emergence of a flexible mode of production, relying on freelance work.

§11.04 WHAT WORKERS WANT: AN ANALYSIS ON THE DEMAND SIDE

This section examines how workers articulate their interests and the demands they formulate concerning their employment statuses and working conditions. The first element to be highlighted is a strong individual focus in terms of how workers define their demands. This is probably connected to the diffusion of freelance work, but also to the particular characteristics of the two sectors. In the graphic design industry, professionalism is central to workers' self-identification, and the connected aspiration to autonomy, self-expression and self-fulfilment tends to reduce the likelihood of interests being articulated collectively. In the videogame industry, the lack of a collective dimension might depend on the relative 'newness' of the sector, which has no collective legacies or previous representation structures. The workers perceive those somehow connected with the sector (as we will see below, the metalworkers' unions signed the collective agreement most widely applied by video game companies) as being too far from their experience. Still, the absence of collective structures as an inhibitory factor to the collective articulation of workers' interests is also visible in graphic design. Apparently, the transformations that took place in this sector (companies' fragmentation and outsourcing) have dismantled those collective institutions which characterised the industries (publishing and printing) from which graphic design originates. Furthermore, in both sectors, the small size of companies, managerial styles (with a diffused presence of open-door policies) and work organisation (characterised by flat organisational structures) coalesce in favouring the development of informal relationships between workers and employers. This, in turn, fosters individualised approaches and reduces the perceived need for collective action.

Still, both sectors seem to be characterised by the predominance of *exit* over *voice* strategies. The interviewees reported several instances in which, confronted with working conditions that they considered unacceptable or not meeting their expectations, they responded by leaving the company. This suggests that, notwithstanding open-door policies, workers are quite aware of the power relations characterising their workplaces and the difficulty of expressing grievances or producing changes in the way companies operate.

Only rarely do workers express the need for changes in the way work is regulated. In graphic design, specifically, complaints are related to concrete problems of freelancers, whose work and income discontinuity implies, for instance, difficulty in paying insurance contributions in due time, not compensated by protections in case of unemployment, illness or maternity. In this regard, a designer, a 50-year-old woman, reveals the perception of an unfavourable cost-benefit ratio:

> As a freelancer, I must give all the money to the INPS [the National Social Security Institute]. [...] But it doesn't give me anything, zero. If I get sick or pregnant, I get nothing. But I have paid 27 per cent [contributions]... [Graphic design, freelancer, Int. 17]

This leads the workers to adopt a 'pragmatic' attitude and focus on 'urgent' needs – that is, raising or maintaining income levels, as a younger graphic designer testifies:

> I don't care about the pension. [...] The accountant gave me an opportunity ... he told me that with my taxation regime I could pay 30 per cent less [of contributions] ... but I would be covered for 9 months instead of 12. Yes, I said. Let's do it. [Graphic design, freelancer, Int. 22]

Second, we identified two somewhat contrasting stances among workers in the two industries. On the one hand, several interviewees expressed a feeling of resignation concerning working conditions. They often perceived the acceptance of relatively poor working conditions as the price to pay for being able to do a job they love. Expressions like 'That's simply the way it is if you want to work in the sector' [Videogame development, employee, Int. 25], 'We're not here for the money' [Videogame development, employee, Int. 34] or 'It's our passion, it doesn't really look like working' [Graphic design, employer, Int. 20] were, in fact, rather common. Still, while important, this argument needs to be qualified and related to other aspects, such as the configuration of the labour market and workers' characteristics (skills and competencies, age and family status). Indeed, this trade-off seemed to play out differently across different groups of workers in the two industries. This attitude seems to be widely diffused among younger workers, who still enjoy the support of their families and do not have family responsibilities of their own. The existence of different phases in workers' life courses and the influence of those phases on how workers strike a balance between *intrinsic* and *extrinsic* motivations towards work is highlighted by the words of a video game programmer, who argued:

> Passion for our work is here and will always be, but when the time comes when you have to choose whether to start a family, to buy a house etc., or to remain in the sector ... then, you may also decide to leave the sector, if things do not change. [Video game development, employee, Int. 34]

Such a resigned attitude seemed to be widespread, especially among workers with a weaker labour market position. Across the two industries, it seemed to be more diffused in graphic design rather than video game development and, within the latter, among artists rather than programmers.

At the other extreme is a robust entrepreneurial mentality and a keen perception of being able to 'do it alone'. This approach can be traced back to the idea that good working conditions are a consequence of the individual capacity to stay in the market and, conversely, that poor working conditions are a sign of personal failure. This attitude seems to be stronger in the video game industry and is probably due to the fact that this is a new and boosting industry, predominantly composed of young workers, with a significant share of workers, particularly programmers, with strong competencies and strong positions in the labour market. These characteristics sustain a way to look at labour market issues focused on individual capacities and strength. For example, concerning the risk of not having a pension when retiring, a freelance worker, which is also the founder of a start-up, argued:

> If I get to 60-70 years of age, and I need a pension to survive, this means that I have done something wrong. [...] If things work, I should be able to put enough money aside for my old years. [...] I never thought that I would need a pension to survive when I'm old. [Video game development, freelancer, Int. 45]

In the video game industry, the idea that working conditions are intimately connected with sectoral competitiveness and the needs of a sector that is still in its infant phase of development is not limited to freelancers but is diffused among salaried workers as well. Moreover, the perception that workers and employers share the same interests and that working conditions can improve only if the sector develops is quite widespread, as well expressed by the words of an employee, who argued:

> Those who work and those who manage, they basically have the same problems. So, in reality, nothing can be solved by trade unions. It is not that managers exploit the situation to underpay the workers. [...] The issue is to make a common front towards public institutions to try to have facilities and aids. [Video game development, employee, Int. 29]

Hence, competitiveness policies supporting the development of the sector are perceived as the only instrument that can have an impact on working conditions.

Still, the assumption that good working conditions derive from workers' capacity to be successful in the market rather than from market regulation is also common in the graphic design industry. However, in graphic design, it is somewhat counterbalanced by the perception of a lack of social recognition. According to several interviewees, clients' deficiency of competencies, together with the diffusion of easy-to-use do-it-yourself design tools, led to an undervaluation of the profession and the spreading of practices that contributed to deteriorating the market, such as race-to-the-bottom competitions or free-of-charge contests for design activities. The awareness of challenging market conditions, though, generally translates into a claim of recognition of the professional nature of work in the industry, which mainly takes the form of a demand for certifications of professionalism. Hence, in both sectors, workers' requests are not connected to issues of regulation, but rather to initiatives enabling them to strengthen their positions in the market. As we will see below, this influences the configuration of interest representation significantly.

The last element worth noting is workers' search for support by their peers. Both industries are, indeed, characterised by extensive informal interactions among the workers, which often take place in both online and offline communities as well as in physical sectoral events. These 'communities of coping' respond to different demands: first, the need to avoid isolation and the lack of sociability, closely connected with the broad diffusion of freelance work, which reduces room for interaction among the workers, through the exchange of experiences and the feeling of being part of a community; second, the request of practical, work-related support, informal training and information exchange - for example, on technical matters and market dynamics. These informal communities might be interpreted as a functional substitute for more formal ways of collectively articulating workers' interests but, again, are focused on providing resources for navigating the market. Indeed, they rarely qualify as platforms for organising workers around labour issues.

§11.05 WHAT COLLECTIVE ORGANISATIONS DO: AN INSIGHT INTO THE SUPPLY SIDE

The way workers articulate their interests and formulate their demands is mirrored in the configuration of interest representation in the two sectors, namely the actors populating it, their specific weight, their logics of action and practices.

To begin with, the *actors of industrial relations* – i.e., trade unions and employers' associations – play a limited role. Union membership is negligible, and companies tend not to join employers' associations. This is, of course, truer for graphic design, which is dominated by self-employment with a marked professional character, although video game development is also characterised by a high share of self-employed workers and small firms. As a matter of fact, the target groups of these organisations are still salaried workers and larger firms, respectively. In both sectors, however, the social partners play an 'indirect' role: they sign the industry-wide agreements that companies apply, although these agreements are not devised for the two sectors. In this sense, companies engage in a sort of 'institutional shopping', borrowing forms of regulation developed for other sectors. This occurs more frequently in the case of video game companies, because of the higher proportion of salaried workers in the sector. As reported by key informants, these mostly refer to the metalworking or retail agreements. Small graphic design firms, instead, apply different collective agreements, depending on the reference market segment. Besides, creative workers benefit from the outcomes of social negotiation on welfare issues, which takes place at the cross-industry level.

Experimental forms of trade unionism can, however, be found that are targeted to freelance workers. Two examples are given by the Professional Workers' Council of CGIL (the Italian General Confederation of Labour) and vIVAce (community of indipendent workers), an association affiliated to CISL (Italian Confederation of Workers' Trade Unions). These are peculiar cases in the Italian landscape which are nevertheless most likely to have an indirect impact on employment relations in the two sectors, basically through lobbying activities aimed at influencing public policies or, in the case of Vivace, the provision of services addressed to freelancers overall.

Here, a remark must be made about the workers' unawareness of what trade unions do. Few interviewees, indeed, referred to collective agreements, none to strikes or workplace representation bodies nor to the new organisations just mentioned. Some of them perceive these actors as absent: 'Perhaps it's my fault, but I don't see them' [Graphic design, freelancer, Int. 19]; 'Trade unions represent other categories of workers' [Graphic design, freelancer, Int. 18]. Others complain that trade unions do not comprehend the nature of their work or are very detached from their experience: 'I feel like they don't understand me' [Graphic design, freelancer, Int. 17]; We are with the metalworkers union, but we have nothing to do with that, at all [Video game development, employee, Int. 34].

Professional and trade associations are the dominant actors in the realm of interest representation within the two sectors, also widely recognised by the workers interviewed. In the graphic design industry, the leading role is played by AIAP (the Italian Association of Visual Communication Design), a professional association of graphic designers which performs the dual function of cultural promotion and professional regulation, although in a 'soft' sense, since neither a specific education or qualification nor associative membership are necessary conditions to practise the profession. This regulatory function, nevertheless, focuses more on ensuring that market actors recognise (and, thus, adequately remunerate) professional competencies, rather than on setting standards and rules. In the video game industry, the most significant role is played by AESVI, a trade association affiliated to Confindustria, which focuses on promoting the development of the sector. Even though they are different from each other in their characters and functions – AIAP represents professionals (i.e., individuals), AESVI organises businesses – these organisations have relevant similarities in their strategies and modes of action. None of them engages in collective bargaining, while both carry out lobbying activities to influence the public policies that might have an impact on the sectors. Two examples are the extension of the tax credit policy applied to the film and audiovisual industry to video game companies, fostered by AESVI, and the process of institutionalisation started by AIAP under Law No. 4/2003, which indeed should lead the association of graphic designers to exert a 'soft' regulatory power through the release of a certification of quality. In the video game industry, particularly, AESVI's approach has a broad consensus also among the workers, the development of the sector being considered as the best way to improve working conditions. Moreover, both associations engage in the provision of services (e.g., information, training, legal assistance and, in the case of AESVI, mentorship in the phase of business start-ups, and support for internationalisation), aimed at either enabling or strengthening the individual capacity to stay in the market, which is particularly important for freelancers and small firms. They are also active in cultural promotion, mostly exercised through the organisation of exhibitions and events, e.g., Design Per, the Italian Game Developer Summit (IGDS) and the Milan Games Week. Both associations tend to concentrate their efforts in the promotion of the sectors themselves, hence representing all the subjects involved therein, irrespective of their employment status. Even though it is formally a business association and organises companies, for instance, most workers employed in the video game industry consider AESVI their only representative organisation:

> I know one that is AESVI, which is the representative of Italian video game developers and it's responsible for raising [...] the problems of video game development, also at the level of professional figures, conditions ... [Video game development, employee, Int. 33]

Similar activities are carried out by emerging actors, such as ACTA (Italian association that gives representation to high-skilled self-employed workers), which represents freelancers on a cross-industry basis. What is worth noting about ACTA is its pragmatic attitude, translating into protest actions targeted to specific issues, carried out through innovative methods (e.g., occupations, flash mobs, tweet and fax bombing). This gives ACTA greater visibility and allows it to be recognised as an influential actor, above all in the graphic design industry: 'ACTA is the only association that has some merit, because it fought to avoid the increase of insurance contributions from 27 to 33 percent' [Graphic design, freelancer, Int. 17].

The tendency towards the individualisation of employment relations, the absence of specific trade unions and the structural weakness of other relevant organisations, associated with a certain reluctance of both workers and employers to join any form of collective action, contribute to explaining the existence of a 'latent' demand for representation. This demand finds responses in new forms of organisation and modes of regulation of a 'communitarian' type. The latter provides several forms of support to the workers, again strengthening their individual capacity to stay in the market by counterbalancing market dynamics, although not being involved in market regulation.

A first example is given by *online and offline communities* (e.g., I Pirati Grafici and Roba da Grafici among graphic designers; Gameprog, Indievault and Gameloop among video game developers), some of them based on Facebook groups (e.g., Grafici Creativi, Develop Gamez, and Indie Game Developers). Their main goals are to provide information on cultural events, job and training opportunities and deal with other issues relevant to people working in the two sectors. Besides, they are platforms for the exchange of experiences and, as such, they are key agents in the process of building professional communities 'from the bottom'.

A second case is represented by *mutual cooperatives*. The most interesting experience is that of Smart-It, an independent branch of a not-for-profit organisation born in Belgium in 1998, with almost 90,000 working members in Europe, whose role is likely to grow, especially among graphic designers. In brief, the philosophy of

Smart-It is to 'hire' artists and creatives to give them the same protection as salaried workers. The role of Smart-It is, indeed, recognised by key actors, such as ACTA, but, at the time of writing, has no relationships with the unions.

§11.06 WHAT IMPACT ON WORKING CONDITIONS?

What emerges from the research is the limited capacity of the actors of interest representation in the two sectors to influence working conditions. As we have seen, an indirect role is played by the traditional actors of industrial relations for salaried workers. In effect, companies in the two sectors – and, more systematically, those in the video game industry – do apply collective agreements. Still, we are facing, here, a case of 'regulation without representation', since employers and workers neither take part in negotiations nor are 'under the radar' of representative organisations. Non-traditional organisations do not focus on the issue of working conditions, although they exert an indirect influence on them by strengthening individuals' positions in the market. Hence, other factors than dynamics connected with interest representation play a dominant role in influencing them. We show that the type of organisation workers are employed in, the contract they are employed with, and the skills they possess are crucial for explaining variance in this regard.

The first source of segmentation, particularly evident in the video game industry, is constituted by *professional profiles*. This industry includes a variety of figures, with different skills and power resources, such as game developers (programmers), game designers, artists and animators, and administrative staff. Programmers represent the strongest segment, as their competencies are highly requested both in the video game industry and in other, better paying and more secure industries. Artistic work, however, seems to suffer from a lack of recognition, which contributes to explaining why artists are more exposed to lower wages. Similarly, in graphic design, two main types of freelancers can be identified, differing in the market position and related power resources: those who have 'direct' clients and those who do not. In both cases, they can be either in exclusive or multiple licensing, the former not necessarily meaning bogus self-employment – it could also be a case, for instance, of a job for a big client taking all the time, but ensuring high earnings.

The diversity of employment status is reflected in various aspects of working conditions, namely career development, working hours, earnings and access to welfare. In both sectors, *careers* are characterised by frequent changes of employer as well as transitions to and from self-employment. However, the insecurity deriving from discontinuity mostly affects workers employed by smaller firms or self-employed, while those in larger firms more often change their employment status voluntarily. In video game development, the main difference is, again, between programmers and artists, the latter being more exposed to free work. In graphic design it is more common for the reiteration of experiences of unpaid internships and bogus self-employment to translate into a 'precarisation trap', mostly affecting younger generations.

Working hours are a controversial issue. In graphic design, freelancers – especially in early years – tend to work often on weekends and bank holidays and more hours per day than those required by standard contracts. At the opposite end, larger firms require more commitment from their employees, which may translate into longer working hours. Small teams and firms have a more flexible organisation. Generally, growth in size can solve the problems related to the organisation of time and gives graphic designers more power in negotiations with clients, but nevertheless does not preclude that they may carry out practices of 'self-exploitation'. In video game development, working hours are ordinarily long and unpredictable, often extending into the weekends, especially during 'crunch times' (i.e., when deadlines for development milestones are approaching). Freelancers and small teams reported longer working hours and a frequent recourse to work during the weekends, while large video game companies adopt management strategies to avoid excessive working hours.

Earnings are also reported to be comparatively low, though to different extents and with some exceptions. In graphic design, employment relations are highly individualised. The outcomes of negotiations, therefore, vary greatly, depending on the type of client, the project and, even, contingencies. In video game development, the situation is more clearly stratified, with employees enjoying higher earnings and freelancers and workers in small teams earning little money. If we look at the professional profile, programmers working in the video game industry are penalised compared to similar figures working in other sectors, while artists and game designers, paradoxically, find the best-paid employment opportunities in the video game industry, especially when they are in salaried positions.

Concerning *access to welfare*, especially among graphic designers, freelancers do not seem to be fully aware of their vulnerability in terms of ability to manage the risks related to periods of unemployment, sickness or maternity. Some of them, when interviewed, stated that they will deal with these problems if needed, and that, if they cannot work, they will outsource part of their work to colleagues, stressing the importance of informal networks. A similar attitude was found among video game developers. Some interviewees, while expressing a certain 'disinterest' due to the temporal distance between the current phase of their career and the end of it, expressed their pessimism about the probability of being granted an adequate pension when they retire.

§11.07 CONCLUSIONS

Based on the study of two distinct sectors within the creative industries, namely graphic design and video game development, this contribution has analysed the relationship between the way workers articulate their interests, the configuration of interest representation, and working conditions. We have shown that workers in both sectors tend to represent their situations and define their demands in an individualistic manner, with minimal collective orientation. This tendency is further supported, especially in video game development, by the presence of flat organisational hierarchies and close (often personal) relationships between workers and employers, which, in larger organisations, are also fostered by specific human resource management strategies, such as open-door policies. Professionalism, instead, seems to be the dominant logic in graphic design, where workers' aspiration to autonomy and desire for self-expression and self-fulfilment tends to reduce their propensity to organise collectively. These individualistic attitudes are strongly connected with two partially contradictory stances expressed by the workers: fatalism regarding working conditions, considered the price to pay for being able to do a job workers are passionate about, and a robust entrepreneurial mentality, which considers working conditions as the result of individual success (or lack thereof). Both stances further reinforce the appeal of individualistic, market-supporting demands over collective, market-regulating ones.

The way workers articulate their interests is crucial for explaining the specific configuration of interest representation in the two sectors. The traditional actors of industrial relations, in effect, play a marginal and mostly indirect role in these industries, probably because their logic of action – relying on a collective approach to regulation – indeed, is not attuned to creative workers. Other actors, particularly trade and professional associations, seem to be more in line with how these workers perceive their situations and, therefore, tend to play a dominant role. Their representation strategies are remarkably different from those of traditional actors: while the latter concentrate on market regulation, mostly by engaging in collective bargaining, the former focus on fostering workers' and companies' capacity to stay in the market, supporting them through the provision of services and carrying out lobbying activities.

The configuration of interest representation, in turn, contributes to explaining the limited impact of collective action on working conditions. In effect, this is not due, as generally implied by the specialist literature, to the *absence* of collective organisations (which are, in fact, present) but to their *inherent characteristics*. Because they are focused on helping workers to navigate the market and supporting individual careers, these organisations do not affect the way the labour market works and, consequently, workers' employment statuses. As we have shown, these are influenced by other factors, such as the type of organisation workers are employed in, the contract they are employed with, and the skills they possess.

Lastly, our findings have basically confirmed the centrality of passion for work and self-fulfilment through work for creative labourers, as well as the existence of a trade-off between the possibility to do the job they love and the acceptance of relatively poor working conditions. But they have also revealed that there is a wide variation in working conditions across the two sectors studied and different groups of workers. This implies that, in order to account for working conditions in the creative industries, we need to qualify the character of creative labour as a 'labour of love' (McRobbie 2002) and take into consideration not only individual motivations and behaviours (Gill and Pratt 2008), but also, and more prominently, labour-market and organisational dynamics. In this sense, this paper responded to calls for more empirically grounded and nuanced representations of creative labour and for going beyond accounts which emphasise the exceptionality of creative labour as trapped in a trade-off between passion and poor working conditions (Smith and McKinley 2009; Thompson et al., 2016).

REFERENCES

Antcliff V., Saundry R., Stuart M. (2007), Networks and Social Capital in the UK Television Industry: The Weakness of Weak Ties, *Human Relations*, 60(2): 371-393.

Bellini A., Burroni L., Dorigatti L. (2018a), *Industrial Relations and Creative Workers. Country Report: Italy*, IR-CREA Project, Research Report.

Bellini A., et al. (2018b), *Industrial Relations and Creative Workers. Overall Report*, IR-CREA Project, Research Report.

Dardot P., Laval C. (2009), *La nouvelle raison du monde. Essai sur la société néolibérale*, Paris: La Découverte.

Gandini A. (2016), Digital Work. Self-Branding and Social Capital in the Freelance Knowledge Economy, *Marketing Theory*, 16(1): 123-141.

Gill R., Pratt A. (2008), In the Social Factory? Immaterial Labour, Precariousness and Cultural Work, *Theory, Culture and Society*, 25(7-8): 1-30.

Greer I., Samaluk B., Umney C. (2018), Better Strategies for Herding Cats? Forms of Solidarity Among Freelance Musicians in London, Paris and Ljubljana, in V. Doellgast, N. Lillie, V. Pulignano (eds), *Reconstructing Solidarity. Labour Unions, Precarious Work, and the Politics of Institutional Change in Europe*, Oxford: Oxford University Press, 166-187.

Heckscher C., Carré F. (2006), Strength in Networks: Employment Rights Organisations and the Problem of Co-ordination, *British Journal of Industrial Relations*, 44(4): 605-628.

Heery E., Adler L. (2004), Organizing the Unorganized, in C. Frege, J. Kelly (eds), *Varieties of Unionism: Strategies for Union Revitalisation in a Globalizing Economy*, Oxford: Oxford University Press, 45-69.

Hesmondhalgh D., Baker S. (2011), *Creative Labour: Media Work in Three Cultural Industries*, London-New York: Routledge.

McRobbie A. (2002), Clubs to Companies: Notes on the Decline of Political Culture in Speeded up Creative Worlds, *Cultural Studies*, 16(4): 516-531.

Parker R., Cox S., Thompson P. (2014), How Technological Change Affects Power Relations in Global Markets: Remote Developers in the Console and Mobile Games Industry, *Environment and Planning A*, 46(1): 168-185.

Ross A. (2003), *No-Collar: The Humane Workplace and Its Hidden Costs*, New York: Basic Books.

Saundry R., Stuart M., Antcliff V. (2007), Broadcasting Discontent – Freelancers, Trade Unions and the Internet, *New Technology, Work and Employment*, 22(2): 178-191.

Smith C., McKinley A. (2009), Creative Industries and Labour Process Analysis, in A. McKinley, C. Smith (eds), *Creative Labour: Working in the Creative Industries*, Basingstoke: Palgrave Macmillan, 3-28.

Sullivan R. (2010). Organizing Workers in the Space Between Unions: Union-Centric Labor Revitalization and the Role of Community-Based Organizations, *Critical Sociology*, 36(6): 793-819.

Thompson P., Parker R., Cox S. (2016), Interrogating Creative Theory and Creative Work: Inside the Games Studio, *Sociology*, 50(2): 316-332.

Umney C., Coderre-Lapalme G. (2017), Blocked and New Frontiers for Trade Unions: Contesting 'the Meaning of Work' in the Creative and Caring Sectors, *British Journal of Industrial Relations*, 55(4): 859-878.

Ursell G. (2000), Television Production: Issues of Exploitation, Commodification and Subjectivity in UK Television Markets, *Media, Culture and Society*, 22(6): 805-825.

ANNEX

Table 1 List of Interviews

No.	Type of interviewee or sector	Type of Organisation or Occupational Status
01	Stakeholder	Association of freelancers
02	Stakeholder	Employers' association (video games)
03	Stakeholder	Professional association (graphic design)
04	Stakeholder	Employers' association (high-skilled services)
05	Stakeholder	Employers' association (cross-industry)
06	Stakeholder	Trade union (cross-industry)
07	Stakeholder	Trade union (trade and services)
08	Stakeholder	Higher-education institute (graphic design)
09	Stakeholder	Online community (graphic design)
10	Stakeholder	University (video games)
11	Stakeholder	Regional government
12	Stakeholder	Trade union (high-skilled services)
13	Stakeholder	Trade union (high-skilled services)
14	Stakeholder	Mutual cooperative
15	Stakeholder	Trade union (cross-industry)
16	Graphic design	Freelancer
17	Graphic design	Freelancer
18	Graphic design	Freelancer
19	Graphic design	Freelancer
20	Graphic design	Employer
21	Graphic design	Employee
22	Graphic design	Freelancer
23	Graphic design	Employee
24	Graphic design	Employee/Freelancer
25	Video game development	Employee
26	Video game development	Employee
27	Video game development	Employee

No.	Type of interviewee or sector	Type of Organisation or Occupational Status
28	Video game development	Employer
29	Video game development	Employee
30	Video game development	Freelancer
31	Video game development	Employer
32	Video game development	Employee
33	Video game development	Employee
34	Video game development	Employee
35	Video game development	Employee
36	Video game development	Freelancer
37	Video game development	Employer
38	Video game development	Freelancer
39	Video game development	Freelancer
40	Video game development	Employee
41	Video game development	Employee
42	Video game development	Employee
43	Video game development	Employer
44	Video game development	Employee
45	Video game development	Freelancer

CHAPTER 12

Lay Labour Court Judges as Industrial Relations Actors In Germany, Great Britain and France. Can Field Theory Contribute to Comparative Research?

Pete Burgess, Susan Corby, Armin Höland, Hélène Michel & Laurent Willemez

In Germany, Great Britain and France employment rights disputes are adjudicated in labour courts in which lay judges play a decisive role. This chapter outlines the key findings of a recent study into lay labour court judges in these three countries.[1] It then explores how these might be understood as industrial relations (IR) actors and whether field theory might help in understanding the relationships between the IR and legal fields in the selected countries.

§12.01 INTRODUCTION

Labour courts are a central institution for resolving employment rights disputes and with this a core element in both employment regulation and IR. Labour courts in the three selected countries deal with a total of some 600,000 fresh claims each year, although the proportion of cases that go to a full hearing in a labour court is much smaller. Dismissal claims dominate in France and Germany, but there are many other significant areas, notably pay; and in Great Britain, there is a particular focus on discrimination. In France, judgments at the first merits hearing are mostly made by lay judges without the involvement of professionals, who only preside if the lay judges cannot agree. In Germany and Great Britain, lay judges will always sit with a

1. Burgess et al., 2017.

professional. And in Great Britain, uniquely, most contested dismissal cases are now heard by a professional judge sitting alone.[2]

Based on recent research, this chapter explores whether lay judges might be classified as 'industrial relations actors' located, for varying amounts of time and with varying intensity, in the 'juridical field' (Bourdieu, 1987), and what implications this might have for understanding the relationships between these spheres. This has an institutional and comparative aspect, given the differences between IR and labour courts as between the three countries. It also has a 'subjective' aspect in terms of the, sometimes contrasting, perspectives of both interviewees and researchers. In this context, we consider the variant of field theory developed by Fligstein and McAdam (2012). Interest in this approach emerged from a critical appreciation of Bourdieu's depiction of the juridical field and analyses of Bourdieu (*see* Hilgers and Mangez, 2015).

The chapter begins with an overview of the context and main findings of the research (sections §11.02 and §11.03). Drawing on this, in section §11.04 the chapter then turns to the issue of whether these findings support the characterisation of the 'juridical field' advanced by Bourdieu (1987) or whether alternative versions of the field-theory approach are more appropriate.

§12.02 CONTEXT

There are some 14,500 lay judges in France, (approximately one *employee* lay judge per 3,000 employees), some 24,000 lay judges in Germany (roughly one employee lay judge per 3,000 employees), and some 1,000 lay judges in Britain (roughly one employee lay judge per 56,000 employees). These ratios give an initial indication of the relationship between the IR field and the labour court field in the three countries, crystallised in the volume of lay judge recruitment required in each country from their respective institutions to maintain the desired numbers.

Labour courts were found to have been subject to actual or potentially disruptive change in all three countries, highlighting the relationships with other fields. In France, recent changes have seen a switch from a system under which lay judges were elected to one in which lay judges will be nominated by trade unions and employer organisations. In this respect, the bond between the IR and labour court fields will remain a close one.

In Germany, lay judges are appointed by the authorities after nominations from trade unions and employer associations. A public debate in the early-2000s centred on the merits of abolishing labour courts as a separate system. This was not 'state-led', but did find some support, at least temporarily, from some business organisations. This debate has since abated, arguably due to recent improvements in relationships between the main labour market actors after the financial crisis.

2. We refer to non-legally qualified judges as 'lay judges': local designations include 'ehrenamtliche Arbeitsrichter', 'conseillers', 'juges', and 'lay members'.

In Great Britain, lay judges are appointed by the judicial authorities via open competition after applications from individuals. Before 1999, lay judges were nominated by trade unions and employer associations. A transformation took place under the 1997-2010 Labour government, in part as a reform in access to all public appointments but also reflecting a weakening of intermediate institutions, when the right of unions and employer associations to nominate candidates was abolished. More recently, lay judges have been effectively removed from deciding on most stand-alone dismissal claims, which are now mainly heard solely by a professional judge. Because of a fall in the number of cases requiring lay participation, no new recruitment occurred between 2009 and 2019, leading to an ageing cohort.

§12.03 COMPARATIVE RESEARCH ON LAY LABOUR COURT JUDGES: SELECTED FINDINGS[3]

This chapter builds on a study of lay labour court judges in France, Germany and Great Britain, carried out in 2015-2017, which aimed to compare the resources available to lay judges, investigate how lay judges perceive their role; examine relationships between professional and lay judges, and understand the lay judges' contribution to the judicial process. Data was collected via c.180 semi-structured interviews with lay and professional judges, supplemented by 'expert' interviews for detail on institutional aspects. Below we briefly review the findings and their implications for some of the main areas of relevant theory.

[A] The Influence of National IR Systems

The main influence on lay judges was the IR system in each country (with its associated impact on the route to nomination), mediated by labour court structures and operations. Lay judges generally have experience of organised IR in France and Germany. The position is different in Britain, where candidates for lay judge office nominate themselves and are formally evaluated by the authorities, weakening the link between the IR system and the labour court system: for example, of the forty-one British employee lay judge interviewees, fourteen were not (no longer) union members and nearly a quarter (ten out of forty-one) said that they were self-employed/partially retired and so had no *current* experience of organised IR.

National IR systems have been assigned to a range of typologies. Typically, Germany is seen as corporatist, Britain voluntarist, and France adversarial. Lay judges' reports often reflected these models. Individualism appeared higher in Britain than elsewhere. German interviewees' reports were marked by their experience of workplace codetermination. Some lay judges also referred to how labour courts stood in relation to the wider constitutional system, which they were keen to help sustain as a

3. Interview quotes can be found in the final reports. The 'Working Paper' is available on https://www.boeckler.de/64509.htm?produkt=HBS-006695&chunk=1&jahr and an extended version of the report on https://halshs.archives-ouvertes.fr/halshs-01616783/document.

form of civic engagement. And French employee interviewees tended to view trade unions as the sole legitimate channel for representation. What the adversarial model for France does not sufficiently capture, however, is the aspiration for agreement between employee and employer lay judges, rooted in both a desire to keep professional judges at a distance and preserve the distinctive lay quality and independence of the French labour court with its roots in IR but also a commitment to apply the law.

[B] Motivations

Lay judges reported a range of motives – instrumental, normative, personal – with some national patterns. In Germany, the most common motive for seeking office was to improve legal knowledge and transfer it back to the workplace. In France, employee lay judges had close links with trade unions: for some, being a lay judge was part of a wider 'career' as an employee representative. In Great Britain too, there was a link to workplace representation, but also evidence of individual motives, especially for employer lay judges involved in HRM/consultancy. Some British lay judges also took up the role later in their careers or following a redundancy, with lay judge activity seen as part of the reconfiguring of their professional and civic lives.

This multiplicity of motives chimes with the argument that lay activity results from a combination of 'instrumental' and 'normative' elements (Hollstein, 2015). These motives fit less well with the distinctive notion of *interest representation*, however, highlighting the intersection of the legal and IR fields in labour courts. Wanting to act as a representative is not reducible to 'instrumentalism' or 'altruism'. 'Instrumental' might be understood as 'rational-purposive' (being a 'better representative') or self-interest ('helping my career'). And representing a social interest (on occasions seen in class term) is more complex than 'altruism'.

[C] Adaptation to the Labour Court Role: Maintaining Impartiality

Lay judges, not only but especially from the employee side, might arguably experience and need to resolve a clash between their role as a representative ('partisan') and as a judicial decision-maker ('neutral'). This led us to look at actor-centred and micro-sociological theories, such as cognitive dissonance and 'self-consistency' theory, and interactionist theories of role (Festinger, 1957; Aronson, 1992; Goffman, 1961). At the same time, these theories raised their own difficulties; in some instances, they appeared to be incompatible.

We found that being a lay judge was generally not seen as interest representation; or rather any such sense became modified through exercising judicial office and being exposed to the culture of the court. Nevertheless, there were national differences. In Germany, adaptation took place quite swiftly, despite the lack of a mandatory induction procedure; lay judges from both sides reported the influence of the culture of workplace codetermination. In Britain, distance from a representative role is officially stipulated and reinforced in the mandatory and joint induction by professional judges.

Partisanship in France seemed more overt and persistent. For employee lay judges, maintaining a consistent identity was possibly aided by the acceptability of an adversarial environment in which reaching a judgment could be cast as an 'agreement', with undertones of collective bargaining.

[D] Lay Judges and Professional Judge Dominance

Much of the literature on the role of lay judges in labour courts contends that they are generally passive in hearings, with the professional judge (and other 'repeat players', such as lawyers) dominant, a contention often supported by reference to the high degree of unanimity in judgments.

Our findings suggest that this needs to be qualified as far the hearing is concerned; moreover, lay judges were found to play an active (and unseen) part in *deliberations*.

Lay judges in France exercise a role for which there is no direct comparison in the other two countries: they manage the court, conduct hearings, and determine and write judgments (supported in the latter process by legally-qualified court clerks, the *greffiers*).

In terms of *hearings*, lay judges in Great Britain and Germany play a complementary role to the professional judge. In Britain, this is due to some, largely contingent, aspects of hearings (lay judges take written notes of proceedings as a record but also in the event of an accusation of bias against the professional judge). This creates scope for lay involvement and endows them with some latent power.[4] In Germany, lay judges can, on occasions, help bring about a voluntary settlement. In short, although the professional judge, as chair of the proceedings, was dominant in hearings in both countries, this was qualified by their occasional dependence on the lay judges.

In contrast, lay judges play a key part in *deliberations* in Germany. This is, first, because German professional judges have a direct career track after legal qualification and so are reliant on their lay judges to provide specific (technical) and general (workplace) knowledge; and second because dismissal cases, where workplace norms are often a key consideration, dominate. As we note in section §11.04, lay judges' role in deliberations was highlighted by both lay and professional judges.

In Britain, the role of lay judges in deliberations is arguably somewhat less salient for three reasons. First, legal precedent, typically conveyed by the professional judge, circumscribes judicial reasoning and forbids all judges, lay and professional, from putting themselves 'in the shoes of the parties' in unfair dismissal cases. Second, British lay judges typically sit on discrimination cases which are subject to complex legal provisions (such as the burden of proof) and in which workplace norms are not a consideration. And third, where lay judges do sit on unfair dismissal cases, they are not alone in their workplace knowledge. British professional judges are not career

4. Lay judges in Britain noted interactions with the professional that qualified this dominance, such as suggesting that a professional judge alter their courtroom behaviour, responding to a request by the professional to confirm the record, and jointly deciding who should ask which questions of the parties.

judges. They will have been lawyers previously and thus built up a knowledge of workplace practice, albeit indirectly, from being instructed by their clients.

Constrained by the pressures towards unanimity, discussion in both Germany and Britain was typically steered by the professional judge and there was an acceptance by lay judges that the professional was the law expert. However, the possibility that lay judges might outvote the professional, an event that some professional judge interviewees in Britain had experienced, meant that persuasion was often needed to obtain unanimity and perhaps make an appeal less likely in practice.

[E] Knowledge and Skills

Previous research into lay judges (Corby and Latreille, 2011; Höland et al., 2007) suggests that lay judges' main contribution is the provision of 'workplace knowledge' and a 'balance' between a legal and a workplace perspective. We asked lay and professional judges for their assessment of this.

We found that lay judges offered distinctive skills and knowledge. Some of this was explicit and specific (how pay systems operated, for example), but also often tacit, acquired experientially and involved not only 'facts' but also workplace norms ('fairness'). Such knowledge is, in principle, unavailable to, and valued by, professional judges. Lay judges injected multiple perspectives into deliberations, potentially improving decision-making (Nemeth, 1995). Lay judges also reported that they enhanced their representational and professional skills, suggesting an 'education function' (Machura, 2016). This is most likely in France, given strong organisational links. There is also a close link with representation in Germany: in our sample, 76% of employee lay judges had a background in workplace codetermination.[5] The potential educative function has shrunk in Britain, however, as organisational nominees retire.

[F] Gender

Gender issues played a role in motivation and nomination in Britain, where some female interviewees said they were motivated to become a lay judge because of their experience of discrimination. A few employee lay judges also reported that they had been blocked from being nominated by their organisations (before 1999) and that self-nomination enabled them to apply direct. In contrast, most employer and employee lay judges in Britain noted that the organisations to which they belonged had encouraged and enabled them to become a lay judge. In Germany, men and women appeared to have different ideas about the nature of their contribution. Whereas men tended to emphasise specialist knowledge, women highlighted a 'social perspective'.

5. *See* too Höland et al. (2018).

§12.04 THE JURIDICAL AND IR FIELDS

One area of theorisation which formed a backdrop to this study was whether Bourdieu's characterisation of the 'juridical field' in 'The Force of Law' (1987), and field theory more generally, was relevant and applicable to our research. This centred on two aspects, elaborated below. First, Bourdieu's characterisation mainly draws on examples from France: our research, by contrast, was designed as comparative and our findings suggested national variation in both structures and reported experiences.[6] Should field theory be deemed useful, it would need to be able to accommodate or depict such differences. And second, although Bourdieu's critique of a highly deterministic account of the law and assertion of its complex formal and real autonomy is apposite,[7] his characterisation of the demarcation (and conflict) between fields, and between lay and professional actors in this field, does not accord with our findings, suggesting that some qualification might be needed.

The concept of 'field' in social analysis can be traced back to the work of Kurt Lewin in the 1930/1940s (Lewin, 2010 [1951]) when Lewin was reflecting on experimental work in psychology that used concepts drawn from mathematics and physics, such as 'vector', for experimental investigations into the strength of association in psychology. Lewin's definition of 'field' states that, as a conceptualisation of 'the total situation':

> (a) behaviour has to be derived from a totality of coexisting facts,
> (b) these coexisting facts have the character of a 'dynamic field' in so far as the state of any part of this field depends on every other part of the field (ibid. 187).

At its core, this is a relational theory that emphasises mutual 'interdependence' (*ibid.* 274) within an overall 'constellation' that is characterised by both a 'structure and forces' (*ibid.* 275).

Although Lewin wished to emphasise the scientific nature of 'field' in psychology, he also noted its heuristic aspect as a 'pedagogical device' (Lewin, 2010: 172). This metaphorical aspect also has a value in using fields as a comparative tool, and especially as a visual prompt to recognise similarities and differences between systems (as illustrated in Figure 12.1). The relational aspect emphasised by field theory also makes this a useful approach given that much of the interview data obtained turned on social interactions and the structures in which these occurred.[8]

---

6. Bourdieu certainly allows for such comparison in his observation in 'The Force of Law' that the hierarchies of legal actors might vary across 'juridical traditions' that might emerge through 'the comparative history of law' (Bourdieu, 1987: 821).
7. *See* too Pashukanis (1978 [1929]) for an earlier comparable characterisation of the distinctive quality of 'juridical form'.
8. Space forbids a fuller exploration of field theory and its variants. On this, *see*, for example, Suckert (2018).

[A] Bourdieu and the Juridical Field

'For Bourdieu a field is a relatively autonomous domain of activity that responds to rules of functioning and institutions that are specific to it and which define the relations among the agents' (Hilgers and Mangez, 2015: 5). This autonomy is the basis for the emergence of elites who exercise domination within each field by virtue of their control over operational rules, regulations and access to positions through control of eligibility – ultimately, the monopolisation of the sources of legitimacy in that field.

As Hilgers and Mangez (op. cit.) indicate, Bourdieu's understanding of fields was based on his interest in theorising the bases of institutional differentiation and the creation of distinct social spaces. These spaces become 'closed' in proportion to the degree of autonomy and the power of elites within spaces to distance themselves from 'lay' – that is, non-professional – criteria for legitimacy. As the Introduction to the English translation of 'The Force of Law' (Terdiman, 1987) also emphasises, Bourdieu also sees the law as closely tied to other 'social realms' but is notable for its resistance to other competing forms of social practice leading 'to the deceptive *appearance* of autonomy' (*ibid.*, 808). The issue of the 'boundaries' between fields is, therefore, a central but somewhat unresolved issue (*see also* Suckert, 2018).

For Bourdieu, the juridical field ('a specific social universe', *ibid.* 815) was characterised by a stark social division between lay people and legal professionals, and was subject to a process of rationalisation that privileged judgments based on law over 'naïve intuitions of fairness' (*ibid*: 817), on occasions leading to 'the disqualification of the non-specialists' sense of fairness' (*ibid.* 828). Such a tension was evident in our study in many of the reported experiences not only of lay judges but also of some professionals, who had to apply ('enforce') the law in deliberations despite (sometimes shared) misgivings about whether this served wider notions of 'fairness'.

While Bourdieu argued that the juridical field was characterised by a sharp separation between professional jurists (lawyers, judges, officials) and non-professionals, our findings suggest that the location of labour courts at the intersection of other fields, and in particular the legal/IR fields, softens this separation when compared with other areas of the law. Moreover, the nature of this intersection varies between countries. In this respect, Bourdieu's concept is both too wide and too narrow. One might argue that the 'labour court field', which differs from country to country, is a *sub-field* within the wider 'juridical' field, and has specific features to which a general characterisation of the legal field does not apply. In this respect, the 'juridical' field is too broad. But by excluding the specific features of labour courts, it is also too restrictive.[9]

The theory of 'strategic action fields', developed by Fligstein and McAdam (2012), points to an alternative conception of fields. For Fligstein and McAdam (2012: 9), a 'strategic action field' is a:

9. In Bourdieu and Wacquant (1992: 97), Bourdieu argues that fields are 'relatively autonomous social microcosms' with a 'logic and necessity' that is 'specific and irreducible' to those of other fields.

> constructed meso-level social order in which actors (who can be individual or collective) are attuned to and interact with each other on the basis of shared (which is not to say consensual) understandings about the purposes of the field, relationships to others in the field (including who has power and why), and the rules governing legitimate action in the field.

Fields can be embedded in other fields and 'the ties between fields highlight the interdependence of strategic action fields and their very real potential to effect change in one another' (*ibid.*). How might this apply to labour courts, considered as a 'strategic action field'?

[B] Institutions

Lay labour court judges in France, Germany and Great Britain exercise full judicial powers when making judgments in court. In this respect, they are part of the legal field and subject to its rules, conventions, and hierarchies. At the same time, lay judges typically originate in the IR arrangements of their respective countries and in this respect might be seen (also) as IR actors and imbued with its distinctive rules and conventions. When acting as lay judges they bring with them differing notions of legitimacy and contribute particular resources ('workplace knowledge') and 'social skills'. These resources are central to their capacity to function in the IR field but, as professional judges stated in our interviews, are transferred to other fields and affect the operation and outcomes of labour courts and the way in which power is exercised in them (on 'social skills', *see* Fligstein and McAdam, 2012: 45ff).

The distinctive character of labour courts is also a feature of the fact that, to varying degrees, labour courts in the three countries have been *generated* in their current form by the IR field in an interaction with the state; they are not simply 'emanations' of a general juridical field.[10]

This is most emphatically the case in France, where the composition of labour courts ('parity') is the product of a long-running struggle by French trade unions to ensure that existential decisions affecting employees were not made by employers alone. In Germany, the establishment of labour courts, in broadly their current shape, took place during the period of the Weimar Republic (1919-1933), reflecting an aspiration to accommodate labour and forge a new and progressive constitutional settlement in the wake of the collapse of the Wilhelmine state and the 1918 German revolution. In Britain, labour courts, originally conceived as administrative tribunals to resolve disputes over state funding between employers became *party v party* labour courts as a result of a recommendation by a Royal Commission on Trade Unions and Employers' Associations in 1968 (Donovan, 1968) in response to a sustained period of industrial conflict when trade unions had considerable organisational strength. This contrasts with France, where trade union workplace strength was weaker.[11]

10. This is not the universally case, but is found in a number of other countries (such as Sweden).
11. *See* Emmenegger (2014). This might be one explanation for the relatively muted resistance to the removal of union and employer nomination rights in 1999. By contrast, labour courts are seen as having a fundamental place in the 'constitutional order' by unions in France and Germany.

In all three countries, therefore, there is a complex and nationally-specific set of interactions between the legal field in general, as a 'state field', the 'labour court field', with its specific characteristics and origins, and the 'industrial relations field', defined as the field of interactions between (primarily) collective but also individual actors that governs the regulation of employment relationships and distributive matters that have been assigned to this field (and which will vary as between differing IR systems).

For Fligstein and McAdam (2012), states are 'a set of strategic action fields that claim to make and enforce authoritative rules over a specified geographic territory' (*ibid.*, 68) with 'tremendous potential to shape the prospects for change and stability in virtually all non-state strategic action fields within those geographic coordinates' (*ibid.*). For their part, fields within the state (and on occasions the state itself) are characterised by contestation from challengers and the response of incumbents, as evident in the shifting boundaries in the regulation of employment.

In line with this approach, the IR field itself can also be seen as a set of 'nested' fields, varying as between countries. In Germany, it will include statutory workplace and board-level codetermination, a field that includes customary IR actors but also shareholder representatives. In France, it would include individual (and competing) trade unions. In Britain, and in contrast to Germany, it would include official mechanisms for dispute resolution (Acas).

Figure 12.1 sets out a simplified depiction of some of the fields involved, the strength of the relationships, and the overlaps (implying dominance) of related fields.

Figure 12.1 Main Fields in Relation to Labour Courts in France, Germany and Great Britain

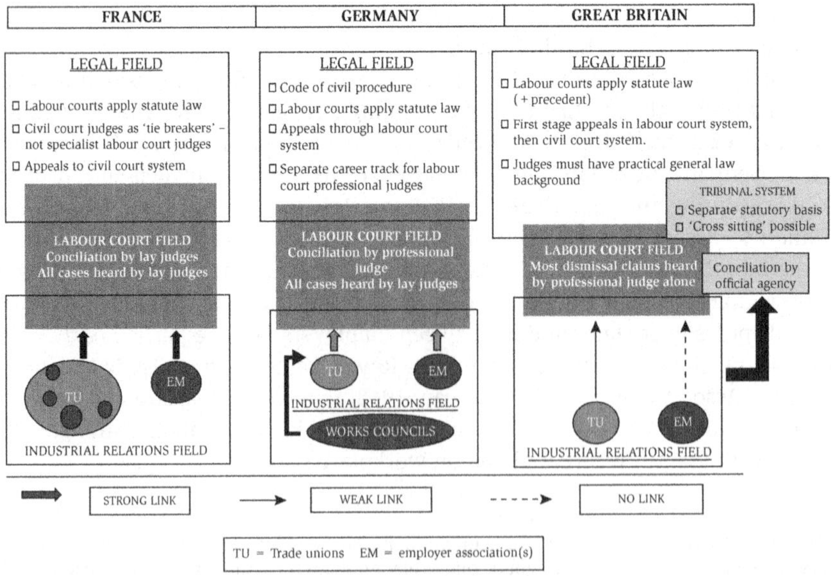

[C] Interactions

Fligstein and McAdam (2012: 11) emphasise that fields are not only characterised by power and hierarchy, but also by 'shared understandings about the nature of the "rules" in the field' and that actors 'understand what tactics are possible [and] legitimate'. The overlap between the juridical and IR fields, that is their intersection within the labour court field, is also illustrated in the interactions that reveal such 'shared understandings'. For lay judges, some of these understandings are imported from the workplace, while others are either acquired through socialisation into court life or imposed by the rules that govern the judicial system that are set by the state (and conveyed by professional judges). In this sense, Bourdieu's 'logic' of the juridical field remains a powerful factor. Compared with many of the meso-level fields noted by Fligstein and McAdam, labour courts are subject to external rules in the form of statute law that determines their composition and operation, other operational rules,[12] and legal precedent. In this respect, they constitute relatively 'settled' fields from an internal perspective in that the immediate actors cannot reconfigure the field. At the same time, as noted above, labour courts have been buffeted by actual or threatened disruption from external actors, with varying degrees of resistance. On the whole, however, resistance has not taken the form implied by Bourdieu: that is, generated from within the legal field.

One further aspect noted by Fligstein and McAdam, which serves to distinguish their view from Bourdieu's emphasis on power and hierarchy, is the scope for cooperation between actors in maintaining and reproducing fields. As noted above, labour courts can be, and in some circumstances are, the sites both of a clash between and a productive combination of lay and professional knowledge. For example, professional judge interviewees in Britain saw themselves as on occasions in an antagonistic relationship with lay ('naïve') norms,[13] but also at times welcomed the scope to make law jointly, as the injection of workplace knowledge enabled them to arrive at well-founded judgments in which the exigencies of the law could be made as consistent as possible with 'common sense' conceptions of fairness. And as lay and professional judges noted in Germany and Britain, intervention by lay judges could change the direction of a case. The scope for this appears wider in Germany than in Great Britain, where there are more constraints on the reasoning that can be applied in deliberations.

One German employee lay judge noted:

> There are not that many differences between us, I think. We all want to resolve a conflict. All three of us work together collectively, both the professional judge ... the judge from the employer side, and me ... If I could say this, we fit with each other.

12. In Great Britain, 'practice directions' issued by the judicial authorities or in Germany, codes of procedure.
13. 'They think of unfairness in a rather more generalised sense. I think the law is quite clear ... and that's what you have to apply. And it's sometimes with a clenched jaw' (British professional judge).

A German employer lay judge similarly said:

> It depends on the judge, of course. But most judges don't push the fact that they are full-time professionals or behave like schoolmasters – it's much more of a partnership. There are naturally exceptions, as always, but most judges treat it like a partnership.

Another German employer lay judge commented:

> It's not in every case, *but in 10 or 20 per cent the professional judge sometimes doesn't know what to do next*. If we're all sitting in the room as a trio, we can look for a solution because we all want to conclude the case that day. And sometimes the professional judge doesn't know how.

Lay judges in both Great Britain and Germany were seen as providing some support and certainty to the professional judge by acting as a 'sounding board' (British professional judge) for the professional judge's view. On compensation, for example, one British employee lay judge noted: 'I think the judge is interested (...) I remember the [professional] judge not setting a figure, waiting to see what we both said before he would come in with his view'.

In Germany, professional judges highlighted contested dismissals as cases in which lay judges' assessments, through knowledge of workplace practice, could play a significant role, 'when it's a matter of a gut feeling'. Similarly, a professional judge posed the question of compensation to lay judges in stark terms: 'Is that enough or not enough?'. Agreement between the two lay judges was seen as suggesting the correctness of a decision: professional judges referred to it as a 'surety for correctness', a 'useful corrective', and 'as a kind of sanity check, when we can't see the wood for the trees any more'. One professional judge commented that agreement between the two lay judges made them 'much more confident in the solution'.

The collegiality reported in Great Britain by both lay and professional judges[14] is also possibly rooted not only in etiquette but also the fact that professional judges need to collaborate with the lay judges during proceedings in their capacity as observers and note-takers during the hearing. Moreover, compared with professional judges in Germany, British professional judges have a lower informational advantage in relation to lay judges in that they receive case papers later in the development of a claim and often only shortly before these are made available to lay judges on the day of a hearing. Lay and professional judges then read the case papers together (often with some exchange during this process, although this was reportedly mostly low key).

Finally, cooperation between professional and lay judges can constitute joint efforts to defend the field as such from 'exogenous shocks' (Fligstein and McAdam, 2012: 19-21). This is arguably comparable with Bourdieu's notion of 'resistance' but has a more political quality. For Fligstein and McAdam, these are typically understood as 'episodes of contention' in which incumbents are confronted by challengers. Such shocks seem to present themselves differently in the labour court context, in the following respects.

14. 'We work as a collegiate team' (British employee lay judge).

First, changes in the composition and operation of labour courts will alter the roles (and balance of power) between lay and professional actors. For example, as noted above, British professional judges now determine most stand-alone dismissal claims although they have discretion in prescribed circumstances to include lay judges.[15] Interestingly, some British professional judges we interviewed regretted the absence of lay judges in most dismissal cases.

In France, employee and employer lay judges were faced with a dilemma: should they vote for the party of their own 'side'? If so, they risk a stalemate and the case being taken to a hearing with a professional judge (*juge départiteur*) breaking the tie. This potentially weakens the lay quality of the labour court and empowers the professional, both immediately but potentially structurally.

§12.05 CONCLUSION

This chapter represents an initial attempt to understand labour courts in the three selected countries as a strategic action field 'nested' within other significant proximate fields, principally the state and the IR field. This approach was motivated by a realisation that the emphasis in Bourdieu's classic 1987 paper differed from the more nuanced perspective that emerged from our comparative study. Lay judges in France and Germany, and in particular employee lay judges, are primarily IR actors for two reasons. First, except for a minority of French lay judges who are presidents of chambers, most lay judges spend more time on their IR role than on their labour court role. Second, French and German lay judges' origins and specific contribution to the judicial process is primarily derived from workplace knowledge. Great Britain has evolved away from this construction inasmuch as state action has transformed the operation of labour courts and has led to a much-reduced recruitment of fresh labour court lay judges with a background in organised IR, weakening the link to the IR field, perhaps permanently.

REFERENCES

Aronson, E. (1992). 'The Return of the Repressed: Dissonance Makes a Comeback', *Psychological Inquiry*, Vol. 3, No. 4, 303-311.

Bourdieu, P. (1987). 'The Force of Law: Towards a Sociology of the Juridical Field', *The Hastings Law Journal*, Vol. 38, July 1987, 805-853.

Bourdieu, P. and Wacquant, L.J.D. (1992). *An Invitation to Reflexive Sociology*. Cambridge: Polity Press.

Burgess, P., Corby, S., Höland, A., Michel, H., Willemez, L., Buchwald, C. and Krausbeck, et al. (2017). *The Roles, Resources and Competencies of Employee Lay Judges: A Cross-National Study of Germany, France and Great Britain*. Working Paper Forschungsförderung, Hans Böckler Stiftung, Düsseldorf, ISSN 2509-2359.

15. This arrangement was met by surprise by some senior German professional judges when interviewed for a previous study.

Corby, S. and Latreille, P. (2011). *Survey Evidence: ET and EAT Judges and Lay Members*. http://www2.gre.ac.uk/about/schools/business/research/centres/weru/publications.

Corby, S. and Burgess, P. (2014). *Adjudicating Employment Rights: A Cross-National Approach*. Basingstoke: Palgrave.

Donovan (1968) *Royal Commission on Trade Unions and Employers' Associations 1965-1968, Cmnd 3623*, London: Her Majesty's Stationery Office.

Emmenegger, P. (2014). *The Power to Dismiss: Trade Unions and the Regulation of Job Security in Western Europe*. Oxford: Oxford University Press.

Festinger L. (1957). *A Theory of Cognitive Dissonance*. Evanston: Row, Peterson and Company.

Fligstein and McAdam (2012). *A Theory of Fields*. Oxford: Oxford University Press.

Goffman, E. (1961) *Encounters: Two Studies in the Sociology of Interaction*, New York: Bobbs-Merrill.

Hilgers, M. and Mangez, H. (eds) (2015). *Bourdieu's Theory of Social Fields: Concepts and Applications*. London and New York: Routledge.

Höland, A., Kahl, U. and Zeibig, N. (2007). *Kündigungsprozess und Kündigungsschutz im Arbeitsverhältnis*. Baden-Baden.

Höland, A. and Buchwald, C. (2018). *Ehrenamtliche Richterinnen und Richter in der Arbeitsgerichtsbarkeit und in der Sozialgerichtsbarkeit. Ergebnisse einer repräsentativen Befragung in Baden-Württemberg, Berlin und Sachsen-Anhalt*. Forschungsbericht aus dem zsh 18-01. ISSN: 1617-299X, Zentrum für Sozialforschung Halle e.V., Halle.

Hollstein, B. (2015). *Ehrenamt verstehen. Eine handlungstheoretische Analyse*. Frankfurt/New York: Campus Verlag.

Lewin, K. (2010 [1951]). *Field Theory in Social Science*. First edition 1951. Reprinted in 1997 by the American Psychological Association. 2010 Kindle Edition. Page references are to the latter edition.

Machura, S. (2016) 'Civil Justice: Lay Judges in the EU Countries', *Onati Socio-Legal Series* [online].

Pashukanis, E. (1978 [1929]). *Law and Marxism: A General Theory*. London/Ink Links, with an introduction by Chris Arthur. Translated by Barbara Einhorn.

Suckert, L. (2018). 'Same but different. Die Feldtheorien Fligsteins und Bourdieus und das Potenzial einer wechselseitig informierten Perpsektive für die Wirtschaftssoziologie', *Berliner Journal für Soziologie*, published online 27 June 2018.

Terdiman, R. (1987). 'Translator's Introduction' to 'The Force of Law: Towards a Sociology of the Juridical Field', *The Hastings Law Journal*, Vol. 38, July 1987, 805-853.

Wagner, D.G. and Berger, J. (1993). 'Status Characteristics Theory: The Growth of a Program', in Berger, J. and Zelditch, M., *Theoretical Research Programs: Studies in Theory Growth*. Stanford.

Willemez, L. (2013). 'French Labor Tribunals and the Making of Labor Law. Towards a Sociology of Judicial Roles', *Sociologie du Travail*, 55 e67-e87.

Part III The Future of Work: Challenges

CHAPTER 13

Is Forced Labour the New Normal?*

Richard Hyman

§13.01 WHAT IS FORCED LABOUR?

In 1930 the International Labour Organisation (ILO) adopted Convention 29, which defined forced labour as 'all work or service which is exacted from any person under the menace of any penalty and for which the said person has not offered himself voluntarily'. Subsequently, it argued (2019) that 'forced labour refers to situations in which persons are coerced to work through the use of violence or intimidation, or by more subtle means such as manipulated debt, retention of identity papers or threats of denunciation to immigration authorities'.

The ILO stresses that the phenomenon is widespread, estimating that 16 million people are subject to forced labour in the private economy (just over half involving debt bondage) and a further 4 million subject to state-imposed forced labour; while the numbers affected by the broader category of 'modern slavery' covers 40 million (ILO and Walk Free Foundation 2017). But forced labour tends to be viewed officially as peripheral to 'normal' capitalist work relations, for example involving trafficking for sex work or agricultural labour in non-industrialised countries.

Yet is involuntary labour so peripheral? Convention 29 contains a range of exceptions to the ILO definition of forced labour: compulsory military service, work 'which forms part of the normal civic obligations of the citizens', prison labour and work required in cases of emergency. Similar provisions exist in the European Convention on Human Rights. These exemptions allow considerable elasticity in interpretation. For example, Topo (2016) shows how they can be used to deprive individuals of any effective choice of whether and how to work, which might be a reasonable test of whether labour is voluntary; she discusses, in particular, the

* This article derives from work undertaken in 2018 as a Visiting Fellow at the Zentrum für interdisziplinäre Forschung (ZiF), Bielefeld.

conditionality increasingly attached to eligibility for social benefits ('workfare'), but also identifies a range of other 'grey areas' where work is at best quasi-involuntary.

Hence there is no binary divide between voluntary and involuntary, or free and unfree labour; rather there are degrees of (un)freedom. Correspondingly, there are many varieties of violence and coercion. Physical violence is relatively straightforward to identify, though threats of coercion may be less so, and the broader category of psychological violence is more diffuse still. But all are embedded in interpersonal relations, involving 'abuse of power' as specified in the ILO Convention. However, it is increasingly recognised that coercion and violence can be embedded in the social framework within which interpersonal relations are played out.

Half a century ago, Galtung (1969: 173) distinguished between 'personal' and 'structural' violence: 'personal violence *shows*. The object of personal violence perceives the violence ... Structural violence is silent, it does not show.' Galtung also analysed 'cultural violence' which 'makes direct and structural violence look, even feel, right – or at least not wrong'. There are clear parallels with Bourdieu's notion of 'symbolic violence': cognitive structures, perhaps deliberately imposed, which encourage the perception of systems of domination and social damage as natural and inevitable. In the context of industrial relations, the absence of alternatives to bad jobs or indecent work can be viewed as an expression of cultural and symbolic violence. If such alternatives are reduced, is labour increasingly unfree?' I return to these questions later.

§13.02 WHAT IS FREE WAGE LABOUR? FICTITIOUS COMMODITIES AND REAL COMMODIFICATION

In the conclusion of his discussion of the sale and purchase of labour power, Marx (1976: 280) ironically described the labour market as 'a very Eden of the innate rights of man. It is the exclusive realm of Freedom, Equality, Property and Bentham'. Shortly before this, Maine (1861: 101) wrote of a historical progress from a system of social relations predefined by feudal and familial constraints to one based on the 'free agreement of individuals'. But whereas Maine viewed wholly positively the capacity of market actors 'to settle rules of conduct for themselves with a liberty never allowed to them till recently', Marx stressed to contradictions between the form of 'free agreement' and the reality of asymmetrical dependency. Equality before the law did not denote equality in practice. As many other authors emphasised, workers were often in competition with each other for jobs, entailing a downward pressure on wages; and because of their limited resources, even a short spell without work could entail severe deprivation, even starvation. Conversely, employers often possessed sufficient capital to survive longer without workers; and they could more easily act collectively.

Moreover, the freedom of 'free labour' was double-edged. While workers were free *to* sell their labour power for whatever wage they could obtain, with the rise of capitalism they were increasingly free *from* any alternative means of subsistence. This could be the consequence of the structural violence of unfettered market competition: for example, the independent Lancashire hand-loom weavers, whose products were undercut by cheaper factory production and who were therefore driven into dependent wage-labour. But it could also be the outcome of the personal violence of land-owners, capitalists or governments. Polanyi (1944: 92) examined the impact of 'enclosures of the commons and consolidation into compact holdings' in rural Britain. 'The war on cottages, the absorption of cottage gardens and grounds, the confiscation of rights in the common deprived cottage industry of its two mainstays: family earnings and agricultural background. As long as domestic industry was supplemented by the facilities and amenities of a garden plot, a scrap of land, or grazing rights, the dependence of the laborer on money earnings was not absolute.' While beyond the scope of my discussion here, the violence of colonialism involved even more forcible and systematic dispossession.

Polanyi (1944: 73) described labour, land and money as 'fictitious commodities' because while they were all subject to market forces, unlike real commodities they were not produced for sale on the market. In the same year that Polanyi's book was published, the ILO in its Philadelphia Declaration affirmed as the first of its 'fundamental principles' that 'labour is not a commodity'. For Marx, of course, labour as such was not a commodity; but in the context of capitalist employment, labour *power* – the capacity to perform productive work – was indeed commodified. It was the difference between the exchange value of labour power, and the value of the products of the labour performed, which provided the source of profit. The specific activities of individuals with distinctive competences (concrete labour) became reduced to quantifiable, and hence marketable, phenomena (abstract labour). This marginalised the humanity of actually existing workers.

§13.03 DOUBLE MOVEMENTS: THE CONQUEST OF SOCIAL RIGHTS?

For Polanyi, the rise of industrial capitalism imposed a commodity status on workers; but the resulting social dislocation precipitated a counter-movement, and eventually a new framework of social rights was established. Subsequently, Esping-Andersen (1990) wrote of 'decommodification', the protection of workers from the vagaries of market forces.

In post-war Europe, 'labour markets' became subject to a range of regulations which ensured that they constituted markets only in limited respects. In essence, employment was treated as a status rather than a mere contract, one which could be terminated only for good cause and through due process. Public policy typically encouraged collective bargaining, and collective agreements usually had priority over individual employment contracts. The public provision of social welfare systems protected the vulnerable from the vagaries of the labour market and reduced downwards competitive pressures on the standards of the core labour force.

Where did workers' rights come from? Polanyi regarded the counter- movement as 'a spontaneous reaction', but it would be a serious mistake to assume that national labour regimes derived from consensus on the architecture of employment regulation. The systems emerging in each country typically reflected a contingent historical balance of class forces: rights were usually achieved as a negotiated accommodation between class interests or as a set of concessions by those in power to dampen protest from below.

Across Europe, the institutionalisation of workers' rights was a major social achievement. But such institutionalisation was never sufficient to prevent regression when circumstances changed. Formal rights acquire substance only through a process of interpretation and application, and their meaning is constantly reconstructed and renegotiated. It is often easier for those who wish to weaken citizenship rights to erode their practical effect rather than to attack them frontally.

§13.04 GLOBALISATION AND FINANCIALISATION: POST-DECOMMODIFICATION?

Decommodification involved an accommodation between *national* labour movements and their interlocutors. Employers were primarily national in terms of corporate ownership and production strategies, and governments were to a large degree autonomous in social and economic policy. The world has changed. First, globalisation has removed the dominant capitalist agglomerations from national control. Second, the liberalisation of financial markets has spawned an array of exotic fictitious commodities which Polanyi could never have imagined. It is now possible, and indeed more effective, to generate a surplus without producing value: money can be expanded without the production of commodities as traditionally understood. Corporations have themselves been transformed into commodities, increasingly bought and sold: for growing numbers of workers (and their unions), it is no longer even clear *who* is the employer.

There has been a parallel reconfiguration of the role of the state. In recent decades, neoliberal globalisation has provided an alibi for anti-social policies by governments that insist that there is no alternative to submission to international markets. On the one hand, policies have aimed at 'rolling back the state', and restricting social protections to those that can be justified on grounds of productivity and competitiveness; on the other, new and repressive forms of intervention have been required to impose the sway of market forces. The EU, once often viewed as a defender of decommodification, has become one of the key drivers of this process. National economies and national labour markets are thus increasingly *disembedded* from effective social regulation. Where significant productive and infrastructural assets were in public hands, in most countries these have now been largely privatized. These trends can be understood, within Polanyi's framework, as a *counter*-counter-movement, a *third* phase involving the deliberate unravelling of the regulatory web constructed in previous decades. The norm of insecurity, widely believed to have been overcome in the mid-20th century, is increasingly re-imposed. The crisis which began in 2007-2008 brought a rapid increase in unemployment, which in many countries persists. For many, and in some countries most new labour market entrants the only available employment opportunities are precarious.

For several decades, the wage share in national income has declined and inequality has increased, in some countries dramatically. Even before the recent (and current) crisis, government budgets had been squeezed, to an important. Closely associated is the growth of the so-called informal economy. Systems of institutionalised industrial relations were traditionally founded, at least in industrialised countries, on what was often termed the 'normal' employment relationship. Those whose situation was seen as most evidently appropriate for collective organisation and representation, and certainly as providing the most favourable support for union recruitment and retention, were employed full-time on more or less permanent contractual terms; typically also in larger organisations and in occupations where collective withdrawal of labour could have a persuasive impact. The stereotypical trade unionist possessed 'industrial muscle'. But the workforce has become, and has been recognised as, increasingly diversified - in terms of gender, ethnicity and employment status. 'Atypical' employment has become increasingly typical, in particular for new labour market entrants, with fixed-term contracts, agency work, subcontracting, dependent self-employment and unpaid internships. The rise of the 'platform economy' has brought a return to spot contracting in the labour market. For an expanding proportion of the workforce, the available options are no work, bad work or often indecent work in its many guises.

§13.05 MODERN SLAVERY AS A BUSINESS MODEL

When, and how, does bad work constitute forced labour? Often, unfree labour is regarded as primarily a problem of 'developing' countries, but one exported to 'developed' economies through migration flows which themselves may be sustained through violence in the form of trafficking. It is also often seen as exclusively linked to the 'illicit economy', involving such activities as organised prostitution and the drugs trade: 'a separate and specific category of labour relations' (Barrientos et al., 2013: 1037-1038). Yet 'unfreedom ... needs to be understood as a continuum of exploitation to which any worker might be subject, but to which particular groups and individuals have particular vulnerabilities' (Strauss 2012: 141).

According to Crane (2013: 59), 'the threat of violence is a definitional condition of modern slavery. Without it, labour practices may be inhumane and exploitative but will not constitute slavery because the victim has the opportunity to walk away.' Yet this 'opportunity' may be precluded without the threat or exercise of direct physical violence. One contemporary example is the *kafala* system in the Arab Gulf states, Lebanon and Jordan. 'Foreign nationals must have a local sponsor, or *kafeel*, who is in most cases the employer, in order to obtain residence and work permits. During the term of service, the worker does not have the right to quit except under specific circumstances, and in most cases cannot change jobs or choose a new employer without the sponsor's consent .... Within this framework, migrants are effectively bonded to their employers (Frantz 2013: 1072).

In the absence of access to formally enslaved labour, employers may have many functional alternatives. Brown and van der Linden (2010: 6-7) note that 'after the slave trade had gradually been abolished in Africa and the Americas, employers invented many tricks to guarantee the ongoing supply of bonded workers.' Nor is this a problem of distant history and faraway countries: it is important to recognise 'the unclear divide between "free" and "unfree" work' and to question 'the *telos* implicit in the understanding that "unfreedom" belongs to the past, while "proper" capitalism is based on "free" wage labour' (Sarkar 2017 173).

As Phillips argues, (2013: 178), 'in contemporary global production, unfreedom is primarily constituted not by coerced entry but by precluded exit. These conditions are often established by indebtedness and/or the withholding of wages until the end of a contract, which may be combined with such abuses as imprisonment and restrictions on physical movement, threatened or actual violence (both psychological and physical, and both against a worker and against her family or co-workers) and/or the confiscation of documents and possessions.' Much more generally, variants of the *kafala* system have been implemented in many 'developed' countries: work permits for many occupations are dependent on a specific job offer, and may be revoked if the worker leaves the sponsoring employer (O'Connell Davidson 2013: 183; 2015: 144).

Unfreedom is often closely linked to the role of labour market intermediaries: 'labour contracting is increasing, and that its worst forms are associated with the rise of unfree labour within contemporary globalised production ... Labour contractors often charge migrant workers high fees for transport, training, provision of 'documents', and also charge high 'interest' on loans for these 'services'. These are often on top of large payments to agents for 'travel' to the country of destination. Undocumented migrant workers have few channels for claiming their rights and fear loss of work and deportation if they complain (Barrientos 2013: 1059-1061). Hence 'bonded labour' is not simply a historical, third world problem; nor, in 'developed' countries, is it simply associated with trafficking and people smuggling. Allain et al. (2013) provide detailed documentation of the interlinkages between global value chains and 'modern slavery', specifically examining construction, food and cannabis production. Forced labour, they argue, makes business sense for specific actors within these supply chains; not only do unscrupulous employers and intermediaries benefit, but so do the supermarket chains and consumers who enjoy lower costs than would otherwise be possible. Hence 'modern slavery' is not an aberration but is rather integral to contemporary business models. The pressure which it can place on the wages and conditions of 'free' labour across supply chains can, in turn, be seen as a form of structural violence.

§13.06 STATES, VIOLENCE AND RESISTANCE

'Forced labour' is not merely the outcome of (illicit) private activities; states must be viewed 'as actors who play a causal role in shaping the conditions that give rise to it' (LeBaron and Phillips 2018: 2). What counts (and does not count) as forced labour is usually specified in law, and statutory definitions vary considerably across jurisdictions (Skrivankova 2010). Within the USA, Steinfeld (2009: 4) shows that in some states, courts have defined 'involuntary servitude' only in terms of entry into a labour contract, while in others they have considered limitations on exit. In Britain, for most of the 19th century, the first of these statutory interpretations prevailed under the

Master and Servant laws. As Price (1986: 39-42) indicates, these laws were used as mechanisms of social and industrial discipline. They were an important means of outlawing individual exit from the oppressive and exploitative enforcement of individual contracts. For example, coal miners and other occupations who were commonly subject to twelve-month contracts could suffer imprisonment with hard labour for individual breaches of contract. Nor was this simply an anachronistic residue of feudal employment regulation: in the two decades before the repeal of the laws in 1875, in an era when capitalist wage labour was firmly established, prosecutions actually intensified. Perhaps exceptional within the modern EU is the 2018 'slave law' implemented by the Orbán government in Hungary, which allows employers to force employees to work overtime, but analogues of Master and Servant are still to be found elsewhere.

LeBaron and Phillips (2018), drawing empirically on recent US experience, focus on how state policy, through acts of commission or omission, can facilitate unfree labour both by increasing the pool of vulnerable workers and by enhancing the incentives to adopt a business model based on forced labour. Both are predictable outcomes of neoliberalism. The 'modernisation' of labour markets and social security systems, through the weakening or abolition of employment protection legislation and social safety nets and their replacement by recommodification and workfare, drastically restricts the options available to workers and forces many into unwanted work situations. Reducing 'burdens on business' by weakening regulatory regimes, cutting back on inspectorates and failing to prosecute (or imposing minimal penalties for) illegal practices makes resort to forced labour an increasingly profitable option.

An important aspect of state policy is the construction of migration regimes. LeBaron and Phillips (2018: 7) show how the tightening of US border controls, rather than preventing 'illegal' immigration, has increased the cost of securing entry through traffickers and people smugglers; while those seeking work still cross the border. 'The extent of the debt accrued in the context of a highly policed border enforcement regime augments the unfreedom that can be imposed on a migrant worker'. Much more generally, variants of the *kafala* system have been implemented in many 'developed' countries: work permits for many types of workers are dependent on a specific job offer and may be revoked if the worker leaves the sponsoring employer. Well-grounded fears that complaints to the authorities may result in deportation can tie such workers to relations of forced labour. In the UK, government efforts to create a 'hostile environment' for foreign workers (or those who may look foreign) clearly reinforce such unfreedom.

Is forced labour the new normal, or can financialised global capitalism be re-regulated? Neoliberalism emerged from the 2007-2008 crisis – which surely demonstrated the practical bankruptcy of its recipes – stronger than ever, partly because it serves powerful vested interests, but also because of the lack of widespread conviction, even among its opponents, that there is an alternative which is both practical and inspirational. To resist the spread of forced labour, a radically different logic is required, of sustainability, solidarity, equity and dignity. Creating a strategic vision which might counteract the advance of unfreedom is a massive challenge. It requires new forms of engagement with those most affected by the destruction of once seemingly secure freedoms and opportunities. But it also requires a willingness to move beyond the limits of pragmatism to the possibilities of utopia. In this, there is a crucial role for public intellectuals and engaged scholars, to show how there *is* an alternative to the new normality of forced labour.

REFERENCES

Allain, J, Crane, A, LeBaron, G and Behbahani, L (2013) *Forced Labour's Business Models and Supply Chains.* York: Joseph Rowntree Foundation.

Brown, C and van der Linden, M (2010) 'Shifting Boundaries Between Free and Unfree Labour', *International Labor and Working-Class History* 78: 4-11.

Crane, A (2013) 'Modern Slavery as a Management Practice: Exploring the Conditions and Capabilities for Human Exploitation', *Academy of Management Review* 38(1): 45: 69.

Esping-Andersen, G (1990) *The Three Worlds of Welfare Capitalism.* Cambridge: Polity Press.

Frantz, E (2013) 'Jordan's Unfree Workforce: State-Sponsored Bonded Labour in the Arab Region', *Journal of Development Studies* 49(8): 1072-1087.

Galtung, J (1969) 'Violence, Peace, and Peace Research', *Journal of Peace Research* 6(3): 167-191.

Galtung, J (1990) 'Cultural Violence', *Journal of Peace Research* 27(3): 291-305.

ILO (2019) *What Is Forced Labour, Modern Slavery and Human Trafficking.* https://www.ilo.org/global/topics/forced-labour/definition/lang--en/index.htm.

ILO and Walk Free Foundation (2017) *Global Estimates of Modern Slavery: Forced Labour and Forced Marriage.* Geneva: ILO.

LeBaron, G and Phillips, N (2018) 'States and the Political Economy of Unfree Labour', *New Political Economy* doi.org/10.1080/13563467.2017.1420642.

Maine, HS (1861) *Ancient Law: Its Connection With the Early History of Society, and Its Relations to Modern Ideas*. London: John Murray.

O'Connell Davidson, J (2013) 'Troubling Freedom: Migration, Debt, and Modern Slavery', *Migration Studies* 1(2): 176-195.O'Connell Davidson, J (2015) *Modern Slavery: The Margins of Freedom.* London: Palgrave Macmillan.

Phillips, N (2013) 'Unfree Labour and Adverse Incorporation in the Global Economy: Comparative Perspectives on Brazil and India', *Economy and Society* 42(2): 171-196.

Polanyi P (1944) *The Great Transformation.* New York: Rinehart.

Price, R (1986) *Labour in British Society.* London: Croom Helm.

Sarkhar, M (2017) 'Constrained Labour as Instituted Process: Transnational Contract Work and Circular Migration in Late Capitalism', *European Journal of Sociology* 58(1): 171-204.

Skrivankova, K (2010): *Between Decent Work and Forced Labour: Examining the Continuum of Exploitation.* York: JRF programme paper.

Steinfeld, R (2009) *Coercion/Consent in Labour.* Oxford: COMPAS Working Paper 66.

Strauss, K (2012) 'Coerced, Forced and Unfree Labour: Geographies of Exploitation in Contemporary Labour Markets', *Geography Compass* 6(3): 137-148.

Topo, A (2016) 'Obbligo di lavoro e libertà di lavoro: Quando lavorare è un dovere "sociale"', in M Brollo, C Cester and LMenghini (eds), *Legalità e rapporti di lavoro: Incentivi e sanzioni*. Trieste, EUT Edizioni Università di Trieste, 2016, pp. 177-203.

CHAPTER 14

The Development of Employee Involvement in the EU: Lessons to Be Learned

Manfred Weiss

§14.01 INTRODUCTION

The European Union (EU) from the very beginning has been confronted with the diversity of the Member States' systems. Some countries had no systems of workers' participation whatsoever. They refused cooperation and relied exclusively on antagonism and conflict. And where systems of employee involvement in management's decision-making existed, they were different from country to country. These differences referred to the degree of participation, ranging from information and consultation up to co-determination. It also referred to the level of participation, ranging from the shop-floor level up to the headquarters of the company or group of companies. Only some countries even had established employees' representation in company boards. One of the most important differences between the Member States referred to the relationship between bodies of workers' representation and trade unions. And some Member States rejected the philosophy of participation in management's decision-making and relied exclusively on conflict and collective bargaining.

The relationship between institutionalized systems of workers' participation and collective bargaining again differs from country to country. It has to be stressed that differences between systems of workers' participation taken as an isolated phenomenon are by no means a reliable indicator for the degree of workers' influence on management's decision-making. The extent of such influence depends on the overall assessment of industrial relations, including collective bargaining and the legal framework as well as the factual possibilities for strike and other mechanisms of conflict resolution. The culture and tradition within a country also plays a significant role in this context. Therefore, even in countries which totally reject the philosophy of workers' involvement in management's decision-making and rely exclusively on conflict and collective bargaining, the workers' pressure on management can, of course, also be high.

The question for the European legislator was whether it might be better to just accept this diversity and leave it as it is or to intervene and try to regulate industrial relations at least to a certain extent in favour of participative schemes. As we all know the European legislator chose the latter option because it expected positive effects for the European economy as well as for the relationship between business and labour.

The positive effects of the system of employee involvement in management's decision making are well documented by many empirical studies. To just mention a few features: It leads to a change of focus from shareholder value to stakeholder value and tends to promote sustainability instead of short term effects at the stock markets. It has a big advantage compared to unilateral decision-making by the mere fact that management, who has to justify towards workers' representatives what it wants to do and why it wants to do it, tends to prepare the decisions much more carefully than it would be the case without this obligation. This leads evidently to better decision-making. The consciousness that workers' representatives are involved in management's decision making and that workers' interests are taken into account tends to increase the employees' motivation and thereby the company's productivity. Last not least the permanent dialogue between management and workers' representatives leads to mutual trust, changes the attitudes of both sides and absorbs conflicts.

I do not intend to reproduce the sequence and the content of the different Directives on workers' participation which you know quite well. I rather would like to reflect on the question what we can learn from the failure of specific proposals and from the way they were overcome. This might help us to speculate on future possibilities to further EU legislation on employee involvement in management's decision making.

The main examples I choose to illustrate failure and success are the Directive on European Works Councils (EWCs) and the Directive on employee involvement in the European Company.

§14.02 THE DIRECTIVE ON EWCs

Evidently national institutional arrangements on employee involvement can operate only within the national framework. If the decisions are taken by the headquarters outside the country concerned, information and consultation rights become useless. The first attempt to overcome this shortcoming was the so-called Vredeling proposal of 1980, amended in 1983. The proposal did not affect the given structure of employees' representation. The actors in the case of information and consultation were 'the employees' representatives provided for by the laws or practices of the Member States'. The chain of information had to go down from the parent company to the subsidiaries where information and consultation were supposed to take place. The content, the procedure and the frequency of information and consultation were prescribed in detail.

Within a moratorium of thirty days after the beginning of consultations management was prohibited to take the respective decision.

This proposal met strong resistance by employers' associations and chambers of commerce, including those from USA and Japan. It was considered to be an intolerable imposition on management's decision making. Due to the increasing pressure, the proposal had no chance to become a Directive. The attempt was given up in the mid-eighties: A funeral first class.

The Directive on EWCs of 1994 is the result of fresh efforts to revitalize social policy. Thanks to the President of the Commission Jacques Delors the notion of the 'European Social Dimension' became a key issue in the discussions on the realization of the internal market. In addition, the institutional strengthening of the social dialogue at the EC (European Community) level by the Single European Act's amendment of the Treaty led to an increased involvement of the social partners throughout the Community. This explains why the initiative to adopt a Community Charter of Fundamental Social Rights of Workers enjoyed widespread public attention and became the subject of very heated and controversial debates.

When in December 1989 in Strasbourg the Charter was adopted by eleven Member States the content was reduced to a minimum on which practically everybody could agree. Hence, the topics contained in the Charter were also agreed upon by at least the majority of business organizations and their spokesmen. It is important in this context to mention that section 17 of the Charter reads as follows: 'Information, consultation and participation for workers must be developed along appropriate lines, taking account of the practices in force in the various Member States. This shall apply especially in companies or groups of companies having establishments or companies in two or more Member States of the European Community'. And in the Commission's Social Action Programme to implement the Charter the introduction of a Community instrument on employee information, consultation, and participation procedures in transnational undertakings was proposed. In short, and to make the point: Both the legitimacy of such an instrument and the pressure to introduce it had increased tremendously compared to the period when Vredeling was being debated.

The Directive on the establishment of a EWC seeks to achieve the same goal as the Vredeling proposal but uses a very different strategy: the change of paradigm from substantial detailed regulation to a merely procedural solution. The focus of the Directive is on the establishment of a body representing the interests of all employees of the undertaking or group of undertakings within the Community: the EWC. In order to establish such an EWC a relatively complicated procedure is provided for. First, the employees' representatives in each undertaking or each group of undertakings covered by the Directive must form a so-called Special Negotiating Body (SNB) composed of representatives of each Member State in which the Community-scale undertaking or group of undertakings employs at least 100 employees. Then the EWC has to be set up by written agreement between the central management of the Community-scale undertaking or of the controlling undertaking of the group on the one hand and the SNB on the other. If a Community-scale undertaking or group of undertakings has its central management or its controlling undertaking outside the EU, the EWC must be set up by written agreement between its representative agent within the EU or, in absence of such an agent, the management of the undertaking or of the group of undertaking with the largest number of employees on the one hand and the SNB on the other.

This agreement must determine specific matters: the nature and composition of the EWC; its functions and powers; the procedure for informing and consulting the EWC; the place, frequency, and duration of its meetings; and, lastly, the financial and material resources to be allocated to the EWC. Whether such an agreement is concluded, and in what manner, depends entirely on the parties on both sides. If the SNB decides by a two-thirds majority not to request such an agreement, that is already the end of the matter. Only if the central management refuses to commence negotiations within six months of receiving such a request or if after three years the two partners are unable to reach an agreement do the subsidiary requirements of the Annex to the Directive apply.

These subsidiary requirements are the only form of pressure available to the SNB. They regulate in detail the composition of the EWC, the establishment of a specific committee for certain topics and situations, the frequency of information and consultation, the content on which the EWC is to be informed, the question of who bears the costs as well as the possibility of access to expert knowledge. In short: these subsidiary requirements contain all the detailed substantial prescriptions for which the Vredeling proposal turned out to be non-acceptable. They are supposed to be a threat to the bargaining parties. And it works. From the more than 1,100 EWC only very few were formed by recourse to subsidiary requirements, all the others are the result of negotiations.

In addition to the change of paradigm from substantial to procedural regulation the Directive introduces a further element which explains its success compared to Vredeling Proposal. Vredeling was intending uniform patterns: the same topics for information and consultation, the same frequency of information and consultation and the same procedure for information and consultation. This now is different: the results of negotiations between SNB and central management differ significantly and lead to very heterogeneous structures. The variety of patterns not only allows each company and group of companies to develop the pattern fitting best to its specific conditions but also offers an opportunity to find out best practices by experience, an ideal setting for learning from each other.

The system of EWCs has developed dynamics of its own and gone far beyond information and consultation towards negotiations, leading to agreements. These agreements refer to a whole variety of topics: health and safety; environment; fundamental rights, in particular, trade union rights and data protection; corporate social responsibility, equal treatment at work, job security, codes of conduct, mobility management; mergers; closures; relocations and restructuring. They are found in quite a few sectors, among them the chemical industry and therein, in particular, the pharmaceutical industry, the banking industry, the food industry, the oil industry, the metal industry and therein, in particular, the automobile industry, and even the tourism industry. The most spectacular agreements were concluded in the automobile industry of which the agreements at Ford and General Motors are the most prominent and far-reaching ones. These agreements lead to another question, namely whether

Directives on workers' involvement may also be understood as a sort of stimulus for further developments of industrial relations.

§14.03 THE HISTORY OF EMPLOYEE INVOLVEMENT IN THE EUROPEAN COMPANY

The second example I want to present you, the Directive on employee involvement in the European Company, has an even longer history which dates back to the late sixties of last century. When the Commission of the European Communities in the mid-sixties asked two eminent experts, (Pieter Sanders and Gérard Lyon-Caen), for an expertise on a possible structure of the EC, it looked as if the Commission would be willing to build its proposal on the insights of expert knowledge. This, however, was not the case. In spite of the fact that in view of the existing huge differences between the systems of industrial relations within the Community Lyon-Caen stressed the impossibility of a uniform pattern of workers' participation in company boards, the Commission's proposal of a European Company Statute of 1970 insisted on a uniform model: a mixture of the German and the Duch system of workers' representation in company boards was to be imposed on each European Company, no matter in which country its seat would be.

This strategy not only ignored the existing differences of the systems of industrial relations in the different Member Countries, but it also ignored the fact that for many countries this would mean a total reconsideration of their traditional pattern of company law: The model as contained in the proposal only made sense in a two-tier system with a management board and a supervisory board, but not in a system where both functions of these separate boards are contained in one single board, in the so-called one-tier system. Hence it was not astonishing at all that this first draft met nothing but strong resistance. The Commission, however, decided to remain stubborn: even the amended version of the European Company Statute of 1975 maintained the original pattern of employee board representation. Compared with the first draft, which provided only a representation of one third from the workers' side as against two thirds for shareholders' representatives, the new draft merely changed the board composition: one third workers' representatives, one third shareholders' representatives, and another third reserved for persons agreed upon by the other two groups.

The maintenance of this uniform pattern is even more surprising if linked to another activity of the Commission in the same year 1975. Based on the controversial debate which marked the beginning of a real awareness of the differences in the basic structures of company law, differences in trade union structures and trade union policies, and differences in the role played by law in industrial relations in the various Member States, the Commission presented a highly sophisticated Green Paper on Employee Participation and Company Structure in the EC. This paper served as a very informative and stimulating input to this debate, in the course of which the heterogeneous nature of the industrial relations' landscape throughout the community became even more evident and was discovered to its full extent. Against this background, it became more and more apparent that future drafts and amendments would have to abandon the approach of imposing one identical model on all who wanted to make use of the European Company as an option. Otherwise the chances of realization in the political process would tend towards zero.

It took quite a long time until the Commission pushed a new initiative. For a long time, the Commission was focusing on another, even more ambitious project: the harmonization of national company law by a Fifth Directive on the Structure of Public Limited Companies. There again in a first draft of 1972, the Commission presented the same pattern of workers' participation as contained in the proposal for the European Company. When it turned out that this approach had no political chance whatsoever the Commission presented a new proposal in 1983. This new draft no longer offered only one fixed menu for all the Member States seated around the Community table but replaced it by a sort of cafeteria system in which each Member State is able to choose whatever best suits its taste. First of all, it contained models for the one-tier structure of company law as well as for the two-tier structure. It, however, has to be stressed that the one-tier system somewhat was supposed to be modified to look like a two-tier system. The board of directors was supposed to be divided into a smaller number of managing members and a larger number of monitoring members, thereby arriving at a division of labour similar to that between a management board and a supervisory board in a two-tier structure.

As far as the two-tier was concerned, there was a choice of four models, the representation of workers German-style, leaving each Member State free to fix the proportion of workers' representation at between one third and a half, in the latter case providing a casting vote for the shareholders' representatives. This option also included the alternative of three groups as previously contained in the amended draft of the European Company Statute of 1975. Secondly, a model as used in the Netherlands could be chosen: the supervisory board co-opts members who are neither workers' nor shareholders' representatives. According to the third model, a separate body representing the company's employees has to be established. This body has the right to regular information and consultation on the company's situation. The rights of this separate body were, in essence, the same as the information rights of the supervisory organ appointed by the general meeting. Furthermore, this body had to be consulted the same way as the supervisory organ. The separate body was supposed to meet prior to each supervisory board meeting and had to provide all the documentation and information relating to the agenda for the supervisory board meeting. Lastly, the fourth model tried to introduce workers' participation by way of collective agreements. Where, however, such an agreement could not be reached within a certain period, Member States were supposed to regulate workers' participation in accordance with one of the other options. If the one-tier system was chosen, the same rules applied, at least in principle.

The proposal not only offered a significant degree of variety but also allowed workers' participation to be circumvented altogether: if the majority of workers voted against it, a participation model did not have to be introduced.

Even if this proposal was much more flexible than the first one, it quickly turned out that even this offer of many options politically had no chance. The European Trade Union Confederation (ETUC) opposed it for the reason that it was possible to get rid of participation by majority vote. And for the Employers' Confederation of European Industries (UNICE = Union des Industries de la Communauté Européenne, now Business Europe) the pattern still was too imposing for countries so far not acquainted with any employees' board representation whatsoever. In view of the opposition of both sides - which of course related in addition to many other points not mentioned here - it was no surprise at all that this amended proposal had to share the destiny of its predecessor: it was very soon considered to all intents and purposes moribund.

The failure of the strategy to harmonize national company law meant at the same time a new starting point for an attempt to realize the project of a European Company. The more it proved that the integration of workers' participation into the national company law structure remains illusionary, the more efforts were renewed to introduce workers' participation in a Community scale by way of redefinition of the European Company Statute. Consequently, in the Commission's White Paper of 1985 on completing the internal market the European Company Statute was mentioned as one of the goals to be achieved by the end of 1992. Therefore, in 1987 the European Council requested the relevant bodies 'to make swift progress with regard to the company law adjustments required for the creation of a European company'. Urged by these initiatives, in 1988 the Commission drew up a memorandum in which the key problems of a Statute for a European Company were listed. In this memorandum the European Parliament, the Council, and the two sides of industry were invited to express their views. On the basis of the feedback obtained from these actors, the Commission prepared a new proposal, which was presented in August 1989. In order to achieve the necessary flexibility, the element of workers' participation was now separated from a Statute proper, which was supposed to be contained in a Regulation: workers' participation was to be covered by a Directive. There were, however, safeguards that the Regulation could not be passed without the Directive. Both were closely interrelated. This pattern of division between Regulation and Directive and the interrelation between the two has survived and become also the basis of the now existing legislation in this area.

The proposal of 1989 contained a range of options which was very similar to the alternatives provided in the last draft of the Fifth Directive: first, the German model in which the workers' representatives were supposed to have a minimum of one third and a maximum of one half of the seats, without a casting vote for the shareholder's side in the latter version; secondly the Dutch model of co-optation; thirdly the separate body for workers' representation with specific rights of information and consultation; and last systems agreed by collective agreements. Where in the latter case such an agreement could not be reached, the most advanced national model in the respective Member State was supposed to be applied. In case such a model did not exist, the draft Directive stipulated a set of minimum standards for information and consultation. Most importantly, the possibility of opting out of workers' participation altogether was abolished.

In spite of the fact that this new proposal offered different options to be chosen, it soon turned out that it still was considered to be too rigid to be politically acceptable. Therefore, in the early nineties the hope that the European Company Statute with a scheme of workers' participation might be realized, became weaker and weaker.

Finally, it somehow passed away. It seemed to be just impossible to reconcile the peculiarities and philosophies of national industrial relations patterns with a transnational structure of workers' participation whatever it might look like. The project seemed to be dead for ever.

The revitalization of the project of a European Company is due to the success of the Directive on EWCs and the change of paradigm from substantial regulation to proceduralization. The Commission impressed by the success of the Directive on EWCs was considering whether the method applied there could not be repeated in the case of workers' participation in the European Company. It established in 1996 a group of experts on 'European Systems of Worker Involvement' chaired by the former Deputy President of the Commission, Etienne Davignon. The Davignon-group presented its report in 1997: its recommendations were based on the logic and on the principles of the Directive on EWCs. It defined actors for negotiation and left in principle everything to these negotiations. As in the Directive on EWCs for the case of failure of such negotiations a safety net, so-called subsidiary requirements, was suggested, guaranteeing the workers' representatives at least one fifth (in any case two) of the seats in the supervisory board or the corresponding body.

In spite of the very positive reaction the Davignon report got throughout the EU it soon became pretty clear that it still was very difficult to transfer the ideas of this report into legislation. The crucial point of controversy was the level of workers' board representation guaranteed by the subsidiary requirements. Member States with a higher amount of seats were reluctant to accept such a low proportion of workers' representation. Therefore, in a first phase, the attempt to turn the Davignon report into law mainly failed because of the German and Austrian opposition. Under the United Kingdom's presidency in the first semester of 1998, a compromise was developed in order to overcome this resistance. According to this new version the highest level of board representation of a company participating in a merger has to be decisive and to be guaranteed by the subsidiary requirements. If for example, a German company would engage in a merger, the German level of workers' representation would be extended to the new European Company if not a different pattern would be the result of negotiations. This maintenance strategy, however, has been combined by a trade-off: there is no need for workers' board representation at all if there was none in the pre-existing companies. This pattern – for a long time opposed by Spain – has survived when finally after quite a few futile attempts in Nice in December 2000 agreement on the content of the draft Directive was reached by the Council.

It is important to stress that also in the case of the European Company The subsidiary requirements are merely functioning as a threat. To my knowledge so far all negotiations ended with a positive result. Recourse to the subsidiary requirements was not necessary.

§14.04 LESSONS TO BE LEARNED

This very enlightening history of workers' participation in the EU teaches us important lessons. Since each system of industrial relations does have its own history embedded in the respective country's culture and institutional framework, there can be no harmonization or uniformity of institutional arrangements all over the EU. It is particularly impossible to impose one country's system to all the others, as the early history of workers participation in the European Company demonstrates. But even predefined options seem still to be too rigid to fit in the overall framework of a given country, as is shown by the later proposals for the European Company and the fifth company law Directive. And as the Vredeling proposal teaches us, substantive prescriptions on what has to be done within the companies have no chance to be politically accepted.

The way out of this dilemma is proceduralization, establishing a framework for negotiations in order to elaborate compromises fitting to the needs of the respective companies and employee representatives. The result is not uniformity but utmost variety.

Finally, the Directive on EWCs teaches another important lesson: Once such a scheme is established by a Directive it develops its own dynamics exceeding by far the intention of the legislator. Or to put it differently: legislation is only the beginning, depending on the actors' strategies the schemes can grow beyond the limits drawn by the legislator. This scenery is not to be perceived as static but as highly dynamic.

CHAPTER 15

The Dark Side of the Labour Market: Institutional Change, Economic Crisis and Undeclared Work in Greece

Horen Voskeritsian, Panos Kapotas, Andreas Kornelakis & Michail Veliziotis

§15.01 INTRODUCTION

Undeclared work is a problem that has increasingly attracted the attention of both policymakers and academics. In 1998 the European Commission published its first Communication on undeclared work (COM(98) 219 final) and the topic started gaining momentum in the European agenda. Following this, the item was prioritised as one of the ten Employment Guidelines of the revised European Employment Strategy, while the Council also adopted a Resolution on 'transforming undeclared work into regular employment' in 2003. Subsequently, the European Commission published another Communication at the end of 2007 (European Commission, 2007) encouraging member-states to pursue policies and engage in mutual learning from best practices. Finally, the 2010 Recommendations of the Council to Greece on tackling the sovereign debt crisis included a recommendation to take 'immediate measures to fight undeclared work'.

Apart from the increasing importance attached to the topic from European policymakers, undeclared work has also attracted the interest of academics. Crucially, the literature does no longer only examine the prevalence of the 'shadow economy' in developing and transition countries, but also looks at the incidence of undeclared work within advanced European countries (Williams and Windebank, 1998; Pfau-Effinger et al., 2009). Recent scholarly work on this topic has examined several themes such as: the motives for undeclared work and explanations for its persistence (Kimmel and Conway, 2001; MacDonald, 1994; Ram et al., 2007) different 'varieties' or 'geographies' of undeclared work (Pfau-Effinger, 2009; Williams, 2009); efforts to measure the extent of the shadow economy (Hussmanns, 2004; Schneider, 2004), and finally, the range of policies available to tackle the problem (Sepulveda and Syrett, 2007; Williams, 2005; 2008).

Addressing undeclared work and other unlawful practices in the labour market was among the priorities of the consecutive Memoranda of Understanding (MoU) between the Greek state and the Troika (European Commission, 2010; 2012; 2015). Nevertheless, limited progress had been made in this regard, especially in the early years of the crisis, despite the fact that combating undeclared work remains one of the few policy-issues that enjoys widespread consensus among the social partners. It is (almost) the perfect win-win game, since (almost) everyone seems to benefit from eliminating this phenomenon: increased revenues from reduction of tax-evasion and insurance contributions-evasion for the government; increased security, healthcare coverage, and pension rights for the workers; increased productivity from effort/loyalty effects and penalties-avoidance for firms.

The introduction of a law in 2011 (Law 3996/2011) aiming to reform the operation of the Labour Inspectorate did little to confront the problem at its source. Although the rationalisation and better functioning of the Labour Inspectorate are very important in tackling undeclared work, a bundle of policies of measures are required to prevent employment relations actors in engaging with such unlawful activities. The 2016 road map that the Greek government constructed in collaboration with the International Labour Organization (ILO) is a fruitful first step in this direction (ILO 2017).

In line with the rationale of the ILO report on Undeclared Work in Greece (ILO 2016), this chapter aims to shed some light on the changing nature of illegality in the Greek labour market during the Memoranda years and to try and understand why such practices persist. It should be stressed that what follows is just a first approximation to a very complex phenomenon, and in no circumstances do we make the claim that our results and considerations depict the full reality of illegal labour practices in Greece. To better appreciate the extent and nature of illegality, and to offer targeted and specific recommendations for its abatement, further research is necessary.

We follow a qualitative critical case study research design, having conducted interviews with key informants in Greek employment relations. In total, we interviewed seventeen participants from the tertiary social partners' institutions (GSEE, SEV, GSEVEE, ESEE, SETE)[1], the Ministry of Labour, the Labour Inspectorate (SEPE) and the Organisation for Mediation and Arbitration (OMED). All interviews took place between July and August 2016.

The chapter is structured as follows. The next section presents the relevant theoretical framework structured around the state morality versus civil morality dichotomy. The third section presents data documenting the incidence and prevalence

1. GSEE (Greek Confederation of Employees) is Greece's peak level trade union confederation. SEV (Hellenic Federation of Enterprises) represents big firms from various sectors of the economy. GSEVEE (Hellenic Confederation of Professionals, Craftsmen and Merchants) represents SMEs and its members are federations from various sectors of the economy. ESEE (Hellenic Confederation of Commerce and Entrepreneurship) represents SMEs in the retail sector. SETE (Association of Greek Tourism Enterprises) represents the Hotel and Tourism industry.

of undeclared work in different sectors of the Greek economy. It also seeks to inform the discussion of the prevalence of undeclared work with insights from primary interviews with key actors. The fourth section wraps up the arguments to provide a first explanation of the incidence of undeclared work and the reasons behind other unlawful activities in the Greek labour market. The final section concludes.

§15.02 THEORETICAL FRAMEWORK

A prominent theoretical framework that has been used in the relevant literature to explain illegal practices (and undeclared work more specifically) is the 'state morality' versus 'civil morality' dichotomy (Helmke and Levitsky, 2004; Williams, 2015; Williams and Horodnic, 2015a, b). According to it, it is the failure of formal (i.e., state) and informal (i.e., civil society) institutions to be aligned that lead to the emergence of illegal practices. Hence, illegality emerges when there is a misalignment of the interpretations of the 'rules of the game' as set by these different institutions. There are four types of formal institutional failings: formal institutional voids (e.g., non-existence of a welfare state, which forces people to undeclared work to compensate for the lack of income); formal institutional inefficiencies (e.g., when formal institutions seek to protect or appear to be protecting the interests of an elite); formal institutional uncertainty; and formal institutional weaknesses and instability (i.e., lack of capability to enforce legislation) (*see* Webb et al., 2009).

Although this framework may offer plausible explanations regarding the behaviour of the parties in the employment relationship, it lacks in two respects: first, it does not adequately consider the complex social dynamics that may define the rules of the game in an employment relations system, disregarding for instance the role of other institutions – such as the trade unions or the employers' associations – that occupy a 'middle ground' position in between the state and the civil society. Second, it does not consider the importance of power in formulating certain behaviours in society. In a social setting where the power balance between capital and labour has been disturbed (for whatever reasons), illegality may become more prominent as a means of redefining one's position in the employment relations arena.

Said limitations notwithstanding, the state morality versus civil morality theory does offer some interesting breakthroughs, especially regarding the role of formal and informal institutions in determining an actor's behaviour and actions. In what follows, we will see that both approaches have merit in the Greek case. Before proceeding, however, it is imperative to set out some preliminary definitions.

[A] Preliminary Definitions: Types of Illegality in the Labour Market

- Undeclared work: work that generates value but is not revealed to the appropriate authorities either for taxation or social security reasons or because its nature or its products are illegal (e.g., human trafficking, drug dealing, smuggling etc.). For the sake of simplicity we will employ the European Commission's definition of undeclared work – which is also the one adopted by Article 32 of Law 3996/2011: 'productive activities that are lawful as regards their nature, but are not declared to the public authorities, taking into account the differences in their regulatory systems between the Member States' (European Commission 2007: 2).

- Undeclared employment: waged employment that generates value but is not revealed to the appropriate authorities for reasons of taxation, social security contributions or labour law (for instance, so as not to generate rights and responsibilities associated with one's categorisation as an 'employee'). It is a narrower concept than undeclared work, as it is only concerned with waged employees/workers. Hence in this category, we do not include self-employed people (such as doctors, lawyers, etc.). The question of bogus self-employment is of particular interest here. For taxonomical purposes, these activities are to be considered undeclared work.
- Under-declared employment: employment that is not declared in its totality to the appropriate authorities. This may be (i) under-declaring an employee's wages; (ii) under-declaring an employee's working hours. In the first case, an employee may receive part of one's wages 'under the table' (envelope wages), and in the second an employee may be working for more hours than the ones officially declared for (for instance, working an eight-hour shift while they are registered as working a four-hour shift; working unpaid overtime etc.). Whether the employee receives compensation for the undeclared part of one's working hours is an empirical question, which does not affect the classification of this practice as under-declared employment.
- False declaration of employment: the practice of declaring an employee as doing one particular type of job (e.g., working as a secretary) while in reality doing another (usually more specialised) job (for instance, working instead as an accountant).

As can be appreciated, the boundaries between these categories can be quite blurred and usually a person may be classified as belonging to more than one category. Hence, the declaration of a student as an 'intern' (when, in reality, this person works full-time for the company), is both a false declaration of employment and undeclared (or under-declared) employment. As it will become evident in the analysis of our interviews, the blurring of the boundaries is a common practice in various sectors and creates multiple problems both for the practice of employment relations and for tackling illegality.

[B] Illegal Practices in Greek Employment Relations

Illegal practices in the labour market are by no means a new phenomenon in Greece. They preceded the crisis and, in all certainty, they will outlive it. As the ILO report on undeclared work in Greece states, 'the undeclared economy in Greece in 2013 was the equivalent of 24% of GDP, which puts Greece among the countries with one of the largest undeclared economies in Europe' (ILO 2016: 22). Within this context, it is not surprising that undeclared work and other illegal practices prevail in the labour market.

Official statistics about unlawful labour practices are primarily derived from the Greek Labour Inspectorate (SEPE). Between 2009 and 2013 SEPE published an annual report that included detailed information about its activities, and detailed statistics on the various violations that were observed in the market. This annual report has since been discontinued and has been replaced by a summative report taken from the ARTEMIS database, which is only concerned, however, with instances of undeclared work.

According to the latest ARTEMIS report (Ministry of Employment and Social Affairs 2015), in between the fourth quarter of 2013 and January 2015, *13%* of all inspected companies employed undeclared workers (*see* Table 15.1). Undeclared workers constituted *4.2%* of the sample (2.7% were Greek nationals and 1.5% migrant workers).

Table 15.1 Undeclared Employment in Greece September 2013-January 2015

	15 September 2013-31 January 2015	*1 January 2015-31 January 2015*
Inspected enterprises	36,007	1,854
No of enterprises employing undeclared workers	4,672 (12.98%)	267 (14.40%)
Total no of workers	180,856	5,649
No of undeclared workers	7,544 (4.17%)	460 (8.14%)
Total amount of fines (€)	€78,672,952	€4,854,043

Source: Adapted from Ministry of Employment and Social Affairs (2015: 5).

The ILO report on undeclared work in Greece (ILO, 2016), supplements the above picture by reference to a recent Eurobarometer survey (conducted in 2013), which adopted a more reliable and robust methodology. According to this (ILO 2016: 26):

> 67.3% of all undeclared work was waged employment, of which: 13.3% was wholly undeclared waged employment, and 54% was under-declared employment. 10.2% was under-declared self-employment, and 22.5% paid favours conducted for close social relations, such as kin, friends, acquaintances and neighbours.

Undeclared and under-declared employment is concentrated in certain industries that occupy an almost permanent position in the relevant statistics, although the magnitude of these practices varies from one year to another. Figure 15.1 presents the industries with the greater instance of undeclared employees between 2013 and 2015, while Figure 15.2 presents the same data for January 2015.

Figure 15.1 Undeclared Employees per Sector September 2013-January 2015 (Results of Labour Inspections)

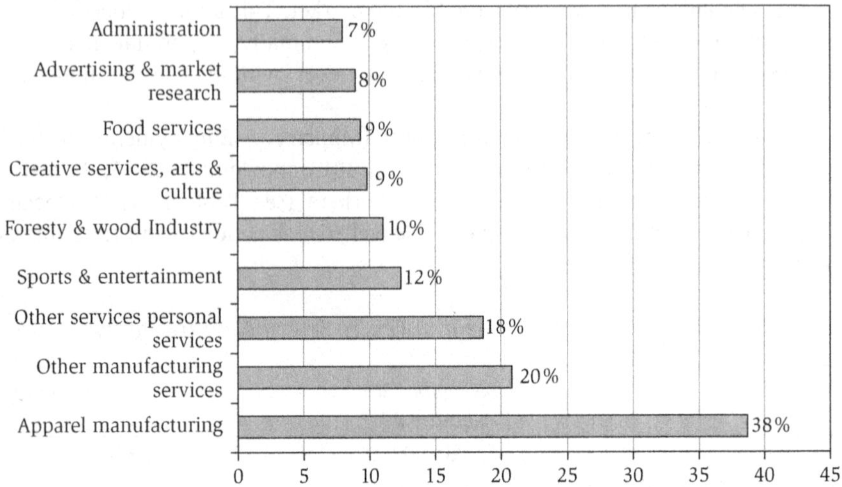

Source: ILO (2016:25).

Figure 15.2 Undeclared Employees per Sector, January 2015 (Results of Labour Inspections)

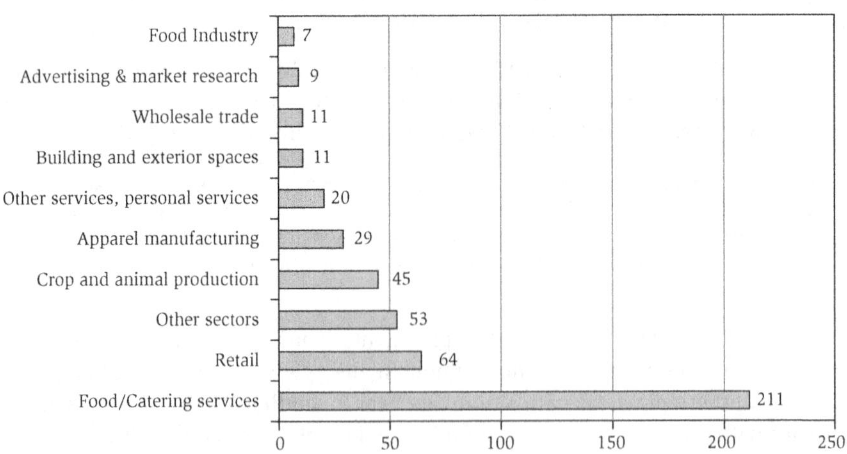

Source: Ministry of Employment and Social Affairs (2015: 26).

Most of the firms that participate in such activities (although by no means all of them) have certain common characteristics: they are small or very small firms, engaged in production activities that may require the use of flexible forms of employment, and usually employ low-skilled workers since they have a very simple (or simplistic) labour process that does not require the use of experienced personnel. Food services (such as catering, bartending, table waiting) or apparel manufacturing are two prime examples.

Our interviews with the social partners shed some additional light to the realities of illegality in the Greek labour market. Four themes clearly emerged from our discussions: the first concerned the issue of *undeclared work and employment* and the reasons for its occurrence; the second concentrated on instances of *under-declared work* (especially regarding envelope wages and under-declared working time); the third focused on the *false declaration of employment*, while the fourth raised the issue of the *delay in the payment of wages*.

Undeclared work and employment were a reality that all our interlocutors considered to be a common characteristic of the sectors they represented. Their view was that the official figures – as published in SEPE's reports – actually underestimate the extent of the issue, something that was not surprising per se. The structural characteristics of the Greek economy, which is dominated by very small and small enterprises, mostly family-owned, contributes to the persistence of the phenomenon.

The family-oriented nature of small businesses in Greece is an important factor to be considered when discussing illegality for two reasons: first, the social relationships that develop between the firm-owner and the firm's staff are such that allow the development of a mutual 'understanding' about the condition of the firm and the realities of the market in which it operates. Hence, it is much easier for the employer or the employee to agree on the implementation of an illegal practice that serves both ends. This is particularly important in the case of under-declared employment, as will be shortly analysed. Second, the vast majority of family-owned businesses usually employ family members (typically first-degree relatives – wife/husband, son/daughter, mother/father), who may voluntarily agree not to appear as the company's employees. Family businesses may constitute, at least for the owner's family members, a parallel source of (illegal) income, in addition to their legitimate employment. As one of our interviewees from GSEVEE stated:

> Most of the self-employed also work in 'black employment', which comes either from non-relatives but primarily from relatives. An emerging issue, therefore, is what kind of motives [to abstain from undeclared work] you provide to the relative who works in a business, and may be also registered as unemployed, to have social security (GSEVEE interviewee, 5/8/2016).

The reference to the self-employed is of particular interest in this respect. As other interviewees also commented, in recent years the number of 'self-employed' has increased exponentially. The question, however, which is not adequately addressed by the existing data, concerns the nature of self-employment. Thus, apart from the 'true' self-employed persons (like doctors, lawyers, software engineers etc.), many can be classified as 'bogus' self-employed. Employers may have a preference for self-employed personnel, as they do not incur social security contributions for the employer, and the wage rate does not depend on a specific collective agreement but is freely determined in the market. It is, therefore, possible (although more research is required to establish this) that bogus self-employed persons may be paid below the national minimum wage. Consequently, reverting to the family business to supplement their income can be a fruitful way forward.

An interesting finding from our research concerned the process through which one finds itself working illegally. Two reasons became apparent: the first, and the one that could be expected under conditions of high unemployment, is the pressure that the employers themselves may exert on the employee to take up undeclared or under-declared employment. Fear of losing one's job, or of not finding alternative employment, is central to this scenario, allowing, therefore, the emergence of exploitation. Second, and this is particularly important especially regarding the policies to tackle the phenomenon, many employees voluntarily request, and agree with, their employer to be employed in the 'black market'.

The explanations brought forward to 'justify' the turn to illegality focused around the issues of taxation and non-wage costs. On the one hand, employers do not have to pay social security contributions (or may only have to pay a small amount), whereas employees increase their 'take home' income as this is not be taxed and they do not pay social security contributions. Our interviewee from SEPE argued that this is a result of the deregulation of the labour market, of incomplete controls, and of the destruction of a 'social security consciousness':

> when you cannot enforce even the minimum compliance of both the employers and the employees in legality, when there is absolutely no motive to comply with the minimum requirements of labour law, when there is no social security consciousness, when the prospect of receiving a decent pension fades away then ... all the measures [we are discussing] are at best fragmentary that may somehow improve things but do not address the problem (SEPE interviewee, 25/7/2016).

Similarly to undeclared work, ***under-declared employment*** appears to be quite prevalent in the labour market. Under-declared employment manifests itself in two different ways: first, through the payment of *'envelope wages'* and, second, through the *under-declaration of working time* (or *concealed full time employment*).

The aforementioned practices are not, of course, new in the Greek labour market. However, the crisis and the changes in the institutional framework of employment relations seem to have accentuated their use. As an interviewee from GSEVEE argued:

> In the official data it may appear that ... in our country companies have adopted the 586 euro [i.e. the national minimum wage], in practice however this is not the case. This had as a result to use the national minimum wage as a measure to reduce non-wage costs but not so much wage costs. To be more specific I will give you an example: if the wage in a sector was 1,000 euro, it remained 1,000 euro under the table but on paper it appeared as having dropped to 586 euros (GSEVEE interviewee, 4/8/2016).

Although one cannot easily determine the full extent of this practice – and indeed as our SEPE interlocutor argued, these numbers do appear excessive – it was a common belief across the spectrum of the social partners that such behaviours do persist. Apart from the reasons previously discussed (i.e., avoidance of taxation and social security contributions, and an increase in 'take-home' income), two more reasons were put forward to explain this phenomenon: first, the family nature of the Small and medium-sized enterprises (SMEs), as previously discussed and, second, the attempt by the employer to retain the skill base in the company and to avoid dissatisfaction that may lead to informal conflicts or sabotage in the company. This appears to be a 'win-win' situation for both parties: the employee sacrifices social security for the net value of his or her wage and retains his or her job, while the employer saves money, retains human capital, and avoids conflicts that could have arisen if the wage had been decreased. It is important to note, however, that this is only one possible manifestation of the phenomenon in the labour market, the extent of which cannot be determined, and which is not necessarily a faithful representation of reality. The very existence of under-declared employment, however, is an index of endemic pathogenies in the Greek labour market and should inform any discussion on addressing 'envelope wages'.

In the case of *under-declared working time*, similar considerations apply. It seems that the substitution of full-time employment for 'bogus' flexibility is a common practice in the Greek labour market. As an interviewee from SEPE commented:

> What we also constantly observed, and to me this constitutes the Greek paradox, [is that the employers] used flexible forms of employment, either temporary employment or part time employment, to reduce wage costs. They declared, for example, the employee as working part time for 4 hours, they paid him and insured him for 4 hours, but they asked him to work for 8 hours ... we tried to fight this, but it was not easy (SEPE interviewee, 28/7/2016).

Another practice that can be classified under this category is the exploitation of the institutions of internships by certain employers, especially those in the tourism industry (although it may be possible that similar practices exist in other industries as well, where internships or apprenticeships are in common use). Our SEPE interviewee provided a typical example:

> I remember we had a very good collaboration with the island of Rhodes because all the legitimate employers felt that they were being undermined by the methods that the others [i.e. the non-legitimate ones] were using, and they provided us with all the information regarding these methods. I remember, for instance, the 'jobbery' according to which they declared employees from ex-communist countries as interns and they paid them for the whole season 120 euros plus food, water etc. (SEPE interviewee, 28/7/2016).

As in the case of the envelope wages, two scenarios seem to account for this practice: first, that there is some kind of voluntary or involuntary cooperation between the two parties of the employment relationship; and second, that many of these actions constitute exploitation on the part of the employer of the adverse conditions in the labour market.

This seems to be the case in instances of ***false declaration of one's employment***. As a respondent from the GSEVEE commented:

> A profession is ... what the employer says it is! What the employer does, for instance, is the following: for example, an audit firm has a big contract and requires staff. If it hired 100 people as accountants, it should give them the wage that is set by the accountants' occupational-level collective agreement. It hires

> them, therefore, as secretaries with 586 euros but they agree that they will work in accounting (GSEVEE interviewee, 4/8/2016).

The same respondent argued that this appears to be a common practice among firms, leading among other things to the destruction and devaluation of occupations, with adverse consequences for the country's human capital. The pertinent question, in this case, is why employees agree to this practice. Our SEPE interlocutor provides an answer: in times of high unemployment the employee will do anything necessary to gain or retain his or her employment status – even work for free (SEPE interviewee, 25/7/2016).

Unthinkable as it may seem, 'working for free' also appears to be a practice that prevails in the Greek labour market. This may take three general forms: the first, which we did not explore in detail, has to do with forced labour – with prominent examples being the exploitation of trafficking victims predominantly in the sex industry. The second, which closely resembles the first, is the employment of undocumented migrants in certain jobs (usually low skilled and of temporary nature) and their subsequent reporting to the relevant migration authorities once the job is completed (resulting, of course, in the non-payment of any outstanding wages). Again, this was an issue that fell outside the scope of our current research project, but several infamous cases have been widely reported in the Greek media and some have also been the subject of judicial scrutiny (as, for example, the case of the workers in the strawberry fields of Manolada). The third form is the ***delay in the payment of one's wages***, which amounts – if one typically examines it under the lens of labour law – to 'unpaid work'. Both our SEPE interviewees agreed that wages in the labour market are not always paid on time, the delay ranging from one week to a year. As one of them argued:

> According to estimates by INE-GSEE [i.e. the institute of employment of the General Confederation of Greek Workers], [there exist] 1 to 1,2 million employees who are unpaid for 2 to 15 months. It is a huge number. There are legal consequences, but how can you enforce them? The wage is protected both under civil and under criminal law. But how can you impose this protection when this phenomenon has acquired a certain universality and has been transformed to a social phenomenon? (SEPE interviewee, 25/7/2016).

By the phrase 'social phenomenon' our interlocutor meant that this is such a common practice nowadays that carries with it a certain 'social legitimacy', rendering said behaviour acceptable (or, at least, understandable) by both parties of the employment relationship. The social legitimacy of illegality is linked to the 'state mentality/civil mentality' framework but is not necessarily directly explained by it. For, in this case, we do not observe a common front of the civil sphere against the will and actions of the political sphere, but a (partial) justification of the actions of the employer as a 'natural' consequence of the wider socio-economic environment in which (s)he operates. Such a behaviour can become a crucial obstacle to tackling any form of illegal action, as the 'victim' identifies with the interests of the 'abuser' and constructs a rationalisation framework that prevents them from taking action against their employer.

§15.03 EXPLAINING ILLEGALITY IN THE GREEK LABOUR MARKET

According to the *ILO Diagnostic Report on Undeclared Work in Greece*, the view of the Greek stakeholders on the determinants of undeclared and under-declared work in Greece can be summarised as follows (ILO, 2016: 39):

- High levels of self-employment and the small size of enterprises and family businesses
- High unemployment rates, especially among young people
- Seasonality and dispersion of operations, especially in agriculture and hospitality
- The immigration flow into the Greek labour market
- High levels of non-labour costs – social security contributions for both employers and employees
- High tax rates
- Changes in the determination of wages through legislative means rather through social dialogue
- The reduction of real wages and
- The lack of trust in state mechanisms and the mind set developed because of these factors.

Indeed, as the preceding analysis revealed, most of these points emerged in our research as well. However, although the above may constitute the causes behind specific instances of illegality, they do not adequately explain the emergence of illegality as a phenomenon. In other words, the question is what is the mechanism that links, for instance, the lack of trust in the state to the adoption of illegal practices? As already mentioned, a comprehensive answer to this question requires further research into the causal mechanisms of illegality, as well as a different methodological approach: one which would allow us to better appreciate the motives behind illegal activities. Although we did not pursue this line of enquiry so far, we firmly believe that it offers fruitful grounds for future research. The material deprivation of the parties involved in such activities – and the opportunity to potentially improve their circumstances – could constitute a promising starting point. The same may be the case with regard to the current socio-economic environment (high unemployment in a deregulated labour market with problematic enforcement mechanisms) that provides ample opportunities for ill-willing powerful actors to exploit the weaker parties of the employment relationship with little, if any, fear of being challenged.

The ILO report partially supports this conclusion; contrary to a standard narrative that blames undeclared work on high tax rates, the authors of the report provide evidence to suggest that there is actually a correlation between undeclared work 'the lack of trust in the state and [the] belief that they [employers and employees do not] receive appropriate public goods and services for the taxes they pay' (ILO 2016: 35). Given that Greece is a country where citizens tend not to trust the state, where the 'effectiveness of social transfers in reducing poverty is considerably lower than in the European Union (EU) as a whole' and where income inequality has considerably increased in recent years (*see* ILO 2016: p.32ff), the prevalence of undeclared work is hardly surprising. The earlier discussion about the divergence between state morality and civil morality seems to be applicable in this case and to explain illegal behaviours.

However, in our view, this framework is not in itself adequate to make evaluative judgments regarding a rather complex situation in the case of Greece. Although there is indeed ample evidence to argue that society may define its own *modus operandi* in contrast to the one promoted by the state, for reasons that have to do with culture, the economy or one's financial state, one should also consider the *role of power dynamics* in determining certain actions. It would be a mistake to ignore or underestimate the role of exploitation and power politics in persuading an employee to engage in an illegal activity or even in changing an employee's cognitive structure and perception about the legitimacy of a course of action. The fact, for example, that an employee is afraid to denounce the employer when (s)he is engaging in illegal activities or the fact that an employee may be willing to accept certain (illegal) actions as 'legitimate' (both of which became apparent in our interviews) points in this direction.

Another interesting view voiced by one of our interlocutors was that, perhaps, the state/civil morality dichotomy may not necessarily exist in Greece:

> I do not agree with this interpretation [i.e. the state morality vs civil morality dichotomy]. For here, in Greece, these two moralities coincide with each other. The state never wanted to fight illegality and undeclared work, it considered it a factor of development, especially with regards to migrants in the 2000s; and secondly both the employers' and the employees', and the society's, consciousness has concurred with any form of illegality ... this points to the following, that in Greece this divergence between the state and civil morality does not exist (SEPE interviewee, 25/7/2016).

Although this point of view may exaggerate or over-generalise the situation, it highlights a possible analytical dimension that should, in our view, be the subject of further research. For, as the same interlocutor argued:

> 'All three MoU included an obligation to reduce illegality in the labour market. Let me, therefore, ask a provocative question: all 3 MoU included an obligation to reduce labour costs. Were they reduced? Yes. They also included an obligation to deregulate dismissals. Were they deregulated? By all means. They also included the clause to combat illegality. Was this achieved? No. Why? How can you be successful in all but miss one? And this [i.e. tackling illegality] would be the easiest of the three, since there is a relevant commitment and the agreement of the social partners, of the IMF, the ILO, the World Bank, and the ECB etc. In this case, therefore, where everybody agrees we cannot do anything about it, but where we disagree the MoU succeeds' (SEPE interviewee, 25/7/2016).

Admittedly, the above analysis does not necessarily take into account a series of factors that would ensure the successful implementation of anti-illegality policies. It does, however, raise an interesting point that merits further investigation: namely, an evaluation not only of the policies that have been diachronically used to address the issue but, primarily, an evaluation of the motivation to tackle illegality.

§15.04 CONCLUSION

The prevalence of undeclared work and other illegal activities in the Greek labour market is consistent with the high level of undeclared economy in Greece. Undeclared work is encountered in sectors across the economy and has been a permanent feature of the Greek labour market even before the advent of the crisis. However, the decline in economic activity and the general economic slump since 2010 further accentuated the prevalence of this phenomenon. Undeclared work appears to be concentrated in specific sectors of economic activity, namely, Retail, Food services (such as catering, bartending, table waiting) or Apparel Manufacturing. Common characteristics of firms engaged in undeclared work are their small or very small size and the fact that they operate in production activities that may require the use of flexible forms of employment and low-skilled or unskilled workers.

Although undeclared work and employment is perhaps the most dominant form of illegal labour practices, three additional sub-types of this phenomenon are also widespread in the Greek labour market: the under-declaration of employment, the false declaration of employment and the non-payment of wages or salaries. The theory of state versus civil morality can help explain the prevalence of these practices. According to this theory, illegality emerges when there is a misalignment between the interpretations of the 'rules of the game' as set by these different institutions. However, our research has also revealed that when dealing with illegality one also needs to consider the structural characteristics of the capitalist system and the influence of power in shaping the employees' behaviours.

Hence, although employees and employers may come to a 'common understanding' and engage in forms of undeclared work – for reasons outlined by the state/civil morality theory – it is also the case that many employees are forced into this situation by employers who take advantage of the adverse economic and labour market environment to impose their will and dominate the employment relationship. To protect their employment status, employees may either reluctantly agree to enter into such arrangements or they may 'rationalise' their situation, thus further enhancing the employers' hegemonic position in the labour market.

REFERENCES

European Commission (2007). *Stepping up the fight against undeclared work* COM(2007) 628 final. Brussels: European Commission.

European Commission (2010). *The Economic Adjustment Programme for Greece.* Brussels: European Commission, Directorate-General for Economic and Financial Affairs.

European Commission (2012). *The second economic adjustment programme for Greece.* Brussels: European Commission, Directorate-General for Economic and Financial Affairs.

European Commission (2015). *Memorandum of Understanding Between the European Commission Acting on Behalf of the European Stability Mechanism and the*

Hellenic Republic and the Bank of Greece. https://ec.europa.eu/info/sites/info/files/01_mou_20150811_en1.pdf.

Helmke, G. and Levitsky, S. (2004). 'Informal Institutions and Comparative Politics: A Research Agenda', *Perspectives on Politics*, 2(4): 725-740.

Hussmanns, R. (2004). 'Measuring the Informal Economy: From Employment in the Informal Sector to Informal Employment', *Policy Integration Department Working Paper #53*, Geneva: International Labour Office.

ILO (2016). *Diagnostic Report on Undeclared Work in Greece*. Geneva: ILO.

ILO (2017). 'Road Map for Fighting Undeclared Work in Greece', *Policy Brief Series, No. 2*, Geneva: ILO.

Kimmel, J. and Conway, S. (2001). 'Who Moonlights and Why? Evidence from the SIPP'. *Industrial Relations*, 40(1): 89-120.

MacDonald, R. (1994). 'Fiddly Jobs, Undeclared Working and the Something for Nothing Society', *Work, Employment and Society*, 8(4): 507-530.

Ministry of Employment and Social Affairs (2015). *'ARTEMIS'. Action Plan for Addressing Undeclared Employment*. Athens: Ministry of Employment and Social Affairs.

Pfau-Effinger, B. (2009) 'Varieties of Undeclared Work in European Societies', *British Journal of Industrial Relations* 47(1): 79–99.

Pfau-Effinger, B., L. Flaquer and P. Jensen (2009) (eds), *Formal and Informal Work in Europe. The Hidden Work Regime*. London and NY: Routledge.

Ram, M., Edwards, P. and Jones, T. (2007). 'Staying Underground: Informal Work, Small Firms, and Employment Regulation in the United Kingdom' *Work and Occupations*, 34(3): 318.

Schneider, F. (2004), 'The Size of the Shadow Economies of 145 Countries all over the World', *IZA Discussion Paper # 1431*, December 2004.

SEPE (2009) *SEPE's Activity Report for 2009*. Athens: SEPE.

SEPE (2010) *SEPE's Activity Report for 2010*. Athens: SEPE.

SEPE (2011) *SEPE's Activity Report for 2011*. Athens: SEPE.

SEPE (2012) *SEPE's Activity Report for 2012*. Athens: SEPE.

SEPE (2013) *SEPE's Activity Report for 2013*. Athens: SEPE.

Sepulveda, L. and Syrett, S. (2007) 'Out of the Shadows? Formalisation Approaches to Informal Economic Activity', *Policy & Politics* 35(1): 87-104.

Webb, j.W., et al. (2009). 'You Say Illegal, I Say Legitimate: Entrepreneurship in the Informal Economy', *Academy of Management Review*, 34(3): 492-510.

Williams, C. (2005). 'Fostering Community Engagement and Tackling Undeclared Work: The Case for an Evidence-Based 'Joined-Up' Public Policy Approach', *Regional Studies*, 39(8): 1145-1155.

Williams, C. (2008). 'A Critical Evaluation of Public Policy Towards Undeclared Work in the European Union', *Journal of European Integration*, 30(2): 273-290.

Williams, C. (2009). 'Formal and Informal Employment in Europe: Beyond Dualistic Representations', *European Urban and Regional Studies*, 16(2): 147-159.

Williams, C. and Windebank, J. (1998). *Informal Employment: Implications for Work and Welfare in the Advanced Economies*. London: Routledge.

Williams, C.C. (2015). 'Explaining the Informal Economy: An Exploratory Evaluation of Competing Perspectives', *Relations Industrielles/Industrial Relations,* 70(4): 741-765.

Williams, C.C. and Horodnic, I. (2015a). 'Evaluating the Prevalence of the Undeclared Economy in Central and Eastern Europe: An Institutional Asymmetry Perspective', *European Journal of Industrial Relations,* 21(4): 389-406.

Williams, C.C. and Horodnic, I. (2015b) 'Explaining the Prevalence of Illegitimate Wage Practices in Southern Europe: An Institutional Analysis', *South European Society and Politics,* 20(2): 203-221.

CHAPTER 16

Workers' Involvement in Collective Redundancies in EU Law: What for? a Case Study

Silvia Rainone

§16.01 INTRODUCTION

This contribution aims at unveiling the approach of the Court of Justice of the European Union (hereinafter 'CJEU', or 'the Court') with regards to contractual freedom in the field of labour law and, more precisely, with respect to the rules concerning collective redundancies, as defined in Directive 98/59/EC.

The relevance of this enquiry lies in the widespread perception that, at least since the last fifteen years, business freedoms find more and more space within European Union (EU) labour law, while workers' prerogatives have not substantially progressed.[1] In line with this perception, the analysis of policy-making documents on the social dimension of EU integration shows that there has been a change of focus and rhetoric. If originally the Commission's Communications were referring to the importance to ensure an upward convergence of labour standards across the EU, more or less since the mid 1980s labour and social policies have increasingly been portrayed as functional to economic growth. The depiction of labour policies as essentially subordinated to competitiveness and market integration reached its peak in the Green Paper on Modernising Labour Law, where the Commission highlighted that '*stringent*

1. Among others: E. Gill-Pedro, '*Freedom to Conduct a Business in EU Law; Freedom from Interference of Freedom from Domination?*', (2017) European Journal of Legal Studies, 2; S. Giubboni, '*Libertà d'impresa e Diritto Del Lavoro nell'Unione Europea*' (2016) Costituzionalismo.it.; J. Prassl, '*Business Freedoms and Employment Rights in the European Union*' (2015) 9 Cambridge Yearbook of European Legal Studies; F. Laagland, '*Member States' Sovereignty in the Socio-Economic Field: Fact or Fiction? The Clash Between the European Business Freedoms and The National Level of Workers' Protection*' (2018) 9 European Labour Law Journal (ELLJ) 50.

employment protection legislation tends to reduce the dynamism of the labour market', and that '*rapid technological progress, increased competition stemming from globalization, changing consumer demand [...] have shown the need for increased flexibility*'.[2]

During the past five years, the Juncker Commission has made an effort to give the EU a more socially oriented outlook, as the adoption, in November 2017, of the European Pillar of Social Rights shows.[3] However, the Pillar does not seem to be, yet, a turnaround point. On the one hand, the Pillar undoubtedly has the effect of restoring the attention of EU institutions on social and labour matters. On the other hand, both the Communication that has preceded the Pillar[4] and the Pillar itself suggest that the labour priorities have been formulated with an eye for economic and business interests.[5]

Alongside this (de-)evolution in the overall approach towards social and labour rights, it appears that the EU economic freedoms are undergoing an expansive process. Article 16 of the Charter of Fundamental Rights of the EU (CFR)[6] combined with CJEU case law has allowed private parties to refer in judicial proceedings to their freedom to conduct a business and their freedom of contract to limit the effects of EU (labour) law.[7]

In light of this context, it is interesting to narrow the focus on whether the interpretation of the CJEU portrays a similar shift in the approach to labour rights and, in case, to what extent. Directive 98/59/EC on collective redundancies represents a good case study. First, the Directive was adopted with the intention to counterbalance the employers' (stronger) contractual freedom with regards to the decision to terminate employment contracts. Second, the Directive entered into force in the 1970s, during the so-called golden years of EU labour law,[8] and has remained basically unchanged until today. This allows to track eventual interpretative evolutions in the CJEU's reasoning.

2. Green Paper COM(2006)708 final, *Modernising labour law to meet the challenges of the 21st century*.
3. The European Pillar of Social Rights was adopted in the form of an interinstitutional proclamation on the 16 November 2017, in occasion of the Gothenburg Summit for Fair Jobs and Growth. On the possible Pillar's contribution to EU social dimension: F. Hendrickx, '*The European Social Pillar: A First Evaluation*' (2018) 9 European Labour Law Journal (ELLJ) 1.
4. COM(2016)127, *Launching a Consultation on a European Pillar of Social Rights*.
5. For instance, Principle 5 of the Pillar on flexible and secure labour contracts specifies that '*the necessary flexibility for employers to adapt swiftly to changes in the economic context shall be ensured*'. *See also*: Z. Rasnaca, '*Bridging the Gaps or Falling Short? The European Pillar of Social Rights and What it Can Bring to EU-Level Policy Making*', ETUI Working Paper, 2017 and S. Giubboni, '*Appunti e Disappunti sul Pilastro Europeo dei Diritti Sociali*', in Quaderni Costituzionali, a. XXXVII, n. 4, December 2017, p. 953.
6. The Explanations relating to the Charter of Fundamental Rights (2007/C 303/02) indicate that Article 16 CFR covers the concepts of freedom to exercise an economic or commercial activity, freedom of contract (as defined by the CJEU case law), as well as the concept of free competition, recognized in Article 119(1) and (3) of the TFEU. The Explanation also specify that the freedom to conduct a business is a right that is to be exercised with respect for EU law and national legislation.
7. Judgment of 21 December 2016, *AGET Iraklis*, C-201/15, ECLI:EU: C:2016:972; judgment of 18 July 2013, *Alemo-Herron*, C-426/11, ECLI:EU: C:2013:521; Judgment of 27 April 2017, *Asklepios*, C-680/15, ECLI:EU:C:2017:317; judgment of 14 March 2017, *Samira Achbita*, C-157/15, ECLI: EU:C:2017:203; judgment of 14 March 2017, *Asma Bougnaoui*, C-188/15, ECLI:EU:C:2017:204.
8. De Smyter, Colucci, Engels, Salas, Hendrickx, *Institutional Changes and European Social Policies after the Treaty of Amsterdam*, (ed.) R. Blanpain, Kluwer Law International, 1998, p. 105.

Therefore, an analysis of the CJEU's decisions consents to determine whether there has been a significant evolution in the approach to labour rights, at least with reference to the norms prescribed in this Directive.

The hypothesis that underpins this Chapter is that the analysis of the case law on Directive 98/59/EC consents to determine whether the CJEU's reasoning is coherent with the approach of the policy documents, that tend to place a strong accent on business freedoms -among which the contractual freedom of the employer, when definying labour policies. The intuition is that if a similar stance also characterizes the CJEU's interpretation, this would be reflected in rulings that provide a narrow reading of those labour rights that substantially interfere with the employer's contractual freedom.

The structure of this contribution is the following. Section §16.02 presents the rules established in Directive 98/59/EC, section §16.03 provides a brief reflection on the importance to focus on the interpretation of the concept of contractual autonomy in order to determine the (evolution in the) rationale of labour legislation, and section §16.04 is dedicated to the analysis of the CJEU's reasoning throughout time. Section §16.05 interprets the result of the analysis and advances a couple of considerations on the CJEU's understanding of the purpose of workers' right to information and consultation.

§16.02 DIRECTIVE 98/59/EC ON COLLECTIVE REDUNDANCIES

Directive 98/59/EC (originally Directive 75/129/EEC[9]) was the first piece of legislation implementing the 1974-1976 Social Action Programme,[10] which aimed at providing a more social dimension to the European Communities.[11] The Directive was drafted in a context where national rules on collective dismissals diverged considerably from Member State to Member State, with differences in the degree of workers' protection which affected the costs that the employer had to bear in connection with the termination of employment contracts.[12]

The Directive was conceived to partially harmonize national rules on collective redundancies with a twofold objective. On the one hand, the EC was acting as an economic regulator, since the Directive was the first step towards the establishment of a level playing field in the area of business restructurings.[13] The differences in national rules had indeed a direct effect on the functioning of the internal market, as those disparities affected the conditions of competition among business actors. On the other hand, the Directive had the purpose to provide labour protection, in view of the fact

9. Directive 75/129/EEC of 22 Feb. 1975 OJ [1975] L 48.
10. Social Action Programme COM(73)1600.
11. European Parliament - Document de séance 1972-1973 - Rapport fait au nom de la commission politique sur les résultats de la Conférence au sommet des Chefs d'Etat ou de gouvernement des Etats membres de la Communauté élargie qui s'est tenue á Paris les 19 et 20 octobre 1972.
12. Commission Proposal COM(72)400 final.
13. *Ibid.*

that the (partial) convergence of rules on collective dismissals was also directed at improving the living and working conditions of workers.[14]

In particular, the Commission specified that the aim of the Directive was to strike a balance between the need to protect workers and the necessity for enterprises to maintain a sufficient room for manoeuvre when conducting their businesses.[15] The adopted rules were (and still are) predominantly procedural and do not touch upon substantial matters, such as compensation rights or the definition of the grounds that allow, or rather preclude the execution of collective redundancies.

The Directive applies when the employer is '*contemplating collective redundancies*',[16] which are defined on the base of quantitative thresholds,[17] and provided that the employment contract is terminated for reasons that are not related to the individual workers concerned.[18] In those circumstances, the Directive prescribes the observation of a specific procedure that, albeit only to a limited extent, enables the workers' representatives to react to the employer's decision to proceed with the reduction of the workforce.

The first procedural duty is set out in Article 2, which establishes the obligation to inform and consult the workers' representatives, in good time and with a view to reach an agreement. The consultation should concern '*means of avoiding collective redundancies or reducing the number of workers affected, and of mitigating the consequences by recourse to accompanying social measures aimed, inter alia, at aid for redeploying or retraining workers made redundant*'.[19] It is worth noting that Directive does not impose on the employer and on the workers' representative the obligation to actually reach an agreement.

The other procedural rule prescribed in the Directive concerns the employer's duty to notify the competent national authority of any projected collective redundancy.[20] This notification shall contain all the relevant information concerning the projected collective dismissals and the consultation with workers' representatives. Article 4 specifies that the notification to the national authority has the effect to 'freeze' the collective dismissals, which will take effect not earlier than thirty days after such notification. The purpose of the notification and the subsequent suspension period is to allow the competent authority to help the employer and the workers' representatives to seek solutions to the problems raised by the projected collective redundancies.[21]

It is interesting to consider that in the initial Commission's proposal the authority had the competence to scrutinize the legitimacy of the employer's decision to operate dismissals and could eventually prevent the dismissals to take place, were those based

14. M.R. Freedland, '*Employment Protection: Redundancy Procedures and the EEC*', (1976) Industrial Law Journal, 5; Catherine Barnard, '*Collective Redundancies and Employees' Rights on the Employer's Insolvency*' in '*EU Employment Law*', fourth edition, Oxford University Press, 2012, pp. 629-656.
15. COM(72)400 final.
16. Article 2(1) Directive 98/59/EC.
17. Article 1(1)a Directive 98/59/EC.
18. *Ibid.*
19. Aricle 2(2) Directive 98/59/EC.
20. Article 3 Directive 98/59/EC.
21. Article 4(2) Directive 98/59/EC.

on non-valid grounds. Instead, the final version of the Directive does not contemplate this competence, since the only power that is attributed to the authority is that of extending the thirty days suspension period in case such an extension might increase the chances to reach an agreement between the employer and the workers' representatives.[22]

Finally, Article 5 allows the Member States to adopt rules that are more favourable to workers and that go beyond the procedural requirements established by the Directive. This implies that the national implementations of the Directive can legitimately prescribe norms that limit the contractual freedom of the employer in a more substantial manner.

§16.03 FREEDOM OF CONTRACT AND THE FUNCTION OF LABOUR RIGHTS

The intention of this contribution is to frame the analysis of the evolution of the CJEU's reasoning on Directive 98/59/EC within a broader reflection on the employers' contractual freedom in the context of labour rules. Therefore, a few words should be spent on the relationship between labour law and contractual freedom, and on how a change in the approach to contractual freedom can affect the rationale of labour norms.[23]

First of all, we should depart from the consideration that labour law finds its ontological justification in the uneven distribution of the bargaining power among the employer and the workers.[24]

The original rationale of labour law can then be defined as the attempt to repair a situation of inequality between the parties of the employment relationship: even if *formally* both parties dispose of contractual freedom, the contractual freedom of the employer is substantially superior and dominates that of the worker, since the employer has a stronger bargaining position.[25] In order to correct this unbalance, labour law is conceived as pursuing two possible functions.

The first function is to establish limitations to the contractual freedom of the employer, the stronger contractor.[26] Labour law thus performs a protective function, as

---

22. Article 4(3) Directive 98/59/EC.
23. S. Sciarra, '*Market Freedom and Fundamental Social Rights*', EUI Working Paper, 2002, and, with more specific reference to the CJEU's case law, J. Prassl, '*Freedom of Contract as a General Principle of EU Law? Transfer of Undertakings and the Protection of Employer Rights in EU Labour Law Case C-426/11 Alemo-Herron and Others v. Parkwood Leisure Ltd*' (2013) 42 Industrial Law Journal.
24. B. Veneziani, '*The Employment Contract*', in '*The Transformation of Labour Law in Europe – A Comparative Study of 15 Countries 1945-2004*', (ed.) B. Hepple, B. Veneziani, Hart Publishing, 2009, pp. 99-126.
25. L. Wedderburn, '*Labour Standards, Global Markets and Labour Law in Europe*', in '*International Labour Standards and Economic Interdependence*', by International Institute for Labour Studies, 1994, pp. 247-253 and A. Neal, '*Comparative Labour Law and Industrial Relations: "A Major Discipline? – Who Cares?"*', in '*Labour Law and Industrial Relations at the Turn of the Century*', Kluwer Law International, 1998 among others.
26. R. Dukes, '*Hugo Sinzheimer and the Constitutional Function of Labour Law*', in '*The Idea of Labour Law*', (ed.) G. Davidov, B. Langille, Oxford University Press, 2011, pp. 57-68; M. Weiss,

its role is to set minimum standards of protection for workers. An example of an EU labour provision with a protective function is Directive 2001/23/EC on transfers of undertakings. This Directive prescribes that in case of a transfer of a business or part of it, the transferee has the obligation to take over all the employment contracts of the workers employed by the transferor at the moment of the transfer.[27] In addition to that, the new employer (the transferee) is prevented from altering in a pejorative manner the terms and conditions of employment of the transferred workers.[28]

The second function that is generally ascribed to labour law is that of uplifting the bargaining position of the workers.[29] In this case, labour law aims at counterbalancing the unequal bargaining power that naturally exists within the employment relation not by interfering with the freedom of contract of the employer, but by enabling the workers to become stronger contractors.[30] Directive 98/59/EC on collective redundancies is predominantly an expression of this second function. Indeed, by conferring to the workers' representative information and consultation rights, the Directive intervenes on the contractual position of the workers and reinforces it. The employer's obligation to notify the competent public authority serves a similar purpose, as the authority is in charge to ensure that the information and consultation duties are carried properly, and to promote the definition of shared solutions between the workers' representatives and the employer.

Once determined that Directive 98/59/EC attains to the function of labour law of uplifting the negotiation power of the workers, the intention and relevance of the analysis of the CJEU's case law, that will follow in the next section, should also be clearer. We can now assume that if the Court adopts a restrictive interpretation of the employer's obligation to inform and consult the workers' representatives, it will enhance the freedom of contract of the employer, thus distracting the Directive from its objective to act as a counterforce in favour of the workers, the weaker contractors. Similarly, a narrow reading of the national authority's competences would reach the same effect. On the contrary, if the case study reveals a broad interpretation of the employer's obligations to inform and consult, the Court indirectly expands the negotiating position of the workers. In this case, the CJEU interpretation would have the result of reaffirming the Directive's function to intervene in the allocation of bargaining power among the employer and the workers with a counterbalancing intention.

It is finally important to note that the CJEU's approach has implications for the rationale of the labour norms at issue. In other words, the case study that will be presented in the next section provides indications on whether the Directive (as interpreted by CJEU) still shares the original justification pertaining to labour law,

'Re-Inventing Labour Law?' in *'The Idea of Labour Law'*, (ed.) G. Davidov, B. Langille, Oxford University Press, 2011, pp. 43-56.

27. Articles 3 and 4 of Directive 2001/23/EC on transfers of undertakings.
28. Articles 3.1 and 3.3 directive 2001/23/EC on transfers of undertakings.
29. P. Davies, M. Freedland, *'Kahn-Freund's Labour and the Law'*, Stevens & Sons, 1983.
30. B. Hepple, *'Introduction'*, in *'Social and Labour Rights in a Global Context'*, Cambridge University Press 2002.

namely to react to the uneven distribution of bargaining power among the employer and the worker.

§16.04 CASE STUDY ON DIRECTIVE 98/59/EC

This section is dedicated to the analysis of the CJEU's case law on the Directive on collective redundancies.

All the Court's decisions on Directive 98/59/EC (and its preceding versions, Directive 75/129/EEC and Directive 92/56/EEC) have been considered, a total of twenty-six cases. Among those rulings, eleven are pertinent for the case study, as only in those the CJEU was asked to interpret the aspects of the Directive that concern information and consultation rights or the role of the competent national authority in supporting the proper execution of those rights. As mentioned in the previous section, those are the provisions of the Directive that directly pertain to the employer's contractual freedom.

The relevant cases have been analysed as follows. At first, the arguments and statements of the Court have been extrapolated from the decisions, and have therefore been de-contextualized. This means that it is possible that a single case is related to more than one argument or statement. Then, the different arguments of the Court have been classified into two categories. On the one hand, there are those arguments that have the effect of uplifting the bargaining position of the workers, and that thus promote a more substantial equivalence of the freedom of contract of the employer and that of the workers (letters from A to F). On the other hand, there are those arguments that produce the opposite result, as they indicate an expansive understanding of the employer's freedom of contract (letters from G to L). In this second category of cases, the CJEU appears to disregard the Directive's purpose of strengthening the bargaining position of workers.

The CJEU's arguments have been rephrased and summarized in order to make them more understandable in a de-contextualized setting. The division of the reasonings in two groups allows to identify eventual conflicting positions of the Court and to recognize fluctuations in the Court's approach throughout time.

The Court's arguments that fall in the first category and that unveil a rather broad interpretation of the employer's information and consultation duties are those listed here below:

A. The employer has to begin the consultation process with the workers' representatives not only when the redundancies are a direct consequence of his will, but also in presence of circumstances that reasonably will lead to the termination of the employment contract of a consistent portion of the workforce.
B. Consultation rights shall not be dependant on the employer's discretion to recognise or rather not to recognise the establishment of a body of worker's representatives. The fact that the law of a Member State allows the employer not to formally accept the role and activity of workers' representatives should not represent an obstacle for the correct exercise of the workers' rights to

receive information and to be consulted. Therefore, Member States have to adapt their national rules on the designation of workers' representatives and on the system of employees' representation to the extent that is necessary to guarantee the effectiveness of the rights established in the Directive;

C. The consultation process between the employer and the workers' representatives should be carried out *before* the employer takes the decision to terminate the employment contracts;
D. Consultation rights correspond to the employer's duty to re-create the conditions for an effective and fruitful negotiation;
E. The consultation process should get started even if the employer does not dispose yet of all the information listed in Article 2;
F. The employer can terminate the employment contracts only at the conclusion of the consultation process, not earlier.

The arguments that belong to the second category, inasmuch as they reflect a rather broad interpretation of the employer's freedom of contract are:

G. The employer is free to decide whether and, eventually, at what point, to define plans for collective redundancies, as it is solely up to his discretion to launch the collective redundancies' procedure and to begin the consultation. More specifically, the Court ruled that circumstances such as the business' severe financial difficulties are not sufficient reasons to compel the employer to open the collective dismissals process;
H. Even at the end of the consultation process, the employer shall preserve its discretion in choosing to enforce its decision to dismiss;
I. The employer must be able to assert its interest effectively in the negotiating process into which he is part. It descends that a national measure that confers to the competent authority the power to scrutinise and eventually veto the employer's decision to proceed with redundancies shall not affect the essence of the employer's freedom to conduct his business;
J. Member States are allowed to impose limitations to the individual workers' right to challenge the compliance of the employer's behaviour with the information and consultation procedure established by the Directive, as those information and consultation rights are conceived to be collectively and not individually exercised;
K. The information and consultation process has to be carried out exclusively by the "direct employer", meaning the legal or natural person with the highest degree of proximity with the workers. This applies also when the business is part of a corporate structure, and even when the "direct employer" has not been involved in the decision-making process that leads to the collective redundancies. In this case, it is evident that there are severe obstacles to the proper implementation of the information and consultation rights, as crucial decisions are taken elsewhere, at a different management level;
L. In connection to the previous indent, in presence of a corporate structure, the "direct employer" has to begin the information and consultation process only

once the parent company or the central management has decided the establishment where the reduction of the workforce should take place and the details thereof. Also in this situation, it is difficult to imagine how the "direct employer" might be able to take part of a genuine negotiation process, having no influence on the strategic decision that leads to collective redundancies.

Figure 16.1 Graphic Representation of the CJEU's Reasonings on Information and Consultation Rights in the Case Law on Directive 98/59/EC

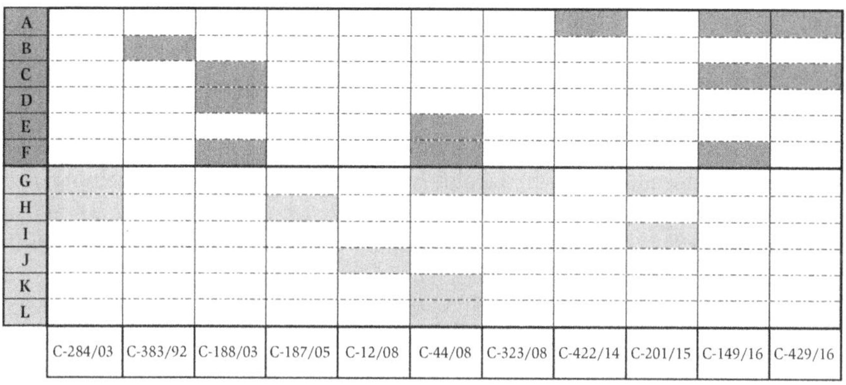

§16.05 CJEU'S APPROACH TO CONTRACTUAL FREEDOM AND DISTRIBUTION OF THE BARGAINING POWER

The case study, graphically illustrated in the previous section, does not show signs of meaningful development throughout time, differently from what has been argued with respect to the general EU policy-making attitude towards labour and social rights, as well as in merit to other EU labour law provisions.[31]

The reason might be that while the inclination of the EU official documents has progressively turned in favour to preserve business freedoms from excessive limitations, Directive 98/59/EC does not actually directly encroach the employer's freedom of contract. It indeed appears that the presence of divergent attitudes of the CJEU vis-à-vis the workers' bargaining position does not depend on a transformation of the Court's overall approach to the function pursued by the Directive. Rather, the reasoning seems to change on a case-by-case basis, without revealing any interpretative trend.

31. The evolution of the general policy-making towards social and labour matters has been pointed out in the introduction, while a more narrow analysis of the evolution of the CJEU's approach towards labour rights in case of transfers of undertakings, *see*: R.M. Beltzer, '*The Transfer of Undertakings and the Importance of Taking over Personnel – a Vicious Circle*' (2007) 23 International Journal of Comparative Labour Law and Industrial Relations (IJCLLIR), 16; S. Rainone, '*Labour Rights in the Making of the EU and in the CJEU Case Law, a Case Study on the Transfers of Undertakings Directive*' in European Labour Law Journal (ELLJ), (2018) 4, p. 299.

Despite the fact that the case study does not provide indications of particular patters or evolution in the jurisprudence, it is nevertheless possible to advance a couple of considerations. The first pertains to the CJEU's approach with respect to the function of the labour provisions enshrined in the Directive (section §16.05[A]); the second concerns the apparent absence of awareness of the CJEU regarding the fact that its interpretation of the rules on information and consultation have an impact on the overall balance between the contractual positions of the workers and that of the employer (section §16.05[B]).

[A] CJEU's Approach on the Function of Directive 98/59/EC

The case study graphically represented in *Figure 16.1* shows that the CJEU rulings do not reflect a particular interpretative approach towards Directive 98/59/EC, as it is not possible to identify a clear trend that confirms or rather reject the Directive's function of uplifting workers' contractual position. Indeed, six times the CJEU developed arguments that appear in line with the objective of strengthening the bargaining power of the workers, while in six other instances the CJEU adopted a different attitude and read the Directive in a way that predominantly focused on the importance to preserve employer's discretion vis-à-vis the projected redundancies.

The Court thus is quite neutral with respect to the Directive's function of re-equilibrating the contractual weight of the parties in the employment relationship. It is interesting to note that there are instead indications that the Court is not so neutral when the Directive is interpreted as to perform not merely an uplifting or enabling function with respect to workers' bargaining position, but is interpreted also to attaining a protective function, with the effect of interfering more substantially with the employer's contractual freedom.[32]

That was the case with the Greek transposition of the Directive, that – in line with Article 5 – established rules that were more favourable to workers.[33] In particular, the Greek law on collective redundancies attributed wider competences to the national authority (the Minister of Labour): upon a scrutiny of the overall circumstances and of the reasons that the employer indicates to justify his decision to dismiss, the authority could deny to grant the employer the authorization to proceed. The authority could base its refusal on three grounds: the situation of the labour market, national economic interests and the employer's situation. Asked about whether EU law precluded or rather allowed an implementation that limits the employer's discretion in the manner that Greek law established, the CJEU ruled that the Greek law went too far.[34] In the *AGET Iraklis* case, the CJEU indeed argued that the national transposition of the Directive should not affect the essence of the employer's freedom to conduct his business.[35] This implies that, with reference to Figure 16.1, the Court's responded positively to the argument represented by the letter I.

32. *See* section §16.03.
33. Article 5 of Law No. 1387/1983.
34. Judgment of 21 December 2016, *AGET Iraklis*, C-201/15, ECLI:EU: C:2016:972.
35. *Ibid.*, paragraph 84.

This reasoning, despite being, for now, an isolated case with regards to Directive 98/59/EC, embeds an understanding of labour rights as not being allowed to trespass what is necessary to preserve the freedom to conduct a business and, therefore, the freedom of contract of the employer.[36]

It descends that in the *AGET Iraklis* case, the Court showed its reluctance to accept the protective function of labour law, and this reluctance can be explained with reference to what has been described in section §16.03: labour law, when performing its protective function, inevitably clashes with the employer's freedom of contract, and therefore risks to go beyond what is consented by EU law.[37] As mentioned above, the situation appears instead different when the legislation is functional to the pursuit of the other objective of labour law, that of counterbalancing the stronger bargaining power of the employer by strengthening the contractual position of the workers. With respect to that function, the case study indeed shows that the CJEU's approach fluctuates and does not reflect a clear antagonistic or rather benevolent stance.

[B] The CJEU's Inconsistency: What Is the Function of Information and Consultation Rights in EU Law?

The second consideration that can be advanced in light of the case study is that the Court seems to lack awareness on the importance of adopting a coherent approach on the Directive's rules on information and consultation rights. Despite the fact that the Directive's provisions confer only procedural prerogatives to the workers affected by collective redundancies, those norms are crucial for elevating the contractual position of workers vis-à-vs the termination of their employment contract.

In section §16.03 it was indicated that if those information and consultation rights are correctly implemented and enforced, the Directive pursues the function of uplifting the bargaining position of the workers, so to re-balance that of the employer. Since the analysed case law contains legal argumentations that oscillate between those that provide a broad interpretation of Articles 2 and 4 and those that instead concentrate more on the employer's contractual freedoms, it is not clear whether the Court is conscious about and, eventually, if it gives any importance to the attainment of such uplifting function.

The case study indicates that the CJEU changes approach on a case-by-case basis and that, as a consequence, the jurisprudence on Directive 98/59/EC presents evident contradictions. For instance, one of those contradictions is evident when noting that the Court's has, throughout its case law, interchanged the arguments described in section §16.04, under the letters A and G. Both arguments relate to the moment where the employer has to start the information and consultation procedure, and to the

36. I. Antonaki, '*Collective Redundancies in Greece: AGET Iraklis*', (2017) 54 Common Market Law Review (CMLR), 1513-1534 and K. Polomarkakis, '*A Tale of Two Approaches to Social Europe: The CJEU and the Advocate General Drifting Apart in C-201/15 AGET Iraklis*', (2016) 23(3) Maastricht Journal of European and Comparative Law (MJECL) 424-2017.

37. G. Orlandini, '*Libertà Di Stabilimento Versus Diritto Al Lavoro: Ancora Un Bilanciamento "Sbilanciato" Tra Libertà Economiche e Diritti Dei Lavoratori*' [2017] Giornale di Diritto del Lavoro e di Relazioni Industriali 203.

interpretation of the rule established in Article 2(1) according to which '*where an employer is contemplating collective redundancies, he shall begin consultations [...] in good time*'.

Argument A indicates that the obligation to inform and consult becomes effective regardless of the fact that the collective redundancies are actively sought by the employer or that are the direct result of a conscious choice of the employer. This means that the employer is compelled to engage with the workers' representatives as soon as there are elements that suggest that the labour contracts of a consistent portion of workforce will be terminated. These elements might consist in the bad financial situation of the company, that imposes a reorganisation of the business or in the employer's decision to unilaterally modify in a substantially pejorative manner the terms of employment, to which a resignation of part of the workforce will presumably follow.[38]

Argument G instead confers to the employer more room to avoid informing and consulting the workers' representatives, as this argument defends the employer's margin of appreciation concerning whether and, in case, when defining plans for redundancies. In particular, while adopting this position, the Court has also indicated that the definition of such plans constitutes necessary conditions for the implementation of the obligation to inform and consult the workers.[39]

It is rather clear that when the CJEU chooses the first interpretation (A), it is more likely that the workers' representatives dispose of an appropriate amount of time to adopt an informed position and to conduct fruitful negotiations with the employer. Therefore, the Directive is read in line with the function of enhancing the contractual position of workers. When the CJEU instead adopts the second interpretation (G), the workers' representatives are involved -if involved- only at a later stage, when there is actually no longer a margin to avoid the collective redundancies. In this case, the Directive's rules do not appear effective in reaching the objective to strengthen the workers' bargaining position with respect to the termination of their employment contract.

Despite the different implications of these two interpretative approaches (A and G), the CJEU has alternated them, with negative repercussions on the overall coherence on the application of the Directive.

Even if both the focus and the length of this contribution do not allow an extensive digression, one may wonder about the possible causes for the Court's inconsistency. This requires that a few words are spent on the EU policy context, especially when it addresses the worker's information and consultation rights in situation of collective redundancies and business restructurings. Indeed, it is interesting to point out that the analysis of the EU institutions' position on workers'

38. Judgment of 11 November 15, *Rivera*, C-422/14, ECLI:EU:C:2015:743; judgment of 21 September 2017, *Socha*, C-149/16, ECLI:EU:C:2017:708, paragraph 32 and judgment of 21 September 2017, *Ciupa*, C-429/16, ECLI:EU:C:2017:711, paragraph 35.
39. Judgment of 12 February 1985, *Dansk Metalarbejderforbund*, C-284/83, ECLI:EU:C:1985:61, paragraph 15.

involvement and business reorganizations reveals a rather uncertain framework, similarly to the CJEU's case law.

On the one hand, the EU has produced policy documents that highlight the importance of social dialogue and the effective involvement of workers' representatives in the business reorganization process.[40] Moreover, in its Social Agenda 2005-2010, the Commission expressed the intention to conduct an assessment (so-called 'Refit') of EU law on workers' rights in the event of business restructurings. In particular, the Commission advanced the idea to intervene on specific provisions of EU labour law, among which also Directive 98/59/EC, to strengthen and harmonize the EU's *acquis* on information and consultation rights.[41] In 2015, the Commission adopted a consultation document where it announced an initiative to consolidate EU information and consultation rights through a new Recast Directive, with the intention to give more visibility and legal certainty about workers' participation in business reorganizations.[42] Furthermore, it is worth noting that the European Pillar of Social Rights includes a principle on the importance of social dialogue and the involvement of workers, with specific reference to collective redundancies.[43]

On the other hand, the Commission's proposals did not develop into binding acts. The idea of a consolidation of the existing provisions was not favoured by the social partners,[44] and it seems that after some years the Commission decided to abandon the project, as indicated by the absence of further references to that strategy in the subsequent Commission's working programmes. Moreover, besides the inconclusive epilogue of the Commission's initiative, it should be noted that policy documents on business restructurings often stress the centrality of enhancing the dynamism, the business freedom and competitiveness of enterprises, and highlight that the current conditions of the market require a limitation of burdens on businesses.[45]

In conclusion, it appears that the ambivalent CJEU's interpretation of Articles 2 and 4 of Directive 98/59/EC is in line with the rather disaggregated constellation of EU policy documents on workers' involvement in case of business restructurings. In light of that, it is not surprising that the CJEU case law reflects the absence of a clear vision on the (importance of the) role of information and consultation rights. As seen, this leads to the consequent ambiguity on the Directive's function, since the Court is not

40. Commission, 2002, First phase of consultation of the Community cross-industry and sectorial social partners on Anticipating and managing change: a dynamic approach to the social aspects of corporate restructuring; Resolution of the European Parliament, '*Restructuring and Employment*', 2005/2188(INI).
41. Communication from the Commission on the Social Agenda. COM(2005)33 final.
42. COM(2015)2303 final, First phase of consultation of Social Partner under Article 154 TFEU on a consolidation of the EU Directives on information and consultation of workers.
43. European Pillar of Social Rights, Principle n. 8.
44. The European Trade Union Confederation expressed a negative opinion in relation to the launch of an initiative to revise the existing directives on information and consultation rights when the revision is limited to issues of definition and scope, as proposed by the Commission. *See*: 'First Phase Consultation on a Consolidation of the EU Directives on Information & Consultation of Workers – ETUC Answer', 18.6.2015.
45. COM(2015)120 final, Communication from the Commission: Restructuring and employment, anticipating and accompanying restructuring in order to develop employment: the role of the European Union, p. 3.

clear about the degree in which the employer's contractual power shall be counterbalanced by means of effective information and consultation rights.

§16.06 CONCLUDING REMARKS

This contribution has investigated the CJEU's approach to the information and consultation rights established in Directive 98/59/EC, with the aim to unveil whether those rights are interpreted as to constitute an adequate counterbalancing reaction to the (substantially predominant) freedom of contract of the employer. The hypothesis that has informed this Chapter is that if the Court's understanding of labour rights is aligned with the policy-making documents, we would see that reflected in a clear trend resulting from the case study. The hypothesis was not confirmed inasmuch as the case study has shown that the Court does not adopt a uniform approach towards the workers' rights prescribed in the Directive. It was suggested that the reason might lay in the fact that the Directive was conceived with the objective to enhance the workers' bargaining capacity, rather than to directly limit the employer's freedom to operate its business. This entails that, ontologically, the Directive does not interfere substantially on the freedom of contract of the employer, meaning that eventual changes in the CJEU's towards labour rights limiting the economic prerogatives of the employer would not be reflected in the case law on Directive 98/59/EC. While the case study does not provide information on the CJEU's approach towards the protecting function of labour rules, it tells us that the case law reflect a quite neutral stance vis-à-vis labour rights that respond to the function of uplifting workers' bargaining position.
Moreover, it has been noted that the presence of divergences within the Court's reasoning is not the result of a jurisprudential evolution but rather the consequence of a systemic lack of coherence across the case law.

This analysis, finally, suggests that the absence of a CJEU's firm vision with respect to the ultimate purpose of the Directive's rules on information and consultation rights can be read alongside the rather fragmented EU policy on workers' involvement in situation of business restructurings.

CHAPTER 17

Work Incapacity and Disability Coinciding?: The Role International and Supranational Understanding of Disability in Member States' Labour Law

Miet Vanhegen

§17.01 INTRODUCTION

The issue of (long term) work incapacity due to illness or disability is a topic that has been the centre of economic and employment policies for several decades now. Health problems and disabilities are indeed major causes of early exits from labour markets in European countries and worldwide.[1] Medical conditions, or problems labelled as such by societies and policy systems, are hindering the labour market participation and allow for a significant increase in public expenditures. In order to tackle these adverse effects, the need to address the 'medicalisation' of labour market problems and to promote labour market participation was recognised by many and, in particular, Organisation for Economic Co-operation and Development (OECD) countries. Many persons who experience difficulties to perform their normal professional duties due to their health condition, often referred to as employees with an incapacity for work, can indeed work and want to work in ways compatible with their health condition.[2] An important catalyst for the employment rights of these employees might be found in

1. S. Widding, *Modernising and activating measures relating to work incapacity – Synthesis Report*, Work Research Institute, EU Commission Employment, Social Affairs and Equal Opportunities, Madrid, 2010, 2, available at: http://ec.europa.eu.
2. ILO, *The price of exclusion: the economic consequences of excluding people with disabilities from the world of work – Employment working paper No. 43*, Geneva, 2009, available at: https://www.ilo.org; OECD, *Sickness, Disability and Work: Breaking the Barriers: A Synthesis of Findings across OECD Countries*, OECD Publishing, Paris, 2010, 3.

anti-discrimination law, and more specifically in the protected ground of 'disability', that has undergone a paradigm shift, and the idea of the accommodated workplace.[3]

This shift in perception was primarily initiated by the United Nations (UN) Convention on the Rights of Persons with Disabilities (hereafter: UNCRPD) of 2006,[4] which abandoned the medical understanding of disability, which primarily focuses on the clinical and medical diagnosis of the impairment, and illustrates the move towards a focus on the social and environmental barriers which may hinder full and effective participation in society. This social model of 'disability' is also reflected, although prudently, in the way the Court of Justice of the European Union (CJEU) conceptualised disability discrimination within the labour context. In the light of this social perspective, the line between disability and illness has become extremely blurred in the sense that not only congenital or accidental handicaps are included in the scope, but also long-term -curable or incurable – illnesses and other conditions that prevent a person to participate fully in the workplace (i.e., work incapacity). The impact of this broad interpretation is significant for employees who become unable to pursue their professional activity since the qualification as a person with a disability often guarantees better protection in the workplace. In particular, the obligation to provide reasonable accommodations for persons with a disability makes this qualification crucially important. The purpose of this paper is therefore to examine if the CJEU and certain Member States (namely France, Belgium and the Netherlands) have indeed fully embraced the social approach of the concept of 'disability' when it comes to understanding work incapacity and the role environmental and socially constructed circumstances play in hindering the participation on the labour market.

§17.02 INTERNATIONAL AND SUPRANATIONAL CONCEPTUALISATION OF DISABILITY

[A] The UNCRPD and the Social Understanding of 'Disability'

In the international context, the emergence of fundamental social rights and the idea of equal treatment and inclusion of persons with disabilities led to the abandonment of the medical idea regarding disability, namely that legislation should be aimed at repairing and curing the disability and compensating the loss of income because of that impairment, in favour of the development of a new social model of disability. This social model departs from a socio-political point of view that an individual physical, sensory, intellectual, or psychological limitation or impairment as such does not constitute a disability, but the failure of the social environment to adjust to the needs

3. F. Hendrickx, 'Disability and reintegration in work. Interplay between EU non-discrimination law and labour law' in R. Blanpain and F. Hendrickx (eds), *Reasonable Accomodation in the Modern Workplace. Potential and Limits of the Integrative Logics of Labour Law*, Alphen aan den Rijn, Kluwer Law International, 2016, (61) 62-63 (hereinafter: F. Hendrickx, 'Disability and reintegration in work').
4. UN Convention on the Rights of Persons with Disabilities, 13 December 2006, A/RES/61/106, 46 I.L.M. 443 (2006) (Hereinafter: UNCRPD).

of persons with an impairment does.[5] In this light, the UNCRPD must be regarded as the most important international legal instrument that represents this paradigm shift from a medical understanding of disability, which focuses on the clinical and medical diagnosis, towards a focus on the barriers which may hinder full and effective participation in society, including the labour market.[6] When defining the notion of 'disability', the UNCRPD refers explicitly to the given that disabilities result from the interaction between long-term impairments and un-adapted physical, social and environmental factors that hinder the full and effective participation in society on an equal basis with others.[7] Disability, in the sense of this social understanding, is, therefore, a participation problem that should be remediated through adaptions, f.eg. in the workplace, rather than a medical condition.[8] This opens up the personal scope of the Convention to a broad range of people, including those suffering chronic and long term diseases.[9] As clarified by the UN Office of the High Commissioner for Human Rights, the definition must not be regarded as a definition in the strict sense, but it more as a guidance that is intended to clarify the UNCRPD's application.[10] In any case, Member States should be less restrictive about the notions of 'disability' and 'persons with disabilities'.[11]

The UNCRPD entails the obligation for States Parties to recognise and ensure protection of the right to equality and non-discrimination.[12] Article 2 of the UNCRPD gives substance to the concept of discrimination on the basis of disability, which is

5. Read more: M. Oliver, 'If I had a hammer: The social model in action' in C. Barnes (ed.), *Implementing The Social Model of Disability – Theory and Research*, Leeds, the Disability Press, 2004, 18-31.; C. Thomas, 'How Is Disability Understood? An Examination of Sociological Approaches', *Disability & Society* 2014, Vol. 16, No. 6, (569) 579-580; L. Waddington and A. Lawson, 'Disability and non-discrimination law in the European Union. An analysis of disability discrimination law within and beyond the employment field', EU Commission, Directorate-General for Employment, Social Affairs and Equal Opportunities, Luxembourg, 2009, 16 (hereinafter: L. Waddington and A. Lawson, 'Disability and non-discrimination law in the European Union').
6. G. Quinn, 'A short guide to the United Nations Convention on the rights of persons with disabilities' in G. Quinn and L. Waddington (eds), *European Yearbook of Disability Law Vol. 1*, Antwerp, Intersentia, 2009, 89; M.A. Stein and J.E. Lord, 'Future prospects for the United Nations Convention on the rights of persons with disabilities' in O.M. Arnardóttir and G. Quinn (eds), *The United Nations Convention on the Rights of Persons with Disabilities. European and Scandinavian Perspectives*, Leiden, Martinus Nijhoff Publishers, 2009, (17) 25 (Hereinafter: M.A. Stein and J.E. Lord).
7. Preamble e) and Article 1 UNCRPD; M.A. Stein and J.E. Lord, *supra* note 6, 25.
8. *See* T. Mladenov, 'The UN Convention on the Rights of Persons with Disabilities and Its Interpretation', *European Journal of Disability Research* 2013, Vol. 7, (69) 78.
9. L. Waddington, *Disability, Employment and the European Community*, Antwerp-Apeldoorn, Maklu, 1995, 34; M.A. Stein and J.E. Lord, *supra* note 6, 25; L. Waddington, 'Breaking new ground: The implications of ratification of the UN Convention on the rights of persons with disabilities for the European Community' in O.M. Arnardóttir and G. Quinn (eds), *The United Nations Convention on the Rights of Persons with Disabilities. European and Scandinavian perspectives*, Leiden, Martinus Nijhoff Publishers, 2009, (111) 115.
10. UN Office of the High Commissioner for Human Rights, Monitoring the Convention on the rights of persons with disabilities. Guidance for human rights monitors, New York and Geneva: United Nations, 2010.
11. M.A. Stein and J.E. Lord, *supra* note 6, 25.
12. L. Waddington, 'The influence of the UN Convention on the rights of persons with disabilities on EU non-discrimination law', in U. Belavusau and K. Henrard (eds), *EU Anti-Discrimination Law*

broadly defined as '*any distinction, exclusion or restriction on the basis of disability which has the purpose or effect of impairing or nullifying the recognition, enjoyment or exercise, on an equal basis with others, of all human rights and fundamental freedoms in the political, economic, social, cultural, civil or any other field. It includes all forms of discrimination, including denial of reasonable accommodation*'.[13] The importance of this definition lies within the fact that it explicitly states that a refusal to make reasonable accommodation must be equated with discrimination on the grounds of disability. This makes the Convention the first international human rights convention to explicitly refer to the lack of reasonable accommodations as a form of discrimination. According to the UN Convention, reasonable accommodations must be understood as 'necessary and appropriate modification and adjustments not imposing a disproportionate or undue burden, where needed in a particular case, to ensure to persons with disabilities the enjoyment or exercise on an equal basis with others of all human rights and fundamental freedoms'.[14]

[B] The CJEU: A Prudent Shift Towards a Social Model of 'Disability'

In the European context, the right to equal treatment for persons with disabilities, within the restricted area of employment and occupation, is guaranteed by Council Directive 2000/78 establishing a general framework for equal treatment in employment and occupation (hereinafter: Directive 2000/28/EC).[15] Although Directive 2000/78/EC was adopted prior to the formal conclusion of the UNCRPD by the European Union (EU),[16] the Convention has had a significant impact on the way disability and disability discrimination are interpreted within the employment context. Directive 2000/78/EC does not in itself include a definition of disability or guidance on who falls within the personal scope of the Directive, nor does it refer to the law of the Member States. This indeterminate nature of the legal concept of 'disability', made it susceptible to the interpretation by the CJEU.

The demarcation of the notion 'disability' is however not a purely theoretical matter, but also substantial for the rights of the 'disabled' employee in the workplace. The Directive only prohibits discrimination on the grounds of an exhaustive list of protected categories and only in the area employment and occupation. When it comes to health-related characteristics, only disability is protected as such within the directive, with illnesses not explicitly incorporated in the list of discrimination grounds. One of the most significant innovations within the Directive 2000/78/EC is however the duty placed on employers to '*take appropriate measures, where needed in a particular case, to enable a person with a disability to have access to, participate in, or advance in*

Beyond Gender, Oxford, Hart Publishing, 2018, 3. (hereinafter: L. Waddington, 'The Influence of the UN Convention on the Rights of Persons with Disabilities').

13. Article 2 UNCRPD.
14. Article 2, 4) UNCRPD.
15. Council Directive 2000/78/EC establishing a general framework for equal treatment in employment and occupation, 27 November 2000, *OJ* 2 December 2000, L303/16. (hereinafter: Directive 2000/78/EC).
16. Council Decision 2010/48/EC concerning the conclusion by the European Community of the United Nations Convention on the Rights of Persons with Disabilities, 2009 O.J. (L23) 35.

employment, or to undergo training, unless such measures would impose a disproportionate burden on the employer'.[17] This provision entails that the employer, in order to ensure material equality of opportunity for employees with disabilities, has to address work practices and barriers which exclude or disadvantage those employees and has to take appropriate measures, where needed, to enable them to have access to, participate in, or advance in employment, or to undergo training, unless such measures would impose a disproportionate burden on the employer.[18] In this light, persons with disabilities often enjoy better protection in the workplace against discrimination than persons who are understood to be 'merely' sick. The qualification as a disability is therefore paramount for persons who are confronted with a work incapacity due to (long-term) health problems.

Over the years, an evolution is noticeable in the way the CJEU interprets the notion of 'disability'. As the EU ratified the UNCRPD, the Convention became a part of European law. Therefore, when defining the legal concept of disability in the sphere of EU anti-discrimination law, the CJEU has to seek consistency with the broad social notion of 'disability' of the UNCRPD. This has resulted in a prudent transition from a narrow medical to a broader social model of disability in the CJEU-case law, which in itself is still evolving.

One of the first rulings of the Court of Justice regarding the scope of the concept of disability as stipulated in Directive 2000/78/EC was the *Chacón Navas*-judgment in 2006, thus before the EU acceded to the UNCRPD.[19] In this case, the Court concluded that an employee who has been dismissed by her employer solely because she was certified as unfit for work on grounds of sickness and was not in a position to return to work in the short term, could not be regarded as a person with a disability, reflecting the medical model of disability.[20] By using the concept of 'disability', the European legislator deliberately chose a different term from 'sickness', according to the Court, so '*the two concepts cannot therefore simply be treated as being the same*'.[21] The fact that the Court opted for a medical approach to the concept of disability was mainly due to the fear that an extensive interpretation of the notion would have far-reaching consequences, given the fact that the identification of a prohibited inequality of treatment on the base of disability always encompasses a claim to equal access, continued employment or the availability of reasonable accommodations for persons with disabilities.[22] This case raised a great deal of controversy, with the judgment largely being criticised for the fact that both the CJEU and Advocate General GEELHOED gave an inherent medical definition to the concept of disability which focuses primarily on the individual defects of the person concerned and not on the limitations of

17. Article 5 Directive 2000/78/EC.
18. J. Clifford, 'The UN Disability Convention and Its Impact on European Equality Law', *The Equal Rights Review* 2011, Vol. 6, (11) 15 (hereinafter: J. Clifford).
19. *Chacón Navas v. Eurest Colectivadas SA*, Case No. C-13/05, 11 July 2006, EU:C:2006:456 (hereinafter: *Chacón Navas v. Eurest Colectivadas SA*).
20. *Id.* paragraph 25.
21. *Id.* paragraphs 43-46; J. Clifford, *see supra* note 18, 18; N. Betsch, 'The Ring and Skouboe Werge Case: A Reluctant Acceptance of the Social Approach of Disability', *European Labour Law Journal* 2013, No. 2, (135) 140.
22. Opinon A.-G. Geelhoed, paragraph 56.

interaction with the environment. The dichotomy between 'illness' and 'disability' and the option of a particularly narrow definition of disability certainly provoked a debate.[23] It was argued that this Court of Justice ruling was completely contradictory to the general international and European social perception of persons with disabilities. All Community institutions had made clear that they recognised the need to base policy and legislation on the social model of disability.[24] The view of the CJEU in *Chacón Navas* was especially called into question when the EU ratified the UNCRPD on 23 December 2010. Ratifying the Convention meant that it became an integral part of European law. Given that, in addition, Directive 2000/78/EC does not provide a concrete definition of disability, the CJEU has to seek consistency with the UNCRPD when interpreting secondary EU law.[25]

The first milestone judgment[26] that has shown the effect of the UNCRPD in the CJEU's case law was the *HK Danmark* case,[27] in which the Court first referred to the concept of 'disability' as defined in the UNCRPD and thus, unlike the *Chacón Navas* judgment, adheres to a more social model of disability.[28] In its opinion, Advocate General Kokott added that the scope of Directive 2000/78/EC is therefore not limited to congenital or accidental disabilities, but also includes curable or incurable diseases, if it brings with it a long-term limitation.[29] The fact that an employee is able to perform his work to a limited extent does not prevent his state of health from being covered by the concept of disability, according to the Court. Stating that the concept of disability should be interpreted as any obstacle to being active in a professional activity and not as total impossibility to pursue a professional activity, the Court clarified the relation between disability and work incapacity. Any other interpretation would be incompatible with the objective of the directive, which is to enable a person with disabilities to

23. L. Waddington, *Disability, Employment and the European Community*, Antwerpen-Apeldoorn, Maklu, 1995, 33; F. Hendrickx, 'Disability and reintegration in work', *see supra* note 3, 65; L. Waddington and A. Lawson, 'Disability and non-discrimination law in the European Union', *supra* note 5, 16.
24. *See* i.a. Resolution of the Council and the representatives of the Governments of the Member States meeting within the Council of 20 December 1996 on Equality of opportunity for people with disabilities, *OJ* C 12, 13.1.1997; Communication from the Commission of 30 October 2003, *Equal opportunities for people with disabilities; A European Economic Action Plan*, COM(2003) 65 final.
25. Article 216(2) TFEU; F. Hendrickx, 'Disability and reintegration in work', *supra* note 3, 67; L. Waddington, 'The Influence of the UN Convention on the Rights of Persons with Disabilities', *supra* note 12, 4.
26. The first explicit reference to the UNCRPD-definition can however be found in the case law of the European Court of Human Rights (EctHR); see Application No. 13444/04, *Glor v. Switzerland* (30 April 2009), Application no. 38832/06, *Alajos Kiss v. Hungary* (20 May 2010) and Application no. 2700/10, *Kiyutin v. Rusland* (10 March 2011) in which the EctHR recognised that, respectively, diabetes, manic depression and a HIV-positive status fall within the scope of the UN Convention and are protected against discrimination on grounds of disability.
27. *Ring and Skouboe Werge v. Danks Arbejdsgiverforening*, No. C-335/11 and C-337/11, 11 April 2013, ECLI:EU:C:2013:222. (Hereinafter: *HK Danmark*).
28. *HK Danmark*, paragraphs 37-38.; N. Betsch, 'The Ring and Skouboe Werge Case: A Reluctant Acceptance of the Social Approach of Disability', *ELLJ* 2013, No. 2, (135) 135; L. Waddington, 'HK Danmark (Ring and Skouboe Werge): Interpreting EU Equality Law in Light of the UN Convention on the Rights of Persons with Disabilities', *European Anti-discrimination Law Review* 2013, afl. 17, (11) 13-16.
29. *HK Danmark*, paragraph 40; Opinion A.-G. Kokott, paragraph 32.

have greater access to employment or to participate in it.[30] Moreover, the Court held that refusal to provide the employees with a disability with reasonable accommodations in itself amounted to discrimination.[31] The nature of the accommodations, such as a reduction in working time, does not determine whether there is a disability or not, but instead such measures must take account of the needs of persons with disabilities and are therefore the mere consequence of the concept of disability and, thus, do not constitute an essential part of it.[32]

Although the CJEU cautiously represents the paradigm shift when defining disability, by referring explicitly to the definition given in the UNCRPD when applying Directive 2000/78/EC i.a. in *HK Danmark* case, there are still some arguments that the CJEU does not fully adhere to the importance of the role which environmental and socially constructed circumstances play in creating disability. In a way, the CJEU still holds on to the physical and medical limitations of employees when examining the hindrances to full professional participation, although the emphasis in the social model of disability clearly lies on the interaction with environmental aspects. This is demonstrated in the fact that the CJEU restricted itself to the conclusion that disability included 'a condition caused by an illness medically diagnosed'.[33] Moreover, Advocate General Kokott adds that not until there is a **prognosis** of permanent limitation can there be any question of a disability.[34]

In 2014 and 2018 the CJEU had to rule on the scope of 'disability' in the light of two discrimination cases regarding obesity. In the *Kaloft* case,[35] an employee invoked Directive 2000/78/EC to challenge his dismissal, which he claims took place on the basis of his body weight. However, obesity is not explicitly mentioned as a ground for discrimination in Directive 200/78/EC. Referring to the definition of 'disability' it had already given in the *HK Danmark* judgment, the Court concluded that obesity can constitute a disability if, under given circumstances, the obesity of the worker concerned entails a limitation which results in particular from physical, mental or psychological impairments that in interaction with various barriers may hinder the full and effective participation of that person in professional life on an equal basis with other workers, and if the limitation is a long-term one.[36] The Court however added that only when the obesity of the worker hindered his full and effective participation in professional life on an equal basis with other workers on account of reduced mobility or the onset of medical conditions preventing him from carrying out his work or causing discomfort when carrying out his professional activity, the obesity could

30. Directive 2000/78/EC does not explicitly state that the failure to provide reasonable accommodations amounts to a discrimination; *HK Danmark*, paragraphs 43-44.
31. *Id.* 65-68.
32. Point 16 Considerans Council Directive 2000/78/EC; *HK Danmark* paragraphs 45-46.
33. *HK Danmark*, paragraph 47.
34. Opinion A.-G. Kokott, paragraph 37; L. Waddington, 'Saying All the Right Things and Still Getting it Wrong. The Court of Justice's Definition of Disability and Non-discrimination Law', *Maastricht Journal of European and Comparative Law* 2015, Vol. 22, No. 4, (576) 580 (hereinafter: L. Waddington, 'Saying All the Right Things and Still Getting it Wrong').
35. *Kaloft v. Kommunernes Landsforening*, No. C-354/13, 18 December 2014, ECLI:EU:C:2014:2463 (hereinafter: *Kaloft*).
36. *Kaloft*, paragraphs 59-60; F. Hendrickx, 'Disability and reintegration in work', *supra* note 3, 65.

constitute a disability.[37] Mr Kaloft, however, was not fired because there was a hindrance to his participation in professional life, but allegedly for the mere fact that he was obese. The Court remarkably left it to the domestic court to determine whether Mr Kaloft could be qualified as a person with a disability, but in the light of this interpretation of the CJEU, this would doubtfully be the case.[38] These principles were repeated in the recent CJEU judgment of 18 January 2018.[39] In this case where an employee was dismissed by reason of his intermittent but justified absences caused by i.a. his obesity, the Court ruled that in the event that, in given circumstances, the obesity of the worker concerned entails a limitation of capacity that hinders his full and effective participation in professional life on an equal basis with other workers on account of reduced mobility or the onset, in that person, of medical conditions preventing him carrying out his work or causing discomfort when carrying out his professional activity, this health state is covered by the concept of 'disability'.[40]

In a judgment of 18 March 2014, the Court set out yet another limit to the broad concept of disability.[41] In this case, an employee who was unable to conceive naturally and decided to rely upon a surrogate mother to carry their child was not entitled to paid leave, equivalent to maternity leave, according to Irish labour law. She, therefore, claimed before the national court that she is a disabled person within the meaning of Directive 2000/78/EC and that she is therefore entitled to reasonable accommodation in the form of maternity leave. The Court held that there is, in fact, a long-term limitation which is the result of a physical, mental or psychological condition and which may be a source of great suffering.[42] However, the Court adds that the concept does presuppose that the limitation of the person in interaction with various thresholds must prevent the person concerned from participating fully, effectively and on an equal footing with other workers in professional life.[43] Following the opinion of Advocate General WALH, the Court concluded that the impossibility of Mrs Z to give birth naturally does not in itself prevent her from having access to or participating in employment or pursuing a career and therefore cannot be qualified as a disability. If this condition were to be brought under the term 'disability' within the meaning of Directive 2000/78/EC, this would not constitute an 'interpretation in conformity with the Treaty', but rather an extension of EU law beyond the legislator's control.[44] The Court acknowledged that Mrs. Z's condition might qualify as a disability under the

37. *Id.* paragraphs 60-64.
38. *Kaloft*, paragraph 62.
39. *C.E. Ruiz Conejero v. Ferroser Servicios Auxiliares SA en Ministerio Fiscal*, No. C-270/16, 18 January 2018, ECLI:EU:C:2018:17 (hereinafter: *C. E. Ruiz Conejero*).
40. *C.E. Ruiz Conejero/Ferroser Servicios Auxiliares SA en Ministerio Fiscal*, paragraph 30; (hereinafter: L. Waddington, 'Saying All the Right Things and Still Getting it Wrong', *supra* note 34, 580).
41. *Z./A Government Department*, No. C-363/12, 18 March 2014, ECLI:EU:C:2014:159; Opinion A.-G. WAHL.
42. *Z./A Government Department*, paragraph 79; L. Waddington, 'The Influence of the UN Convention on the Rights of Persons with Disabilities', *supra* note 12, 7.
43. *Z./A Government Department*, paragraph 80.
44. *Z./A Government Department*, paragraphs 82-90; Opinion A.-G. WAHL, paragraphs 49-48.

UNCRPD, but concluded that it did not amount to a disability for the purposes of Directive 2000/78/EC.[45]

Another judgment of the CJEU that could suggest that the Court still holds on to the physical and medical limitations of employees when determining if a certain impairment constitutes a disability is the *Daouidi* case.[46] The court was asked whether the condition of an employee, who was dismissed while temporarily unable to work, as defined in national law, for an indeterminate period of time, is covered by the notion of 'disability' within the meaning of Directive 2000/78/EC.[47] While referring to the definition of the UNCRPD,[48] the Court adds that it is necessary to assess whether that limitation to his capacity, which in interaction with various barriers may hinder the full and effective participation of the person concerned in professional life on an equal basis with other workers, is 'long-term'.[49] The long-term duration of the limitation may be derived from the fact that, at the time of the allegedly discriminatory act, the incapacity of the person does not display '*a clearly defined prognosis as regards short-term progress or the fact that it is likely that the recovery time will be significantly prolonged*'.

When examining the aforementioned cases of the CJEU, one could indeed question that the Court fully adheres to the importance of the role which environmental and socially constructed circumstances play in creating disability. As argued by WADDINGTON, there is still a strong emphasis on the physical nature of the condition possibly resulting in disability and the reliance on medical evidence in the CJEU's case laws, which might reflect the reluctance of the CJEU to fully commit to the social model of disability.[50] This stance is however problematic in cases where the permanent or long term nature of the limitation cannot be medically diagnosed (yet), e.g., a breast cancer survivor suffering from fatigue after treatment.[51] Moreover, as the cases have shown, the Court also maintains an emphasis on the 'limitation' of the disabled persons, resulting from both individual factors and the work environment, which has to affect his or her ability to perform his or her job. It is however quite plausible that there are other attitudinal and social barriers that may hinder professional participation, such as negative attitudes and prejudices of the employer.[52] The question thus remains to what conclusion the Court would have come if an employee would have been dismissed because the employer assumed e.g., that his or her health status would lead to possible absences in the future, irrespective of the employee's true health

45. *Z./A Government Department*, paragraph 93; Opinion A.-G. WAHL, paragraph 49.
46. *Daouidi v. Bootes Plus SL*, No. C-395/15, 1 December 2016, ECLI:EU:C:2016:917 (hereinafter: *Daouidi*).
47. *Id.*, paragraph 36
48. *Id.*, paragraphs 42-44.
49. *Id.*, para. 48
50. L. Waddington, 'The Influence of the UN Convention on the Rights of Persons with Disabilities', *see* note 12, 9.
51. *See* more elaborately: L. Waddington, 'Saying All the Right Things and Still Getting it Wrong', *supra* note 34, 579-580; C. Hießl and G. Boot, 'The Application of the EU Framework for Disability Discrimination in 18 European Countries', *ELLJ* 2013, Vol. 4, No. 2, (119) 125 (hereinafter: C. Hießl and G. Boot).
52. L. Waddington, 'The Influence of the UN Convention on the Rights of Persons with Disabilities', *supra* note 12, 8.

status. In the purely social perception of disability, an individual who does not experience any impact on his work capacity, can become disabled because of false assumptions and prejudice of others and therefore should be protected against discrimination.[53]

A possible explanation for this remaining focus on medical limitations when performing a professional activity might, however, be the fact that EU-antidiscrimination law is designed to remedy certain forbidden discriminatory behaviour, and only within the limited area of employment and occupation, while the UNCRPD encompasses a whole range of civil, political, social and cultural rights to facilitate participation in society as a whole and therefore departs from proactive models to advance social inclusion that are much broader than anti-discrimination legislation.[54] It has been argued that the broad social understanding of 'disability' in the UNCRPD might be too broad when establishing whether an individual was discriminated against on the ground of his disability in an employment context. When it comes to applying anti-discrimination laws, i.a. through litigation, defining who belongs to the group that has to be covered by such measures is indispensable, therefore there is a need to focus on the actual impairment. The reference for the interpretation of disability within the context of employment discrimination is for this reason often the (hindered) participation in the more limited field of professional life due to individual limitations and environmental barriers, and thus involves a more narrow notion of disability.[55] Only when it is clear that a (long term) medical condition might prevent a person to participate fully in the workplace, the case law of the CJEU shows that environmental barriers, such as an unadapted workplace, are effectively taken into account when evaluating the obligation to provide reasonable accommodation.

§17.03 WORK INCAPACITY AND DISABILITY IN NATIONAL (CASE) LAW

As shown above, the ratification of the UNCRPD by the EU, resulted in the fact that the CJEU has to interpret EU anti-discrimination in conformity with the Convention and thus when defining the legal concept of disability in the sphere of EU anti-discrimination law, the CJEU has to seek consistency with the social notion of 'disability' as proclaimed by the Convention. Although many questions remain about the direct effect of the UNCRPD in national legal systems, the Convention has an enforcement mechanism through EU anti-discrimination law and the application thereof. As the Directive 2000/78/EC has horizontal direct effect, national courts are

53. Opinion A.-G. Jaaskinen, paragraph 52; L. Waddington, 'The Influence of the UN Convention on the Rights of Persons with Disabilities', *supra* note 12, 9.
54. *See* more elaborately: L. Waddington, 'The Influence of the UN Convention on the Rights of Persons with Disabilities', *supra* note 12; G. De Beco, 'Is Obesity a Disability? The Definition of Disability by the Court of Justice of the European Union and Its Consequences for the Application of EU Anti-discrimination Law', *Columbia Journal of European Law* 2016, Vol. 22.2, (381) 396 (hereinafter: G. De Beco).
55. G. DE BECO, 397-398.

obliged to interpret legislation in conformity with EU anti-discrimination (case) law with regard to the grounds of discrimination contained in Directive 2000/78/EC.[56]

This makes it quite interesting to investigate whether the social understanding of the equal treatment of persons with a disability in employment relations has trickled down into national (case) law regarding disability and work incapacity. For the purpose of this paper, three Member States were selected, namely France, Belgium and The Netherland. However, the spill-over effect of the social understanding of disability in the legal frameworks as developed by national courts and lawmakers relies heavily upon the question whether the national implementation legislation of the Directive 2000/78/EC contains a closed definition of 'disability'. As far as the national legislature does not contain a national definition, it is for the national courts to interpret the implementing provisions in conformity with the criteria given by the CJEU when dealing with questions of disability discrimination.[57]

[A] France: Remnants of a Medical Approach

When it comes to disability in the (employment) discrimination context, the French legislation contains well-defined (medical) concepts of disability. The first legal definition can be found in the Law of 11 February 2005 on equal rights and opportunities, participation and citizenship of people with disabilities, which states that '*a disability, under this law, is constituted by any activity limitation or any restriction to participation in life in society to which a person is subjected in his or her environment due to substantial, durable or definitive alteration to one or more physical, sensorial, mental, cognitive, or psychological functions, or to a polydisability or to a disabling problem of health*'.[58] Although the 2005 law rests on a new paradigm of disability as a possible condition for every individual, and not as a personal tragedy, and thus represents a move towards a more social model of disability, the definition given in the law failed to fully embrace the social model of disability by not adopting an interactive definition and instead ignoring the link between disability and environmental barriers.[59]

The principle of non-discrimination is also a core aspect of French Labour law. The French Labour Code contains several provisions on discrimination and lists all grounds of prohibited discrimination, which include not only disability but also medical condition and physical appearance, contrary to the EU Directive 2000/78/EC.[60] Although 'reasonable accommodation' is not a familiar notion in French labour law, the obligation to take 'appropriate measures' for disabled workers was

56. Article 8 Directive 2000/78/EG, *see* note 15; *Irmtraud Junk/Wolfgang Kühnel*, Case no. C-188/03, 27 January 2005, ECLI:EU:C:2005:59;
57. C. Hießl and G. Boot, *supra* note 51, 120, 127.
58. Article 2 Law no 2005-102 of 11 February 2005 on equal rights and opportunities, participation and citizenship of people with disabilities, implemented by Article L114 Code de l'Action Sociale et des Familles.
59. L. Bertrand, V. Caradec and J.-S. Eideliman, 'Situating Disability. The Recognition of "Disabled Workers" in France', *European Journal of Disability Research 2014*, Vol. 9, 270.
60. Article L.1132-1 Labour Code.

added to the Labour Code since the implementation of Directive 2000/78/EC. These measures must be taken in order to have access to, or retain employment corresponding to their qualification, and to participate in or advance in such employment unless the costs resulting from their implementation are not disproportionate.[61] However, according to French labour law, only a few categories of disabled employees are entitled to certain appropriate measures, namely those whose disability status[62] is recognised by a special Commission[63] which is responsible for the rights of persons with disabilities in general, workers for which a work accident resulted in a disability estimated at 10% or more, disability pensioners, war veteran pensioners, holders of a disability card and recipients of the Disabled Adult Allowance.[64] The fact that French legislation has delineated the notion of 'disability' in various legislative documents, leaves little to no room for the domestic courts to interpret the notion in a more social light. Case law on the matter is therefore virtually non-existent in France.[65] Its often medical and individual focus on disability and the requirement to be officially recognised by an administration in order to be entitled to reasonable accommodation however might lead to future infringement procedures by the Commission

Besides disability, health problems are also included in the personal scope of French anti-discrimination law, however, it only prohibits decisions that are directly or indirectly based on grounds of health and does not entail an obligation to provide for reasonable accommodations in case of health problems as such.[66] In their search for legal protection, employees who have become unfit to perform their work tasks due to health issues, can however rely in many instances on legislation which requires their 'reclassification'.[67] In the context of health and disability at work, employers have a duty to look for another position for those employees and must strive to maintain employment by looking for accommodations.[68] Only when the employer can prove that this is 'impossible', he can terminate the employment contract. In this sense, there is a certain obligation to provide for 'appropriate' accommodations on behalf of the employer and that obligation does not only apply in the limited case of 'disability'. However, the scope of this obligation is much more limited than the reasonable accommodations obligation, as it seems to focus on the question of dismissal on the basis of the unfitness for work much more than on the question of remaining in suitable

61. Article L 5213-6 Labour Code; French law does not refer to a disproportionate 'burden' but rather 'disproportionate costs', thus focusing entirely on the financial aspects of the situation.
62. Also known as the *Reconnaissance de la Qualité de Travailleur Handicap* (Recognised Disabled Worker Status).
63. The CDAPH (*Commissions des droits et de l'autonomie des personnes handicapées*) or Commission for the Rights and Independence of Disabled People.
64. Article L 5213-6 and L 5213-13 Labour Code; L. Bertrand, V. Caradec and J.-S. Eideliman, *supra* note 59, 271.
65. C. Hießl and G. Boot, *supra n*ote 51, 120, 121.
66. S. Robin-Olivier, 'Reasonable Accommodation for Religion and Other Motives, in French Labour Law: Testing the Possibility of a Legal Transplant', in R. Blanpain and F. Hendrickx (eds), *Reasonable Accommodation in the Modern Workplace. Potential and Limits of the Integrative Logics of Labour Law*, Alphen aan den Rijn, Kluwer Law International, 2016, (145), 155. (hereinafter: S. Robin-Olivier).
67. *Id.* 152.
68. Article L 1226-2 and 1226-10 Labour Code.

employment. Moreover, the 'reasonableness' of these measures in France is not subject to appropriate judicial review.[69]

[B] First Steps Towards a More Social Approach: Belgium

A clear example of the spill-over effect of the UN's social model of disability into the employment context is Belgium, where there is no legal definition of disability in its implementation legislation of Directive 2000/78/EC.[70] Several attempts to introduce a definition were rejected, as the Belgian government wanted to avoid that a restrictive definition of 'disability' would give rise to a discussion about who should be qualified as a person with a disability from a medical point of view or not. The choice was made for a broader, more social understanding of disability that does not so much emphasize the limitations of the person, but rather focuses on the possibilities of participation provided that adjustments are made to the environment.[71] The absence of a concrete definition of disability left some room for the Belgium national courts to develop the concept of disability in accordance with the CJEU rulings. Unlike Directive 2000/78/EC, the Belgian anti-discrimination act includes not only the protected ground of 'disability' but also physical properties and current or future health status.[72] However, qualification as a disability is crucial, as Belgian employers are in theory only obliged to make reasonable adjustments if there is a disability within the meaning of the Anti-Discrimination Act.

Over the past decade, there has been an increase in the number of cases in which the Labour courts were asked to clarify the relationship between a temporary disability, an illness and a disability in itself in the context of anti-discrimination in labour relations.[73] The notion was initially interpreted in line with the *Chacón Navas* judgment, following a medical approach, and thus precluding employees affected by an illness or temporary condition from the protection by the legal framework to combat discrimination on grounds of disability.[74] However, in a few more recent judgments, a broader interpretation of the concept of disability was applied, leading to judgments where chronic conditions such as diabetes[75] and chronic back pain[76] were found to constitute a disability that hinders professional participation. The focus was however still on establishing the existence of a medical condition and the fact that it has a

69. S. Robin-Olivier, *supra* note 66, 155.
70. Directive 2000/78/EC was implemented through the law of 10 Mai 2007 regarding combatting certain forms of discrimination (hereinafter: Anti-Discrimination Act).
71. Report of the Commission for Justice, *Parl.St.* Kamer 2001-02, nr. 1578/8, 31.
72. Article 2 Anti-Discrimination Act.
73. *See* M. Vanhegen, *Arbeidsongeschiktheid en re-integratie in het arbeidsrecht*, Brugge, die Keure, 2017, 24-27.
74. *See* e.g., Labour Court of Antwerp, 3 September 2008; Labour Court of Hasselt 28 Mai 2009, AR nr. 2051589, www.unia.be; Labour Court of Bergen 7 December 2012, AR 11/409/A, www.unia.be; Labour Tribunal of Tongeren, 29 Juin 2006, AR 3503/2004.
75. Labour Court Antwerp 21 November 2011, AR 2010/AA/334/A, *NB Arbeidsrecht* 2011/9 en *Soc.Kron.* 2012, 21.
76. Labour Court Brussels 18 December 2012, AR 2011/AB/1089, www.unia.be.

long-term nature.[77] Since the CJEU's landmark judgment in the *HK Danmark case* however, the courts began to display a more social understanding of the concept of disability. In a case of 2015, it was clarified that '*a disability relating to employment is a long-term and important problem of participation in working life that is due to the interplay between functional disorders of a mental, psychological, physical or sensory nature, limitations in carrying out activities and personal and external factors*'. In doing so, the Labour Court explicitly referred to the definition of disability developed by the Court of Justice in the *HK Danmark* judgment and the definition in the UNCRPD.[78] This paved the way for more labour courts to adopt the definition the CJEU formulated in *HK Danmark*, which led to judgments where medical conditions such as obesity,[79] a psychological condition,[80] chronic pains,[81] a shoulder injury[82] and the consequences of a cancer treatment[83] were qualified as a disability within the meaning of Directive 2000/78/EC and the Anti-Discrimination Act. The courts acknowledged that the Directive should be interpreted as broadly as possible in accordance with the UNCRPD and therefore, the (long-term) limitation in participation in professional life should also be examined in the light of the interaction between the impairment and various external barriers. The courts followed the view that a disability does not necessarily imply total exclusion from work or working life and a person's (partial) work incapacity for a particular job could also constitute a disability. In this case, the employer must examine the possibilities for that employee to enable him or her again to carry out certain tasks with the help of reasonable accommodations.[84]

However, in all these cases, it was quite clear from the start that the medical conditions constituted disabilities. The courts therefore never really elaborated on the social aspect of the definition, but merely referred to the *HK Danmark* definition, still focusing on the medical evidence of a long-term medical condition that forms an obstacle to full and effective participation in professional life. In all the aforementioned cases, the courts looked for evidence of reduced mobility or the fact that the pathology prevented the normal performance of work or led to discomfort. In the Belgian case law, it therefore remains unclear whether obstacles originating essentially in the stigmatisation of the person or prejudices concerned by their environment would be subsumed under As such as the hindrance of work performance and normal day-to-day activities by a physical impairment.

Outside the area of disability discrimination, the UNCRPD and the CJEU case law has also affected the way other aspects of Belgian labour law were shaped. One of the main examples is the introduction of new legislation on the reintegration in the workplace of persons confronted with work incapacity due to health issues through

77. Labour Tribunal Antwerp 8 May 2014, AR 13/469/A, www.unia.be.
78. Labour Tribunal 22 January 2015, AR 14/642/A, www.unia.be.
79. Labour Tribunal Luik 20 June 2016, AR 15/167/A, www.unia.be.
80. Labour Court Brussels 21 February 2017, www. unia.be.
81. Labour Tribunal Luik 9 March 2018, AR 17/22/C www.unia.be.
82. Labour Tribunal Brussel 24 June 2016, AR 2105/AB/920, www.unia.be.
83. Labour Court Brussels 28 February 2018, AR 2016/AB/959, www.unia.be.
84. Labour Court Antwerp 12 May 2009, AR 2070100.

adaptation to the work or workplace.[85] When drawing up the legislation, the Belgian government explicitly referred in the explanatory memorandum to the obligation to carry out 'reasonable accommodation' with regard to workers who are unable to pursue their tasks due to health reasons.[86] The purpose of the procedure for the reintegration of disabled employees is precisely to determine the extent to which employees with health issues can continue to be employed in the enterprise, in particular by giving them temporary or permanent adapted or alternative work, unless this is technically or objectively impossible or cannot reasonably be required for well-founded reasons.[87] Although the legislation primarily envisages to encourage the resumption of activity of workers who have been ill for a long time but who have retained certain residual capacities, employees for whom it is not quite sure how long their health issues will last or who are temporarily unable to work, must also be granted access to jobs in adequacy with their disability or illness.[88] However, the effectiveness of the provisions is somewhat negated by the lack of a strong enforcement mechanism.

[C] Embracing the Social Model of Disability: The Netherlands

The same evolution is also noticeable in the Netherlands, where national jurisdiction is increasing, mainly because a special 'Human Rights Council' (HRC, before 2012 called the Equal Treatment Commission) is competent to deal with questions of disability discrimination next to the civil courts, and is able to give non-binding rulings with regard to the qualification as disability.[89] The disability provisions of Directive 2000/78/EC have been transposed in the Netherlands by the Equal Treatment on the basis of Disability or Chronic Disease Act *(Dutch:WGB h/cz)*.[90] However, contrary to the Directive 2000/78/EC, this law prohibits not only discrimination on the grounds of disability, but also on the grounds of chronic illness, as a result of which national legislation has already cleared the way for a broader scope of anti-discrimination legislation.[91] According to the Dutch government, both protected grounds show so many similarities and involve so many comparable situations that it was logical to bring both grounds within the personal scope of the law. After all, the Dutch government took the position that the term 'disabled persons' as developed in the

85. Royal Decree 28 October 2016 regarding the amendment of the Royal Decree of 28 May 2003 on the health supervision of employees with regard to the reintegration of disabled employees.
86. Explanatory memorandum, draft law of 16 November 2016 on various provisions on employment law in connection with incapacity for work.
87. Article I.4.72-I.4.82 Codex Wellbeing at Work.
88. Article I.4.72 Codex Wellbeing at Work.
89. C. Hießl and G. Boot, *supra* note 51, 120; J. Goldschmidt, 'Reasonable Accommodation in EU Equality Law in a Broader Perspective', *ERA Forum* 2007, No. 8, 47 et seq.
90. Equal Treatment on the basis of Disability or Chronic Disease Act of 3 April 2003.
91. Article 1 *'In this Act the following definitions apply: a. distinction: direct and indirect distinction; b. direct distinction: distinction between persons on the basis of a real or perceived disability or chronic illness* [...]'; L. Waddington and M.H.S. Gijzen, '(Her)definitie van het begrip "handicap" in de EG en Nederlandse gelijke-behandelingswetgeving', *NTER* 2006, No. 12, (270) 273-274 (hereinafter: L. Waddington and M.H.S. Gijzen).

international context, like the UNCRPD, is a collective term for both persons with disabilities and persons with chronic illnesses.[92]

Like in Belgium, the national implementation legislation of Directive 2000/78/EC does not contain a definition of the concept 'disability', nor 'illness'. One of the reasons for the lack of definitions of the notions was that the question of whether a person is hindered by disability or chronic illness does not depend solely on the disability or chronic illness as such, but also on the context in which a person operates.[93] Indeed, the legal obligation to make reasonable accommodation is a recognition of the fact that disability cannot be explained in purely biological terms. Disability is a social construction, in the sense that it is often created by the society/environment itself.[94] This shifted the attention away from the medical condition of the individual disabled person, towards the 'unequal treatment' itself.[95] In any event, it is undisputed that the concepts of disability and chronic illness may include physical, mental or mental disorders. In addition, it was indicated that disability is, in principle, irreversible, whereas a chronic disease is sometimes not. However, both are of a long-term nature.[96] Furthermore, Art. 1 of the Dutch Act on Equal Treatment forbids making a direct difference in treatment on grounds of a real or ***presumed*** disability or chronic illness. The reason to add the words 'presumed' is that prejudices against chronically ill persons may exist even if the illness does not manifest any more, e.g., prejudices against a recovered cancer patient.[97] The concept of alleged or presumed disability or chronic illness may also be invoked at the outset of a disability when it is not clear what the course will be and what recovery possibilities will present themselves. For the persons concerned, it is thus not necessary to prove that the alleged disability is long-term or irreversible.[98]

As proven above, the Dutch notion of 'disability' reflects the impact of the social model of disability. However, when there is any uncertainty, the civil courts and the Human Rights Council are able to give guidance on the question whether a certain medical condition constitutes a disability or a chronic illness in the sense of the Equal Treatment Act. When looking at the rulings of the HRC and the civil courts with regard to the disability qualification, several examples are to be found of the adherence to a broad social definition of disability and chronic illness in the Netherlands.[99] Medical conditions such as agoraphobia,[100] AHDH,[101] diabetes,[102] morbid

---

92. Explanatory memorandum, II, 2001-2002, 28 169, nr. 3, p. 9; L. Waddington and M.H.S. Gijzen, *see* note 91, 274-275.
93. Kamerstukken II 1999/2000, 24 170, nr. 55; Explanatory memorandum, II, 2001-2002, 28 169 nr. 3, p. 9; B.H.M Werker, 'Wet gelijke behandeling op grond van handicap of chronische ziekte: met vallen en opstaan vooruit', *Tijdschrift Recht en Arbeid* 2008, No. 7/8, (46) 46-47.
94. M.H.S. Gijzen, 'Thema's in het gelijkebehandelingsrecht: een veellagige rechtsvergelijkende analyse van Europees, Engels en Nederlands recht', *NCJM-Bulletin* 2007, Vol. 32, No. 6, 809.
95. L. Waddington and M.H.S. Gijzen, *see* note 91, 275.
96. Kamerstukken II 2001/02, 28 169, nr. 3, p. 9 en 24; *See* HRC Ruling n° 2013-139.
97. MvT, II, 2001-2002, 28 169 nr. 3, p. 24.; HRC Rulings n° 2004-7, 2007-6, 2017-39, 2017-93 and 2018-19; L. Waddington and M.H.S. Gijzen, *see* note 91, 275.
98. A.C. Hendriks, *Werken met een handicap (WGBH/CZ)*, Deventer: Kluwer 2007, 30-31.
99. *See* L. Waddington and M.H.S. Gijzen, *see* note 91, 276.
100. HRC Ruling n° 2005-133, r.o. 5.5 (chronic illness).
101. HRC Ruling n° 2005-02, r.o. 5.3 and 2017-120 (disability).
102. HRC Ruling n° 2006-03.

obesity,[103] post-traumatic stress disorder,[104] alcohol addiction,[105] burn-out,[106] cancer[107] and the consequences of whiplash[108] are all regarded as a chronic illness or disability and thus fall within the personal scope of the Equal Treatment Act.

More general, the HRC takes into account the purpose of the Dutch Equal Treatment Act, namely the protection of persons who, with or without effective adaptations, can participate in (parts of) social life, including working life. In other words, the law aims to offer individual legal protection to persons who can function, but who are regularly confronted with prohibited discrimination on the grounds of (their) disability or chronic illness, for example in the form of prejudices, stigmatising ideas or (unconscious) refusal to provide reasonable accommodation.[109] In this sense, according to the Dutch case law, disability and chronic illness do not necessarily coincide with work incapacity, as not all persons with disabilities are completely unfit for work. An employee can, therefore, invoke the protection of the Equal Treatment Act if he or she doesn't suffer from a medical condition but the employer wrongly believes that he or she is chronically ill.[110] In some (individual) cases, however, there may be a (causal) link between a person's absence due to illness/incapacity for work on the one hand and disability or chronic illness on the other.[111] Indeed, a person's incapacity for a particular job may be the result of a particular disability or chronic illness. In that case, the employer must first examine the option whether, with the help of reasonable accommodations, someone can be made capable to carry out certain work.

Similar to Belgium and France, the shift in perception regarding sickness and disability was also made in other Dutch labour provisions.[112] In order to reduce absence from work due to illness or disability, measures were introduced which made the employer responsible for the reintegration of a sick or disabled employee into the workplace, regardless of the duration of their impairments or the fact that the work incapacity is partial or full. The employer must do all he reasonably can to improve the individual's chances of returning to work and reintegrate the employee into the employment process, even if it is unclear it is unclear how long the work incapacity will take.[113] This clearly reflects the 'reasonable accommodation' obligation as included in the UNCRPD and Directive 2000/78/EC, but even goes further, as it imposes the obligation to provide reasonable accommodation also for employees with temporary health-related work restrictions.

103. Rb. Breda 23 September 2011, JAR 2011/239; HRC Ruling n° 2014-158, 2015-18 and 2016-18; A.C. Hendriks, 'Hof van Justitie ontwikkelt nieuwe visie op begrip handicap- en daarmee op non-discriminatie', *NtER* 2015, No. 7, (232) 235-236.
104. HRC Ruling n° 2005-176, r.o. 5.13.
105. HRC Ruling n° 2017-150.
106. HRC Ruling n° 2017-36.
107. HRC Ruling n° 2011-159, 2014-45.
108. HRC Ruling n° 2005-234, r.o. 5.7.
109. HRC Rulings n°2005-177, 2004-145, 2005-77, 2005-133, 2005-176; L. Waddington and M.H.S. Gijzen, *see* note 91, 276.
110. *See* HRC Ruling 2017-36.
111. HRC Ruling n° 2015-20.
112. I.a. Gatekeeper Improvement Act of 29 November 2001.
113. Article 7:658a lid 1 BW.

§17.04 CONCLUDING REMARKS

When looking into the impact of the UNCRPD, with its social approach on disability, on the way the CJEU has developed its case law regarding the concept of disability and disability discrimination, it is clear that the identifying disability is not straightforward. Although the first steps towards a social approach of disability have been taken by the CJEU, blurring the delineation of disability from other categories like illness and work incapacity, it seems that the CJEU left some other rather fundamental questions unanswered. In practice, it remains somewhat opaque who would come under the concept of disability. This is, nonetheless, important seen the obligation of employers to make reasonable accommodation.

It could be argued that the CJEU still does not fully adhere to the importance of the role which environmental and socially constructed circumstances play in creating disability. In a way, it still holds on to a medical model of disability by focusing on the medical evidence of the long-term limitations of employees when examining the hindrances to full professional participation, rather than on the discriminatory treatment. This raises the question whether the Court would fully consider the social approach of disability, in conformity with the UNCRPD, if a decent medical prognosis on the real development of the employee's health condition is not readily possible, e.g., a breast cancer survivor suffering from fatigue after treatment. The same question can be raised if the potential barriers to full participation would stem from negative attitudes or prejudices of the employer, e.g., in the case of dismissal because the employer assumed that the health status of an employee would lead to possible (future) absences, irrespective of the employee's true health status.

National systems cause similar debate. The French legislator still holds on to well-defined medical concepts of disability, which leaves little room for a more social understanding of disability. Case law on the matter is therefore virtually non-existent in France. The obligation of reasonable accommodation of the employer is limited by a closed list of categories in the Labour Code. This makes the scope of application of the obligation to provide reasonable accommodation more limited than suggested by the CJEU's case law.

In Belgium, the absence of a concrete definition of disability left some room for the courts to develop the concept of disability in accordance with the CJEU rulings. This paved the way for a more social definition, as formulated in *HK Danmark*. However, while the array of conditions that can be categorised as a potential disability has expanded throughout the years, Belgian courts rarely elaborate on the possible environmental and socially constructed barriers. They merely refer to the *HK Danmark* definition, still focussing on the medical evidence of a long term medical condition that forms an obstacle to full and effective participation in professional life. This is not the case in the legislation in the Netherlands, which grants protection to a more broadly defined category of persons, much more in line with the social model of disability.

The personal scope of Dutch legal protection against discrimination also includes ***presumed*** disability or chronic illness. For the persons concerned, it is thus not necessary to prove that the alleged disability is long-term or irreversible.

The debate thus continues. The remnants of the medical model of disability still enforce an additional precondition in order to be qualified as a disability and therefore fall within the scope of protection offered by disability discrimination law, namely the condition that the employee must provide medical evidence that his medical condition entails a long-term or permanent limitation which hinders, in interaction with various barriers, his full and effective participation of the person in professional life. It is imaginable that there are situations where workers become unable to pursue their professional activity and it is not yet clear what the course of their health status will be and what recovery possibilities will present themselves. A plausible explanation as to why these persons are still excluded from the scope of disability discrimination protection is that they are not perceived as an identifiable group that needs fundamental protection in terms of reintegration into work. However, it can be argued that this latter group of employees has also very distinct needs that require accommodation in order to have access to substantive equality in the workplace.[114] As seen in the examined cases, national labour legislation often provides for a separate legal protection mechanism outside the area of disability discrimination for employees confronted with work incapacity due to health issues, even when they are temporary or when it is not sure how long the health issues will last. This protection often consists of the obligation for employer to temporarily or permanently adapt the workplace or work tasks of the sick or disabled employee in order to maintain employment, which is, in fact, a reflection of the obligation to provide for reasonable accommodation as developed in anti-discrimination law. In many instances, the protection by an additional legal ground, such as disability discrimination law, is paramount for employees confronted with a work incapacity due to health reasons. Although the aforementioned health and safety provisions indeed entail obligations to reintegrate employees with health issues, regardless of the duration of the impairments, these measures are often characterised by unwieldy procedures which require the intervention of e.g., an occupational physician and often lack effective enforcement. One of the strongest means of protecting disabled and sick employees still lies in the general principle of non-discrimination which prohibits any employer from treating an employee differently on the basis of certain grounds including, *inter alia*, the employee's health situation and disability. This additional legal ground makes their claim to accommodating measures in order to have access to and remain in employment much more tangible.

114. *See also* G. Davidov and G. Mundlak, 'Accommodating All? (or: "Ask Not What You Can Do for the Labour Market; Ask What the Labour Market Can Do for You")' in R. Blanpain and F. Hendrickx (eds), *Reasonable Accommodation in the Modern Workplace. Potential and Limits of the Integrative Logics of Labour Law*, Alphen aan den Rijn, Kluwer Law International, 2016, (191) 206.

Part IV Industrial Relations in the Low Countries: Belgium and the Netherlands

CHAPTER 18

Social Dialogue in the Low Countries: Institutional Reconversion and Legal Challenges in Belgium and the Netherlands

Valeria Pulignano, Frank Hendrickx & Marc van der Meer

§18.01 INTRODUCTION

In 1977, Harvie Ramsay published 'Cycles of Control: Worker Participation in Sociological and Historical Perspective' in *Sociology*. Since then, it has been one of the most influential contributions in the field of industrial relations. Ramsay's theoretical framework departs from the assumption that relations between representative organizations of employers and workers are fundamentally antagonistic. This is why, in his view, a win-win situation is never a real option.

The inherent conflict in industrial relations puts limits to the sustainability of systems based on social dialogue. When Ramsay developed his theory, the Keynesian welfare state was challenged in the international political economy given the decreasing economic growth rates, a rise of inflation and structural and high unemployment. This brought the question how in countries with a practice of centralized collective bargaining and social concertation would respond to the rise of monetarist theory and supply-side economics which argued that less state intervention and more individual responsibility were needed.

As long as countries were sovereign in executing monetary policy, social dialogue still proved its value, since national central banks could make 'deals' with social partners to define wage levels at the benefit of economic prosperity and socially fair outcomes. With the European monetary integration and the growth of the European internal market, national states however no longer could easily engage in such wage-deals with social partners. The Great Recession associated with export decline and an international financial crisis of 2008 and 2009 (and again 2012-2013) had a severe impact on the fabric of various systems and institutions of social dialogue. Particularly, the crisis hit at the 'core' of social dialogue, with the European Council recommending at austerity in the social domain and modifications of decentralization of multi-employer collective bargaining systems in order to increase competitiveness. Simultaneously, collective bargaining and social dialogue have to deal with the agenda of the future of work and employment relations. New forms of flexible work and Industry 4.0. urge both employers' and workers' organizations to set an agenda for research and development, training and institutional arrangements to guide the mobility of workers to keep them in the work process. Moreover the question of the international climate change and carbon crisis and thus the sustainability of the model of economic production has arrived at the top of the agenda.

The Low Countries, where workers and trade unions were already since the Second World War involved in economic participation and decision-making processes at various levels (national, sector, company) are good examples of how national concertation has dealt with these changes. In these small and open economies, where the cyclical swings in the international economy determine strongly the course of politics, political decision-makers know what they may expect from social partnership. The two countries are similar in many ways, with a small difference with substantial consequences (Mok 1985). In Belgium, the rate of union membership -due to the Ghent system of social security- is much more elevated than in the Netherlands (53% versus 18%).

The social dialogue in the Netherlands originates from the fight against the water (in Dutch: 'polderen'), but the 'great trade-off' in 1945 between the unions and politics is significant, where the former let the business enterprise to the employers in exchange for political representation in the national bodies of the bipartite Foundation of Labour (1945) and the tri-partite Social-Economic Council (1950). In both countries, social dialogue and the involvement of 'social partners' have produced several waves of economic progress, where the state shared its political space to bridge apparent 'contradictory' interests, but also made these organizations responsible for the execution of particular government tasks in social policies.

In the Netherlands these periods include the reconstruction of the country after the Second World War with a relatively centralized state-led wage policy and also the period after the now-famous Wassenaar agreement of 1982, where wage moderation and decentralization of wage setting has been exchanged for labour time reduction, which served as the basis for the transformation of the welfare state into the direction of activation policies, which was negotiated at the national level of concertation (*see* Visser and Hemerijck, 1997; Van der Meer a.o. 2003). More recently in spite of a context of deep economic and political uncertainties, since 2010 with de facto minority positions, governments are searching for new alliances to find societal support (Hemerijck and Van der Meer, 2019).

Social dialogue in Belgium has its basis in the Social Pact of 1944, which established the foundations of a comprehensive system of social security with the common goal to improve the living conditions of the population as a whole through economic prosperity. In line with this, social dialogue foresees that sharing of productivity gains between wages and profits should be determined at sector level

(Cassiers and Denayer 2010). Thus, a centralized and strongly coordinated bargaining system, which guarantees wage indexation, as well as policy concertation with changing government coalitions are important institutional pillars of the Belgian system of social dialogue (Leonard and Pichault 2016; Van Gyes et al. 2017). Like in the Netherlands, there have been high levels of polarization at times, and sometimes it took long for dialogue to compromise, it is widely acknowledged that the institutional apparatus has tended to remain intact along the different years within a situation of relative social peace. Following these national experiences, social dialogue became also a key component of the European social market economy (European Commission (EC) 2016).

The fall of Lehman Brothers however had a direct impact on the world economy and thus effected the social dialogue in Belgium and the Netherlands. Under the introduction of the new European Semester approach in 2009 social dialogue in Belgium was transformed into an informal process with the consequent reduction in the political influence by the social partners. The crisis was felt in the Belgian debate with reform plans, such as the revision of the wage indexation system and the use of 'opt-out' clauses from sectoral collective agreements was envisaged, in order to align wage growth and labour productivity at the local level. Trade unions opposed both employers' and government's attempt to constrain wage growth by organizing several strikes and therefore safeguarding the right to collective action as at the core of the strategies for trade unions renewal in Belgium. This is because – as the general secretary of ACV-CSC Marc Leemans states in his contribution in this volume 'negotiating and strike action are two sides of the same medal. If necessary, one has to show his teeth'.

The Dutch trade union leader, Erik Pentenga, arrives at a similar conclusion that social dialogue requires social action. In the Netherlands, where unions are weaker but strongly institutionalized, the economic crisis resulted in a direct response: At the eve of the economic crisis the social partners called two social pacts in 2008 and 2009 in which the traditional recipe of wage moderation was augmented with a partial labour time reduction to prevent companies to shed labour and a regulation for knowledge workers to keep their employment. A new pact on the future of pensions in 2010 resulted in a deep crisis of the trade unions. In 2013 a broad social pact has been negotiated to change labour market policies, followed by a number of 'ad hoc' domain pacts on technology, housing, education, health care, and energy. In 2019 various broad pacts have been negotiated on the future of Europe, the economic sustainability in the Climate Accord and after ten years of deliberation also a broad Pension Pact has been negotiated. In all these agreements there has been involvement of the government and leading representatives of the employers' associations and the trade unions.

We discuss in this chapter whether it is still true that in consensus-oriented political economies, because of their 'public status', employer and employee organizations are better able to mitigate social conflicts and manage balanced policy responses to the economic crises, to achieve better socio-economic performance (*see* e.g., Crouch 1993; Visser & Van der Meer 2011). Or does the sluggishness of socioeconomic consultation due to organizational obstruction, with the social partners acting as insiders in the policy system in relation to other societal interests hamper the adjustments that are needed (cf. Schmidt 2013). Our question thus is how the two countries have responded to the crisis. Is Belgium with relatively stable centralized institutions and even slightly increasing trade unions power, which enjoy a large support by the workforce, better able to mitigate the economic crisis and the challenges of the future of work than a country with centralized consultation where trade union power is relatively weak? How have both countries dealt with the instability inherent of post-war European models of social compromise which tended to impose a certain self-restrain on employers. So what are the challenges for social dialogue and collective bargaining, departing from the experiences in the low countries, Belgium and the Netherlands? What were the main responses to the crisis? Has the process of social concertation been able to improve itself? What future lies ahead?

§18.02 DRIVERS OF CHANGE

When the crisis emerged, Belgium and the Netherlands faced the same challenges as many other European economies.[1] First, these challenges include the globalization of economic production and the liberalization of financial markets, of which European economic integration became one important element. The mid-20th century saw a qualitative shift to the crucial (dominant) role of multinational corporations and the development of what may best be called global surplus value chains, in which corporate strategists subject actual producers to constant pressures to cut costs, the free movement of labour and the increased competition for jobs in the Single European Market. This concurred to remove the dominant capitalist agglomerations from national control, whereas also an array of commodities, such as hedge funds, private equity, leveraged buy-outs, credit default spawned. The raise of the global platform economy introduces new challenges in the way in which it imposes a new 'dominant global order' where transactions are conducted via on-line platforms where 'one-person' micro-providers - and not anymore the multinational - play a crucial role serving clients around the world (Lehdonvirta, 2016). Corporations have themselves been transformed into commodities or goods to be increasingly bought and sold, creating new source of value and combined to this generating new modes of insecurity through restructuring. In the crisis also the structure of foreign and homegrown multinational companies (MNCs) has substantially changed. Overall, in accordance with the ERM (European Restructuring Monitoring) restructuring accounted for over 60% of the total announced job losses in Belgium in the period 2008-2010. In the period 2014-2019 (March 2019 as the latest data available) restructuring under the form of offshoring/ delocalization in manufacturing was responsible for 13.47% of job losses in Belgium.[2]

Traditional Dutch and Belgium companies are increasingly in foreign hands and external shareholders have taken the lead in operational management of many

1. Hemerijck and Van der Meer (2016) distinct three 'pillars' on which social consultation is built: the political, the societal and the international, which are all altering.
2. https://www.eurofound.europa.eu/nl/topic/restructuring accessed 1 March 2019.

companies.[3] Both countries suffered from major restructuring in both traditional manufacturing (e.g., the car industry) and private services (e.g., financial and banking). An important difference is that the Netherlands attracts a lot of financial holding companies, whereas Belgium has less popularity as financial heaven for MNCs (Pulignano and Deckoker 2014). The banking system was extremely vulnerable, and immediately after the outbreak of the crisis, the Belgium-Dutch Fortis-bank had to be split into a separate Belgium and a separate Dutch Branch. Connected to the international banking crisis and the limitation to capital, the economic recession put the stability of the monetary system to the test. The so-called European Semester (2010), connected to the agreements on sharpened budget-monitoring by the EC in the context of the Euro Plus Pact (2011), the Two-Pack (2011), the Six-Pack (2011) and the Fiscal Compact (2012), has granted an elementary authority of sovereign states – the right to budget – subordinate to the administrative authority of the EC. This is a watershed (Hemerijck and Van der Meer 2016). Only the European Council of Ministers can intervene in this process with qualified majority. For example, the EC is now evaluating in Spring 'ex ante' the planned concept-budget for Euro-countries, including the mandate to propose policy adjustments. This argument for decentralization, deregulation and flexibilization substantially limits the room for political manoeuvring for county-specific macro-economic flexibility and ignores the fact that European economies differ fundamentally in terms of sector structure, trade balance and institutional order (*ibid*).

Secondly, the reconfiguration of national politics and the role of the state itself is an important driver of change. In the post-war period, governments were stable coalition supported by social partners. The state itself became a major employer, typically committed to supporting high labour standards. However, since the turn of the century, political stability is hard to find in both countries given the rise of populist parties at the right and left-wing end of the political spectrum. A fundamental change behind the functioning of the state is the revision of political decision-making. Increasingly the parties in the middle have gained less votes in elections, whereas fragmentation has occurred both at the left and right wings of the political spectrum. In Belgium, even more than in the Netherlands, regional disparities between the Flemish- and the French-speaking regions reinforce waves of emergence of right wing (Flemish-nationalist) populist parties. Since the 1980s government policies have been aimed at 'rolling back the state', and restricting social protections to those that can be justified on grounds of productivity and competitiveness. Not only European Union (EU) (i.e., 'new economic governance') but also national governments ('new public management') have become the key drivers of this process which increasingly targets social welfare and employment protection by imposing policy measures which increase ambiguity by escalating insecurity and inequality in labour markets. This challenges the post-war compromise in multiple ways where the web of individual employment rights and the collective representation of worker interests through trade unions and

3. *See also* the contribution of Laurens Harteveld in this volume.

works councils where no longer automatically buttressed and welfare regimes were revised.

Third, given all these changes, the social partners themselves were looking for new sources of legitimation and renewed strategies to represent their interests. This was particularly the case since 2014 when under the Charles Michel's government, labour market reforms represented an important change of direction for the country and sparked discussions, protests and power struggles, not the least between the social partners themselves. Within the Dutch trade union movement, 'organizing principles' gained foot in the course of 2007 and 2008, when some informal union leaders argued that trade unions were miscalculating their position and are basically solving HR-problem for management instead of raising workers' demands. In the context of increasing flexibilization of labour and strong rise of self-employment, these arguments have gained in importance in the union ranks and in the debate on pensions in 2010-2011, even a split between the 'poldering' and 'organizing' orientations occurred within *Federatie Nederlandse Vakbeweging* (FNV). The organizers argued that concession bargaining and giving-in at national agreements deteriorates the position of the unions. In 2016, principal negotiator for the Metal industry, Roel Berghuis, even argued that 'nothing is to be gained from national consultation anymore' and in the same year the social-democratic union FNV, the Christian union (CNV), medium and higher staff union (VHP) warned in a letter 'for the race to the bottom'. In spite of this reflection, trade union membership has declined over the period since the crisis, and the trade union are finding themselves involved in court cases with employers in concession bargaining and are facing internal reorganizations. The uncertainty within the trade union movement, is reflected among employers too, that compete in product market and for scarce innovation capital. During the crisis, the leadership of the federation for small and medium-sized enterprises (SMEs) was replaced twice, given the fierce competition between larger and small-sized companies about the importance of labour costs.

§18.03 THE PRESSURE ON WAGE-SETTING IN BELGIUM

Under the new European Semester in 2009, social dialogue lost political consensus as indicated by all Belgian contributors in this special issue, i.e., Paul Windey (Chair of the National Labour Council); Marc Leemans (General Secretary ACV-CSC) and Paul Soete (former Agoria Chairman). In particular, the Elio Di Rupo's socialist government during 2011-2014 was the first to embark upon a range of austerity measures to reach agreement with the EC on the path of fiscal consolidation. EC recommendations for structural reforms repeatedly concerned key areas in which there is a clear tradition of social dialogue in Belgium. These included the long-term sustainability of State finances; the (cost) competitiveness of the economy through wage-setting, including wage indexation and the 1996 Law on competitiveness; the need for labour market reforms (e.g., increase in the retirement age) and for shifting taxes from labour to other incomes.

However, during the same period (2011-2014), social partners were asked by the government to discuss a number of 'partial agreements' covering the technical implementation of the wage freeze, the reduction of labour costs, the reduction by tax redemptions, and the recurring decision to adapt social allowances to cost-of-living changes, improve the minimum wage, and abolish the age-discriminatory youth minimum wage. Thus, a consensus was reached and social dialogue also delivered on a proposal to make working time calculations more flexible ('annualisation' and 'counting overtime'). Specifically, in July 2013, an agreement was reached between the social partners about the (partial) harmonization of the two main employment statutes, namely the statutes of blue- and white-collar workers (*see* further below). In 2014, the new Charles Michel-government, consisting of a centre-right coalition of the New Flemish Alliance (N-VA), the Christian Democratic and Flemish (CD&V), the Open Flemish Liberals and Democrats (Open Vld) and the Reformist Movement (MR) pushed for new labour market reforms which clearly hit once more and more deeply at the core of key areas of social dialogue (i.e., the increase of the age of early retirement to 66 by 2025 and to 67 by 2030; the temporary freeze of the automatic wage indexation; the increase in working hours flexibility; the degressivity of unemployment benefits; the disincentive of temporary unemployment; the creation of flexi-jobs), trade unions raised serious concerns about the quality of social dialogue and the limited bargaining room left by the government in negotiating on the new measures. A wave of trade union protest followed, with a mass demonstration (comprised of 120,000 people) in Brussels, regional strikes and a general strike on 15 December 2014, immediately after the inauguration of the government. Political strikes followed during 2015-2019. Recently, on the 13 February 2019 trade unions called a national protest after disagreement on a framework wage agreement proposed by the Central Council for Business (CRB) to limit the wage increase to a mere 0.8% for the next two years, and in addition to the automatic index rise to compensate for inflation. Following the strike a new agreement was reached on the 26 February 2019. The agreement fixed at 1.1% the margin for wage increase during 2019-2022. It also indicated an increase of 1.1% of minimum wage and overtime, it guaranteed additional flexibility to employers in return for more runways and mobility allowances and it reduced to 58 the age for early retirement under restructuring.

The increase in unilateral government regulation in Belgium in the post-crisis period confirms this. As aforementioned, in the period 2011-2012 Belgium came under fire from the financial markets and under close supervision of the EU semester. Since then politics and government have taken the lead in a program of austerity and structural reforms, of which cuts, an increase in retirement age and wage moderation are important aspects that touch upon key elements of existing agreements between social partners. Centralized wage coordination fell under the direct supervision of the government in 2013. Negotiations between employer and employee representatives during 2009-2010 were difficult. The negotiations in 2011-2012 have failed and the government decided unilaterally not to allow extra wage increases over automatic wage indexation. For the period 2015-2016, this arrangement was reversed with a plan to skip a 2% indexation, imposed by the government and a negligible room of 0.5% for sectoral negotiations. These interventions took place amid continuing discussions and disagreements about automatic wage indexation and possible revision of the 1996 law, also in accordance with the recommendations made within the European semester as of 2012. In December 2016, the Michel government proposed a new and stricter revision of the 1996 law, which was adopted by parliament in March 2017. Under the proposal to fix at 0.8% the wage increase in 2019 trade unions went on strike. It was followed by a tentative negotiation whose outcomes are currently still under scrutiny and discussion within each organization of interests (trade unions and employers) which have been responsible for making that agreement.

The de-construction of social protection and pressure – particularly on wages – by the different national governments in Belgium since the beginning of 2000s have greatly hit the stability of the function of social dialogue, i.e., striking the balance between the apparently 'antagonistic' interests of workers and employers by promoting agreements and policy measures to address socio-economic and labour markets issues of mutual relevance. This is because this pressure destabilizes national economies by preventing a solid sustainable economic upturn underpinned by scares quality jobs. One of the most relevant indicators of job quality is 'wages' (Organisation for Economic Co-operation and Development (OECD) 2010). Currently, wage growth remains too low and too slow in several European countries. In accordance to the European Trade Union Institute in Brussels in nine EU countries – including Belgium – working people were still earning less – or not much more – in 2017 than they did in 2010. Moreover, and conversely to the Netherlands where real wages have slightly grown, Belgium is indicated as one of the ten EU countries where real wages have not grown enough between 2009 and 2018. The continuous decline of the wage share of GDP fuels wealth inequalities as much of the benefits of economic growth go to the side of the capital (cfr. ETUI, *Benchmarking Working Europe* 2018 in Pulignano, 2019).

§18.04 WAGE SETTING AND PENSION REFORM IN THE NETHERLANDS

After the fall of Lehman Brothers in 2008, the first response of the social partners was to sign a Social Agreement entitled 'Doing what we can together' ('*Samen doen wat mogelijk is*'). The parties came to an agreement met by reaffirming the existing consultation agenda. Following Dutch tradition, they ensured 'responsible wage growth' (at the level of inflation) in order to avoid a wage-price spiral. The aim of this agreement was to contribute to stability and mutual control by coordinating the policy agenda aimed at improving employment (Van der Meer & Visser 2010). When export levels decreased by 8% and financial capital became scarce for companies to invest, the Netherlands Bureau for Economic Policy Analysis (Centraal Planbureau: CPB) negatively adjusted its growth forecasts for 2009 (a contraction of 3.5% was expected). In response, the social partners concluded a new 'Spring Agreement' (Voorjaarsakkoord) in 2009, aimed at controlling wage costs with a maximum of 1% in 2009, and 0% in 2010; *see* Hartveld 2012 & this volume). In addition, some additional labour market policies were polished: for knowledge workers, a regulation was introduced to keep working, while companies could also benefit from a part-time unemployment regulation, which resulted in substantial labour hoarding, people were not dismissed but could continue working.

Ever since, no central agreements have been negotiated on wage-setting and overall wage developments have been very moderate.[4] In Spring 2019, the Dutch Statistics published that average real wage had not risen during the last ten years. During the crisis, less collective wage contracts were negotiated or it took more time to achieve them, whereas employers were discovering pay-arrangements for flexible staff outside the traditional collective agreement. An example is the construction industry, were many construction workers became self-employed during the crisis, and the collective agreement for the construction sector was stripped into a bleak agreement discussing wages and hours, without the sectoral agreements on training and quality of work, that were are all cancelled.

For the unions, the major concern was to keep employment conditions at standard, i.e., the levels of compensation equivalent to that of a wage-earner in a permanent employment contract. As before, FNV has continued to apply a standard formula for wage coordination, which was relaxed upwardly in 2017 and 2018. At the same time, the unions had to accept a strong growth of self-employment and flexible employment contracts, at lower rates. The system of youth wages has been altered form 2015, when the younger fractions of the unions initiated an alternative approach and gave up weekend-bonuses in exchange for wage increase.

In connection with wage-setting, a second issue became apparent at the start of the great recession: the future of pensions. Both the ageing of society and the lowering funding ratios of the pension that regularly fell below the formally needed minimum of 105%, made the Fourth Balkenende cabinet (2007-2010) to put the future sustainability of the pension system on the agenda. Two issues were dealt with at the same time: the age of general retirement (*Algemene Ouderdomswet*, AOW, paid from the State budget) and the change of the sectoral pension fund into a defined contributions system (based on saved earnings by employers and employees). The proposals for raising the retirement age led to much resistance that the social partners were instructed to come up with alternative proposals themselves within six months to save 'the best pension system in the world' (Van der Zwan, 2016). When this didn't work, two advisory committees were set up to prepare the way to a pension agreement, which was signed in the Labour Foundation on 4 June 2010 after the fall of the Fourth Balkenende cabinet (CDA-PvdA-D66). However, one year later - in June 2011 - it turned out that there was no political support for the increase specified in the pension agreement of the state pension age to 67 years of age (with a transitional arrangement for current cases). Both the trade unions, the left-wing political parties and the PVV (supporting the First Rutte liberal VVD-CDA-cabinet minority government) felt that this was unacceptable: no one should have to work past the age of 65. The price of the

4. There have been more social pacts, on which we return later in this text. For Keune en De Beer (this volume) the stalemates in central negotiations and the difficulties in pursuing decentral bargaining, even led to the (premature) conclusion of erosion of the Dutch model of social dialogue.

pension agreement also turned out to be extremely high: the entire Dutch Trade Union Confederation FNV was administratively abolished when the FNV chairman, Agnes Jongerius, was unable to ward off the dissenting vote of *Abvakabo* FNV and FNV *Bondgenoten*. Without an agreement, pension reform became issue of unilateral government policy, and -given the economic crisis- also of the austerity measures of the European Semester. As a result, the retirement age was stepwise raised to 67 after a political agreement between the cabinet in resign, the 'constructive' political opposition and Brussels in April 2012. It would take another seven years, until June 2019 when the government and the social partners have negotiated a new pension agreement, in which people will work longer (retirement at 67 from 2024), with a longer transition path whereas for persons with demanding work early retirement remains possible.

§18.05 LEGAL PRESSURES ON SOCIAL DIALOGUE

The omnipresent technological changes and digitalization of work processes also lead to challenges of the legal environment of social dialogue. The regulation of social dialogue and the agenda of collective bargaining will not escape the question of how the concept of a 'worker' or an 'employee' is to be understood and how working conditions can be shaped. There is some experience in Belgium with overcoming the distinction between blue and white-collar workers. The Belgian Constitutional Court has expanded its equality case law in employment matters over the years and has not hesitated to shake up the Belgian industrial relations system in light of constitutional equality. In 2011 it decided that the legal distinction between white-collar and blue-collar workers was unconstitutional. The legislator intervened in 2013 with a reform of the law on dismissal, where the distinction was seen as most problematic. However, the distinction between blue-collar and white-collar workers has remained important over the years, and still is, in the structures of collective bargaining, where there exist separate branches and collective bargaining agreements depending on the sector. In light of the constitutional equality principle, but also given new workplace realities, the government and the social partners are gradually taking steps towards harmonizing working conditions of white and blue-collar workers and thus phasing out the historical distinction.

With regard to social dialogue and collective wage-setting, another question is whether and how self-employed persons are to be covered by collective bargaining.

In the Netherlands today only 60% of employees are working in standard contract, 40% is flexible. In Belgium, the percentage of standard contracts is about 65.5%.[5] According to a Dutch government-committee, the issue of social protection, disability insurance and pensions of self-employed and flexible low-skilled persons is 'the social issue' *('sociale kwestie')* of our times (June 2019). There are many examples which vary in nature and complexity. Construction workers that become self-employed

5. The way of organizing flexibilization varies in both countries, for an early contribution *see*: Sels and van Hootegem, 1999.

is just one case. As the Dutch trade union leader Erik Pentenga (this volume) makes clear, in international market companies make use of chains of subcontracting and labour provision, where the responsibility for individual workers is often diffuse and the premiums for social security can be made either in the home or in the guest country. It is for this reasons, that the Dutch social partners have recently negotiated in the Social Economic Council an national agreement about a 'fair Europe' (May 2019).

But more is at stake. The platform economy for example, also referred to as the collaborative economy or the gig economy, is creating forms of work which are much less capable of being recognized by more traditional modes or patterns of labour law (De Stefano 2016). The EC has analysed the issue of the collaborative economy in its Communication of 2016 and described it as a number of 'business models where activities are facilitated by collaborative platforms that create an open marketplace for the temporary usage of goods or services often provided by private individuals' (COM(2016)356 final). Typical examples of this new economy are Uber, Airbnb or Deliveroo. The question is not only whether and how labour law is responding to the work performed via such platforms. The question is also whether this properly qualifies as work since many tasks are irregular and sometimes referred to as 'micro-work'. The Uber-litigation in different jurisdictions gives a good illustration of how employment law questions arise in light of technology-based platform work (Sanders & Pattison 2016).

The way how work is organized in the gig economy triggers questions about the application of labour law and about whether gig workers have employment status, self-employed status or something in between. It is obvious that the gig economy brings about work forms that are quite new and different from the regular forms of work that we usually see or have known. Looking at platform work, we are struggling with the fact that this form of labour may be really different from how we have considered labour in the past, including the organization of work. Gig work is characterized much more by the functioning of an intermediary or even an app running on a digital platform, providing fragmented work or specific and subdivided tasks, resembling 'piece' work, leaving workers in principal free to engage in the work or to decline it. From this perspective, it may seem that the classical notions and principles, even rules of labour law, do not easily match with these new forms of work. It would, however, be misleading to conclude that, for this reason of mismatch, labour law cannot be applied and should thus not be applied. It would equally be problematic if social partners would keep gig workers out of the bargaining agenda.

Reforms are thus necessary for the legal environment. As is known, the classical model of labour law came already under pressure in the eighties and the nineties of the former Century, due to factors such as globalization, economic competitiveness and the rise of the service economy. At that time, the flexibility question strongly came to the fore, following new needs in our economies and working patterns undergoing change (Atkinson 1984; Pollert 1988). It is clear, since the eighties and nineties, that deviations from the standard form of work have been argued for and adaptations have also been made. The clear examples are the regulating of flexibility in working time, the regulation of fixed-term work, part-time work, or temporary work. It is no surprise that these new work patterns are commonly debated. They concern 'deviations' from the standard norm. Non-standard forms of employment potentially have become all kind of work situations falling outside the standard reference (M. Koch 2013, 30).

The new forms of work often referred to as a-typical work, also imply deviations from standard protection. The benchmark, however, has remained full-time and lifetime employment and labour law provisions are still mainly oriented towards this model. The introduction of a legal principle of equal treatment of non-standard workers or a-typical workers compared to 'standard' workers seems to confirm this (S. Peers 2013). The definition of the scope of labour law is not unproblematic but has not yet lead to a major rethinking of categories of work.

The particular category of dependent self-employed persons is economically dependent on their principle. Workers in the gig economy may be a good example of self-employed people that actually work quasi as employees. In principle, these workers have always be seen as falling outside the scope of labour law. In legal terms, they do not work under the authority of an employer. But in practice, they may be working in a position of dependence vis-à-vis the principal, because they have to respond to all kinds of conditions of work volume, quality, personal availability. They are not always near to free and independent entrepreneurship.

Why would this 'dependent self-employed' worker or this 'autonomous' worker need to be excluded from the protection of labour law? It is evident that the full application of the regulation of the standard model of protection does not always make sense in these categories. But why would those workers not be entitled to wage protection, holiday pay, well-being at work, dismissal protection, information and consultation rights, trade union and bargaining rights?

§18.06 COLLECTIVE BARGAINING FOR THE SELF-EMPLOYED?

One of the major legal issues in collective bargaining for self-employed persons concerns the role of anti-trust law and the European agencies controlling this. There are many examples of self-employment, that can be covered by a collective agreement. For example, the tariffs and stipulations of self-employed architects have been integrated into the Dutch collective agreement (for 'labour' and for 'work orders of self-employed') of architects, but the Dutch Market Authorities evaluated this practice as unacceptable given the European competition regulation.

The leading jurisprudence of the European Court of Justice on this issue also comes from the Netherlands. In the *FNV Kunsten*-case,[6] the Court had to deal with a Dutch collective agreement providing for minimum rates of pay for substitute orchestra members. The collective agreement laid down minimum fees, not only for substitutes hired under an employment contract but also for substitutes who carry on their activities under a contract for professional services, who were thus not regarded as 'employees' for the purposes of the agreement itself and who were seen as 'self-employed substitutes'.

6. Court of Justice EU, 4 December 2014, nr. C-413/13, FNV Kunsten Informatie en Media.

The question is whether such an agreement, providing prices for self-employed service providers, is to be seen as a form of prohibited price-fixing under EU anti-trust law. The European Court of Justice rules that the agreement is exempted from EU anti-trust law only when the self-employed service providers are in fact 'false self-employed', in other words, service providers in a situation comparable to that of those workers.

This judgment is, of course, important, as it seems that the Court is willing to look at a broader scope of application of a collective agreement – and looks further than the classic notions of worker and employer. Although the court referred to the notion of 'false self-employed' persons to which collective agreements may apply while falling outside EU anti-trust law, there is room to bring up an autonomous worker notion in EU law that could lead to the adoption of leeway to collective agreements for dependent self-employed workers. The fact that self-employed persons can be part of collective bargaining processes and be covered by collective agreements is fully recognized by the International Labour Organization. In its recent 'Digest' (2018), the ILO-bodies make clear that also self-employed persons have the right to enjoy trade union freedoms without the need to establish a classical employment relationship.[7]

How self-employed persons need to be involved in collective negotiations remains, of course, a question for the social partners and their structures. Will they be part of the trade union movement, of the employers' organizations, or will they form their own structures. With whom self-employed persons will negotiate is also a challenging issue. In principle, there is not necessarily an employer as a counter party, but rather a group of principals or even clients or consumers. The legal thinking of collective bargaining with self-employed is not yet fully mature, but the regulation questions seem unavoidable. The importance of this way ahead is already made clear in practice. The gig economy examples show that also self-employed persons need to collectively set rules and conditions on wages, safety and health, insurance, dispute settlement and so on (Forsyth 2018).

§18.07 SOCIAL DIALOGUE WITH FOCUS ON THE FUTURE: DIGITALIZATION AND THE GREEN ECONOMY

The changing context of social dialogue and collective bargaining is clearly not limited to the Low Countries. As Thorben Iversen and David Soskice argue in their historical and comparative study 'Democracy and prosperity' (2019), marketization and regional innovation are dependent upon excellent education, company training, innovative connections between schools and the labour market and a good R&D-infrastructure. The international climate change must be added to that agenda. It's an empirical question how the renewal of the social concertation practice can adjust to new issues that come up, and ask for regulation, either at the local or national level or even beyond

7. *Cf.* ILO, *Freedom of Association. Compilation of Decisions of the Committee on Freedom of Association*, ILO, Geneva, Sixth Edition 2018, nrs. 330, 387 en 389.

borders at a European of global scale. We give two examples before we arrive at our conclusions.

[A] Industry 4.0

The first aspect is digitalization and robotics. In April 2013, in the Netherlands, a broad social pact was negotiated on the reform of labour market regulation. It aimed to strike a new balance between flexibility and security and open new regional windows for labour market policy, under the double title 'Out of the crisis' and 'perspective for a social and entrepreneurial country'. Associated with this so-called Mondriaan-agreement (named after the VET-college in The Hague where it was signed) a number of 'ad hoc' domain agreements have been negotiated at national level, on technology, education, housing, health care and energy, which all extend beyond the government's horizon (Hemerijck and Van der Meer 2016). An example is the Technology Pact of 13 May 2013 which builds on the introduction of the Topsector industrial policy which was initiated in 2010. The technology pact is the result of many parties: three Ministers (Economic Affairs, Education, Culture and Science (OCW) and Social Affairs and Employment, and one State Secretary, all school organizations and the various social partners. The Pact was signed by a total number of sixty associations, including the technical branches of industry around the Confederation of Netherlands Industry and Employers (VNO-NCW); the national SME Federation; the three trade unions confederations FNV, CNV, VHP; the Dutch Council for Training and Education (NRTO) in the field of private education; several researches and development funds have put their signature as well (including the Training and Development Fund for the Temporary Work Sector) and the new Cooperation Organisation for Vocational Education, Training and the Labour Market (S-BB). Astronaut André Kuipers serves as ambassador of the Pact. This 'Hands-on Pact' focuses on learning and working with technology, for all young people aged 4-18, across the full breadth of education and the labour market. The aim is to learn skills such as creativity, entrepreneurship, problem-solving, collaboration, initiative, leadership and IT-skills, to be implemented at the regional level. In reality, the initiatives bundled under this banner were already functioning cooperative programs in areas such as Twente, Brainport Eindhoven, Limburg, Wageningen, Haaglanden, et cetera (Van der Meer a.o, 2017). In 2016, the Technology Pact was extended until 2020 in order to strengthen the position of science and technology in education. Next to the technology pact a similar approach has been introduced in the health care sector, and later on also in construction and the defence sectors.

A further example concerns the skills agenda.[8] The Netherlands was not part of the influential OECD study 'Learning for jobs' in 2010, so repair work was definitely needed. In 2012 it enrolled as a case-study in 'Skills beyond school' (OECD 2014). Since then skills and training have become pivotal issues. In 2013 the SER issued the analysis

8. The Anglosaxon concept of 'skills', which is commonly used today in Dutch language, is in the daily practice of continental Europe to be understood as competencies, the combination of knowledge, capabilities and attitude.

of the crafts-based economy, in a combined analysis of entrepreneurship and of VET. In 2014, The SER initiated a series of meetings on the future of labour market (robotization and automation) and learning practices (initial education, life-long development, informal learning), in which more than 100 participants of different companies and social organizations (including local government, business, management and schools) have participated. The result is a wide overview of factors that determine the intertwining areas of learning and working, as also follows from the joint OECD-SER Skills' Agenda for the Netherlands (2017). Ever since, life-long development is national concern, also in collective bargaining in sectors and companies, as well as for social policy in municipalities, to achieve a break-through, especially for those categories of lower-skilled and flexible workers than benefit from the current provisions in a much lesser extent than incumbent, high-skilled employees.

Similar initiatives have been taken in Belgium too, though above all on the sector-level. In many branches of activity there is much room for initiative and creativity in social dialogue. A conference of the Federal Ministry of Labour of 13 November 2019, celebrating the 50th anniversary of the law on collective agreements (dating from 5 December 1968), gave a showcase of sector initiatives concerning 'workable work'. These arrangements suppose new deals of internal flexibility, giving workers more autonomy in the organization of work and making flexibility in working time also supportive of the workers' work-life balance. It is a theme that has been promoted by government and the legislator, but it seems to give inspiration to the sectoral social partners and has led to agreements in different sectors. These successes and optimism shows that the sector level of collective negotiations is still the point of gravity of the Belgian social model. It is clear that new themes are coming to the fore with which social partners need to deal: the right to privacy, time and place independent work, telework, work-life balance, the right to disconnect and time pressure. Skills development and training are clearly topics for the future bargaining agenda. In this way, the flexibilization agenda of the past century may be replaced by a digitalization agenda for social dialogue, stimulating the social partners towards new deals.

[B] The Energy Transition

Another issue is the move towards a sustainable, low-carbon economy. This is a challenge for all EU countries, in fact, our whole globe. De-carbonizing an economy which is still highly dependent on fossil fuels implies, among other things, wide-reaching industrial transformations and technological shifts, the development of new energy patterns, new business models and more circularity in ways of producing and consuming. It will require training of new categories of skilled craft-persons. In other words, it requires a deep and rapid change of the way we produce, move and consume. In many ways, the transition will trigger positive effects. It will improve air quality, reduce energy dependency and it might represent a great vehicle for job creation as well as an opportunity to strengthen European know-how and technological capabilities in environmental innovation. To fully tap this economic potential, investment and policy stability is needed. This is certainly the first added-value that climate policy planning can bring for workers: increasing certainty about the policy framework and investment that are the key prerequisites for moving to a low-carbon economy while creating and maintaining quality jobs across sectors, including in manufacturing industries.

In the Netherlands, a National Energy Agreement for Sustainable Growth (Nationaal Energieakkoord voor duurzame groei) was concluded on 6 September 2013 in the Social-Economic Council by no less than forty-seven organizations after a process of brainstorming sessions, conferences and online consultation. In this investment roadmap, various civil society organizations expressed their willingness to give effect to the 2011 motion of the House of Representatives aimed at arriving at a 'National Energy Transition Agreement'. This integrated approach sets the ambition of savings on final energy consumption of 1.5% per year and a sharp increase in the re-use of energy resources and growth of renewable energy generation in 2020 and 2023. The citizen's initiative NGO 'Nederland krijgt nieuwe energie' ('The Netherlands gets new energy') is seen as the driving force behind the Agreement. In June 2019, a new and more far-reaching Climate Accord has been negotiated in the Social and Economic Council, which has been achieved in a different procedure than in 2013 has been the case. Now five tables with experts on particular issues (electricity, industry, mobility, built environment and agriculture) have granted proposals, that after several rounds of negotiation appeared to be acceptable for each of the parties, after an earlier veto of the environmental and the trade union movement in February 2019. They argued that the distribution of the costs was unfair and 'polluting' companies were granted too favourable subsidy provisions.

From a workers' perspective, the transition will profoundly reshape the labour market in ways that creates both new risks and new opportunities for workers: new jobs but also, in some cases, destruction of jobs (and companies), replacement of some existing occupations by new ones, along with the need for new competencies and skills. Certain sectors and regions, especially the ones that are dependent on carbon intensive industries (Wallonia more than Flanders, may be more negatively impacted than others. In the Dutch 2013 pact, the environmental movement was able to stipulate that the coal-fired power stations of the 1980s would be closed down in exchange for tax exemption on current energy production. It was important for the social partners that the agreement would lead to new investment and thus employment (15,000 additional full-time jobs). The Cabinet invested €150 million in an energy saving fund to elicit private investment, which, supplemented by private investments, amounts to €600 million. In addition, €400 million will be invested in subsidies for energy-neutral renovation in the social housing sector. In 2019, more far-reaching (and necessary) ambitions have been drafted to reduce CO2 with 49% before 2030. For each of the underlying topics, instruments have been proposed to meet the common ambitions. Now it has been estimated that 75,000 new jobs can be created, with makes a combination with labour market policy and training very urgent.

To ensure a 'fair transition' of the workforce as well as the creation of decent and quality jobs, trade union participation in the governance of the policy process is thus of particular importance. The preamble of the 2015 Paris agreement invites parties to 'take into account the imperatives of a just transition of the workforce' which obviously requires worker's participation. ILO guidelines 'for a just transition towards environmentally sustainable economies and societies for all' recommend the consultation and the association of trade unions in the elaboration and implementation of low-carbon policies at 'all possible levels and stages'. In its 'Energy Union Package' of 2015, the EC has underlined the importance of the role of social partners and has invited them to include the energy transition in their social dialogue.

§18.08 CONCLUSIONS

When Harvie Ramsay argued that representative organizations of employers and workers are fundamentally antagonistic, his argument would have been strengthened by the ongoing internationalization of economic and political processes, the changing role of political decision-making and the varying logics of interest associations of employers and employees in response to the flexibilization of labour, we discussed in this chapter. Still however, as the industrial relations actors in Belgium and the Netherlands argue in this volume, the practice of social dialogue continues and social partners value the benefits of social consultation, though trade unions also express a need to manifest political disagreement, in response to the liberalization and flexibilization of employment relations. When governments have enough seats in parliament they can easily sideline trade unions to prevent lengthy and costly negotiations, with a possible burden on the state budget. Conversely, weak governments need trade unions for consensus mobilization and support for retrenchments, which creates opportunities for labour to gain sympathy and strike policy deals to meet their interests (cf. Schmidt 2013, Rathgeb 2018).

Over the course of the past ten years, the social dialogue in the Netherlands mainly served as crisis-mechanism after the outbreak of the great recession (Hemerijck and Van der Meer, 2016, 2019). The wages pacts of 2008 and 2009; the social pact of 2013 and the pension pact of 2019 show that the practice of consensus decision-making is still at stake, though social partners operate within an open European context without the shadow of strong government coalitions. The pension-system and the retirement age are thorny issues with direct effect on the state budget (in the Netherlands retirement at 67 is reached in 2024, much earlier than in Belgium). In new domains, technology, energy, life-long development, also new forms of 'negotiating governance' and social concertation emerge, which illuminate that the government is consciously involving civil-society organizations in the realization of its political goals, thus going back to a long tradition of sharing the political space in Dutch politics. All agreements involve the social partners and thus industrial relations, but often in a different way – less hierarchical and less narrow socio-economically speaking, with a less prominent role for trade unions, though the recent pension agreement has put them in the centre of attention again. The time horizon of the most recent agreements (on the labour market, pensions, technology or on climate change) also extends beyond the horizon of the incumbent cabinet.

In Belgium, the framework of social dialogue has also changed in spite of the institutional continuity through the involvement of trade unions in the Ghent social security system (Van Gyes et al. 2018). Our historical examination portrays a mixed picture with a weakening outcome for social dialogue. Under the EU budget monitoring (2009-2013), 'partial agreements' between the social partners did play a role in some of the reforms pertaining to labour market flexibility (i.e., wage freeze) and social benefits. Under a different political landscape, during 2014-2015, partial agreements did not take place and social partners suffered from lack of autonomy. However, in the key social reforms of the period 2012-2015, namely the pension and retirement age changes, social dialogue played only a minor role, and this was limited to implementation technicalities and transition measures. Within a climate of criticism by the media and politicians, in the post-crisis period, the trade unions took action to participate by launching political strikes and protests for social justice, redistribution and workers' involvement. They also manifested dissatisfaction towards a system which seemed to be standstill under strict EU budgeting monitoring. This has led to agreements between the social partners such as the 26 February 2019 agreement which followed the political strike of the 13th of February. This agreement fixed at 1.1% the wage increase for the coming two years on the one hand and delivered additional flexibility to employers and social allowances to workers as well as it anticipated the age for early retirement under company restructuring on the other hand.

The wage situation has often been seen as a cause for concern for raising inequality between groups of protected (so-called advantaged or insiders) and groups of unprotected (so-called disadvantaged or outsiders) in society. This brings the trade union confederations in an strategic dilemma, to overcome the labour market segmentation between relatively well protected versus relatively unprotected groups, which is increasingly urgent given the flexibilization of labour and the divergent business models encouraging this. As the Belgium and Dutch trade unions show, industrial action and 'organizing' have become -in combination with social dialogue- a main element in the unions' repertoire to illustrate the non-preferred consequences of flexibilization, which is occurring under the label of labour market reforms to foster individual accountability, employability and self-activation. Along the same line, rational economic assumptions about labour market rigidities are being recalled in politics. Today even multi-level collective bargaining is questioned, in order to foster economic recovery and boost employment, particularly of the most disadvantaged ('outsiders') groups in society. It is very urgent to better study the revision of collective agreements and their impact instead of accepting a sudden 'common sense' public truth without considering the implications such claims may have.

In our analysis, we have added the unavoidable interplay between institutional and legal challenges. New forms of work, including a-typical work and platform work in the gig economy, raise fundamental questions about how employment regulation and social dialogue have to be captured in legal terms. Here again, the government is a leading actor, though it requires major rethinking of which categories of work, by which forms of social partnership can be granted particular forms of protection, in legal, political and social-economic terms. One of the challenges is to include self-employed persons within the scope of interest of collective bargaining. The legal question is not only what this means in terms of regulating collective bargaining, but also how this needs to be aligned with, or distinguished from, economic laws such as anti-trust provisions. The right to collective bargaining is a fundamental right and clearly includes legal forms of self-employment.

Given the ageing of society and the related replacement of experience workers for a younger generation, together with the technological changes occurring in work places, we need a more coherent response in social dialogue, that cannot be found in good employment relations at company level alone. There is need for social investment policies instead of austerity, to strengthen citizens and households in an increasingly flexible economy. With hindsight to the technology agenda and the urgency of climate change, the experiences in the Netherlands and Belgium feed the hypothesis that social dialogue can be future proof, as a source of inspiration and experimenting, to respond to common challenges that ask for decent solutions.

REFERENCES

Atkinson, J. (1984). Manpower Strategies for Flexible Organisations, *Personnel Management*, 28-31.

Cassiers, I. & Denayer, L. (2010). 'Concertation sociale et transformations socio-économiques depuis 1944'. in E. Arcq, M. Capron, E. Léonard and P. Reman. *Dynamiques de la concertation sociale.* Bruxelles, CRISP: 75-92.

Crouch, C. (1993). *Industrial Relations and European State Traditions.* Oxford: Clarendon.

De Stefano, V. (2016). The Rise of the 'Just-in-Time Workforce': On-Demand Work, Crowd-Work and Labour Protection in the 'Gig-Economy', *Comparative Labor Law & Policy Journal* 37(3): 471-504.

Forsyth, A. (2018). What Does Collective Representation Look Like in Australia's Gig Economy?, Labour Law Down Under Blog, 27 October 2018 (https://labourlaw downunder.wordpress.com/2018/10/27/what-does-collective-representation-lo ok-like-in-australias-gig-economy/).

Harteveld, L. (2012). Loonvorming in tijden van crisis. *Tijdschrift voor Arbeidsvraagstukken*, 28(2), 138-161.

Hemerijck, A.C. & van der Meer, M. (2016). Nieuw Nederlands polderen: van brede sociale akkoorden naar 'ad hoc' hervormingscoalities. In: M. Keune (red.), *Nog steeds een mirakel? De legitimiteit van het poldermodel in de eenentwintigste eeuw.* Amsterdam: Amsterdam University Press, 167-195.

Hemerijck A.C. & van der Meer, M. (2019). Polderen in de 21^{e} eeuw: Publiek rekenschap gevraagd'. In: *Visies op de polder: essays over de toekomst van het sociaal overleg in Nederland.* Den Haag: Ministerie SZW, 7-28.

Hendrickx, F. (2018). Regulating New Ways of Working: From the New 'Wow' to the New 'How'. *European Labour Law Journal*, 9(2): 195-205.

Hendrickx, F. & De Stefano, V. (eds) (2018). *Game Changers in Labour Law. Shaping the Future of Work, Bulletin of Comparative Labour Relations*, vol. 100, The Hague: Kluwer Law International.

Ibersen T. en D. Soskice (2019). *Democracy and Prosperity, Reinventing Capitalism Though a Turbulent History*, Princeton: Princeton University Press.

Koch, M. (2013). 'Employment Standards in Transition: From Fordism to Finance-Driven Capitalism' in M. Koch and M. Fritz (eds), *Non-Standard Employment in Europe, in Work and Welfare in Europe*. London: Palgrave Macmillan.

Lehdonvirta V. (2016) 'Algorithms That Divide and Unite: Delocalization, Identity and Collective Action in "Microwork"' in J. Flecker (ed.) *Space, Place and Global Digital Work*. London: Palgrave Macmillan.

Léonard, E., & Pichault, F. (2016). 'Belgique: l'adaptation d'un 'modèle' de concertation sociale', in Andolfatto, D. and Contrepois, S. (dir.) *Syndicats et dialogue social. Les modèles occidentaux à l'épreuve*. Bruxelles: P.I.E. Peter Lang, 55-75.

Meer, M. van der, J.Visser, T. Wilthagen en P.F. van der Heijden (2003). *Weg van het overleg. 25 jaar na Wassenaar*, Amsterdam: Amsterdam University Press.

Meer, M. van der & Visser, J. (2010). 'Doing together what is possible- social pacts and negotiated welfare reform in the Netherlands'. In: Ph.Pochet, M.Keune and D.Natali, 'After the Euro and enlargement; social pacts in in the EU'. Brussels; OSE/ ETUI, 251-280.

Marc van der, Jan Peter van den Toren en T. Lie (2017). 'Enhancing Innovation via Public-Private Partnership' in De Bruijn, E, S. Billett, J. Onstenk (eds), *Enhancing Teaching and Learning in the Dutch Vocational Education System – Reforms Enacted*. Berlijn: Springer Verlag.

Mok, A. (1985). Arbeidsverhoudingen in België en Nederland, In: *Tijdschrift voor Arbeidsvraagstukken*, 1 (1), 1-17.

Peers, S. (2013). Equal Treatment of Atypical Workers: A New Frontier for EU Law?, *Yearbook of European Law* 2013, 32(1): 30-56.

Pecinovsky, P. (2019). EU Economic Governance en het recht op collectief onderhandelen, die Keure, Brugge, 583p.

Pollert, A. (1988). The 'Flexible Firm': Fixation or Fact?, *Work, Employment & Society*, 2(3): 281-316.

Pulignano, V. (2019). *Het sluipende gif van tijdelijk werk*, SAMPOL,'1.

Pulignano V. & Dekocker V. (2014). *The Employment Practices of Multinationals in Belgium*. Acco: Leuven University Press.

Rathgeb, P. (2018). *Strong Governments. Precarious Workers*. Ithaca: Cornell University Press.

Ramsie H. (1977). Cycles of Control: Worker Participation in Sociological and Historical Perspective, *Sociology* 11(3): 481-506.

Sanders, E. & Pattison P. (2016). Worker Characterization in a Gig Economy Viewed Through an Uber Centric Lens, *Southern Law Journal* 26(2): 297-320.

Sels L. & van Hootigem, G. (1999). 'België – Nederland strijd om de meeste flexibiliteit', in: J.van Hoof en J.Mevissen (red). *In banen geleid, nieuwe vormen van sturing op de arbeidsmarkt in België en Nederland*, pp. 159-184.

Schmidt, V. (2013). Democracy and Legitimacy in the European Union Revisited: Input, Output, *and* 'Throughput'. *Political Studies*, 61, 2-22.

Van Gyes G., Terlinden, L. & Vandekerckhove, S. (2017). 'Belgian Social Dialogue since the Crisis: The Ups-and-Downs of an Organised System of Industrial Relations' in I. Guardanovich and O. Molina (eds) *Talking Through the Crisis: Social Dialogue and Industrial Relations in Selected EU Countries*. Geneva, ILO, 59-82.

Van Gyes, G., et al. (2018). 'Opposites Attract? Decentralisation Tendencies in the Most Organised Collective Bargaining System in Europe' in Leonardi S. and R. Pedersini. *Multi-employer Bargaining under Pressure – Decentralisation Trends in Five European Countries*, Brussels: ETUI.

Visser, J. & Hemerijck, A. (1997). *'A Dutch Miracle': Job Growth, Welfare Reform and Corporatism in the Netherlands*. Amsterdam: Amsterdam University Press.

Visser, J. & van der Meer, M. (2011). The Netherlands: Social Pacts in a Concertation Economy. in S. Agdavic, Rhodes, M. & J. Visser (eds), *Social Pacts in Europe: Emergence, Evolution, and Institutionalization*. (pp. 203--231). Oxford: Oxford University Press.

Zwan, N. van der (2016). Het pensioenmirakel ontleed. In: M. Keune (red.), Nog steeds een mirakel? *De legitimiteit van het poldermodel in de eenentwintigste eeuw*. Amsterdam: Amsterdam University Press, 143-166.

CHAPTER 19
Belgium: Adapt, or Transform?

Evelyne Léonard

§19.01 INTRODUCTION

In 1944, during World War II and still under German occupation, Belgian central employer associations and trade unions jointly defined the key features of social dialogue in Belgium. Willing to contribute to the reconstruction of the country, they elaborated a 'project of agreement on social solidarity' that set up a system of collective bargaining and concertation benefiting to both employers and workers and aimed at improving living conditions of the population and contributing to prosperity (Cassiers & Denayer 2010). The social pact included elements of mutual recognition, recognition of employers' authority, wages, social security, productivity, prices and cost of living, family allowances, pensions, sickness leaves, unemployment benefits, holidays. It also defined the very comprehensive architecture of industrial relations in three coordinated levels, from cross-industry to company (*see* http://www.ccecrb.fgov.be/txt/fr/1944.pdf).

The characteristics of the 'Belgian system' has remained fairly stable since then: centralised collective bargaining at cross-industry level organising what can be negotiated afterwards in sectors and companies; extensive coverage of all sectors of the industry and services; central bodies for tripartite discussions on labour and on the economy; high degree of representativeness of employer associations and trade union organisations; close interactions with the government whatever the political colour of its composition.

However, like in other countries social dialogue in Belgium currently faces majors challenges, with very limited possibilities to negotiate wage increases; growing interventions by the government; increasing differences between regions within Belgium combined with pressures from multinational companies and from European bodies; deep transformation of systems of production; financiarisation and digitalisation of economies. These trends are combined with profound changes in economies and societies, such as the crisis of democracy, climate change and demographic challenge.

Adopting a slightly provocative viewpoint, this short contribution intends to examine whether the players of Belgian social dialogue, who were strong and wise enough to establish in 1944 a broad social pact to rebuild the country, still have today the capacity to play a key role in transforming societies. In the current context, do they have the capacity to adapt to change, or even, to act as central players to transform the society?

§19.02 ADAPT?

Trade unions and employer organisations in Belgium have demonstrated in many occasions that they have the capacity to adapt their practices to changing environments.

For instance, Faniel (2108) shows how they progressively renewed the process by which they negotiate cross-industry collective agreements that take place every second year since 1960. They can build on very robust institutional settings: membership, regulatory framework, financial resources, architecture of the system, etc. Over the 1980s and 1990s, they have more and more integrated the notion of competitiveness in their bargaining rounds, while the government put growing pressure on wages increases. Several periods of interruption, mostly because the actors could not reach an agreement, did not result in a collapse of the system. Even when successive bargaining rounds failed to generate an agreement, central players tried again to negotiate and, finally, adapted their practice.

Even in a context of increased pressure on competitiveness, more fragmented workforce, strong influence of foreign multinational companies, shifting political power in the government, regionalisation of political bodies or transformation of systems of production, the key players of Belgian industrial relations managed to maintain the architecture of the system and its key processes. Although constraints shifted, they continue to discuss and to negotiate.

The players share a common willingness to maintain social dialogue, both as a tool of regulation between capital and labour and as a means to influence political action. The strong capacity that they have, based on their representativeness, resources and coverage, helps them propose pragmatic responses to the challenges of the moment.

In sum, a key feature of industrial relations in Belgium is certainly their adaptability. Industrial relations remain central in current modes of regulation of labour, employment and work at cross-industry, sector and company levels (Léonard and Pichault 2016).

§19.03 TRANSFORM?

Seven decades after 1944, societies have changed drastically, and they are currently undergoing deep transformation. Are Belgian employer associations and trade unions able, today, not only to maintain the system and adapt to change but also, beyond that, to act purposefully to influence transformation?

Such a role would require several types of responses: trade unions would have to include more 'atypical' workers, such as workers from a foreign origin and younger members; they should probably use new ways of expression and find original responses to strong demands for direct participation in the population; trade unions and employer associations would have to find original responses to 'the new economy' and its competition on wages and working conditions, elaborating original trade-offs between number of jobs, wages and quality of work; they should also be capable of providing coherent answers in a country with more and more distinct regional tracks and, also, in a tiny economy largely open to international competition and submitted to strong influence coming from multinational companies.

From a broader point of view, could the players of industrial relations jointly propose new ways of regulating employment, but also unemployment, in the digital economies facing technological revolutions, ageing and demographic challenges, financiarisation, or climate change?

Employer associations and trade unions do not show signs of clear joint positions on these issues, nor even joint intentions to try to regulate these issues. For instance, climate change or the digital economy seems to happen 'out of the scope' of industrial relations, with debates largely left to the 'civil society' where participants fluctuate and are abroad of institutionalised bodies of social dialogue.

As a consequence, they may appear as occupying defensive positions, trying to maintain not only their own regulatory system but also employment, wages, job quality, social protection.

Doing so, they certainly act as key players of democracy at work, but they risk to be more and more challenged by emerging - and uncontrolled - social movements whose claims concern climate change, for instance, but also traditional issues of labour relations such as revenue.

§19.04 CONCLUSION

Being adaptable, industrial relations actors and bodies are capable to bring adaptation, in the sense of incremental change, for instance in the field of cross-industry collective bargaining where the content of negotiations evolves over time, or in the development of regional-level bodies of bipartite and tripartite social dialogue (Blaise 2010). They can adapt, indeed.

However, beyond adaptation, a crucial interrogation is their willingness, and capacity, to contribute actively to the reforms needed by economic and societal transformation. In short, they do not seem ready to conclude a new social pact.

REFERENCES

Blaise, P. (2010). 'Le cadre institutionnel de la concertation sociale'. in E. Arcq, M. Capron, E. Léonard & P. Reman. *Dynamiques de la concertation sociale. Bruxelles*, CRISP: 44-74.

Cassiers, I. & L. Denayer (2010). 'Concertation sociale et transformations socio-économiques depuis 1944'. in E. Arcq, M. Capron, E. Léonard & P. Reman. *Dynamiques de la concertation sociale*. Bruxelles, CRISP: 75-92.

Faniel, J. (2018) 'Vers un nouveau cycle d'accords interprofessionnels?', *Les @nalyses du CRISP en ligne*, 30 septembre 2018, www.crisp.be.

Léonard, E. & F. Pichault (2016) 'Belgique: l'adaptation d'un 'modèle' de concertation sociale', in Andolfatto, D. & Contrepois, S. (dir.) *Syndicats et dialogue social. Les modèles occidentaux à l'épreuve*. Bruxelles. P.I.E. Peter Lang, 55-75.

CHAPTER 20

Is the Poldermodel Crumbling?*

Paul de Beer & Maarten Keune

§20.01 INTRODUCTION

Since World War II, the Netherlands has established a series of institutions in the field of labour relations, including the tripartite Socioeconomic Council (SER), the bipartite Labour Foundation (STAR), the system of collective agreements that covers most of the labour market, and the system of works councils. In what is often called the poldermodel, employers' organizations, trade unions and sometimes the government deliberate and negotiate about socioeconomic policy and employment conditions, resulting in policy advise, social pacts and yearly hundreds of collective agreements.

The poldermodel has long been considered a proper way to create societal support for common policies and to minimize conflict in society. In the 1990s it was also heralded for its contribution to a successful economy, characterized by a balance between economic and social outcomes. A precondition for these positive functions of the model is however that there is a balance of power between employers and unions and that both sides are willing to not only pursue their own interests but also take those of the other side and of society at large into account, and to reach compromises.

How well is this poldermodel functioning today? We still have the SER and the STAR and collective agreements continue to cover some 80% of employees. At the same time, slowly but surely changes have taken place in the actual functioning of these institutions and the outcomes they produce. In the long run, these changes threaten to erode the foundations of the poldermodel.

* This piece is largely based on P. de Beer & M. Keune, 'De erosie van het poldermodel'. In: *Mens en Maatschappij* 2018, 93(3): 231-260.

§20.02 DISTURBANCE OF THE BALANCE OF POWER BETWEEN EMPLOYERS AND UNIONS

An important change in the poldermodel is the shift of the power balance between employers and unions. This is demonstrated both by the interaction between these two sides and the outcomes of this interaction. A number of elements can be distinguished here:

- *Wage moderation.* Since the late 1970s, the real wages set by collective agreements in the Netherlands have not increased anymore, making them lag behind productivity developments further and further. This can be interpreted as an indication that the trade unions have lost power in relation to the employers. A growing share of the national income is going to the employers and shareholders, at the cost of the employees.
- *The gradual demise of the permanent contract.* Already since the 1970s, but especially in recent years, the share of flexible contracts (temporary contracts, temporary agency work, on-call contracts) and self-employed without personnel in total employment is increasing. Today, 35%-40% of persons working does not have a permanent contract. In this way, employers put the risks and uncertainties in the labour market increasingly on the shoulders of the employees and self-employed. This leads to increased insecurity for a growing group of working people and in many cases includes a worsening of employment conditions. Flexible workers generally earn less and have less access to pensions and training. Also, the growth of flexible work and self-employment without personnel creates competition with the permanent workers and puts their employment under pressure.
- *Insecure occupational pensions.* Although the main characteristics of the system of occupational (second pillar) pensions have not changed, de facto the system does not anymore guarantee a certain level of pension payments. The funding rate of most pension funds has dropped in recent years under the level that allows for the indexation of pensions, and many have not been adjusted to inflation for years now and some have indeed been reduced in nominal terms. The risks of the financial markets in which the funds operate as well as the effects of the ageing of the population are born entirely by the participants (employees and pensioners) themselves, and not by the employers.
- *Difficult collective bargaining.* In recent years, collective bargaining has become more and more difficult and increasingly collective agreements are not signed by the largest trade union FNV (Federatie Nederlandse Vakbeweging) (and sometimes also not by the second-largest union, the CNV (Christelijk National Vakverbond)), but by small (quasi) unions with almost no members. This signals that employers are less willing to do concession to the (established) labour movement and tend to accept more easily that collective agreements are (temporarily) not concluded or that they lack real employee support. Apparently, the employers think that a collective agreement signed by all large unions is less necessary to guarantee stability and labour peace

than in the past. A number of companies has also chosen not to conclude collective agreements with the unions at all anymore and to set up an employment conditions agreement in deliberation with the works council or the employees directly. In this, collective and other agreements change from instruments with which interests of employers and employees are balanced to instruments with which first of all the interests of the employers are served.

§20.03 EROSION OF THE POLDERMODEL AT THE NATIONAL LEVEL

In the relationship between on the one hand the social partners - and in particular the labour movement - and on the other hand the national government, important developments have taken place since the 1980s. The (neo)liberal course that has been dominant since then is characterized by, among others, austerity concerning public services and in particular social security, fostering of market making and competition, privatization of public companies, relative reduction of the minimum wage and the increase of the pension age. The employers have in general supported this course wholeheartedly, but the labour movement sees it as an attack on elementary social rights. It has opposed this course often and vigorously, both at the negotiation table and on the streets. This has often resulted in a reduced speed of the reforms, but most of the time not the direction of the reforms. The continuity of national deliberations is hence accompanied by an ailing influence of the trade unions on government policy.

The SER and the STAR produce a continuous stream of reports and advices, but it appears that the influence of both institutions on the main elements of socioeconomic policy is declining. The unified advices of the SER in recent years often concerned subjects that do not belong to the core competencies of the social partners and also involved other societal organizations: energy policy, health care, the housing market and technology. But on their traditional core competencies like dismissal regulations or wages the polder institutions are in a stalemate and unions and employers less and less manage to achieve consensus. As a result, their joint (but not necessarily their individual) influence on government policy is declining. An exception, to some extent, is pension reform, as after some 10 years of negotiating recently a pension agreement was reached. However, in the aftermath of the agreement is has already become clear that this agreement has not solved the problems of the pension system and new disagreements have again emerged.

§20.04 THE ACTORS OF THE POLDERMODEL

What explains these developments? To an important extent they can be explained by changes concerning the actors of the poldermodel, in particular the unions and employers, and the interaction between the two.

The most obvious trend is the steady decline of trade union density. Around 1980, one out of three workers was member of a trade union. Today this is one out of every six or seven workers. A major reason for this have been the structural changes on the labour market, in particular the demise of the standard contract and of the large manufacturing companies. But also among standard workers with a standard job (white males with a permanent, fulltime job) the percentage of members has dropped. This among others because the growing diversity of the labour market, for example in terms of contracts (fulltime-part time, permanent-temporary, employee-self-employed, etc.) and persons (men-women, low-high education, locals-migrants, young-old, etc.), make it increasingly difficult for the trade union movement to follow one single course that appeals to all groups on the labour market.

On the employers' side there is seemingly more stability. The density of employers - expressed as the percentage of workers that works in a company that is member of an employers' organization – is estimated to be between 60% and 80%, much higher than trade union density. Also, this density seems to be quite stable. Nevertheless, also the employers have a representativeness problem. Of the smaller companies (up to ten employees) much less than half are members of an employers' organization, making them an underrepresented group.

Moreover, the authority of the central organizations is being questioned. Especially large, multinational companies set their own policies and do not automatically follow the advice and guidelines of the main employers' organizations or the agreements made in the Labour Foundation. At the same time, also the differences and contradictions between large and small companies and between export-oriented and domestically-oriented companies seem to grow. This growing diversity makes it difficult for the employers' organizations to develop singular policies that are to the satisfaction of all members.

An outcome of the above-discussed developments is that the relationships between the negotiators of both sides have deteriorated. Distrust has increased. Employers accuse union negotiators of trying to hold on to old-fashioned and expensive rights for workers. Union negotiators in the meantime accuse employers of pursuing a worsening of working conditions under the false flag of 'modernization' and to invent ever-new ways to circumvent the regulations of the collective agreements.

§20.05 AND THE FUTURE?

For how long can this process of erosion of the poldermodel continue? Will it eventually collapse? It seems that it is becoming less and less interesting for all parties involved to maintain the present institutional configuration. Employers have less need for it while unions get less out of it. And the two are less and less able to provide the government with consensual advise and to deliver societal support for socioeconomic policy. Also, the poldermodel seems to generate less positive results in terms of equality, sufficient good-quality jobs and productivity growth.

Is a return to a more balanced poldermodel with better outcomes possible?

The main condition for such a return is that all three actors accept that the poldermodel can only legitimately continue to exist if it is balanced and generates positive outcomes. It has to be balanced in the sense that the actors in the model show the willingness not to put their own interests first but to pursue a broader general interest. It has to generate positive outcomes to maintain its societal legitimacy and to be a superior alternative to a situation without polder institutions. A more balanced poldermodel is also likely to produce more balanced outcomes in terms of wages, inequality, flexibility, productivity and social innovation. This requires first of all more trust and consensus between employers and workers at sector level, to get them to not only divide the cake but also to make the cake grow and become more sustainable.

Another threat to the model is the declining membership of the trade unions. If this trend continues, it twill eventually reach a level at which it is not self-evident anymore that they can, or are allowed to, participate in the polder institutions. This should be a reason to consider alternative ways to represent workers' interests and to determine the importance of the various trade unions, for example through trade union elections. But unions will also have to strengthen their capacity to get members, to connect better with the interests of their members and to cooperate with social movements.

At the same time, employers and their organizations, who now have a much more powerful position, should ask themselves if they, in the long run, do not benefit more from a more balanced relationship with the unions. This would be the way to maintain the traditional benefits of the poldermodel for the economy and for the country's social relationships - which are also in the employers' interest. The same is true for the government, which should ask itself what the effects will be of a society without consensus, with an ever-increasing labour market fragmentation and growing inequality.

CHAPTER 21
Contributions from the Social Partners

Paul Windey, Marc Leemans, Paul Soete, Erik Pentenga & Laurens Harteveld

In this chapter, we present some reflects and contributions to the current and future challenges of industrial relations in the low countries: Belgium and the Netherlands. We had the opportunity to bring together experienced industrial relations actors. This allows us to give insights on the current and future challenges of industrial relations, taking into account the field action itself. From Belgium, the contributors are Paul Windey (National Labour Council (NLC)), Marc Leemans (trade union perspective) and Paul Soete (employers' perspective). From the Netherlands, the contributors are Erik Pentenga (trade union perspective) and Laurens Harteveld (employers' perspective).

§21.01 CONTRIBUTION 1: THE FUTURE OF INDUSTRIAL RELATIONS IN BELGIUM AND THE NETHERLANDS, BY PAUL WINDEY

In the turmoil of the 2008 crisis, social partners and their institutions in Belgium have proven to be major stabilizing factors. With this regards, Belgium has been assessed as a good example by both European and international organizations (i.e., European Union (EU), Organisation for Economic Co-operation and Development (OECD) and International Monetary Fund (IMF)). However, since that period, global competition has put social partnership under pressure. Under budget pressures important industrial relations institutions (e.g., collective bargaining) have been weakened (e.g., Greece, Spain, Ireland, Portugal) and this resulted in wage restraint. On the other hand, the political power of Member States has reduced. Moreover, political power in most EU countries has shifted towards neo-liberalism, raise in populism and decrease of influence of trade unions. Nevertheless, there is nowadays a call for strengthening social partnership by international organizations such as ILO, the EU, OECD, and IMF.

Unlike other European countries, the affiliation degree of Belgian workers to trade unions has been stable over the last twenty years. This is linked to the 'Ghent system', which supports the involvement of social partners in the social security system, but it also relates to that social partners have continued to deliver progress in terms of redistribution, social justice and involvement in decision making through different groups in society. Social partners in Belgium still succeed to compromise which illustrates that industrial relations in Belgium are more than an issue related to politics or market power. Many of the actual topics in industrial relations with regards to workplace and/or branch level cannot be fully dealt with only by political decision making. It is true that the majority of social issues in Belgium are dealt with outside the company, and these are governed by political decisions at different levels (i.e., local, regional-national, international) through multiple scopes (e.g., labour right, social security, non-discrimination, protection of privacy, health and safety, balance between working life and other issues). However, in most of the cases, these same issues intersect with different levels of the industrial relation field.

Lifelong learning, combatting stress/burnout, alcohol and drugs, longtime ill workers, the relation between professional time and non-working time, flexibility in all aspects (i.e., working time arrangements, telework), agency workers, subcontracting, digitalization, have become so complex and multi-level that an overarching approach is needed, between social partners at all levels, including social security institutions, administrations at different levels (national, regional) to find a solution to current problems. This is the role that social partners have taken in Belgium at national-inter-sectoral level by both setting up platforms of all stakeholders concerned or integrating different aspects. This is the case at national level (i.e., in the NLC) but also at regional level (i.e., in the regional economic and social councils). The National Inter-professional Agreement for 2016-2017 is a nice example. Surprisingly, the rate of unanimous opinions at the NLC has been stable at 80% over recent years. However, this remains a difficult task, time consuming and not 'sexy' for (social) media.

Belgian social partners have a longstanding tradition of supporting the EU project and incorporation the EU scope in their activities. Belgian was the first country to implement EU directives in national law through collective agreements of the NLC. Social partners have been part of those activists that realized the Social Chapter of the Maastricht Treaty and the elaboration of a first pillar of social rights in 1990s, through both EU directives (e.g., European Works Councils, protection of pregnant women, prohibition of child work, Posting of workers) and EU social partners agreements (e.g., parental leave, part-time work). Over the last twenty years, however, this result-driven legal activity has weakened and has been replaced by other policy approaches, for example, the Lisbon Strategy, and the EU2020 Agenda. Belgian social partners have tried to incorporate this approach in their activities, however, with variable success or outcome. It is questionable to what extent these outcomes will be able to counter the actual populist tendencies.

The main challenge I see in the future is to find the right balance between the needs of individual workers and the needs of individual companies at the one hand, and the need for a minimum coordination at regional, national and European level in the social and economic sphere, on the other hand. This balance should be kept in mind in order to make the interdependence between the different aspects/issues at stake as well as the different levels of decision making, be it political and industrial relations related, working towards the right direction. Ongoing globalization and digitalization, combined with demographic changes, will further push labour markets to look for new balances. I cannot see politics be able to find the best recipes, life is becoming too complex! Industrial relations will have to find its own role in it. The basic condition is however that trade unions and employers keep fighting to get a mandate of their constituencies.

We hope that the new 'EU Social Pillar Agenda' will be able to deliver and to support social partners legitimacy. Until now, this is what we try at the NLC by regular meetings and discussions, we try to find common views and analysis that can be shared so to help succeeding in finding sustainable solutions.

§21.02 CONTRIBUTION 2: WHEN THE GOING GETS TOUGH: THE STATE OF SOCIAL DIALOGUE, BY MARC LEEMANS

Is social dialogue coming to an end? Allow me to be sceptical about this. Since I started working for the trade union movement, now thirty-seven years ago, it is repeatedly told and written that social partners lose their relevance and that our social model is as good as dead. In fact, these claims are a form of fake news. It is certain that we often face difficult periods. And the word 'often' is merely an understatement. It would be better to speak about 'mostly', or 'always'. But when the going gets tough, there is opportunity for action. There has been a time that reaching an inter-professional agreement was difficult, but then agreements were nevertheless concluded at other levels: in the regions, in sectors, in enterprises, in the NLC and in institutions of social security. Presently, 98% of Belgian employees are covered by a collective agreement. Social dialogue is therefore alive and kicking.

However, social dialogue does not take place on an island. It happens within a political context. When political leaders are hostile vis-à-vis social dialogue, then this is a very problematic factor. This is what we have experienced during the past legislature. With employers who think to gain profit from lobbying with political parties instead of going through social dialogue. With a nationalist right wing in Flanders that has an aversion for federal institutions, so certainly also for federal social partners and federal social agreements. With a political context, with diminished respect for the autonomy of social dialogue, in which compromises of social partners have not always been respected. At the same time, a government might try to make use (some will even call this abuse) of the social dialogue to implement and/or accelerate political decisions without real discussion. Social dialogue is, in doing so, reduced to a mere formalistic instrument rather than a constructive process. A recent example is the pension debate.

Luckily we have – until now – safeguarded the right to strike in Belgium. Because negotiating and strike action are two sides of the same medal. If necessary, one has to show his teeth. And if it really matters, one should be able to bite. Without the right to strike, collective bargaining is collective begging. It is thus a problematic evolution that continuous efforts are done to dismantle the right to strike. As if the dissatisfaction of workers will then just disappear. If it is not through strike action, dissatisfaction will appear in other ways. The movement of the yellow jerseys is a good illustration of this. In order to take away social friction, dialogue with strong partners is needed.

What is the state of the European and international dimension of social dialogue? Increasingly, multinational enterprises take the fore with turnovers bigger than state Gross domestic products (GDP). The economy is globalizing with global supply chains, global value chains, global trade agreements. Capital is ruling the world trade and even the local democracies. Besides the ILO Conventions and Recommendations, there are no worldwide norms regarding labour. At global level, it is positive that ever more multinationals wish to participate in the activities of the ILO. But the employers' organizations are rather hostile towards this. At European level, we have/had a Commission which claimed to be socially triple AAA. Unfortunately, we have seen little from that, and the further prospects are not promising.

[A] How Do We Go Further Down the Road?

The future will be more digital, more virtual, more robotized. It will bring more diversified forms of work. Social dialogue will need to adapt itself to this. Do we have to decentralize our social dialogue system?

Looking back to the past decennia, our social dialogue system has maintained itself quite well. There has been an evolution towards framework agreements with more space for specification at company level; another interplay between central and decentralized dialogue.

If one takes an international comparison, the precarization of work relations in Belgium has stayed reasonably within limits. This is merely due to our social dialogue model. We have convinced employers to avoid derailment and roguishness. Of course, this only works for employment contracts and the last years we see a move towards self-employed labour and even towards a kind of non-status. As a result off the dynamics of internationally operating digital platforms.

But also as a result off the unwillingness of the government Michel I to adjust these forms of work to our norms and values. Instead the governmental policy tended towards *no taxes, no social contributions, no social security* and even *no labour protection*. For example with the exclusion of those activities from the scope of the law on collective agreements. In September 2018 the three Belgian trade unions decided to demand the nullification of the new legislation before the Constitutional Court.

Another contentieux, that we also need to deal with at European and international level, is how to guarantee the right to collective bargaining for dependent self-employed persons and workers of digital platforms? The ILO rules are clear: the right to social dialogue is not a prerogative of employees but is guaranteed for all workers. After discussion in the International Labour Conference in 2016, it has led to a limited legal framework in Ireland. The rest of Europe will have to follow this example.

So there is a lot of work to be done. Strong trade unions, in these insecure times, are more than needed. Because only strong trade unions can deliver results in social dialogue.

§21.03 CONTRIBUTION 3: THE FUTURE OF INDUSTRIAL RELATIONS IN BELGIUM, BY PAUL SOETE

Even if perception may be different from the outside, there has been no impact of the crisis on the social dialogue in Belgium. Nor in quantity nor in quality. Globalization and digitization have had until now no fundamental effects on the social dialogue. However, relationships between the social partners and the government changed fundamentally since the centre right majority came into power in 2014. In particular, the link between unions and political parties became much weaker since right-wing populist parties have no links with trade unions and the former have even started to compete with the latter. To a certain extent, this is also valid for employers organizations, that have been 'bypassed by the right-wing' populist parties in their approach to specific issues, such as profit sharing, tax-free and flexible second jobs. So at the very end, although in different ways, both employers organizations and trade unions in Belgium are threatened by recent political tendencies and in turn consider their possibility to develop new initiatives in the social field as losing terrain. This is disappointing to some extent since actual political top issues are less subject to – as they should instead – of social dialogue. I refer here, particularly to security, migration, climate change.

At the EU level, we see a similar picture, although for different reasons. Social dialogue at the EU level is constraint at the moment. However, the Commission has taken some important initiatives, such as the European Pillar of Social Rights, the new posting directive with the equal pay principle, the work-life balance proposal, the revision of the working state (i.e., transparent and predictable working conditions) directive that will introduce new rights and force employers to give more information and introduce more coordination of social security rules. However, all these initiatives have a common problem which lies in their technical implementation and enforcement.

But the most important impact of the EU level on the social dialogue in Belgium lies probably in the follow up of the European semester. When we talk about the future of the social dialogue in Belgium – we as employers – we know very well what has to change on the union side. Digitization of work and of social relations represent the biggest challenge at the very moment for social partners in Belgium for many reasons. Firstly, the information monopoly of social partners is disappeared already long ago and consultation and decision-making processes should be transformed to alienate with the new needs within the world of work. As a result, traditionally structured organizations can be bypassed. This is because consultations could be launched through the net and democratic decisions could be taken by using flexible structures. Secondly, social dialogue impacts on social media. The use of social media by the social partners between unions and employers organizations, and among them between different countries, may take different forms. For example, in Belgium, we lack an active presence of trade unions leaders in social media. This is different in the Netherlands though. When the fax, the mail and the mobile phone were introduced, unions quite rapidly integrated them in their way of working. With social media, this seems more difficult to be done. Sometimes trade unions consider social media as 'a pool of dirty stuff'. Thirdly, digitization facilitates telework and reduces the importance of the workplace and the working conditions linked to the workplace. This introduces new issues on the table of negotiation such as the right of connection and disconnection which become a new field for rights and obligations for both employees and employers.

Then, what can we expect as the effects of digitalization for social dialogue in the future? The platform economy can develop into systems that are really disruptive for social dialogue. The idea that platform workers are salaried workers is an issue which is currently under legal scrutiny. Some argue that platforms workers are simply workers and that labour law should apply to them even when they are 'self-employed'. But that is not the direction that was taken in the EU proposal concerning predictable and transparent working conditions. At that time, the commission has clearly stated that this directive should not cover the self-employed. Some argue also that platform workers have the right to collective bargaining based on the ILO conventions even if they are not salaried (Article 98). But that point of view is actually not generally shared. Certainly not by the employers organizations. In addition, there is another more tricky issue to be dealt with when talking about platform economy i.e., if there is no employer with whom do trade unions can negotiate? With the algorithm? With the consumer? With the provider of services? With the authorities, to lobby for platform-regulation? The EU definition of employer in the transparent and predictable working conditions proposal is not really very helpful. The employer here is defined as 'one or more natural or legal person(s) who is or are directly or indirectly party to an employment relationship with a worker. And', of course, there will never exist an employers' organization for platforms. A platform that does not want to be considered as an employer will not be eager to become a member of an employers' organization. Personally I do not see this as so negative for both trade unions and employers organization since their main concern should be to play a role in this new field by – for example – revitalizing a return to the medieval 'guilds'. For instance, in Belgium UNIZO is as an organization that was quite successful in defending the rights of liberal professions. Another example is the 'paradoxical' situation of UBER who, conversely, aims at avoiding regulation.

This brings us to the problem of the rules concerning competition and price agreements. Collective agreements are exceptions on market rules but they are legally authorized. What will be the position of the competition authorities concerning agreements on prices of services within the digital economy? The well-known case of the Irish exception for fully dependent journalists and artists explicitly states that there should be no effect on the market nor any distortion of competition. This does not seem to be problematic in the cultural sector or even in the media sector. Some time ago the Belgian competition authorities intervened to prohibit the tariffs of the architects (1995). European case law seems evolving in that field, considering that even real self-employed may conclude collective agreements in some situations. This evolution could change the approach of the activities developed within the platform economy and this is certainly a field for further policy scrutiny.

§21.04 CONTRIBUTION 4: SOCIAL DIALOGUE REQUIRES COLLECTIVE ACTION, BY ERIK PENTENGA (FNV)

[A] Introduction

When we compare the labour market figures of 2019 with 2008, the Dutch labour market seems to have recovered completely from the blow of the Great Financial Crisis in 2008. The number of unfilled vacancies is now higher than ever, and the unemployment rate is even lower than just before the crisis. Viewed from the position of employees however, the labour market is in a substantially worse shape than around 2008. In the Netherlands, only 60% of the workers now have the certainty of a permanent contract. In comparison, the use of the flexible shell of temporary contract workers, temp workers and self-employed workers has grown to 40%, including an explosive growth of the number of self-employed workers without personnel (in Dutch). In addition, the share of zero-hour and on-call contracts has increased considerably. In fact, only the share of temporary agency employees has hardly grown over the years, which is surprising when you look at the intentions of internationally famous 'Flexibility and security'-pact of 1996 that led to the Flexibility and Security Act (1999).

[B] The Emergence of Flexible Work

The recovery of the labour market after the employment crisis in the 1980s and early 1990s was accompanied by the rise of temporary agency work in the Netherlands. Of the total number of working hours per year, the share of agency work rose from 1.8% to 2.5% between 1992 and 1996. In addition, the term *'detacheren'* (secondment) entered the labour market and also the first 'pay-roll services' gained ground. In a brochure of the largest Dutch trade union organization FNV, entitled 'An ordinary job at the temporary work agency; FNV-views on temporary agency work and secondment' (January 1996), the then FNV-chairman Johan Stekelenburg quotes the common view: 'Flexible employment relations are good for the labour market. Modern people want to work flexibly themselves and the modern economy cannot do without. It is only difficult that the trade unions are constantly struggling about it.'

The brochure furthermore reports about a conference day on the subject of secondment: 'Panic at the Hilton!' as more than one hundred people have registered for the meeting.[1] According to the recruitment brochure 'secondment provides major financial benefits, but also entails risks'. And to emphasize the seriousness of the situation, a newspaper clipping with the heading 'FNV wants law on secondment' was added as an illustration.

The brochure continues to wonder: why is agency work so advantageous? They conclude that this is the case as companies don't have to pay certain premiums for temporary agency workers who do not build up pension or are not entitled to early

1. Secondment may also take place via the temp agency.

retirement. Nor do the hiring companies have to pay contributions to training funds or other 'charities' in the industry. The then threatened abolition of the Sickness Benefits Act, whereby an employer runs the risk of having continue to pay six to twelve weeks' pay in the event of illness, also doesn't apply to temporary agency employees. After a waiting period of two or three days, temporary agency workers simply receive a benefit from the business associations (currently by the national labour market agency UWV[2]) instead of from the company. And most importantly: the hirer only has to pay for agency work as long as there is work available.

[C] The 1996 'Flexibility and Security' Social Agreement

At the end of 1995, the Minister of Social Affairs and Employment at that time, Ad Melkert of the Labour Party PvdA, issued a memorandum 'Flexibility and Security', including a package of proposals aimed at putting an end to the prevailing ambiguity on the topic of flexible labour and the legal inequality of flexible workers in comparison with permanent employees. It is a political compromise within the then PvdA-VVD-D66-Cabinet, which in the opinion of the FNV, was unable to bring about a positive change in the precarious balance between 'flexibility and (social) security' and the 'dynamics and social protection'. On 3 April 1996, the requested advice from the bi-partite Labour Foundation (*Stichting van de Arbeid*) followed the joint consultative body of social partners at national level. This advice was published as the 'Flexibility and Security Memorandum', after 'kitchen table negotiations' between the key negotiators of the employers' and the employees' associations at the kitchen table of the then collective bargaining coordinator of FNV, Lodewijk de Waal.[3] Subsequently, the Flexibility and Security Act came into effect on 1 January 1999.

The idea behind the Act is that limited flexibility in companies is required to cope with *'piek en ziek'* (peak workload and sickness of employees). The employment conditions for these flexible employees should be safeguarded as we were accustomed to as social partners: in a collective agreement. And this temporary agency employment agreement should provide more certainty, the longer an employee is in a flexible working relationship. This leads to a phasing system existing of three periods, that is to be included in the collective agreement: the flexibility is greatest in the first 1.5 years and only the hours worked are paid. Then follows a phase in which more certainty is offered to the temp worker by giving temporary contracts for a limited time (2 years, 8 contracts). If you were still working through the temporary employment agency at the end of this phase, the idea is that you either start working at the hirer or at the agency (phase 3). The law and the collective labour agreement (CLA) mentioned working on the basis of a '*uitzendbeding*' or temporary employment clause in the first 1.5 years, and secondment (temporary contracts). In order to provide more certainty in the first

2. In 2002, six organizations that implemented a range of social security programs (Cadans, Gak, GUO, SFB, USZO and Lisv) merged into the UWV.
3. De Waal would later be appointed as FNV-president. For the details: Daphné Dupont-Nivet & Emiel Woutersen (2018, 19 September). 'Terug naar de keukentafel', *de Groene Amsterdammer*, 38.

phase, it was also possible to work with temporary or secondment contracts in that phase. For example, a three-month-contract as a pregnancy replacement gave nevertheless more certainty than the temporary employment clause whereby you could be dismissed at any time.

For a better understanding of the political context, it should be added that at that time, zero-hour contracts were qualified as highly undesirable; certainly in the beginning, advising employment law lawyers posed these contract as 'really no longer acceptable'. Political parties and social partners also agreed that it could not have been the intention of the Dutch welfare state that 12% of the workers worked without a permanent contract. Outside the Netherlands, there was great admiration for the results achieved with the so-called polder model. In 2007 even a prize was awarded by the prestigious German Carl Bertelsmann Foundation to the social partners in the Labour Foundation, for their innovative labour market policy.

[D] Increasing Labour Market Shortages

From the Millennium until the 2008 crisis, the labour market was characterized by low unemployment and increasing shortages in various positions. By the Cabinet established Bakker-committee (2008), forecasted structural shortages on the labour market due to lower birth rates, increasing numbers of early retiring people and a rigid functioning labour market. The committee recommended working longer hours, more flexibility and allowing in more labour migrants.

And then the 2008 financial crisis entered. The labour market developed very differently than was anticipated, stimulated by policy choices that were inspired by the Bakker-committee. In the crisis, local taxes grow and labour costs rise due to changes in social legislation. FNV needs to repair these costs that are the result of political choice, in collective agreements to compensate for the statutory social arrangements.

It then became more and more attractive for employers to not only avoid their own CLA, but also the temporary employment agreement. Ever since, the use of this agreed 'main road' for flexible work (temporary agency work) remained similar, while the use of the other forms of 'no permanent contract', increased substantially.

The evaluation of the Flexibility and Security Act of 1999 showed that the intended build-up to more certainty in three phases was not being pursued. The foreseen interruption period of three months between contracts did not result in an intended incentive to hire the temporary agency worker, neither by the hirers, or by the temporary employment agencies. The distribution over the different phases in temporary agency work has remained roughly the same: 80% does not go beyond the 1st (A) phase, 18% enters the temporary contracts phase (B), and only 2% enters permanent employment at the employment agency (C).

The told story to the temporary workers was: 'you are good, we also want you to come back because the work is there, but the trade unions have forced us to send you home for 3 months'. What the employer of course meant was: 'you are doing well, the work is there, but I refuse to give you a permanent contract'.

[E] Towards a New Social Agreement

A new PvdA-VVD Cabinet (Rutte II, 2012-2017) was needed to arrive at a new major social pact in April 2013 through social dialogue. The reviving 'polder model' had been almost written-off during the four Balkenende cabinets (2001-2010), although the largest trade union demonstration ever took place during this period, on 2 October 2004, with more than 300,000 demonstrators in Amsterdam at the Museumplein. The 2013-pact laid the foundation for among others: the Work and Security Act (WWZ 2015), the Sham Employment Arrangements Act (WAS 2015) and the Assessment of Employment Relationships (Deregulation) Act (DBA 2016).

The 2013 social pact didn't happen by accident.[4] Within the trade union, an ongoing reflection on the strategy of the unions challenged the lack of visibility of the unions in the workplace; unions should not only negotiate national agreements but should also take a role in the compliance and enforcement. The strategy contained the notion that a redesign is needed: the contact with employees in the workplace had to be reintroduced. The result is that the union has become more visible on the topic of daily working conditions and uncertainties, not only in the public opinion but especially in the political arena. The union approach makes use of narratives by ordinary employees, from road transport, distribution centres, meat industry, cleaning, public transport contracted, home care, supermarket, mail and package delivery, et cetera. FNV aims to make visible which sham constructions are used to avoid having to pay the regular collective agreement and to escape from providing permanent contracts.

[F] Flexible Work Is Precarious Work

The Work and Security Act (WWZ) aiming to bring a new balance between flexibility and security has smoothly been implemented in 2015. Remarkably, it has barely been able to show its effects or it is already was disregarded by the current Cabinet (Rutte III 2017) that proposed a new Act (*Work in Balance*), that has been brought through Parliament in Spring 2019. In addition, the enforcement of the DBA Act to clarify when work is done by an employee and when by a self-employed person, was put 'on hold' by the Rutte II Cabinet. Until the present day, it is still kept 'on hold' by Rutte III. Instead, a new national committee on Work Regulation (committee-Borstlap) has been given a prominent position by the Cabinet to find a solution.

FNV is currently politically debating what has become visible by complying and enforcing the collective agreement due to the trade union work at the work floor. Call it 'organizing'. The FNV has succeeded in breaking through the positive framing of flexibility, which had been successfully introduced into the social debate in the 1990s. Flexibility as a modern, young, fresh and most desired lifestyle, is back to what it in reality is: uncertain and cheap. After having kept the image to be the only sour puss in

4. Compare with the introduction text on Belgium and the Netherlands by Pulignano et al., this volume.

a period of optimistic flexibilization world view, the FNV now has gained support from established labour market institutions such as Dutch Technology Research (TNO), Dutch Statistics (CBS), The Central Planning Bureau (CPB) and the WRR (Scientific Council for Government Policy). In its explorative study of the future labour market entitled 'Voor de Zekerheid' (For the Sake of Security 2017), the Dutch Scientific Council for Government Policy uses our assessment that it is no longer about 'flexibility' but about 'as cheaply as possible' and the great uncertainty that this entails for workers.

Better than before (in the pre-Rutte III era), FNV now manages to visualise and gain public recognition for what we call the 'earnings models' of employers behind the sham structures:

- pay-roll work (as temporary agency employment regime that is used for permanent work);
- contracting (below statutory minimum wage level);
- secondment from abroad with A1 (payment of income tax and social contributions in the home country, if at all, instead of the host country);
- the posting of labour migrants and housing yourself in combination with tax provisions such as the ET scheme (which enable working under statutory minimum wage levels);
- zero-hour and on-call contracts (where workers lack certainty about the number of hours one can work, and therefore have no security about their income per week);
- possibilities for avoiding high sector premiums (premium shopping to reduce gross labour costs); and
- disguised employment and sham commissioning with self-employed workers.

[G] Platform Work Intensifies the Self-Employment Discussion

As the newest kid on the block, the platform economy, which is continued by the increasing number of self-employed workers, requires our attention. The constant political enforcement-moratorium of the Assessment of Employment Relationships (Deregulation) Act (DBA) gives these platforms a *carte blanche* to evade the obligations of being an employer. Functions that – juridically seen – obviously can only be performed as an employee with a (temporary) employment contract base, as the work is executed 'under management and supervision' and 'with own materials and resources', in the platform construct these tasks are performed on the basis of self-employment. The contract form is completely placed outside the protection of employment legislation, without social insurance, no pension accrual nor access to training funds. May be workers receive a slightly higher hourly rate, but one actually (and most of them do not) has to purchase individually on the insurance market and pay a more expensive rate than what employees contribute and receive through collective schemes. These costs may even extend the minimum wage to live on. It is not a coincidence that self-employed people are the largest group that now populates the official yearly Dutch Poverty Monitor.

Currently, FNV once again is making the underlying 'earnings model' visible by visiting the Deliveroo riders, the Uber drivers, the Helpling cleaners, the Temper dishwashers and waiters. We talk to our workers and share their story in the public and political arena, in combination with legal proceedings. The first success is that the Cabinet has now asked the Dutch Social and Economic Council (SER) for an exploration of platform work.

Our conclusion: social dialogue cannot do without social action.

§21.05 CONTRIBUTION 5: THE DUTCH POLDER MODEL AFTER THE CRISIS. AN EMPLOYER'S VIEW, LAURENS HARTEVELD (AWVN)

[A] Successful Social Pact in 2009

The employer's organization AWVN is the main business actor in the negotiations of some 500 out of the 800 CLA's in the Netherlands. In this role, we monitor bargaining results in the social dialogue and industrial relations closely.

With the outbreak of the financial crisis in the Fall of 2008, the economic situation turned at an unprecedented velocity from a booming economy in Summer 2008 into a severe economic decline of 3.7% in 2009. Social partners and government reacted with a Social Pact in March 2009.[5] In this pact, the maximum collective wage increase of 3.5% (agreed upon in the Autumn pact just before the outbreak of the crisis[6]) was diminished into the new inflation forecast of 1%.[7] The wage pact was successful: within six months after this national pact the average wage increase actually matched the level of 1%. Without this national pact, the decentral debate on collective wage increase would have been longer and more fierce, resulting in a higher wage increase. In other words: social partners and government reacted quickly and adequately to the threats of the economic crisis.

Individual employers responded to the crisis by labour hoarding: companies did not lay off employees when it otherwise would during the 2009-crisis, with the intention to profit from economic growth in the near future.

Unfortunately, the recovery of the economy did not take place immediately. Instead, the Dutch economy faced a new economic decline in 2012 (-1%) and 2013 (-0.1%). As a consequence, the number of bankruptcies increased in 2012 to an all-time high.[8]

5. https://www.tijdschriftvoorarbeidsvraagstukken.nl/inhoud/tijdschrift_artikel/TA-28-2-138/Loonvorming-in-tijden-van-crisis (in Dutch only).
6. 'The trade unions will ensure that, with a view to responsible wage cost movements, wage claims in the coming collective agreement year will be in line with those of this year.' https://www.stvda.nl/en/~/media/files/stvda/convenanten_verklaringen/2000_2009/2008/20081007_en.ashx.
7. 'Wage movements will be negotiated to match the level of inflation.' https://www.stvda.nl/en/~/media/files/stvda/talen/engels/2009/voorjaarsakkoord_20090325_en.ashx.
8. CBS: https://opendata.cbs.nl/statline/#/CBS/en/dataset/82242ENG/table?dl=16509.

After 2009, the period of cooperation and mutual trust between social actors at central level ends. In 2010, the largest union, FNV, even fell into a severe internal crisis on the subject of pension reforms. In 2013, a new social pact was negotiated on labour market reforms to stabilize the economy and the political climate.[9] However, both the members of trade unions and members of the employers confederations were generally not pleased with the implementation of this pact, resulting in less support for the social dialogue in the years after 2013.

[B] Wage Debate

Today, in 2018 and 2019, the Dutch economy is booming again. In this context, a quite extended debate has emerged about wages that 'do not follow the economic growth sufficiently'. Trade unions refer to the high level of profits of companies in this context. Even the Dutch Prime Minister and the President of the Central Bank have expressed their concerns. According to the employers' association AWVN, reality is less simple than unions suggest for a number of reasons.

First of all, an unwritten convention exists in the Netherlands that collective wages never decrease. Even in the year of 2009, with an economic decline of 3.7%, the average collective wage increase was 1.7% (average according to AWVN-data). After a 1.1% wage increase in 2010 the Dutch economy entered a period of an average annual wage increase of 1.5% to 1.7% until 2017 (Figure 21.1).

9. 'Prospects for a socially responsible and enterprising country: emerging from the crisis and getting back to work on the way to 2020' https://www.stvda.nl/~/media/Files/Stvda/Talen/Engels/2013/20130411-sociaal-akkoord-EN.ashx.

Figure 21.1 Collective Wage Increase (Bars) and Economic Growth (Line), 2008-2019

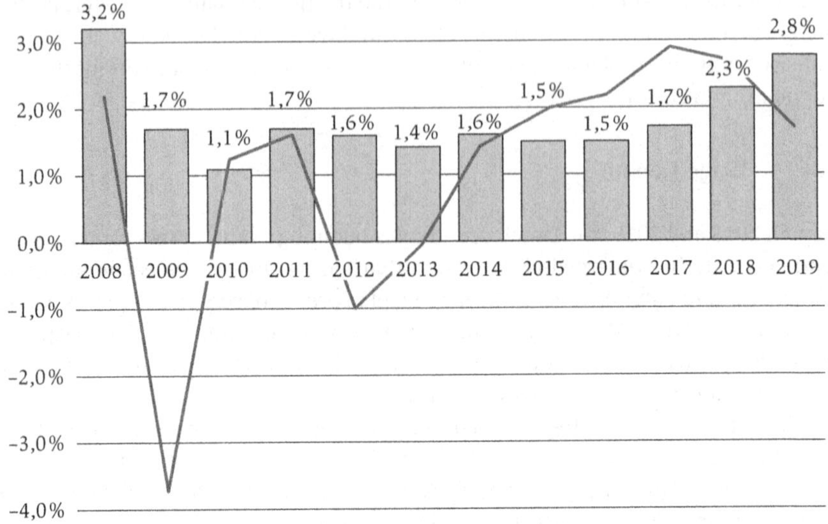

Source: AWVN wage data base (https://cao-kijker.awvn.nl/) and CPB-data on economic growth.

In order to compensate for the wage increase in the years of economic decline (2008-2009 and 2012-2013), the wages in the post-crisis years increased at a lower rate than is normally the case.

If we look at collective wage data over a longer period of time, we must conclude that not only collective wages never decline, but also that the fluctuation of collective wages is less extreme than the fluctuation of economic growth. We also conclude that collective wages follow the economic development with a delay of some eighteen months, that is about equal to the average duration of a negotiated CLA.

Secondly, if we look at the 'labour income share' as part of the national income, we do not see a structural decline since 2000 (figure 21.2). During the crisis, the labour income share indeed has declined, but in recent years the labour income share is increasing again towards the long term average. Recent research shows the statistical complexity of this economic entity and its shortages in the wage debate.[10]

10. http://www.seo.nl/pagina/article/de-aiq-in-nederland-een-overzicht/ (in Dutch only).

Figure 21.2 Labour Income Share in National Income, 1970 to 2019

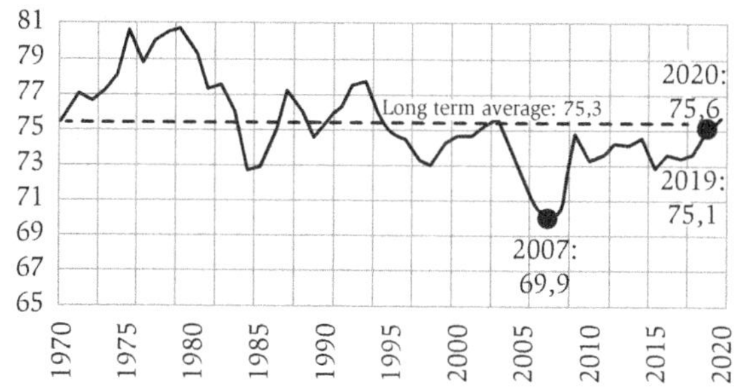

Source: AWVN presentation of CPB-data https://www.cpb.nl/sites/default/files/omnidownload/Appendix_03_kmev20.xlsx).

Thirdly, although the gross wages did increase the last years, the purchasing power of households did not follow. This is the consequence of the policy of central government to increase the tax burden of households from 35% in the beginning of this century to a forecasted 39% in 2019.[11]

Fourthly, the booming profit figures ask for nuance. Indeed, according to national statistics, companies are making higher profits at macro level. But that does not mean that all companies are earning similar (high) benefits. In fact, there are indications that growing shares are limited to a few (larger) companies. Some of these companies earn high profits because of foreign investments in the past, whereas others (like Google, Microsoft, Amazon and Uber) are profitable because of their (global) monopoly power.

Even during the current economic boom period, we witness a lot of companies not making any profit at all. In the retail, for example, companies are facing more severe competition from domestic webshops (open 24/7) and digital purchasing platforms (like Alibaba).

What is not helpful, is that in some collective agreements, the 'result based payment' has disappeared. In the years after the crisis, this 'result based payment' did not result in incidental wage increase because of the lagging or even negative financial results of companies. In reaction to this situation, trade unions wanted to transform this 'result based payment' in a structural payment at a lower level. The employees' preference for more security can be understood, especially in years of crisis, but at the same time prevents that employees can share in higher profits in prosperous times.

Fifth and not least, the wage debate is being blurred by different interests and different wage definitions. Are we talking about wage costs, gross wages or net wages, real wages or nominal wages, structural wages or incidental wages? For example, the call for higher wages from the Dutch Prime Minister can be seen as an attempt to realize the election promise of more purchasing power in times of an increasing tax burden. The call for higher wages from the President of the Central Bank can be seen in the

11. CPB-data: https://www.cpb.nl/en/forecast-june-2019.

context of pursuing an inflation rate of 2% (while the recent ECB policy of monetary expansion was pushing down national inflation rates).

AWVN recommends its members in 2018 and 2019 a 'balanced' wage increase. If the collective wage increase is too low, the employer will face problems attracting new employees in the labour market, when the collective wages rise steeply employers will meet competitive problems in the product market.

The current gap between the central wage demand of the FNV of at least 5% for 2019 and the wage offers of individual employers is large.[12] This can hamper collective bargaining. As a result we register more labour unrest in 2019, more final offers of employers for a new CLA (and less agreements) and less attention on the negotiation table for new investments in employees, necessary to increase (or at least maintain) their value at the rapidly changing labour market, demanding new skills and competencies.

[C] Dutch Consultation Economy: Still Working Though Weaker in the Future?

Social dialogue is still going on and social partners are talking to each other on a regular base. The central government is looking for support for its new policies, and social partners search for opportunities to put specific issues at the government agenda. This system of mutual consultation still works but is facing several threats in recent years that can erode the Dutch polder. For each of the partners, substantial dilemmas are at stake.[13]

First, the trade union confederations lose power because of a declining number of union members. It is commonly understood that the Dutch system of labour relations does not stimulate union membership, given the free-rider issue. Employees will benefit from the collective agreement whether they are union member or not. In theory, as long as unions are representing the interests of all employees (instead of a selected group of – older – members) there is no problem. In the present period, we may note an overall decline in members of political parties, churches, and social organizations, an inevitable trend in times of increasing individualism. In practice, trade unions lose members, which threatens the degree of representation. This may result in a change in the equilibrium of powers at the negotiation table.

Employers' associations on their turn are also facing representation problems. The number of companies that are controlled by foreign capital is increasing rapidly. In terms of employees, almost 20% of all employees in the market sector is working in companies with foreign ownership. In manufacturing, one out of three employees is working in a foreign-owned company. In terms of turn over, even 51% is in foreign

12. *See* for instance the AWVN interim report on CLA trends in the first half of 2019 of https://www.awvn.nl/nieuws/tussenevaluatie-cao-seizoen-2019/ (in Dutch only).
13. Article published in Zeggenschap December 2018 (Laurens Harteveld): 'Model van doorwerking staat onder druk', https://www.zeggenschap.info/zeggenschap/in-het-decembernummer-2018/ (in Dutch only).

hands.[14] With more companies under foreign control, the understanding of the Dutch consultation process and positive attitude towards unions are both declining at company level. Nowadays foreign-owned companies experience a more severe control from the foreign mother company, that is trying to standardize production processes and labour terms in all global production locations by means of uniform spreadsheets and other forms of monitoring and control. This results in less autonomy in labour relations for the individual companies that are part of global conglomerates. At the beginning of this century, the company plants would be closed if it did produce with a loss, nowadays a department will be closed if the profits are less than expected or less than elsewhere in the global conglomerate. Foreign-owned companies have to negotiate twice: first with the mother company about the mandate, then with the Dutch unions about the collective agreement.

Finally, the government is dealing with shrinking powers. In the period 2000 to 2019, Dutch politics counted eight government coalitions. This reflects the underlying societal unrest in the Netherlands. The previous cabinet (2012 to 2017) did manage to fulfil the whole reigning period, but lost powers both to Brussels (due to the European Semester) and to the municipalities (because of the decentralization of social policies). The current government is also quite unstable, with a majority of only one vote in Parliament and a minority in the Senate, since elections in Spring 2019.

In sum each of the tripartite partners is losing position, thereby weakening the whole consultation system. Without support of the external parties, the weakening will be even more visible. This encourages the three parties to continue their tripartite talks like before. At the same time, we do not notice the appearance of serious alternative actors that can fill the growing power vacuum. The government has no alternative yet than consulting increasingly weaker social partners. The advantage of dealing with the social partners is that they can implement a national pact at the decentral level via the instrument of collective bargaining. Other parties lack this implementation power and are therefore less attractive for the central government to consult.

The increasing diversification in the labour market may weaken the consultation model also in other ways. The increasing number of self-employed people makes organizations representing employees less important. At the same time, individualization is weakening the coordination process from top (central pacts) to bottom (collective agreements), since both employees and employers are following their own interests instead of joint collective interests. Both goodwill and support for central deals is lacking in a significant part of the rank and file of both trade unions and employers' associations. This is partly the reflection of individualization processes and partly the result of the disappointment of the benefits of the last central deal in 2013.

Finally, we notice that industries with a high bargaining coverage (construction and manufacturing) are dealing with job losses and sectors with a low bargaining coverage (trade and business) are facing job growth. When these trends will continue, the current degree of bargaining coverage of almost 80% of all employees will

14. CBS Statline: https://opendata.cbs.nl/statline/#/CBS/nl/dataset/81358ned/table?dl=142A6.

decline.[15] In fact, including self-employed people in the working population and excluding the public sector, the degree of bargaining coverage was falling from 72% in 2004 to 56% in 2015.

Overall, the Dutch consultation process did survive the crisis. The benefits of central consultation (support, agenda-setting, influence) and of the collective agreement (economies of scale, equality, transparency) are still too strong for all parties involved. We may conclude that participating actors loose position, but also that other parties have not filled the power vacuum until today. Social partners and government finally reached agreement on a new national pact on pension reforms in Spring 2019.[16] However, despite the joy of the pension deal, a lot of challenges will appear in the decision process about the implementation of the agreement. Also current processes like digitalization and robotization ask for three strong tripartite players with significant internal support, if not, the benefits of central consultation might run the risk to decline or even disappear in the future.

15. Article published in Zeggenschap March 2017: 'Steeds minder werknemers vallen onder een cao' (Geert de Bruin en Laurens Harteveld), https://www.zeggenschap.info/zeggenschap/in-het-maartnummer-2017/ (in Dutch only).
16. *See* https://www.ser.nl/nl/actueel/Nieuws/akkoord-nieuw-pensioenstelsel or https://www.vno-ncw.nl/nieuws/pensioenakkoord-maatschappelijke-en-economische-winst.

BCLR - BULLETIN OF COMPARATIVE LABOUR RELATIONS

Vol. Author/Title/Year/ISBN

1. Roger Blanpain, *Individual Employment Contracts: Collective Agreements*, 1970.
2. Roger Blanpain, *Social Planning*, 1971 (ISBN 90-312-0018-2).
3. Roger Blanpain, *Guaranteed Income Funds*, 1972 (ISBN 90-312-0019-0).
4. Roger Blanpain, *Employee Participation at the Level of the Enterprise*, 1973 (ISBN 90-312-0020-4).
5. Roger Blanpain, *Vastheid van Betrekking: Staking en Bezetting*, 1974.
6. Roger Blanpain, *Labour Law and Industrial Relations (International Bibliography)*, 1975 (ISBN 90-312-0023-9).
7. Roger Blanpain, *Multinational Enterprises*, 1976 (ISBN 90-312-0024-7).
8. Roger Blanpain, *Worker's Participation in the European Company*, 1977 (ISBN 90-312-0044-1).
9. Roger Blanpain, *Women and Labour*, 1978 (ISBN 90-312-0077-8).
10. Roger Blanpain, *European Conference on Labour Law and Industrial Relations: Multinational Enterprises*, 1979 (ISBN 90-312-0091-3).
11. Roger Blanpain, *Job Security and Industrial Relations*, 1980 (ISBN 90-312-0147-2).
12. Roger Blanpain, Greg Bamber & Russell Lansbury, *Technological Change and Industrial Relations: An International Symposium*, 1983 (ISBN 90-312-0205-3).
13. Roger Blanpain, James Janssen van Raay & A. Moulty, *Worker's Participation in the European Community: The Fifth Directive*, 1984 (ISBN 90-654-4187-5).
14. Roger Blanpain, *Equality and Prohibition of Discrimination in Employment*, 1985 (ISBN 90-654-4215-4).
15. Roger Blanpain, *Restructuring Labour in the Enterprise: Law and Practice in France, F.R. of Germany, Italy, Sweden and the United Kingdom*, 1986 (ISBN 90-654-4283-9).
16. Roger Blanpain & E. Kassalow, *Unions and Industrial Relations: Recent Trends and Prospect: A Comparative Treatment*, 1987 (ISBN 90-654-4294-4).
17. Roger Blanpain & Marco Biagi, *Trade Union Democracy and Industrial Relations*, 1988 (ISBN 90-654-4394-0).
18. Roger Blanpain & Jelle Visser, *In Search of Inclusive Unionism*, 1990 (ISBN 90-654-4439-4).
19. Roger Blanpain, *Flexibility and Wages: A Comparative Treatment*, 1990 (ISBN 90-654-4461-0).

20. Roger Blanpain, Stephen Frenkel & Oliver Clarke, *Economic Restructuring and Industrial Relations in Industrialised Countries,* 1990 (ISBN 90-654-4488-2).
21. Roger Blanpain & Friedrich Fürstenberg, *Structure and Strategy in Industrial Relations,* 1991 (ISBN 90-654-4559-5).
22. Roger Blanpain, Amira Galin & Ozer Carmi, *Flexible Work Patterns and Their Impact on Industrial Relations,* 1991 (ISBN 90-654-4572-2).
23. Roger Blanpain, *Workers' Participation: Influence on Management Decision-Making by Labour in the Private Sector,* 1992 (ISBN 90-654-4600-1).
24. Roger Blanpain, Brian Brooks & Chris Engels, *Employed or Self-Employed,* 1992 (ISBN 90-654-4613-3).
25. Roger Blanpain & Tiziano Treu, *Industrial Relations Developments in the Telecommunications Industry,* 1993 (ISBN 90-654-4642-7).
26. Roger Blanpain & Marco Biagi, *Industrial Relations in Small and Medium Sized Enterprises,* 1993 (ISBN 90-654-4696-6).
27. Roger Blanpain & Marco Biagi, *Participative Management and Industrial Relations in a Worldwide Perspective,* 1993 (ISBN 90-654-4769-5).
28. Roger Blanpain, Jacques Rojot & Hoyt N. Wheeler, *Employee Rights and Industrial Justice,* 1994 (ISBN 90-654-4804-7).
29. Roger Blanpain & Ruth Ben-Israel, *Strikes and Lock-Outs in Industrialized Market Economies,* 1994 (ISBN 90-654-4841-1).
30. Roger Blanpain, Kazuo Sugeno & Yasuo Suwa, *The Harmonization of Working Life and Family Life,* 1995 (ISBN 90-411-0064-4).
31. Roger Blanpain & Laszio Nagy, *Labour Law and Industrial Relations in Central and Eastern Europe,* 1996 (ISBN 90-411-0298-1).
32. Roger Blanpain, *Labour Law and Industrial Relations in the European Union,* 1997 (ISBN 90-411-0527-1).
33. Taco Van Peijpe, *Employment Protection under Strain,* 1998 (ISBN 90-411-0528-8).
34. Roger Blanpain, Takashi Araki & Ryuichi Yamakawa, *The Process of Industrialization and the Role of Labour Law in Asia,* 1999 (ISBN 9-041-1104-7-X).
35. Roger Blanpain & Marco Biagi, *Non-standard Work and Industrial Relations,* 1999 (ISBN 90-411-1117-4).
36. Roger Blanpain, *Private Employment Agencies: The Impact of ILO Convention 181 (1997) and the Judgment of the European Court of Justice of 11 December 1997,* 1999 (ISBN 90-411-1118-2).
37. Roger Blanpain, *Multinational Enterprises and the Social Challenges of the XXIst Century: The ILO Declaration on Fundamental* Principles *at Work, Public and Private Corporate Codes of Conduct,* 2000 (ISBN 90-411-1280-4).
38. Roger Blanpain, Ryuichi Yamakawa & Takashi Araki, *Deregulation and Labour Law: In Search of a Labour Concept for the 21st Century,* 2000 (ISBN 90-411-1370-3).
39. Roger Blanpain, *The Council of Europe and the Social Challenges of the XXIst Century,* 2001 (ISBN 90-411-1543-9).

40. Roger Blanpain, *On-Line Rights for Employees in the Information Society, Use & Monitoring of E-Mail & Internet at Work*, 2002 (ISBN 90-411-1626-5).
41. Roger Blanpain, *The Evolving Employment Relationship and the New Economy: The Role of Labour Law & Industrial Relations*, 2001 (ISBN 90-411-1691-5).
42. Roger Blanpain, *Involvement of Employees in the European Union, Works Councils, Company Statute, Information and Consultation Rights*, 2002 (ISBN 90-411-1760-1).
43. Michele Colucci, *The Impact of the Internet and New Technologies on the Workplace: A Legal Analysis from a Comparative Point of View*, 2002 (ISBN 90-411-1824-1).
44. Roger Blanpain, *White Paper on the Labour Market in Italy: The Quality of European Industrial Relations and Changing Industrial Relations*, 2002 (ISBN 90-411-1841-1).
45. Roger Blanpain, Russell D. Lansbury & Young-Bum Park, *Impact of Globalisation on Employment Relations: A Comparison of the Automobile and Banking Industries in Australia and Korea*, 2002 (ISBN 90-411-1850-0).
46. Roger Blanpain & Antoine Jacobs, *Employee Rights in Bankruptcy: A Comparative-Law Assessment*, 2002 (ISBN 90-411-1942-6).
47. Roger Blanpain, Takashi Araki & Shinya Ouchi, *Corporate Restructuring and the Role of Labour Law*, 2003 (ISBN 90-411-1949-3).
48. Roger Blanpain, *Collective Bargaining, Discrimination, Social Security and European Integration*, 2003 (ISBN 90-411-2010-6).
49. Roger Blanpain & Luis Aparicio-Valdez, *Labour Relations in the Asia- Pacific Countries*, 2004 (ISBN 90-411-2239-7).
50. Roger Blanpain & Ronnie Graham, *Temporary Agency Work and the Information Society*, 2004 (ISBN 90-411-2252-4).
51. Roger Blanpain, *The Actors of Collective Bargaining: A World Report*, 2004 (ISBN 90-411-2253-2).
52. Roger Blanpain & Michele Colucci, *The Globalisation of Labour Standards: The Soft Law Track*, 2004 (ISBN 90-411-2303-2).
53. Roger Blanpain, Takashi Araki & Shinya Ouchi, *Labour Law in Motion: Diversification of the Labour Force & Terms and Conditions of Employment*, 2005 (ISBN 90-411-2315-6).
54. Roger Blanpain, *Smoking and the Workplace*, 2005 (ISBN 90-411-2325-3).
55. Roger Blanpain, *Confronting Globalization: The Quest for a Social Agenda*, 2005 (ISBN 90-411-2381-4).
56. Roger Blanpain, Thomas Blanke & Edgar Rose, *Collective Bargaining Wages in Comparative Perspective: Germany, France, the Netherlands, Sweden and the United Kingdom*, 2005 (ISBN 90-411-2388-1).
57. Roger Blanpain & Anne Numhauser-Henning, *Women in Academia & Equality Law: Aiming High - Falling Short?*, 2006 (ISBN 978-90-411-2427-6).
58. Roger Blanpain, *Freedom of Services in the European Union: Labour and Social Security Law: The Bolkestein Initiative*, 2006 (ISBN 978-90-411-2453-5).
59. Roger Blanpain, Frans Pennings & Nurhan Sural, *Flexibilisation and Modernisation of the Turkish Labour Market*, 2006 (ISBN 978-90-411-2490-X).

60. Roger Blanpain & Boel Flodgren, *Corporate and Employment Perspectives in a Global Business Environment*, 2006 (ISBN 978-90-411-2537-X).
61. Roger Blanpain, Shinya Ouchi & Takashi Araki, *Decentralizing Industrial Relations and The Role of Labor Unions and Employee Representatives*, 2007 (ISBN 978-90-411-2583-3).
62. Roger Blanpain, *European Framework Agreements and Telework: Law and Practice: A European and Comparative Study*, 2007 (ISBN 978-90-411-2560-4).
63. Roger Blanpain, Jim Kitay, Leanne Cutcher & Nick Wailes, *Globalization and Employment Relations in Retail Banking*, 2007 (ISBN 978-90-411-2620-1).
64. Roger Blanpain, Russell Lansbury, Jim Kitay, Nick Wailes & Anja Kirsch, *Globalization and Employment Relations in the Auto Assembly Industry: A Study of Seven Countries*, 2008 (ISBN 978-90-411-2698-6).
65. Roger Blanpain & Michele Tiraboschi, *The Global Labour Market: From Globalization to Flexicurity*, 2008 (ISBN 978-90-411-2722-8).
66. Roger Blanpain, Michele Colucci & Frank Hendrickx, *The Future of Sport in the European Union: Beyond the EU Reform Treaty and the White Paper*, 2008 (ISBN 978-90-411-2761-7).
67. Roger Blanpain, Linda Dickens, *Challenges in European Employment Relations: Employment Regulation, Trade Union Organization, Equality, Flexicurity, Training and New Approaches to Pay*, 2008 (ISBN 978-90-411-2771-6).
68. Roger Blanpain, Hiroya Nakakubo & Takashi Araki, *New Developments in Employment Discrimination Law, 2008* (ISBN 978-90-411-2782-2).
69. Roger Blanpain, Andrzej Marian wiątkowski, *The Laval and Viking Cases: Freedom of Services and Establishment v. Industrial Conflict in the European Economic Area and Russia*, 2009 (ISBN 978-90-411-2850-8).
70. Roger Blanpain, William Bromwich, Olga Rymkevich, Silvia Spattini, *The Modernization of Labour Law and Industrial Relations in a Comparative Perspective*, 2009 (ISBN 978-90-411-2865-2).
71. Roger Blanpain, Juan Pablo Landa & Brian Langille, *Employment Policies and Multilevel Governance*, 2009 (ISBN 978-90-411-2866-9).
72. Roger Blanpain, European Works Councils; *The European Directive 2009/ 38/EC of 6 May 2009, 2009* (ISBN 978-90-411-3208-6).
73. Roger Blanpain, William Bromwich, Olga Rymkevich & Silvia Spattini, *Labour Productivity, Investment in Human Capital and Youth Employment: Comparative Developments and Global Responses*, 2010 (ISBN 978-90-411-3249-9).
74. Greg J. Bamber & Philippe Pochet, *Regulating Employment Relations, Work and Labour Laws: International Comparisons between Key Countries*, 2010 (ISBN 978-90-411-3199-7). General Editor: Roger Blanpain.
75. Roger Blanpain, Desislava Nikolaeva Dimitrova, *Seafarers' Rights in the Globalized Maritime Industry*, 2010 (ISBN 978-90-411-3349-6).
76. Roger Blanpain, Hiroya Nakakubo & Takashi Araki, *Regulation of Fixed- Term Employment Contracts*, 2010 (ISBN 978-90-411-3356-4).

77. Roger Blanpain, William Bromwich, Olga Rymkevich & Iacopo Senatori, *Rethinking Corporate Governance*, 2011 (ISBN 978-90-411-3450-9).
78. Roger Blanpain & Frank Hendrickx, *Labour Law between Change and Tradition: Liber Amicorum Antoine Jacobs*, 2011 (ISBN 978-90-411-3424-0).
79. Roger Blanpain, Thomas Klebe, Marlene Schmidt & Bernd Waas, *Trade Union Rights at the Workplace*, 2012 (ISBN 978-90-411-3460-8).
80. Roger Blanpain, William Bromwich, Olga Rymkevich & Iacopo Senatori, *Labour Markets, Industrial Relations and Human Resources Management: From Recession to Recovery*, 2012 (ISBN 978-90-411-4004-3).
81. Roger Blanpain, Hiroya Nakakubo & Takashi Araki, *Systems of Employee Representation at the Enterprise: A Comparative Study*, 2012 (ISBN 978-90-411-4080-7).
82. Roger Blanpain & Frank Hendrickx, *Temporary Agency Work in the European Union and the United States*, 2013 (ISBN 978-90-411-4769-1).
83. Roger Blanpain, Toker Dereli, Y. Pınar Soykut-Sarıca & Aslı en-Tabaı, *Emerging Patterns of Work and Turkish Labour Market Challenges under Globalization: Readings on Labour and Employment Relations*, 2014 (ISBN 978-90-411-4983-1).
84. Roger Blanpain, Pablo Arellano Ortiz, Marius Olivier & Gijsbert Vonk, *Social Security and Migrant Workers: Selected Studies of Cross-border Social Security Mechanisms*, 2014 (ISBN 978-90-411-4770-7).
85. Roger Blanpain & Nikita Lyutov, *Workers' Representation in Central and Eastern Europe: Challenges and Opportunities for the Works Councils' System*, 2014 (ISBN 978-90-411-4746-2).
86. Roger Blanpain, Ulla Liukkunen & Chen Yifeng, *China and ILO Fundamental Principles and Rights at Works*, 2014 (ISBN 978-90-411-4984-8).
87. Roger Blanpain, *The Use of Languages and Employment Relations*, 2014 (ISBN 978-90-411-5606-8).
88. Roger Blanpain, Hiroya Nakakubo & Takashi Araki, *Protection of Employees' Personal Information and Privacy*, 2014 (ISBN 978-90-411-5608-2).
89. Roger Blanpain, Jan Wouters, Glenn Rayp, Laura Beke & Axel Marx, *Protecting Labour Rights in a Multi-polar Supply Chain and Mobile Global Economy*, 2015 (ISBN 978-90-411-5662-4).
90. Roger Blanpain & Stefania Marassi, *Globalization and Transnational Collective Labour Relations: International and European Framework Agreements at Company Level*, 2015 (ISBN 978-90-411-4748-6).
91. Roger Blanpain, Frank Hendrickx & Petra Herzfeld Olsson, *National Effects of the Implementation of EU Directives on Labour Migration from Third Countries*, 2016 (ISBN 978-90-411-6257-1).
92. Roger Blanpain, Frank Hendrickx & D'Arcy du Toit, *Labour Law and Social Progress: Holding the Line or Shifting the Boundaries?* 2016 (ISBN 978-90-411-6747-7).

93. Roger Blanpain & Frank Hendrickx, *Reasonable Accommodation in the Modern Workplace: Potential and Limits of the Integrative Logics of Labour Law*, 2016 (ISBN 978-90-411-6258-8).
94. Roger Blanpain, Frank Hendrickx & Bernd Waas, *New Forms of Employment in Europe*, 2016 (ISBN 978-90-411-6239-7).
95. Roger Blanpain, Frank Hendrickx, Hiroya Nakakubo & Takashi Araki, *The Notion of Employer in the Era of the Fissured Workplace: Should Labour Law Responsibilities Exceed the Boundary of the Legal Entity?*, 2017 (ISBN 978-90-411-8470-2).
96. Elena Sychenko, *Individual Labour Rights as Human Rights: The Contributions of the European Court of Human Rights to Worker's Rights Protection*, 2017 (ISBN 978-90-411-8629-4).
97. William Bromwich & Olga Rymkevich, *Improving Workplace Quality: New Perspectives and Challenges for Worker Well-Being*, 2017 (ISBN 978-90-411-8628-7).
98. Sarah De Groof, *Work-Life Balance in the Modern Workplace: Interdisciplinary Perspectives from Work-Family Research, Law and Policy*, 2017 (ISBN 978-90-411-8630-0).
99. Sylvaine Laulom, *Collective Bargaining Developments in Times of Crisis*, 2018 (ISBN 978-90-411-8999-8).
100. Frank Hendrickx & Valerio De Stefano, *Game Changers in Labour Law: Shaping the Future of Work*, 2018 (ISBN 978-90-411-9953-9).
101. Ivana Palinkaš, *The Legal and Institutional Framing of Collective Bargaining in CEE Countries: Between Europeanisation and Decentralisation*, 2018 (ISBN 978-90-411-9199-1).
102. Jeremy Waddington, *European Board-Level Employee Representation: National Variations in Influence and Power*, 2018 (ISBN 978-90-411-9202-8).
103. Jan Pichrt & Kristina Koldinská, *Labour Law and Social Protection in a Globalized World: Changing Realities in Selected Areas of Law and Policy*, 2018 (ISBN 978-94-035-0093-5).
104. Matthew W. Finkin, *American Labor and the Law: Dormant, Resurgent, and Emergent Problems*, 2019 (ISBN 978-94-035-0654-8).
105. Giuseppe Casale & Tiziano Treu, *Transformations of Work: Challenges for the Institutions and Social Actors*, 2019 (ISBN 978-94-035-0891-7).
106. Miguel De la Corte-Rodríguez, *EU Law on Maternity and Other Child-Related Leaves: Impact on Gender Equality*, 2019 (ISBN 978-94-035-1452-9).
107. Valeria Pulignano & Frank Hendrickx, *Employment Relations in the 21st Century: Challenges for Theory and Research in a Changing World of Work*, 2020 (ISBN 978-94-035-1764-3).

Made in the USA
Monee, IL
18 October 2026

66041383R10177